RELIGION AND COGNITION

Critical Categories in the Study of Religion

Series Editor: Russell T. McCutcheon, Associate Professor, Department of Religious Studies, University of Alabama

Critical Categories in the Study of Religion aims to present the pivotal articles that best represent the most important trends in how scholars have gone about the task of describing, interpreting, and explaining the position of religion in human life. The series focuses on the development of categories and the terminology of scholarship that make possible knowledge about human beliefs, behaviours, and institutions. Each volume in the series is intended as both an introductory survey of the issues that surround the use of various key terms as well as an opportunity for a thorough retooling of the concept under study, making clear to readers that the cognitive categories of scholarship are themselves historical artefacts that change over time.

RELIGION AND COGNITION

A Reader

Edited by

D. Jason Slone

LONDON • OAKVILLE

Published by

Equinox Publishing Ltd.
UK: Equinox Publishing Ltd., Unit 6, The Village, 101 Amies St.,
London SW11 2JW
USA: DBBC, 28 Main Street, Oakville, CT 06779

First published 2006

This selection and introductory material
© D. Jason Slone 2006

British Library Cataloguing-in-Publication Data
A catalogue record for this book is available from the British Library.

ISBN   1 904768 70 9   (hardback)
        1 904768 71 7   (paperback)

Library of Congress Cataloging-in-Publication Data

Religion and cognition : a reader / edited by D. Jason Slone.
     p. cm. -- (Critical categories in the study of religion)
Includes bibliographical references and index.
ISBN 1-904768-70-9 (hb) -- ISBN 1-904768-71-7 (pb)
1. Psychology, Religious. 2. Cognition. 3. Cognitive psychology. I. Slone,
D. Jason. II. Series.
BL53.R433 2006
200.1'9--dc22

                          2005037993

Typeset by ISB Typesetting, Sheffield
www.sheffieldtypesetting.com

Printed and bound in Great Britain by Lightning Source UK Ltd, Milton
Keynes, and Lightning Source Inc., La Vergne, TN

To Betty, Pauline, Irene, Kim, and Amber

CONTENTS

ACKNOWLEDGMENTS

I would like to acknowledge those people who helped with the production of this volume. First, I would like to thank Russ McCutcheon for the invitation to contribute to this series. Second, I would to thank Janet Joyce, Val Hall, Sarah Norman, Iain Beswick, and the rest of the production staff at Equinox for their support and assistance. Third, I would like to thank Shari Schmersal and Dustin Lewis for their tremendously helpful compilation work. Fourth, I would like to thank the staff at the University of Findlay Teaching and Learning Technology Center (TLTC), including Eric Christensen, Jens Hatch, Ray "Big Dawg" McCandless, Beth Stewart, and Scott Trimmer, for their assistance with the technology that made the completion of this project more manageable. Finally, I would like to thank my wife, Brooke, for her editorial eye and for giving me the space and time to work.

I would also like to acknowledge the copyright and reprint permissions that were granted for the collections in this volume.

Barrett. J. L. 2000. "Exploring the Natural Foundations of Religion." Copyright © Elsevier Ltd.

Barrett, J. L., and F. C. Keil. 1996. "Conceptualizing a Non-Natural Entity: Anthropomorphism in God Concepts." Copyright © Elsevier Ltd.

Barrett, J. L., and E. T. Lawson. 2001. "Ritual Intuitions: Cognitive Contributions to Judgments of Ritual Efficacy." Copyright © Brill Academic Publishers.

Barrett J. L., and M. A. Nyhof. 2001. "Spreading Non-Natural Concepts: The Role of Intuitive Conceptual Structures in Memory and Transmission in Culture." Copyright © Brill Academic Publishers.

Bering, J. M., and D. F. Bjorklund. "The Natural Emergence of Afterlife Reasoning as a Developmental Regularity." Copyright © 2004 by the American Psychological Association. Reprinted with permission of the authors.

Boyer, P., and C. Ramble. 2001. "Cognitive Templates for Religious Concepts: Cross-Cultural Evidence for Recall of Counter-Intuitive Representations." © Cognitive Science Society, with permission of the authors.

Evans, E. M. 2001. "Cognitive and Contextual Factors in the Emergence of Diverse Belief Systems: Creation vs. Evolution." Copyright © Elsevier Ltd.

Hirschfeld, L. A., and S. A. Gelman. 1994. "Toward a Topography of Mind: An Introduction to Domain-Specificity." © Cambridge University Press, with permission of the authors.

Kelemen. D. 2004. "Are Children Intuitive Theists? Reasoning and Purpose in Design and Nature." Copyright © Blackwell Publishing.

Knight, N., P. Sousa, J. L. Barett, and S. Atran. 2004. "Children's Attributes of Beliefs to Humans and God: Cross-Cultural Evidence." Copyright © Cognitive Science Society, with permission of the authors.

Lawson, E. T., and R. N. McCauley. 1990. "Explanation and Interpretation: Problems and Promise in the Study of Religion." Copyright © Cambridge University Press, with permission of the authors.

Sperber, D. 1996. "The Epidemiology of Beliefs: A Naturalistic Approach." Blackwell Publishers. Copyright © Dan Sperber.

RELIGION AND COGNITION: AN INTRODUCTION

D. Jason Slone

This volume is designed to introduce readers to the cognitive science of religion through important papers, all but one (Chapter 13) of which have been published since 1990. The volume is divided into two parts. Part I contains four chapters that review the meta-theoretical and theoretical frameworks of the cognitive science of religion, and Part II contains nine chapters that introduce the reader to findings from experimental studies that support core hypotheses in the cognitive science of religion.

1. Part I

Meta-theoretical commitments of the cognitive science of religion are explored in Chapter 1, "Interpretation and Explanation: Problems and Promise in the Study of Religion," by E. Thomas Lawson and Robert N. McCauley. Lawson and McCauley argue that the study of religion is best approached from an *interactionist* meta-theoretical position that welcomes both interpretive and explanatory approaches. This is a change from typical studies of religion that only engage in interpretive, i.e. hermeneutic, endeavors. Hermeneuticists often argue that scientific studies of religion are reductionistic and insensitive to the personal and cultural meanings and values religions provide, and therefore that the job of the scholar of religion is to unpack what religions mean for their followers. On the other hand, explanatory exclusivists, such as the logical positivists in the philosophy of science, argue that interpretive endeavors are merely subjective, personal opinions, and therefore of little epistemological value other than to fulfill the particular curiosities of the scholars involved.

These two positions—hermeneutic and explanatory exclusivism—are in significant ways straw arguments, argue Lawson and McCauley. Explanations themselves require interpretive acts, and interpretations often function as explanations. The interactionist stance sees explanation and interpretation as complementary; they are different cognitive tasks. However, as readers will gather from Chapter 1, Lawson and McCauley argue that an imbalance currently exists in the study of religion because most scholars do exclusively interpretive work. The cognitive science of religion, while welcoming interpretive work, seeks to make explanatory contributions to our understanding of religion and in the process redress the imbalance.

So what exactly are the explanatory theories of the cognitive science of religion? To begin, most operate within the theoretical framework of "cultural epidemiology" outlined by Dan Sperber in Chapter 2. Sperber argues that explanation of widespread cultural forms (including but not limited to religion) must include cognitive considerations. For something to become a "cultural" representation, it must first originate in an individual's mind and then spread to other people's minds (often via material objects, like texts). Thus, a "cultural" representation is merely a private representation that has spread successfully to other members of a population.

Explaining why certain forms recur across populations therefore requires an approach much like viral epidemiology, connecting the "virus" (the mental representation that spreads across a population) with the hosts (the minds of individuals). Just as is the case with viruses, mental representations that fit well with hosts' minds are more likely to be spread than ones that don't. In this way, cognition can be said to constrain what kinds of mental representations become cultural forms. In turn, those types of cultural forms (e.g. religious systems) that recur across cultures can be said to be "fit" cultural forms; that is, they are fit for cognitive consumption. By extension, it is because human minds are basically the same across cultures that we see the same types of cultural forms recur across cultures.

So what is human cognition like such that religion is such a good fit for it? In Chapter 3, Lawrence Hirschfeld and Susan Gelman show that the human mind is domain-specific—a collection of various "modules" that perform specific tasks. Importantly, much of the information each module possesses is non-cultural, but rather part of the cognitive architecture itself. While there is no consensus among cognitive scientists on how many modules minds might possess, it is clear that these modules work together, creating various cognitive systems that allow us to make intuitive sense of the world and its workings. For example, we have a "folk physics" system that tells us (among other things) that solid objects cannot go through other solid objects (e.g. people can't walk through walls). We have a "folk biology" system that tells us that babies resemble their birth parents (i.e. have the same parts/traits). And we have a "folk psychology" system that tells us other people's behaviors are goal-directed, i.e. driven by beliefs and desires (e.g. "Brenda puts on her coat because she believes it is cold outside and desires to stay warm").

These domain-specific cognitive systems are triggered by environmental inputs. For example, when we see a person crying, the perception is likely to trigger the inference that that person is unhappy. When we see a puppy, the perception triggers the inference that the parents of the puppy are similar-looking dogs. When we see a moving object strike into another object, the perception triggers the inference that the object being hit will be launched. Therefore, human minds don't just "soak up" the environment; environmental inputs trigger inferential representations about what is being perceived. The mind is neither a "blank slate" nor a "black box"; it is a domain-specific computational, representational, information processor.

This fact about minds leads to an important question, namely, where does this cognitive information come from? If it is not learned per se, is it innate? Does it develop early in the life span? Is it somehow both learned and developed? The matter itself is far from settled in the cognitive sciences, but the issue is largely immaterial for the study of religion because, regardless of whether these cognitive capacities are innate or develop, they are in place by the time human beings acquire religion from culture. In this way, cognition constrains what kinds of religions will be widespread. If the cultural inputs do not fit with cognition in specific ways, transmission is not likely to be very successful. And a survey of world religions reveals that "successful" religions (i.e. long-lived and/or widespread) possess recurrent patterns of belief and behavior, which can be connected to cognitive capacities that enable their transmission.

In this way, religion—again, at least in the form of religions found to recur across cultures and eras in human societies—can be said to be "natural"; religion is a natural fit for human cognitive consumption. This point is shown in Chapter 4, "Exploring the Natural Foundations of Religion," by Justin Barrett. Barrett points out that, despite variation across and within religious systems, most religions involve a shared system of beliefs and actions concerning supernatural agency (i.e. gods, goddesses, demons, angels, ancestors, etc.). That is, religion involves the belief that supernatural agents exist, and a set of prescribed actions (i.e. rituals) for interacting with those agents.

Why do these features recur across cultures? In short, because of how the mind works. First, why do religions involve belief in supernatural agents? Religious conceptual schemes across the world are believed to be populated by supernatural agents because the mind is primed to detect agents in general. In fact, Barrett argues, the mind is so primed for detecting agents in the world that it is reasonable to say that the mind possesses a "hyperactive agency detection device" (HADD) that predisposes humans to detect agency at work in the world, even where perceptual data do not warrant such representations. When you awaken in the middle of the night and hear a noise in your house, your HADD predisposes you to automatically generate the representation that an agent is in the house and has made the noise. You immediately think, "Is that a burglar?!" (even though it is probably just old floorboards creaking).

The belief in gods and other forms of supernatural agency is the extended application of this natural tendency, with one important difference. Supernatural agent concepts involve ordinary agent concepts (e.g. person, animal) with one or two violations of domain-specific expectations. In other words, gods are mostly like ordinary agents (e.g. they have minds with beliefs and desires) but with one or two "supernatural" capacities (e.g. their minds know everything). As Barrett notes, Pascal Boyer has shown that despite their apparent differences across cultures, most supernatural agent concepts are represented in this way; gods are "minimally counterintuitive" agents.

In turn, once people acquire these concepts of minimally counterintuitive agents, we then interact with those agents, employing the same cognitive system used for social interactions with ordinary agents. That is, religious rituals have the same representational structure as interactions with people, animals, plants, etc., with the only difference being one of the parties involved in the ritual action is (represented as) a minimally counterintuitive agent. In other words, religious rituals conform to the following pattern: Agent → Action → Patient. As a result, only three types of religious rituals are possible: rituals in which minimally counterintuitive agents are represented in the first slot (i.e. as the agent), in the second slot (i.e. in the action), and in the third slot (i.e. as the patient). In this way, religious actions are constrained by ordinary cognition as well as religious beliefs.

Barrett's chapter clearly shows that despite its apparent "super-naturalness," religion can be shown to be a natural product of human cognition. Does this mean the same thing as saying humans are "hardwired" for religion? The answer is "no," Deborah Kelemen explains in Chapter 5, "Are Children 'Intuitive Theists'? Reasoning about Purpose and Design in Nature." What humans do possess, however, are the cognitive prerequisites for acquiring religion.

In Chapter 5, Kelemen reviews a range of literature from developmental and cognitive psychology that suggests children can be viewed as "intuitive theists" in the sense that children develop cognitive capacities that are prerequisites for acquiring theism later.

What are these prerequisites? Kelemen cites three. First, children must develop the capacity to maintain a mental representation of a causal agent (despite its intangibility). Second, children must develop the ability to attribute mental states to that agent, thereby distinguishing it from more commonplace agents. Third, and most importantly, children must develop the basic ability to attribute design intentions to agents, and to understand an object's purpose as being derived from such intentions. Kelemen's literature review shows that children do, in fact, develop these capacities, which allows us to acquire religion.

2. Part II

Like all scientific claims, theories put forth by cognitive scientists of religion need support in order to be taken seriously. Historically, most non-cognitive scholars of religion have relied only on observational empirical support for their claims rather than experimental empirical support, as most scientists do. This is, again, likely because of those scholars' commitments to the meta-theoretical stance of hermeneutic exclusivism (noted in Chapter 1). While plausible, the "naturalness of religion thesis" that cognitive scientists have put forth would—and does—benefit from strong, supportive experimental evidence.

Generally speaking, experimental evidence provides more powerful support for scientific claims than passive observational support for the reason that experiments are controlled tests of potentially causal variables. In other words, experiments allow scientists to isolate variables that are postulated to be the causes of events. If test results fail to disconfirm a claim, those data are taken to be supportive of the claim (and vice versa). Furthermore, this systematic approach allows for a community of scientists to establish the credibility of experimental evidence. If similar results are obtained independently (e.g. by separate test runs, and/or replications by different scientists), this adds to the community's confidence in the claim.

Though only recently emerged, scholars working in the cognitive science of religion have produced a number of experimental studies that support core hypotheses in the field. The articles in Part II present some of those studies.

Chapter 6, "Conceptualizing a Nonnatural Entity: Anthropomorphism in God Concepts," explores the cognitive foundations of the phenomenon of anthropomorphism. As is widely known by students of world religions, the "tragedy of the theologian" is that lay people regularly distort (from the perspective of official theology) god concepts by anthropomorphizing them. The God of Christian theology, for example, is supposed to be (again, from the perspective of official theology) represented as an "essence," not a being, as "omnipresent," not as living in a single location, as "genderless," not as a man, etc. Yet it is common for Christians to represent God as "the big guy in the sky."

Using narrative comprehension and recall studies, in which subjects were told a story and then asked to recall its contents, Justin Barrett and Frank Keil demonstrated that subjects are more likely to (mis-)represent god concepts anthropomorphically than in a theologically correct way in real-time problem-solving situations. Specifically, their studies show that when performing recall tasks that require inferential reasoning processes, people abandon memorized creeds and rely on more "natural" ways of representing gods. In this way, they argue, the specific phenomenon of anthropomorphism, and the more general phenomenon of "theological correctness" (holding ideas that differ from official theologies), are natural by-products of cognitive constraints.

Experimental support for Boyer's "minimal counterintuitiveness" hypothesis is presented in Chapter 7, by Justin Barrett and Melanie Nyhof, and in Chapter 8, by Pascal Boyer and Charles Ramble. Both sets of experiments involve subjects being given concepts that varied in their levels of counterintuitiveness, from intuitive concepts (i.e. concepts that did not violate any domain-specific expectations; e.g. a man who could see right in front of him) to minimally counterintuitive concepts (i.e. concepts with single domain-expectation violations; e.g. a man who can see villages many miles away), and then recalling those concepts after some time had passed. In studies by both, subjects regularly recalled the minimally counterintuitive concepts better than the intuitive ones. The results obtained by Boyer and Ramble are especially important in this regard because they were obtained across different cultures—in France, Gabon, and Nepal. These findings eliminate the possibility that results obtained by Barrett and Keil were unique to the United States, and therefore are merely a product of culture.

In Chapter 9, "Ritual Intuitions: Cognitive Contributions to Judgments of Ritual Efficacy," Barrett and Tom Lawson report results from tests of Lawson and McCauley's "ritual form hypothesis" (reviewed by Barrett in Chapter 4). In these studies, these authors tested ritual participants' judgments about features of ritual performance, such as ritual efficacy and the relative importance of a superhuman agent's participation. In particular, Lawson and McCauley's theory of ritual competence generates three predictions. (1) People with little or no knowledge of any given ritual system will have intuitions about the potential effectiveness of a ritual given minimal information about the structure of the ritual. (2) The representation of superhuman agency in the action structure will be considered the most important factor contributing to effectiveness. (3) Having an appropriate intentional agent initiate the action will be considered relatively more important than any specific action to be performed.

To test portions of these predictions, Barrett and Lawson constructed several artificial rituals (in order to avoid the confounding problem of background knowledge), manipulated several hypothetical scenarios in which the ritual performances were set, and then asked subjects to make judgments about the ritual scenarios. They found that subjects routinely made similar types of judgments about the ritual scenarios, even though they had no background knowledge about the rituals themselves (again, because the rituals were artificially constructed for the purposes of the study) or of the purposes of the test. In other words, these data support Lawson and McCauley's claim that there are non-cultural regularities in how (ritual) actions are conceptualized, which inform and constrain participants' understandings of religious rituals.

The next three chapters, Chapters 10–12, present findings from developmental psychologists who have studied how children reason about religion. In Chapter 10, "Cognitive and Contextual Factors in the Emergence of Diverse Belief Systems: Creation versus Evolution," Margaret Evans reports on data obtained about how children from different backgrounds—those in fundamentalist and those in nonfundamentalist Christian homes—reason about the origins of natural species (i.e. children with "creationist" backgrounds versus those without). She found that pre-adolescent children (like their mothers) embraced the dominant beliefs of their community, whether creationist or evolutionist. However, five- to seven-year-olds in fundamentalist schools endorsed creationism, whereas nonfundamentalists endorsed mixed creationist and spontaneous generationist beliefs. Most interestingly, though, she found that eight- to ten-year-olds were exclusively creationist, regardless of community of origin.

Based on these results, Evans argues that the divergent developmental pattern her data reveal can be explained with a model of "constructive interactionism." Children generate intuitive beliefs about species' origins, both natural and intentional, while communities privilege certain beliefs and inhibit others—thus engendering diverse belief systems. Thus ideas transmitted culturally do not determine, entirely, what an individual thinks. Instead, individuals possess divergent belief systems as a result of cultural acquisition and cognitive inferences.

In Chapter 11, "Children's Attributions of Beliefs to Humans and God: Cross-Cultural Evidence," Nicola Knight, Paulo Sousa, Justin Barrett, and Scott Atran show that children across cultures reason about gods' minds—in particular, about what gods know—using their capacity to mind-read (called "theory of mind capacity" in developmental psychology). Knight et al. employed a commonly-used experimental technique, originally proposed by Daniel Dennett, to study how children understand how other agents' minds work. This technique, which has come to be called the "false belief test," involves (among other versions) showing children an ordinary container, such as a cracker box, and asking them what contents are inside. When given this task, most children say, "crackers." Then, the experimenter in the study opens the box and reveals that the box does not contain crackers, but rather surprising contents such as rocks. Then, the experimenter asks the child to infer what other agents, who don't have access to the information about what is actually inside the box, might think are in the box. For example, "If mommy came in the room right now, what would she think is in the box?"

Children's responses to this false-belief test follow a predictable pattern. Those under the age of four routinely fail the test, saying, "rocks." Those over the age of five routinely pass the test, saying, "crackers." Thus, a child's theory of mind capacity is not fully developed before the age of four, but is so after the age of five.

Knight et al. extended this study to the realm of religion, asking a sample of Yukatek Maya children (in order, like Boyer and Ramble [see Chapter 8], to obtain cross-cultural data) to perform the task, with the additional question of inferring what God might think was in the box. Interestingly, they found that children reasoned about God and other humans in the same way (i.e. same percentage saying God and other humans would think crackers were in the box) up until the age of five, at which point subjects stated that God would know that there were rocks in the box, whereas other humans would falsely think crackers were in the box. This suggests that five-year-olds—but not four-year-olds—understand the theologically correct version of God's mind versus human minds; God is omniscient, whereas humans are epistemically fallible.

In Chapter 12, "The Natural Emergence of Reasoning about the Afterlife as a Developmental Regularity," Jesse Bering and David Bjorklund show—as was shown by the Evans, and the Knight et al. studies—that children reason in religion in different ways depending on their stage of development. In this study, Bering and Bjorklund were interested in understanding how children reason about what happens after death. In particular, given the widespread belief across religious systems that a person's "soul" (or culturally equivalent) continues on after death even though the body dies, they were interested in whether or not people reason that biological functioning ceases at death but psychological functioning does not.

To test this, they told children ranging in ages from four to twelve years old versions of a story in which a mouse was eaten (and therefore killed) by an alligator. Then, they probed the children's death concepts by asking them questions about what was happening (if anything) to the biological and the psychological functioning of the dead mouse. They found that the youngest children were likely to state that both cognitive and psychobiological states continued at death, whereas the oldest children were more likely to state that only the cognitive states continued. Further, they found in subsequent studies that, like the older children, adults were likely to attribute psychological functioning to dead agents as well. These findings suggest that developmental mechanisms underlie intuitive accounts of dead agents' minds. That is, the older we get, the more likely we are to think that psychological functioning continues after death even though biological functioning stops.

Finally, in Chapter 13, "Modes of Research: Combining Cognitive Psychology and Anthropology through Whitehouse's Modes of Religiosity," Rebekah Richert presents findings that support Harvey Whitehouse's "modes of religiosity" theory. The modes of religiosity theory is an account of ritual transmission that describes the existence of two distinct types of religious (ritual) traditions—"doctrinal" and "imagistic"—and attempts to explain this dichotomy (and its related social morphologies) in terms of cognitive processes.

The doctrinal mode of religiosity is characterized by rituals that are repeated frequently, low in emotional arousal, and usually accompanied by verbally transmitted exegesis. By frequently repeating rituals in this mode, the ritual procedures activate semantic memory systems, and make possible the transmission of explicit and complicated doctrinal teachings. The imagistic mode, by contrast, is characterized by rituals that are low in frequency, high in emotional arousal, and often involve terrifying ordeals. These ritual experiences are encoded in episodic memory, and participants spontaneously reflect on the meaning of the ritual through a process of analogical reasoning that continues to unfold over the course of a participant's lifetime. Thus, ritual frequency, levels of emotional arousal, amounts of "spontaneous exegetical reflection" (SER), and concept recall performance (among others) are correlated.

To test predictions made by this theory, Richert and colleagues constructed several artificial rituals for subjects to perform. Subjects performed a ritual only once (thereby controlling for frequency), while the experimenters manipulated the levels of arousal accompanying the ritual in different groups—seeking to test for amount of SER and for recall performance. In other words, two different groups performed the same ritual, with one group doing so in conditions of high sensory stimulation (e.g. loud noises, done outside at sunset, being watched from behind by the experimenter, etc.) and the other in "bland" conditions (e.g. soft noises, in the afternoon, no experimenter watching from behind, etc.). Several weeks after the ritual performance, subjects were interviewed and asked to recall information about the ritual, and to recall their levels of "spontaneous exegetical reflection" (SER). As predicted, subjects in the high arousal groups showed better recall of the ritual scenarios and greater levels of SER than subjects in the low arousal groups.

3. Conclusions and Recommendations

The selections in the book show that the cognitive science of religion is a fresh and exciting approach to the scientific study of religion. They show that there are (1) meta-theoretical stances available to justify explanatory endeavors in the study of religion (for those for whom such justifications are necessary), (2) theoretical frameworks that provide plausible and testable explanations of why certain features of religion recur across human cultures and eras, and (3) experimental findings that provide robust support for core hypotheses in the field. In the end, I hope not only that readers will be impressed by the findings, but also—and more importantly—that readers will be inspired by the selections to explore the field more broadly and more deeply. For such readers, I recommend the following books as places to turn.

References

Atran, S. 2002. *In Gods We Trust: The Evolutionary Landscape of Religion*. New York: Oxford University Press.

Barrett, J. 2004. *Why Would Anyone Believe in God?* Walnut Creek, CA: AltaMira Press.

Boyer, P. 2001. *Religion Explained: The Evolutionary Origins of Religious Thought*. New York: Basic Books.

McCauley, R. N., and E. T. Lawson. 2002. *Bringing Ritual to Mind: Psychological Foundations of Cultural Forms*. Cambridge: Cambridge University Press.

Pyysiainen, I. 2001. *How Religion Works: Towards a New Cognitive Science of Religion*. Leiden: Brill Academic Publishers.

Slone, D. J. 2004. *Theological Incorrectness: Why Religious People Believe What They Shouldn't*. New York: Oxford University Press.

Whitehouse, H. *Modes of Religiosity: A Cognitive Theory of Religious Transmission*. Walnut Creek, CA: AltaMira Press.

Part I

1

INTERPRETATION AND EXPLANATION: PROBLEMS AND PROMISE IN THE STUDY OF RELIGION*

E. Thomas Lawson and Robert N. McCauley

Symbolic-cultural systems are a puzzlement. As forms of thought and types of behavior they seem bizarre. Why do the Dorze of Ethiopia say that the leopard is a Christian animal which observes the fast days of the Orthodox church while protecting their goats from marauding leopards on those same fast days? Why do the Yoruba of Nigeria think that marks on a divining board that a diviner makes and reads simultaneously disclose and determine their future? Why does a marriageable Zulu male regard it as more important to swallow a foul-tasting potion to become attractive to an eligible young woman of his clan than simply relying on special adornment? Why do some Christians assert that bread and wine, once consecrated, become the body and blood of Jesus Christ?

Answering questions such as these requires metatheoretical, theoretical, and substantive reflection. In this chapter we defend two crucial metatheoretical theses. The first is that interpretive and explanatory endeavors need not be antagonistic and, in fact, should interact in the study of symbolic-cultural systems. The second is that the competence approach to theorizing offers a means for developing empirically tractable theories of participants' representations of such systems.

The continuing vigorous debate among social scientists and humanists about the roles that interpretation and explanation play in the analysis of human affairs (and the extremeness of the positions that some adopt) should rapidly eliminate any doubt about the importance of this metatheoretical question for inquiries into symbolic-cultural systems. Most scholars agree that this issue is both serious and unavoidable. They differ widely, however, not only in their views of the relationships between interpretation and explanation, but also about the contents of the terms. Still, most do agree that interpretation involves questions of meaning and that explanation concerns causal relations (in some sense).

Proponents of the extreme positions maintain either that symbolic-cultural systems are only susceptible to interpretation (and not explanation) or that they are susceptible to explanation (and interpretation is irrelevant). The language they use frequently frames the pertinent issues in exclusivistic terms. On the one hand, scientistic thinkers (influenced by logical empiricism) read interpretive approaches as unduly subjective and personal, as speculations without foundation, and as deflecting inquiry from its true purposes—which are to produce law-like causal explanations of human behavior. On the other hand, hermeneuticists regard such scientistic views both as mechanistic (or "reductionistic") descriptions which are insensitive to the role that the investigator's subjectivity, values, and biases play in the pursuit of knowledge and as naive approaches which fail to appreciate the importance of questions of meaning for our understanding of human life and thought. The issue separating these feuding factions is whether or not the subject matter of the human sciences is privileged, hence requiring special categories and methods. Those of scientistic bent argue that no subject matter is privileged, that science is a unified enterprise, and that the only kind of knowledge worth pursuing is that which is produced by the kinds of methods the physical sciences employ. Those with hermeneutic inclinations fight for a privileged status for both subject matter and method and accuse those of scientistic bent of physics envy.

While the appeal to a privileged status for method and subject matter in the human sciences is widespread, it is particularly strong in the thought of those scholars involved in the study of religion and in the history of religions in particular. That field manifests a serious imbalance in favor of interpretation over explanation. For example, Eliade (1963, xiii) says:

> All religious phenomenon will only be recognized as such if it is grasped at its own level, that is to say, if it is studied as something religious. To try to grasp the essence of such a phenomenon by means of physiology, psychology, sociology, economics, linguistics, art or any other study is false; it misses the one unique and irreducible element in it—the element of the sacred.

Eliade, here, is asserting that religious phenomena are sui generis and that they can be "grasped" (understood, interpreted) only if we grant to the category of "the sacred" a unique and irreducible status. From this point of view, explanatory theory, as developed in the social sciences, simply misses the crucial point, namely, that "the sacred" is accessible only by special (interpretive) techniques. In other words, the privileged status of the subject matter requires a special method—hermeneutics.

Eliade's protectionism is not an isolated case. The theologian Rudolf Otto (1958, 8), who had a profound influence on the development of the history of religions as a separate discipline, claimed:

> The reader is invited to direct his mind to a moment of deeply-felt religious experience, as little as possible qualified by other forms of consciousness. Whoever cannot do this, whoever knows no such moments in his experience, is requested to read no farther; for it is not easy to discuss questions of religious psychology with one who can recollect the emotions of his adolescence, the discomforts of indigestion, or say, social feelings, but cannot recall any intrinsically religious feelings.

From Otto's point of view, interpretation of religious phenomena not only excludes explanation but *both presumes and requires* a prior religious experience. Hans Penner (1986) has argued that Otto's appeal to a privileged status for religious experience is theologically motivated and continues to be an unacknowledged assumption in methodological discussions in the history of religions—even when it is explicitly denied!

Examples such as these from the field of the history of religions could be multiplied but would serve little purpose. Our goal is not to excoriate historians of religions but to show that acknowledging the issues which preoccupy them does not require defending the anti-scientific positions most adopt. In fact, we would be derelict in our duty if we did not also acknowledge that the pervasive emphasis on interpretation in the history of religions has encouraged deep sensitivity to the semantic complexities of religious systems and to the diversity and richness of religious forms of experience. Unfortunately, its neglect of explanation has left it bereft of systematic power and prone to highly individualist accounts of religious phenomena.

In addition to historians of religions, many scholars in the larger world of the social sciences and the humanities have taken the development of such sensitivities to the complexities of symbolic-cultural systems as a principled ground for preferring interpretation over explanation. Their views are typically rooted not, as in the history of religions, in claims about the privileged status of "the hole" or "the sacred," but in more extravagant claims about the autonomy of human behavior generally. Their view is that symbolic-cultural systems by their very nature require interpretive rather than explanatory approaches.

By contrast we hold that interpretation and explanation are complementary, and, in light of the imbalance within the study of religion in favor of interpretation that we wish to redress, the proposal of explanatory theories is more likely to advance our knowledge currently. In fact, a number of theoretical approaches are worthy of further attention. Their mere existence belies claims to the effect that plausible theories of religion are impossible.

In the next section we shall first describe the most prominent positions that have been advanced in the relevant literature concerning the relationship between interpretation and explanation. We think that both scientistic and hermeneutic hegemonists are wrong for claiming that the choices are between explanation and interpretation. Nor do we think that explanation is subordinate to interpretation. A more balanced position is not only possible but desirable.

Explanation and Interpretation: Three Accounts

When we are dealing with human subjects, their forms of thought, their types of practice, what are the respective roles of explanation and interpretation, however finely or coarsely they are distinguished? We think that a careful analysis of the debate discloses three views about how they are related. These are the actually occurring options in the literature as opposed to the much larger number of logically possible positions. The first are the exclusive positions to which we have already referred. Both hold that interpretation and explanation exclude one another. Their differences concern which of the two they favor. The second is the inclusive which maintains that explanation is and must be subordinated to interpretation. Inclusivists hold that the enterprise of interpretation always encapsulates explanatory pursuits. The third, which we shall defend, is the interactive. It proposes that interpretation and explanation inform each other. Novel interpretations employ the categories of theories already in place, whereas novel explanations depend upon the discovery of new theories which, in turn, depends upon the sort of reorganization of knowledge that interpretive pursuits involve. On the interactive view these two processes complement one another. We shall discuss each of these positions in order.

Exclusivism

The exclusivist positions are both hegemonistic views. Exclusivism takes two forms, one emphasizing the centrality of explanation, the other the centrality of interpretation. The first group of exclusivists, consisting of behavioral psychologists, sociobiologists, and others, holds that the only methods for systematic inquiry are the methods of the natural sciences. (See, for example, Skinner 1953, 87–90 and Rosenberg 1980.) The second, which focuses on interpretation exclusively, includes such post-modernist philosophers as Rorty (1982, 199) and holds that all inquiry is ultimately interpretive.

(1) For the first group explanation excludes interpretation because human thought and behavior should be studied, like anything else in the world,

according to the strict canons of scientific investigation modeled after inquiry in the physical sciences. Interpretation is irrelevant, if not impossible, for such purposes. Explanation is simply scientific explanation. On this exclusivist view, if the human sciences aspire to be sciences at all, then they should be modeled after the physical sciences. Both should search for causal laws which describe the behavior of the objects in their respective domains. Interpretive factors simply get in the way and introduce needless obscurities. For example, concerns with subjectivity or intentionality only interfere with scientific progress (Rosenberg 1980).

This position was most forcefully developed in the heyday of the logical empiricist philosophy of science. However, its influence has persisted. Richard Rudner's discussion (1966) of the philosophy of social science is a fitting illustration. Rudner maintained that the structure of theories in the study of social and cultural systems should mirror the idealized accounts of theories in the physical sciences that earlier logical empiricists had offered. For Rudner, understanding social worlds (just as understanding the natural world) is essentially a consequence of formulating causal explanations.

More recently, Adolf Grunbaum (1984) has taken up this banner in his attack on recent hermeneutical reinterpretations of Freud by Habermas, Ricoeur, and Klein. For instance, Ricoeur, according to Grunbaum, reduces the object of psychoanalytic theory to the verbal transactions between psychoanalyst and patient and then argues that such verbal transactions require interpretive rather than explanatory approaches. Ricoeur, for example, says: "There are no 'facts' nor any observation of 'facts' in psychoanalysis but rather the interpretation of a narrated history" (1974, 186). Grunbaum argues that such a hermeneutic explication of psychoanalysis as interpretation rather than explanation conforms neither to the intention of Freud nor to the logical structure of his arguments. He argues that psychoanalysis, according to Freud, has the status of a natural science, in virtue of the fact that on Freud's view psychoanalysis proposes law-like generalizations to explain human behavior. Ironically, Grunbaum salvages the explanatory intent of Freudian psychoanalysis in order to scuttle it on different grounds, namely its "genuine epistemic defects, which are often quite subtle" (1984, xii) but which boil down to psychoanalysis' masking a crucial ambiguity about the role that suggestion plays in the psychoanalyst–patient relationship. Clearly, from Grunbaum's point of view, natural science is fundamentally explanatory and includes interpretive elements only incidentally. If psychoanalysis is to be a social *science,* then it should be modeled upon the natural sciences. There is no need to introduce interpretive categories.

What should be noted in this brand of exclusivism is how hermeneuticists such as Ricoeur play right into the hands of the scientistic exclusivists by acknowledging the right of the latter to establish the form and limits of explanation. For example, it is clear from the quotation taken from Ricoeur's work that he concedes to the logical empiricist the "observation of facts" which he then *contrasts* with narrative interpretation. He attempts to purchase autonomy for interpretation at the expense of its ability to contribute to explanation. Not surprisingly, as we shall see next, one form of exclusivism breeds another. Scientistic exclusivism leads to the hermeneutic variety, because it so limits acceptable subject matters and methods that it forces dissenters in response to focus upon just those features of human experience that extreme scientism ignores, such as the affective, the personal, the subjective, the meaningful, the valuable, and the imaginative, to name the most important.

(2) For the second group interpretation excludes the possibility of explaining human behavior, because all inquiry about human life and thought occurs within the ineliminable frameworks of values and subjectivity. This version of the exclusivity thesis is the mirror image of the first position and was partially developed in response to it. In this view human beings are subjects not objects; therefore we should explicate the *meaning* of their thoughts and actions, rather than the alleged causal factors that account for their behavior. Human science reveals its differences from natural science by paying attention to a world of meanings rather than a system of causes. Its approach must be semiotic rather than nomological.

While such a semiotic approach has many exemplars in the human sciences (for example, Lesche 1985), Clifford Geertz (in, at least, some of his moments) has been particularly influential in its defense. While his actual work contains a great deal of creative explanatory theorizing, his methodological pronouncements often have a decidedly exclusivistic ring. We should state at the outset that Geertz's pronouncements about these issues do not *always* follow along the lines we discuss here. Nevertheless, Geertz does enunciate this methodological perspective quite forthrightly in the following passage (1973, 5):

> The concept of culture I espouse and whose utility I now attempt to demonstrate is essentially a semiotic one. Believing with Max Weber, that man is an animal suspended in webs of significance he himself has spun, I take culture to be those webs, and the analysis of it to be, therefore, not an experimental science in search of law but an interpretive one in search of meaning.

Geertz, *here,* clearly advances an exclusivistic hermeneutic agenda; it is the job of the scholar in the human sciences to *interpret* the semiotic patterns of those "webs of significance" spun by humankind rather than to explain their connections. Interpretation does not mean proposing principles that show systematic connections among idealized theoretical objects, nor does it mean identifying causal factors; it means unpacking meanings. Human science should involve the *discernment* of meanings rather than the discovery of laws. A cultural system consists of "socially established structures of meaning." Because it is *socially* established, i.e., a creation of the participants, it does not exist as an entity available for explanation. The only option is for the interpreter to enter it as a world of meaning. The interpreter is in the position of a stranger invited into a home or a reader enticed into reading a book. Explanatory theory is simply not to the point. This methodological perspective is not simply a heuristic strategy in the face of cultural complexity, but a necessary consequence of the character of human interaction—especially interaction across cultures.

Geertz sometimes seems to think that a principled ground exists for justifying the exclusive preference for interpretation in the study of human subjects in their self-woven cultural webs. The alleged problem lies in the very nature of explanation itself. It is not simply that it has a limited value nor that whatever explanations we do come across constrain our interpretations, but rather that our reading of cultural "texts" requires sensitivities to the subjective and semantic dimensions of human thought and action which are absent from explanatory approaches. On this position *the search for explanatory theories with respect to human subjects is fundamentally misdirected.* It fails to acknowledge the autonomy, independence, and uniqueness of the subject matter of the human sciences.

When pursuing this position, Geertz's argument goes something like the following: an examination of the *practices* of anthropologists (those scholars most directly involved with examining symbolic-cultural systems) discloses their fundamentally *ethnographic* approach. What ethnographers do is establish rapport with their subjects. They enter into a hermeneutic relationship with them. In such a relationship they are consistently trying to understand other forms of human meaning. These other forms are not transparent to the ethnographer; their opaqueness requires interpretation. They need to be broken through. Geertz argues that such interpretive analysis involves "sorting out the structures of signification ... and determining their social ground and import" (Geertz 1973, 9). Questions of "import" are questions of interpretation which enlarge the universe of human discourse (1973, 14). Geertz thinks that the mistake made by those scholars who search for explanations is that they view culture as a power—something causally responsible for social events, behaviors, institutions, and processes. Instead, he thinks that a cultural system is a context, something within which the structures of signification can be "intelligibly—that is, thickly—described" (1973, 14).

With such views of culture and of the aim of anthropology there seems little, if any, room for explanatory theory. Interpretation, characterized now as thick description, in the context of the human universe of discourse is all that is possible. Ethnography as the interpretation of cultures excludes explanation. It must stay "much closer to the ground"; in fact, it is incapable of either generalization or prediction (1973, 24–26). Explanation is a matter for the "hard sciences." Ethnography, by its very nature, carves out an exclusive niche for itself, free from a concern with testable generalizations.

By now it should be clear that both forms of exclusivism are in remarkable agreement on at least two issues, namely (1) that explanation is the search for causes and the laws that describe their operation and (2) that the goals and methods of the natural sciences differ radically from our other knowledge-seeking activities. However, they draw exactly opposite conclusions (McCauley 1986a). The advocates of the explanatory methods of the physical sciences regard interpretive projects as superfluous speculations, whereas the advocates of the centrality of interpretation in the human sciences regard these endeavors as indispensable and explanatory projects as foreign and even inimical to understanding human affairs. They disagree only on whether causes and laws are applicable to human thought and action.

We think that the issues of relating explanation and interpretation are much more complex than the defenders of either of these exclusivistic positions willingly acknowledge. More moderate positions are clearly possible.

Inclusivism

The second and more moderate set of views is inclusive but still requires the subordination of explanation to interpretation. Although in principle inclusivism could be a two-way street, in fact it is not. Reliably, it is explanation that is subordinated to interpretation and not the other way around. Such subordination takes a number of possible forms. We shall first discuss three versions of this view. We shall criticize a number of their common assumptions directly in the last part of this section and indirectly in the presentation of the interactionist position which follows.

(1) The first way of subordinating explanation to interpretation involves not so much the goals of inquiry as much as it does explanation's practical unrealizability. This view holds that the barriers to explanation in human matters are practical rather than principled. We may dub this approach "pragmatic modesty" and Edward Shils (1972) is its best representative. He willingly acknowledges the lack of nomological progress in the human sciences and thinks that practitioners in the human sciences cannot do much more at present than set their sights on more modest accomplishments. Perhaps one day the methods, procedures, and concepts of the social sciences will be more sophisticated and refined enough to place social and cultural inquiry on a firmer methodological and theoretical footing. But for now the human sciences are a "heterogeneous aggregate of topics, related to each other by a common name, by more or less common techniques, by a community of key words and conceptions, by a more or less commonly held

aggregate of major interpretive ideas and schemas" (1972, 275). Interpretation is primary; explanation is subordinate.

According to Shils, human beings living in social situations have had to make policy decisions for millennia. The practicalities of such decision-making lead to questions about the principles on which they are made, that is, the basis for choosing one policy rather than another for organizing and enhancing social life. What is the basis for those policies which guide human choices? "Social science" simply makes this complex and intricate project of devising adequate and fruitful policy for the ordering of social life more systematic. It is an essentially interpretive undertaking driven by the practical necessities of life. It is not that interpretation excludes explanation; explanation is allowable but, at present, unreachable. That is not where we need to place our attention.

Shils states his position most forcefully in the following passage (1972, 275–76):

> Most sociology is not scientific. ... It contains little of generality of scope and little of fundamental importance which is rigorously demonstrated by commonly accepted procedures for making relatively reproducible observations of important things. Its theories are not ineluctably bound to its observations. The standards of proof are not stringent. Despite valiant efforts its main concepts are not precisely defined; its most interesting interpretive propositions are not unambiguously articulated.

So, whereas social science is not very scientific in terms of rigorous demonstration, reproducible results, and all the other paraphernalia that accompany natural sciences, as a system of interpretation, "an aggregate of major interpretive ideas and schemes" constraining a severely limited explanatory component, it is capable of effecting human progress.

(2) Some scholars argue that, in the case of human subjects, understanding is not only the *goal* of inquiry in the human sciences but must also be the *method* of inquiry. When human symbolic systems are the subject matter of study, explanatory approaches cannot reach the goal of understanding without first adverting to the rational content of the systems in need of explication, and rational content requires rational analysis. The consequence of that view is that reasons require understanding and not causal explication. The human sciences study reasons rather than causes because human action is, in fact, behavior undergirded by reasons. Reasons require understanding and therefore interpretation; causes require explanation. According to Peter Winch (1958, 23), Durkheim adopted a regressive position when he said:

> I consider extremely fruitful this idea that social life should be explained, not by the notions of those who participate in it, but by more

profound causes which are unperceived by consciousness, and I think that these causes are to be sought mainly in the manner according to which the associated individuals are grouped. Only in this way, it seems, can history become a science, and sociology itself exist.

As Winch recognizes, Durkheim is trying to establish a social science according to the model of a natural science by attempting to locate "more profound causes" than rational contents which are normally held to explain human behavior. From Durkheim's point of view, the ideas of the members of a society are not the subject matter of the social sciences; that subject matter about which scientific generalizations can and should be made are "social relations."

Winch thinks that changing the subject matter in this way is a mistake and proposes, instead, that we look precisely at actions which are performed for reasons. When we analyze such actions we uncover meaningful behavior. "All behavior which is meaningful (therefore all specifically human behavior) is *ipso facto* rule-governed" (1958, 52). Such rule-governed behavior has more to do with the relationships between ideas requiring interpretation than it does with causal relationships involving theoretical explanation. "It is like applying one's knowledge of a language in order to understand a conversation rather than like applying one's knowledge of the laws of mechanics to understand the workings of a watch" (1958, 183).

What is interesting about Winch's view is that it does not necessarily exclude the causal role that reasons might play in accounting for human behavior. After all, reasons can be causes. But Winch is more interested in analyzing the *relations* between reasons than their causal role. Relations between reasons and actions require an analysis in terms of rules rather than an explanation in terms of causes.

Winch's view has attracted ample criticism already (Wilson 1970). In addition, a more sophisticated version of the view has emerged. The reservations we express with Rudolf Makkreel's view discussed below apply with even greater force to the position Winch defends.

(3) Makkreel (1985) asserts that all discussions of human interests and intentions are *fundamentally* interpretive and that, virtually by definition, human interests and intentions pervade all human activity. Hence, as Rorty and other interpretive exclusivists have maintained, even the natural sciences contain an ineliminable interpretive element. However, there is a second sort of higher level, hermeneutic endeavor which recognizes the importance of subjects' *own* views of their interests and intentions, maintaining that they always constitute an additional set of factors which enter in the mix. Although these self-perceptions enjoy no ultimate explanatory privilege, they are also ineliminable in discussions of human affairs. Such interpretive endeavors set

the agenda for any explanatory excursions we may make in our attempts to account for human behavior. This position is not antagonistic to explanation, but it does insist that explanatory projects are always dependent upon and, therefore, subordinated to the interpretive enterprise.

Makkreel states that: "explanation involves subsuming the particular data or elements that can be abstracted from our experience under general laws, whereas understanding is more concerned with focusing on the concrete contents of individual processes of experience to consider how they function as part of *a larger continuum*" (1985, 238, emphasis ours). He thinks that any understanding of human experience will have to subordinate explanatory theories (which are arrived at by *abstraction*) to interpretive endeavors (which are focused on the *concrete* contents of that human experience). These concrete contents have a priority over abstractions from human experience. Furthermore, the point about these contents of experience is not so much what accounts for them as it is their position and role in the "larger continuum." Makkreel does not shrink from the charge of circularity so frequently leveled at hermeneuticists. In fact, he acknowledges the circularity of hermeneutics and argues that it is productive. Its productivity lies in its ability to "widen our framework of interpretation and generate new meaning, so that we will not just refine our original understanding but enrich it" (1985, 247).

Although we thoroughly concur with Makkreel's view of the productivity of interpretation, the position he defends seems incomplete at certain points. Happily, his view widens the hermeneutic circle by focusing on the production of new meaning. But it faces three problems. First, the production of new meaning assumes a great deal of background knowledge (which is both relatively fixed and relatively reliable). Both the fixity and reliability of that background knowledge depend largely upon the stability of previously established explanatory theories. Consequently, the hermeneutical process presupposes, in part, what it allegedly subordinates. The point, in short, is that we cannot expand our meanings without already assuming that we have some knowledge of the world already in place.

Second, the position in question does not deny the possibility of empirical psychology. Presumably, some theories in that field constitute part of the background knowledge which undergirds interpretations. The world that science discloses includes facts about ourselves. Consequently, the priority attributed to self-perceptions of interests and intentions is problematic in the face of scientific findings to the contrary. For example, considerable recent work in social cognition has consistently demonstrated subjects' ready willingness to cite plausible common-sense explanations of their behaviors in terms of standard folk accounts of their interests and intentions, even when, unbeknownst to them, those accounts are thoroughly unrelated to the causal variables experimenters have isolated which are sufficient to explain the overwhelming bulk of the variance in their behaviors. (See Nisbett and Wilson

1977, Nisbett and Ross 1980, Stich 1983, and Churchland 1986.) In light of this research it is unclear why researchers should hold out for the ineliminable importance of subjects' accounts of their intentions and interests in all cases of intentional action.

These self-attributions are informed by our prevailing common-sense view in psychology. But the history of science is replete with examples of new scientific discoveries overthrowing the prevailing common-sense or folk theories. Common sense is theoretical through and through (Churchland 1979). This includes not only common-sense views of the external world but also common-sense views of (even our own) internal, psychological goings-on (Churchland 1988). If common-sense accounts can compete with those of science, then they are subject to correction or even elimination in light of the theoretical upheavals which characterize scientific change (McCauley 1986b).

Third, although the production of new meaning may enrich our knowledge, it cannot account for the production of new *knowledge*. At least some of the time when the world proves recalcitrant to the theories that we propose, neither the stock of meanings we possess nor the interpretations we impose are capable of overcoming the disparity. Rappaport (1979, 139) protests that "as law cannot do the work of meaning neither can meaning do the work of law. The lawful operation of natural processes is neither constituted nor transformed by understanding, and the laws of nature prevail in their domains whether or not they are understood or meaningful." Occasionally, phenomena from the parts of the world that our established theories organize refuse to behave properly no matter how much those theories bend. Every genuinely *empirical* theory has its breaking point, and the incompatibility of some phenomena is too heavy for them to bear. If they could accommodate anything, the theories in question would not be empirical. Although Kuhn (1970), Laudan (1977), and others have documented the many strategies scientists have employed to shelve such anomalies, they concede that in the long run it is precisely the persistence and proliferation of such anomalies that is the single most fundamental force in scientific change. If all theories could accommodate anything (by simply producing new meanings), we could make no sense whatsoever of distinguishing between the relative empirical responsibility of the various disciplines such that it remains uncontroversial when we label some as sciences.

Hence, the development of new explanatory theories has one foot in the hermeneutical circle but another outside it as well at least to the extent that we *presume* a great deal of explanatory knowledge when we contemplate alternative interpretations. This is not to say that interpretation has no role here, but rather that in any inquiry we *must* leave the huge majority of our systematic empirical knowledge unquestioned. Inquiry could not proceed if we left even much of that knowledge up for grabs. Certainly, the generation of new explanatory knowledge does depend, in part, on interpretive endeavors, whose production of new meanings is an important step in that process. It refines and enriches our conceptual resources from which new theoretical proposals emerge. However, that the generation of new theory depends upon the production of new meanings does not imply that explanatory knowledge is uniquely subordinate in some fundamental way to the interpretive enterprise. Indeed, we are suggesting that interpretive pursuits presuppose and, thus, depend just as surely on explanatory knowledge.

Consequently, we maintain that the growth of knowledge depends upon the *interaction* of interpretation and explanation. Widening the circle of meanings is not enough. A satisfactory epistemology must make sense of both the recent psychological findings which bear on our folk theories about the way the mind works and the distinction between scientific and non-scientific pursuits. Still, Makkreel's concern with the problem of understanding the role of individual elements within a larger conceptual system is important. The point is that questions of meaning do not exhaust questions of knowledge. It is our view that both hermeneutic exclusivists and the various inclusivist versions of the relationships between interpretation and explanation have conceded more than they should to the logical empiricists' account of natural science and to their account of scientific explanation in particular. Therefore, they have adopted unduly defensive positions about the relative autonomy (indeed, the priority!) of interpretation and unnecessarily circumscribed the territory in which they think the human sciences can make substantial progress. In our discussion of interactionism we shall suggest that logical empiricism is not nearly as intimidating as it might appear.

Interactionism

The third position, which we call the interactive, neither excludes nor subordinates. It acknowledges the differences between interpretation and explanation and champions the positive values of each. We do not think that explanation is free from interpretive elements. On the contrary, explanation is riddled with interpretation. Nor do we think that interpretation either can or should supplant or supersede explanation, even in the study of human subjects. The temptation to think that it could (to which both hermeneutic exclusivism and inclusivism succumb) is based, in large part, upon overwhelming attention to the model of explanation promoted by the paradigmatic explanatory exclusivists, namely, the logical empiricists. Their attention to the logical empiricist model of explanation has blinded hermeneutic exclusivists and inclusivists to relevant work in recent philosophy of science and psychology. The exclusivist and inclusivist approaches we have discussed fail to appreciate the positive contributions that both interpretation and explanation make in creating understanding.

In the remainder of this chapter we shall briefly examine the general philosophical issues and present a less rigid view of explanation. We open here with a short discussion of the logical empiricist model of explanation and some problems it faces.

Over the last twenty years philosophers of science have thoroughly criticized the model of scientific explanation which the logical empiricists advanced (Suppe 1977). That model focused quite selectively on the *logical features* of explanations in the *physical sciences*. The logical empiricists' pre-occupation with the physical sciences was a function of their covert (anti-) metaphysical agenda and those sciences' rigor and success (Oppenheim and Putnam 1958). Their preoccupation with logical issues was a function of the power and clarity that prior achievements in logic offered for the analysis of claims and the logical empiricists' larger epistemological project which was a version of Cartesian foundationalism with a decidedly empiricist twist.

Their project was foundational, since they maintained that our only justifiable knowledge consisted in the truths of logic and those claims that survived the rigors of empirical verification. Claims which could not be empirically tested must be translatable into those which could. Such translation depended upon ultimately explicating all non-logical notions in terms of some observable predicate or other. This process, which included the reduction of the theoretical to the observable, promised logical empiricism a thoroughly extensional semantics. The logical empiricists confined knowledge to the logically and empirically knowable, and they confined the meaningful to the knowable so defined. On this view, then, the formal and physical sciences are not only the paradigms of human knowledge, they may well exhaust it. Other sorts of human utterances—the poetic, the moral, the political, the metaphysical, and the religious—were expressive at best or, more often, utter nonsense.

The logical empiricists held that scientists explain phenomena when they have formulated theories that employ true causal laws which in conjunction with statements of initial and boundary conditions suffice as the premises of a deductive argument from which a statement about the phenomenon to be explained follows as a deductive consequence. The phenomenon to be explained is the *explanandum*, and the laws and the statement about conditions from which the explanandum is derived constitute the *explanans*. On this view explanation is both deductive and nomological. Explanations which conform to the deductive-nomological (or D-N) model utilize "covering" laws which have the form of universally quantified conditional statements. Such laws claim that for *all* objects, *if* certain initial and boundary conditions obtain, *then* the phenomenon to be explained will as well. The statements in the explanans about the relevant conditions assert that they have, indeed, obtained, so the explanandum follows as the conclusion of a straightforward deductive argument (Hempel 1965).

Critics have objected to nearly every aspect of the logical empiricist program. We will not rehearse all of those criticisms here. Before we briefly discuss some problems with their D-N (or covering law) model of explanation in particular, we will simply list five internal problems with the logical empiricists' epistemology which, even most of them recognized, had utterly resisted satisfactory solution. (See, for example, Carnap 1936–37.) This is *not* to imply that these five points exhaust logical empiricism's weaknesses or problems.

(1) The distinction between theory and observation was pivotal to logical empiricism. It tracked a further distinction between the empirical foundation of knowledge and the theoretical edifice constructed upon it. Unfortunately, as yet no one has satisfactorily formulated either distinction and subsequent research seems to indicate that no one is ever likely to, since evidence mounts from a number of quarters that we make few, if any, observations independently of a theoretical framework (Brown 1979 and Churchland 1979).

(2) Even if they could have forged an acceptable distinction between theory and observation, it became obvious early on that the meaning of most theoretical terms was not exhaustively reducible to observational terms and certainly not by means of the mechanisms that the first-order predicate calculus afforded. They could accomplish very partial reductions, at best. This jeopardized the logical empiricists' goal of developing a thoroughly extensional semantics (and undermined their dismissive view of non-scientific discourse).

(3) Although they rarely singled out the foundational claims of their own position for derision, the logical empiricists' theses on meaning and truth (in particular) failed, just as thoroughly as the most speculative metaphysical claims, to satisfy their own criteria for meaningfulness and truth. (See Putnam 1981, 103–26 and 1983, 184–204.)

(4) Their confidence in science notwithstanding, logical empiricists never offered a convincing solution to the logical problem of induction. For the logical empiricists the premier attraction of science resided in the verification of laws of nature. However, they could not supply adequate grounds to justify their confidence in those laws' truth, since scientific laws are, indeed, conditional claims which apply *universally* (Popper 1972).

(5) Finally, logical empiricism propounded a normative view of science which excluded many of the sciences! Not only did most of the sciences substantially differ from the idealized model of physical inquiry the logical

empiricists championed, some critics suggested that even areas of physical inquiry failed to meet its exacting standards. Probably logical empiricism's most off-putting consequence on this count was its failure to make sense of much of the work in the biological sciences and in the development of the synthetic theory of evolution, in particular. The rigor of their model of scientific explanation came at a heavy price.

These last two points bear directly on problems with the deductive-nomological model of explanation. Item (4) concerned the problem of establishing the truth of universally quantified claims which is one version of the problem of induction. The D-N model of explanation requires not only that scientific explanations use laws but also that those laws are true. Logical empiricism never offered any suitable means for ascertaining how we could ever know that proposed scientific laws met this criterion.

Item (5) discussed how the rigor of the logical empiricists' demands on acceptable science ended up excluding many activities that seemed clearly scientific. Their commitment to the D-N model of explanation also led to profound skepticism among the logical empiricists about those sciences' modes of explanation as well. Consequently, many critics have suggested that the D-N model of explanation is too rigid, when it requires, for example, that an explanation should be "logically conclusive" in the sense that it must offer a sound argument in support of the explanandum (Hempel 1965, 234). Even Hempel recognized that the stringency of this condition disqualified statistical and functional explanations in biology and psychology. In later work he proposed accounts of both as the sorts of logical compromises (relative to the standards of the D-N model) which the complexities of some phenomena seem, at least presently, to demand. (Hempel 1965 discusses functional explanation [pp. 297–330], statistical explanation [pp. 376–412], and other forms of explanation which fall short of the D-N standards [pp. 412–91].)

Many critics, however, maintain that Hempel has not conceded enough and have suggested that these and other "corrupted" forms of scientific explanation are, in fact, the standard forms that scientists employ and, hence, ought to inspire proposed criteria for the acceptability of explanations in science. (See, for example, Salmon 1970; Wimsatt 1972; and McMullin 1978.) Their general complaint is that the restrictiveness of the D-N model is not only excessive, but is rather artificial as well. It captures neither the everyday nor the scientific sense of "explanation." The general consensus is that a science that confined itself to funding sound deductive-nomological explanations would make very little progress.

Ironically, other critics have argued that the D-N model of explanation is not demanding enough. In a now classic article, Bromberger (1966) found the D-N model too weak. The D-N model offers no apparatus for capturing the relation between the problems scientists face and the explanations they seek. The height of a pole can be deduced from information about the length of its shadow, the height of the sun, and a few geometrical and optical principles, but such a D-N account would hardly qualify as an *explanation* of the pole's height nor would it justify any causal attributions. Although Hempel claims that "in no other way than by reference to empirical laws can the assertion of a causal connection between events be scientifically substantiated" (1965, 233), Bromberger's charge, in short, is that the D-N model still does not supply sufficient conditions for a causal explanation.

This objection is of a piece with those of pragmatically oriented critics who charge that the logical empiricists' overwhelming concentration on the logical structure of finished theories and on the context of justification blinded them to considerations of practical problem solving and the role of discovery in scientific research. (See, for example, Laudan 1977.) According to these critics, logical empiricism was unduly taken with the formal, synchronic, and explanatory issues which questions of justification raised about finished theories in the physical sciences. It was, by contrast, almost completely silent on the practical, historical, and problem-solving issues which questions of discovery raise about the production of solutions not only to those theoretical problems but to technological, social, and (even) metaphysical ones as well. If not so obviously in the context of justification, certainly in the context of discovery *interpretive* questions resurface. Our suggestion is that even if scholars could draw a neat distinction between the contexts of justification and discovery, they are not fruitfully considered in isolation from one another. It is with such pragmatic considerations in mind that we offer (in contrast to the rigidity of the logical empiricist account) a less formal, general account of explanation in science. Before we take this project up, though, we need to comment on the multifarious character of explanation.

Explanatory concerns play a fundamental role in everyday life. Common sense provides the various explanatory principles to which we appeal in these everyday contexts. This collection of principles constitutes a rather diverse lot concerning both human behavior and natural phenomena. (The tails of friendly dogs wag; too many cooks spoil the broth; beggars can't be choosers; the sun rises in the east and sets in the west; a red sky at night is a sailor's delight; and so on.) The focus is on explaining *particular* events that occur in the course of everyday life, usually *in service to the interpretation of those events*. The fund of what we have called common-sense explanatory principles that are concerned with the explanation of human behavior is the foundation from which virtually all interpretive projects commence. What is typically missing, though, is a concern for identifying systematic relationships among the explanatory principles. Consequently, these principles inevitably seem largely superficial, if not ad hoc. The crucial point is that even if they are true, the interest of such principles is limited because they lack depth.

Scientific explanation is, no doubt, continuous with everyday explanation, but it surely falls within the more rigorous region of that continuum (certainly, if science supplies, as most would insist, more determinate knowledge). This continuity between scientific explanation and everyday explanation tempts many to obscure the distinction between the two. The dependence of interpretation upon the principles of everyday explanation tempts many to obscure the distinction between these two too. We strongly suspect that it is these two gaffes that open the door to hermeneutic exclusivism (which, we trust, it is obvious that we reject). Since that position minimizes the differences between the two enterprises, they become functionally interchangeable and the choice between them becomes largely a matter of taste. As a consequence we lose our grip on a vast range of pressing epistemological issues, one of the most important of which is ascertaining those features of our inquiries which lead us to regard them as scientific.

All distinctions (except, perhaps, some of those in logic) fall on some continuum or other, and it is in virtue of this that a little philosophical analysis can always offer grounds for obscuring them. Indeed, this is a worthy basis for distinguishing between two styles of doing philosophy. One emphasizes the continuity of concepts in order to obscure the distinctions between them. The other, by contrast, emphasizes the continuity of concepts in order to improve the distinctions between them. We assume that the contents of this paragraph make it clear into which camp we fall.

We distinguish between science and other knowledge-seeking activities (and between scientific explanation and other types of explanation) for perfectly good reasons[1] concerning, among other things, maintaining clarity in epistemological inquiry. One of the most important of those reasons, which we will not defend here, is that it is the emergence of modern science that is the preeminent datum of the past millennium for epistemology. The epistemological preeminence of science rests not in its ability to capture the ultimate causal structure of reality (whatever that might mean) but rather in its ability to provide systematic explanations of phenomena that enable us to tackle the problems that we face. (Ironically, it is by theorizing about abstract worlds removed from the world that is the object of our interpretations that we develop the most effective tools for coping with that world of everyday experience.)

Clearly, we wish to defend making these distinctions, but again we take a less restrictive approach than that of the logical empiricists. The problem with the logical empiricists' view was that they distinguished both science and its explanations too narrowly. While the logical empiricists were correct to focus on explanation *in science*, their D-N model of explanation does not exhaust our insights about causal relations or any other available means for explicating systematic empirical relations among phenomena.

What are uncontroversial regarded as sciences (and their forms of explanation) have proved far more diverse and free-wheeling than logical empiricism and its D-N model ever permitted. Both are unduly confining, as we have indicated above.

By contrast we maintain, in the face of the actual diversity of science, that explanations are more likely to count as scientific to the extent (1) that they operate by means of *systematically related, general principles* that employ concepts at levels of abstraction removed from that by which the phenomena to be explained is currently characterized and (2) that such systems of principles from which explanations proceed are empirically culpable beyond their initial domain of application. This is to say that the clearest cases of scientific explanations are those which stem from independently testable theories. In short, paradigmatic scientific explanation is *theoretical* explanation. In the next few paragraphs we will comment on this portrait of scientific explanation.

Our account indicates that scientific explanations use principles that are *general*. This concerns the quantity of the propositions in question. A term is general if it refers to a class of entities that has more than one member. A principle is general in one sense if it refers to more than one member of a class of entities that has more than one member. It is general in a stronger sense if it refers to *all* of the members of a class of entities that has more than one member, i.e., if it is a universally quantified statement about a class with multiple members. The more general an explanation's principles are the more likely it is, *ceteris paribus*, to count as scientific.

The least controversially scientific explanations issue from *systems* of related principles. Science is concerned with how the world (in all of its specificity) hangs together. Consequently, these explanatory systems in science liberate us from the isolation that characterizes so many of the explanations of common sense. In science that sort of isolation is a vice. Unconnected, explanatory principles can only summarize available knowledge; they *cannot* extend it.

By contrast, a *theory* using *abstract* concepts *can* extend our knowledge. The theoretical systems from which science's explanations follow involve levels of abstraction higher than those that are readily available given existing conceptual schemes—including those of science. Since a theory's various explanatory principles share many of its abstract concepts, no particular explanatory principle fixes a concept's sense or reference. For this reason scientific explanations, unlike those which emerge from common sense, are not conceptually flat. Nor are they conceptually stagnant. In the course of continuing research a successful theoretical proposal inevitably provokes new explanatory problems, which arise from recognizing that its conceptual resources for the description of a phenomenon are deficient in some important respect. Of course, these explanatory problems provoke new explanatory proposals in their turn. It is the combination of this semantic slack and these sorts of vicissitudes and consequences of a theory's empirical application that motivates the theoretical adjustments that contribute to the growth of knowledge. It is the generality of a theory's explanatory principles, then, in conjunction with the abstractness of its concepts (that those principles mutually employ) that insures that the theory will meet the second requirement that it prove *empirically tractable* in domains beyond that to which it was initially applied. It must extend beyond the domain to which it was initially applied because if the theory pertained only to the principal domain that it was forged to explain, it could be tailor-made in an ad hoc fashion.

It should be reasonably clear by now why the first condition in this account of scientific explanation was temporally qualified as well. It is trivial that the level of abstraction "by which the phenomena to be explained is *currently* characterized" cannot be that which the newly proposed, explanatory theory uses. Successfully accounting for the pertinent phenomena in terms of the explanatory principles of a new theory which utilizes concepts of greater abstraction will mark explanatory progress. This additional abstraction permits the new theory to group the phenomena in question systematically with other phenomena to which the extant framework had failed to connect it for the purposes of explanation.

Unlike the D-N model of the logical empiricists, this approach to explanation envisions multiple forms of explanation in science. In addition to covering law explanations, scientists develop statistical, functional, and structural explanations as well. All of these types of explanation are heuristics for increasing our systematic knowledge of an empirical domain. For example, McMullin (1978) argues that if a science has developed D-N explanations, then scientists in that field search for a structural account of the mechanisms which realize the relations that the causal laws spotlight. We have argued elsewhere that functional explanation is a valuable strategy for unpacking complex causal relations and for rendering them susceptible to mathematical modeling and nomological analysis (McCauley and Lawson 1984). It is the search for explanations of the forms that are *not* already available in a science which is often the impetus for important leaps in the progress of research. (Consider the effect of Watson's and Crick's formulation of the double helix model of DNA on the development of molecular genetics.) The quest for deeper and more comprehensive explanation in science is an unending process. *Explanation is never ultimate* (Popper 1963). Where ultimate explanation begins science ceases.

If this approach to explanation is correct, then interpretive endeavors penetrate this process at every turn. Exclusivism forces us into making an unnecessary choice between these two types of cognitive pursuits; and inclusivism overemphasizes one at the expense of the other. Both the dichotomies of the exclusivists and the compromises of the inclusivists each fail to recognize the complex and positive relationships that explanation and interpretation have to one another. In the world in which our knowledge grows they interact with each other in quite specific ways. Novel *interpretations* utilize the categories of theories and models already in place. Novel *explanations* require the discovery of new theories and models. On the one hand, as Makkreel shows, the production of new meanings facilitates the generation of new explanatory theories. On the other, as we show, prior explanatory discoveries inform all good interpretation.

When we seek better interpretations, we *assume* the categories of the theories and models at our disposal (Murphy and Medin 1985 and Lakoff 1987). When we develop better explanations we might very well start off with a set of established categories, but we might have to abandon them in the light of the unexpected implications new models suggest. Interpretations make sense of new experiences on the basis of ready-made conceptual schemes. There is always some view of things already in place. Children are born into a world in which a system of concepts is already at work; the child's job is to discover that system of concepts and to learn how to use it. It is equally true, for child or adult, that no system of concepts suffices for all situations, meets all interests, or serves all purposes.

When people seek better interpretations they attempt to employ the categories they have in better ways. By contrast, when people seek better explanations, they go beyond the rearrangement of categories; they *generate* new theories which will, if successful, replace or even eliminate the conceptual scheme with which they presently operate (McCauley 1986b).

The growth of knowledge is most profound when a better interpretation in terms of existing categories is not enough (because the extant categories simply cannot do the job). In that case, it is not just that proposed interpretations do not stand the tests of life-experience and common sense (for that would simply be another way of presupposing the strong distinction between theory and observation). The failure to acknowledge the theoretical character of common sense invests it with an undeserved epistemological preeminence in the assessment of novel views. It generates the illusion that *within* the hermeneutic circle common sense constitutes a kind of "objective" standard of knowledge—responsible for the stability that our background knowledge displays.

The most provocative discoveries arise in response to the world's continued resistance to established conceptual schemes. These situations require theorizing which exceeds current conceptual structures and which suggests new possibilities. Revolutions in thought do occur. In science, at least, progress can lead to the wholesale elimination of theories that were previously entrenched. These eliminations are a function of the radical discontinuity of the new theory and the old and the increased explanatory and problem-solving adequacy of the new proposals. Those features, in turn, are overwhelmingly assessed on the basis of the new theory's ability to undergo and pass empirical tests. Implicit in the D-N model of explanation and in logical empiricism's focus on completed theories generally is a failure to recognize these two moments in the growth of knowledge (Cummins 1983, 137–38).

Unlike explanation, interpretation is not so obviously concerned with matters of falsifiability. As Sperber (1985, 28–29) says:

> Interpretive generalizations do not in any way specify what is empirically possible or impossible. They provide a fragmentary answer to a simple single question: what is epistemologically feasible? Not: How are things? But: What representation can be given of things? ... Such a statement may be case or hard to corroborate ... but it is beyond falsification.

Note that it follows from this claim that interpretations usually concern more purely conceptual issues (and conceptual relations in particular) than do explanations. Note that it also follows that explanations usually concern more purely empirical issues (and empirical relations in particular) than do interpretations. (Appearances to the contrary, these two claims are not incompatible with the holistic view of semantics. We agree with Quine [1953] that distinctions between empirical and conceptual issues cannot be made once and for all. However, the whole thrust of our constructive argument in this chapter has been to show that *in any particular context of inquiry*, distinguishing empirical and conceptual issues, though still a matter of degree, is not only not impossible, but crucial for an account of the progress of scientific knowledge.) If interpretations are not generally falsifiable as Sperber maintains, then they do not make the kinds of systematic empirical claims in terms of which we have characterized explanation in science. If, typically, they do not make systematic empirical claims, then the function of interpretation is surely different from explanation and it is that very difference that makes it possible for the two to interact (Rappaport 1979, 157–58).

Those who downplay the importance of attempts to distinguish between interpretation and explanation on the basis of their relative empirical tractability wish to emphasize the continuities between our methods of criticizing interpretive and explanatory proposals. However, as we maintained before, merely obscuring distinctions never increases knowledge; the proper goal is to improve upon obscure distinctions by formulating more precise ones (but, then, as Whitehead recommended, remaining ever vigilant in our mistrust of new found clarity).

Explanation and interpretation, then, are different cognitive tasks. They supplement and support one another in the pursuit of knowledge (Sperber 1985, 10). Specifically, interpretations presuppose (and may reorganize) our systematic, empirical knowledge, whereas successful explanatory theories both winnow and increase it. Interpretations uncover unexpected connections in the knowledge we already possess; the success of new explanatory theories establishes new vistas. Consequently, the process of explanation is productive as well. Knowledge is always in the making. The processes *of* interpretation and explanation are interrelated and necessary steps in understanding the world and our place in it. *If* new explanations supplement, modify, or replace existing conceptual schemes, interpretive endeavors reorganize them in order to prepare the ground for further explanation. This interaction is an unending affair.

Our purpose in this chapter has been both to distinguish these two enterprises and to show how they are related. After all, holy matrimony can only join together what were two distinct entities before. We admit the mutual co-dependence of the two activities; however, we refuse to collapse the distinction. (Husband and wife still remain male and female.) Unlike the inclusivists, we refuse to subordinate one to the other. (Sexism is a sin.) Unlike the exclusivist, we recognize the value of both pursuits. (Attempting to maintain the appearance of self-sufficiency yields a lonely life.)

Notes

* This article was originally published in *Rethinking Religion, Connecting Cognition and Culture* (Cambridge: Cambridge University Press, 1990).
1. This is not to say that they are completely different. (To repeat—all distinctions, except for those of logic, fall on some semantic continuum.)

References

Bromberger, S. 1966. Why Questions. In *Mind and Cosmos: Explorations in the Philosophy of Science*, ed. R. Conodny. Pittsburgh: University of Pittsburgh Press.

Brown, H. 1979. *Perception, Theory and Commitment*. Chicago: University of Chicago Press.

Carnap, R. 1936–37. Testability and Meaning. *Philosophy of Science* 3: 420–68 and 4: 1–40.

Churchland, P. M. 1979. *Scientific Realism and the Plasticity of Mind*. Cambridge: Cambridge University Press.

—1988. *Matter and Consciousness: A Contemporary Introduction to the Philosophy of Mind*. 2nd edn. Cambridge: MIT Press.

Churchland, P. S. 1986. *Neurophilosophy*. Cambridge: MIT Press.

Cummins, R. 1983. *The Nature of Psychological Explanations*. Cambridge: MIT Press.

Eliade, M. 1963. *The Sacred and the Profane*. New York: Harper & Row.

Geertz, C. 1973. *The Interpretation of Cultures*. New York: Basic Books.

Grunbaum, A. 1984. *The Foundations of Psychoanalysis: A Philosophical Critique*. Berkeley: University of California Press.

Hempel, C. 1965. *Aspects of Scientific Explanation*. New York: The Free Press.

Kuhn, T. 1970. *The Structure of Scientific Revolutions*. 2nd ed. Chicago: University of Chicago Press.

Lakoff, G. 1987. *Women, Fire and Dangerous Things: What Categories Reveal about the Mind*. Chicago: University of Chicago Press.

Laudan, L. 1977. *Progress and Its Problems*. Berkeley: University of California Press.

Lesche, E. 1985. Is Psychoanalysis Therapeutic Technique or Scientific Research? A Metascientific Investigation. *Annals of Theoretical Psychology*, Volume 3, ed. K. Madsen and L. Mos. New York: Plenum Press.

Makkreel, R. 1985. Dilthey and Universal Hermenetics: The Status of the Human Sciences. *Journal of the British Society of Phenomenology* 16: 234–40.

McCauley, R. 1986a. Searching for a Fully Scientific Psychology. *Contemporary Psychology* 31: 844–45.

—1986b. Inter-theoretical Relations and the Future of Psychology. *Philosophy of Science* 53: 179–99.

McCauley, R., and E. Lawson. 1984. Functionalism Reconsidered. *History of Religions* 23: 372–81.

McMullin, E. 1978. Structural Explanation. *American Philosophical Quarterly* 15: 139–47.

Murphy, G., and D. Medin. 1985. The Role of Theories in Conceptual Coherence. *Psychological Review* 92: 289–316.

Nisbett, R., and L. Ross. 1980. *Human Inference: Strategies and Shortcomings of Social Judgment*. Englewood Cliffs, NJ: Prentice-Hall.

Nisbett, R., and T. Wilson. 1977. Telling More Than We Can Know: Verbal Reports of Mental Processes. *Psychological Review* 84: 231–59.

Oppenheim, P., and H. Putnam. 1958. *Unity of Science as a Working Hypothesis. Minnesota Studies in the Philosophy of Science*, Volume 2, ed. H. Feigl, M. Scriven, and G. Maxwell. Minneapolis: University of Minnesota Press.

Otto, R. 1958. *The Idea of the Holy*. New York: Oxford University Press.

Penner, H. 1986. Structure and Religion. *History of Religions* 25: 236–84.

Popper, K. 1963. *Conjectures and Refutations*. New York: Harper & Row.

—1972. *Objective Knowledge: An Evolutionary Approach*. Oxford: Oxford University Press.

Putnam, H. 1981. *Reason, Truth and History*. New York: Cambridge University Press.

—1983. *Realism and Reason*. New York: Cambridge University Press.

Quine, W. 1953. Two Dogmas in Empiricism. In *From a Logical Point of View*. New York: Harper & Row.

Rappaport, R. 1979. *Ecology, Meaning, and Religion*. Richmond, CA: North Atlantic Books.

Ricouer, P. 1974. *The Conflict of Interpretation*, ed. D. Ihde. Evanston: Northwestern University Press.

Rorty, R. 1982. *Consequences of Pragmatism*. Minneapolis: University of Minnesota Press.

Rosenberg, A. 1980. *Sociobiology and the Preemption of Social Science*. Baltimore: The Johns Hopkins University Press.

Rudner, R. 1966. *Philosophy of Social Science*. Englewood Cliffs, NJ: Prentice-Hall.

Salmon, W. 1970. *Statistical Explanation and Statistical Relevance*. Pittsburg: University of Pittsburg Press.

Shils, E. 1972. *The Constitution of Society*. Chicago: University of Chicago Press.

Skinner, B. 1953. *Science and Human Behavior*. New York: Macmillan.

Sperber, D. 1985. *On Anthropological Knowledge*. Cambridge: Cambridge University Press.

Stich, S. 1983. *From Folk Psychology to Cognitive Science: The Case Against Belief*. Cambridge: MIT Press.

Suppe, F., ed. 1977. *The Structure of Scientific Theories*. 2nd ed. Urbana: University of Illinois Press.

Wilson, B., ed. 1970. *Rationality*. New York: Harper & Row.

Wimsatt, W. 1972. Teleology and the Logical Structure of Function Statements. *Studies in the History of the Philosophy of Science* 3: 1–80.

Winch, P. 1958. *The Idea of a Social Science*. London: Routledge and Kegan Paul.

2

THE EPIDEMIOLOGY OF BELIEFS: A NATURALISTIC APPROACH[*]

Dan Sperber

Abstract

I would like to bring together two sets of speculations: anthropological speculations on cultural representations and psychological speculations on the cognitive
organization of beliefs, and to put forward, on the basis of these speculations, fragments of a possible answer to the question: how do beliefs become cultural? I will
not apologize for the speculative character of the attempt. At this stage, either the
question is answered in a vague, fragmentary and tentative way, or it must be left
alone: there is not enough sound theorizing and well-regimented evidence in the
domain to do otherwise.

&.) Cß

Anthropological Speculations

I use "cultural representation" in a wide sense: anything that is both cultural and a representation will do. Thus, cultural representations can be
descriptive ("Witches ride on broomsticks") or normative ("With fish, drink
white wine"); simple, as in the above examples, or complex, like the common law or Marxist ideology taken as a whole; verbal, as in the case of a

myth, or non-verbal, as in the case of a mask, or multi-media, as in the case of a Mass.

To begin with, two remarks about the notion of a representation. First, "to represent" is not a two-place predicate: something represents something; it is a three-place predicate: something represents something for someone. Second, we should distinguish two kinds of representations: internal, or *mental representations*—for example, memories, which are patterns in the brain and which represent something for the owner of that brain—and external, or *public representations*—for example, utterances, which are material phenomena in the environment of people and which represent something for people who perceive and interpret them.

Which are more basic: public or mental representations? Most cognitive psychologists (see Fodor 1975) see mental representations as more basic: for public representations to be representations at all, they must be mentally represented by their users; for instance, an utterance represents something only for someone who perceives, decodes and comprehends it—that is, associates with it a (multilevel) mental representation. On the other hand, mental representations can exist without public counterparts; for instance, many of our memories (and all or nearly all the memories of an elephant) are never communicated. Therefore, it is argued, mental representations are more basic than public ones.

Most social scientists (and also philosophers such as Ludwig Wittgenstein [1953] and Tyler Burge [1979] do not agree: they see public representations as more basic than mental ones. Public representations are observable, both by their users and by scientists, whereas mental representations, if they exist at all, can only be surmised. More importantly, it is claimed (e.g. by Vygotsky [1965]) that mental representations result from the internalization of public representations and of underlying systems (e.g. languages and ideologies) without which no representation is possible. But if so, public representations must be more basic than mental ones. (This denies mental representations to non-social animals, but holders of this view don't mind.)

There is an obvious sense in which public representations do come before mental ones: a child is born into a world full of public representations, and is bombarded with them from the first moments of her life. She does not discover the world unaided, and then make public her privately developed representations of it; rather, a great many of her representations of the world are acquired vicariously, not through experience, but through communication, or through a combination of experience and communication. Moreover, her very ability to communicate effectively is contingent upon her acquiring the language and the other communication tools of her community. However, those who see mental representations as basic are not (or should not be) denying this point. What they are (or should be) denying is that public representations could be of use to the child if she did not have, to begin with, some system of mental representations with which to approach the public ones.

Conversely, those who see public representations as basic are not (or should not be) merely making the trivial point that each individual is born into a world full of public representations and crucially relies on them. They are (or should be) claiming not only that the physical shape of public representations is public, outside people's heads, there for people to perceive, but also that the *meaning* of public representations is public, out there for people to grasp. On this view, meaning—the regular relationship between that which represents and that which is being represented—is social before being individually grasped; hence, in the relevant sense, public representations are more basic than mental ones. This leads anthropologists, in particular, to consider that "culture is public because meaning is" (Geertz 1973, 12). Most anthropologists study culture as a system of public representations endowed with public meanings, without any reference to the corresponding mental representations.

I have a bias: I am a materialist—not in the sense this word too often has in the social sciences, where a materialist is one who believes that the economic "infrastructure" determines the ideological "superstructure," but in the sense of philosophy and the natural sciences: that all causes and all effects are material. I then wonder: what kind of material objects or properties could public meanings possibly be? I am not persuaded by Geertz when he dismisses the issue thus:

> The thing to ask about a burlesqued wink or a mock sheep raid [two of his examples of public representations], is not what their ontological status is. It is the same as that of rocks on the one hand and dreams on the other—they are things of this world. The thing to ask is what their import is: what it is ... that, in their occurrence and through their agency, is getting said. (Geertz 1973, 10)

I am not persuaded, because the task of ontology is not so much to say which things are "of this world" and which are not, as to say in what manner, or manners, things can be of this world; and regarding cultural things, the problem stands.

We understand reasonably well how material things fit into the world; but we don't know that there are immaterial things, and if there are, we don't know how they fit. Hence, for any class of entities—rocks, memories, or cultural representations—a materialist account, if it is available at all, is preferable, on grounds of intelligibility and parsimony.

In the case of mental things such as memories or reasonings, cognitive psychologists accept at least a form of minimal materialism, which has precise methodological implications. From a cognitive point of view, an appropriate description of a mental phenomenon must, *inter alia*, show that this phenomenon can be materially realized. For example, cognitive psychologists may try to show how a reasoning process could be materially implemented on a computer. Thus, with the development of cognitive psychology, we begin to grasp what kind of material objects mental representations might be.

Now, when it comes to cultural representations allegedly endowed with public meanings, whether we pay lip-service to materialism and declare them to be material too or resign ourselves to ontological pluralism, the truth of the matter is that we have no idea in what manner they might be "things of this world."

The materialist alternative is to assume that both mental and public representations are strictly material objects, and to take the implications of this assumption seriously. Cognitive systems such as brains construct internal representations of their environment partly on the basis of physical interactions with that environment. Because of these interactions, mental representations are, to some extent, regularly connected to what they represent; as a result, they have semantic properties, or "meaning," of their own (see Dretske 1981; Fodor 1987; Millikan 1984). Public representations, on the other hand, are connected to what they represent only through the meaning attributed to them by their producers or their users; they have no semantic properties of their own. In other words, public representations have meaning only through being associated with mental representations.

Public representations are generally attributed similar meanings by their producers and by their users, or else they could never serve the purpose of communication. This similarity of attributed meaning is itself made possible by the fact that people have similar enough linguistic and encyclopedic knowledge. Similarity across people makes it possible to abstract from individual differences and to describe "the language" or "the culture" of a community, "the meaning" of a public representation, or to talk of, say, "the belief" that witches ride on broomsticks as a single representation, independently of its public expressions or mental instantiations. What is then described is an abstraction. Such an abstraction may be useful in many ways: it may bring out the common properties of a family of related mental and public representations; it may serve to identify a topic of research. Mistake this abstraction for an object "of this world," however, and you had better heed Geertz's advice and ignore its ontological status.

From a materialist point of view, then, there are only mental representations, which are born, live and die within individual skulls, and public representations, which are plain material phenomena sound waves, light patterns and so forth—in the environment of individuals. Take a particular representation—witches on broomsticks—at an abstract level: what it corresponds to at a concrete level is millions of mental representations and millions of public representations the meanings of which (intrinsic meanings in the case of mental representations, attributed meanings in the case of public ones) are similar to that of the statement: "Witches ride on broomsticks." These millions of mental and public representations, being material objects, can and do enter into cause-effect relationships. They may therefore play a role both as *explanans* and as *explanandum* in causal explanations. The materialist wager is that no other causal explanation of cultural phenomena is needed.

Consider a human group: it hosts a much wider population of representations. Some of these representations are constructed on the basis of idiosyncratic experiences, as, for instance, my memories of the day on which I stopped smoking; others are based on common experiences, as, for instance, our belief that coal is black; others still derive from communication rather than from direct experience, as, for instance, our belief that Shakespeare wrote *Macbeth*. Common experience and communication bring about a similarity of representations across individuals; or, loosely speaking, they cause some representations to be shared by several individuals, sometimes by a whole human group. This loose talk is acceptable only if it is clear that when we say that a representation is "shared" by several individuals, what we mean is that these individuals have mental representations similar enough to be considered versions of one another. When this is so, we can produce a further version—a public one this time—to identify synthetically the contents of these individual representations.

When we talk of cultural representations—beliefs in witches, rules for the service of wines, the common law, or Marxist ideology—we refer to representations which are widely shared in a human group. To explain cultural representations, then, is to explain why some representations are widely shared. Since representations are more or less widely shared, there is no neat boundary between cultural and individual representations. An explanation of cultural representations, therefore, should come as part of a general explanation of the distribution of representations among humans—as part, that is, of an *epidemiology of representations*.

The idea of an epidemiological approach to culture is by no means new. It was suggested by Gabriel Tarde (1895; 1898). Several contemporary biologists have developed it in various ways. The value of an epidemiological approach lies in making our understanding of micro-processes of transmission and macro-processes of evolution mutually relevant. However, if the micro-processes are fundamentally misunderstood, as I believe they have been in previous epidemiological approaches, the overall picture is of limited value. Whatever their differences and their merits, past approaches share a crucial defect: they take the basic process of cultural transmission to be one of replication, and consider alterations in transmission as accidents.

The view of cultural transmission as a process of replication is grounded not only in a biological analogy—a genic mutation is an accident, replication is the norm—but also in two dominant biases in the social sciences. First, as we have already seen, individual differences are idealized away, and cultural representations are too often treated as identical across individuals through-out a human group or subgroup. Second, the prevailing view of communication, as a coding process followed by a symmetrical decoding process, implies that replication of the communicator's thoughts in the minds of the audience is the normal outcome of communication.

In *Relevance: Communication and Cognition,* Deirdre Wilson and I have criticized this code model of human communication, and developed an alternative model which gives pride of place to inferential processes. One of the points we make—a commonsensical point, really, which would hardly be worth making if it were not so often forgotten—is that what human communication achieves in general is merely some degree of resemblance between the communicator's and the audience's thoughts. Strict replication, if it exists at all, should be viewed as just a limiting case of maximal resem-blance, rather than as the norm of communication. (The same is also true of imitation, another well-known but little understood means of cultural trans-mission, which I won't go into here.) A process of communication is basically one of transformation. The degree of transformation may vary between two extremes: duplication and total loss of information. Only those representa-tions which are repeatedly communicated *and* minimally transformed in the process will end up belonging to the culture.

The objects of an epidemiology of representations are neither abstract representations nor individual concrete representations, but, we might say, strains, or families, of concrete representations related both by causal rela-tionships and by similarity of content. Some of the questions we want to answer are: what causes such strains to appear, to expand, to split, to merge with one another, to change over time, to die? Just as standard epidemi-ology does not give a single general explanation for the distribution of all dis-eases, so there is no reason to expect that these questions will be answered in the same way for every kind of representation. The diffusion of a folktale and that of a military skill, for instance, involve different cognitive abilities, different motivations and different environmental factors. An epidemiologi-cal approach, therefore, should not hope for one grand unitary theory. It should, rather, try to provide interesting questions and useful conceptual tools, and to develop the different models needed to explain the existence and fate of the various families of cultural representations.

Though which factors will contribute to the explanation of a particular strain of representations cannot be decided in advance, in every case, some of the factors to be considered will be psychological, and some will be envi-ronmental or ecological (taking the environment to begin at the individual organism's nerve endings and to include, for each organism, all the organ-isms it interacts with). Potentially pertinent psychological, factors include the ease with which a particular representation can be memorized, the existence of background knowledge in relationship to which the representation is relevant, and a motivation to communicate the content of the representation. Ecological factors include the recurrence of situations in which the representation gives rise to, or contributes to, appropriate action, the availability of external memory stores (writing in particular), and the existence of institutions engaged in the transmission of the representation.

Unsurprisingly, psychological and ecological factors are themselves affected by the distribution of representations. Previously internalized cultural representations are a key factor in one's susceptibility to new representations. The human environment is, for a great part, man-made, and made on the basis of cultural representations. As a result, feedback loops are to be expected both within models explaining particular families and between such models. The resulting complexity is of the ecological rather than of the organic kind. Though "organicism" has disappeared from the anthropological scene, the organicist view of a culture as a well-integrated whole still lingers. The epidemiological approach departs from such cultural holism; it depicts individual cultures as wide open, rather than almost closed, systems and as approximating an ecological equilibrium among strains of representations, rather than as exhibiting an organic kind of integration. It is then of interest to find out which strains of representations benefit one another, and which, on the contrary, compete.

The identification of epidemiological phenomena in classical epidemiology often arises out of the study of individual pathology, but the converse is also true: the identification of particular diseases is often aided by epidemiological considerations. Similarly, when types of mental representations have been identified at a psychological level, the question of their epidemiology arises; and, conversely, when particular strains of representations, or mutually supportive strains, have been epidemiologically identified, the question of their psychological character arises. More generally, as with the pathology and epidemiology of diseases, the psychology and epidemiology of representations should prove mutually relevant.

Psychological Speculations

Anthropologists and psychologists alike tend to assume that humans are rational—not perfectly rational, not rational all the time, but rational enough. What is meant by rationality may vary, or be left vague, but it always implies at least the following idea: humans beliefs are produced by cognitive processes which are on the whole epistemologically sound; that is, humans approximately perceive what there is for them to perceive and approximately infer what their perceptions warrant. Of course, there are perceptual illusions and inferential failures, and the resulting overall representation of the world is not totally consistent; but, as they are, the beliefs of humans allow them to form and pursue goals in a manner which often enough leads to the achievement of those goals.

Anthropologists and psychologists tend to assume that humans are rational, without explaining why. I assume some degree of rationality because it makes good biological sense. Why did vertebrates evolve so as to have more and more complex cognitive systems, culminating, it seems, in the human one, if not because this makes their interaction with the environment (e.g. feeding themselves, protecting themselves) more effective? Now, only an epistemologically sound cognitive system (i.e. one that delivers approximations of knowledge rather than pretty patterns or astounding enigmas) can serve that purpose, and, for that, it must be rational enough. This way of explaining why humans are rational implies that there is an objective reality, and that at least one function of human cognition is to represent in human brains aspects of that reality.

Fitting together reality and reason in this manner may seem common-sensical to psychologists, but many anthropologists—not so long ago, most of them—know better. People of different cultures have beliefs which are not only very different, but even mutually incompatible. Their beliefs from our point of view, ours from theirs, seem irrational. If we want to maintain, nevertheless, that both they and we are rational, then an obvious way out is to deny that there is an objective reality to begin with. Reality on that view is a social construct, and there are at least as many "realities" or "worlds" as there are societies. Different beliefs are rational in different socially constructed worlds. I have argued at length against this view (see Sperber 1974, 1985). Here I will merely state my bias: I find a plurality of worlds even less attractive than a plurality of substances; if there is a way, I would rather do without it.

There is a way, but first we must do a bit of conceptual house cleaning. What are we referring to when we talk of "beliefs"? Take an example: we tend to assume that Peter believes that it will rain if he says so, or assents to somebody else saying so, or, in some cases, if he takes his umbrella on his way out. We do not mistake these behaviors for the belief itself; we take them, rather, as caused in part by Peter having the belief in question and, therefore, as evidence of the belief. We might be tempted to say, then (as many philosophers have—e.g. Ryle 1949), that a belief is a disposition to express, assent to, or otherwise act in accordance with, some proposition. As psychologists, however, we will want to go deeper and find out what kind of mental states might bring about such a disposition. An answer often heard nowadays is that humans have a kind of "data base" or "belief box" (Steven Schiffer's phrase) in which some conceptual representations are stored. All representations stored in that particular box are treated as descriptions of the actual world. When the occasion is right, this yields the usual behavioral evidence for belief: assertion and assent in particular.

The belief box story, however attractive, cannot be the *whole* story. Many of the propositions to which we are disposed to assent are not represented at all in our mind—a well-known point—and many of the propositions we are disposed not only to assent to but also to express and, in some cases, to act in accordance with are not, or not simply, stored in a data base or belief box—a more controversial point.

You have long believed that there are more pink flamingos on Earth than on the Moon, but no mental representation of yours had, until now, described that state of affairs. We may well have an infinity of such unrepresented beliefs, and a large proportion of these are widely shared, though of course they have never been communicated. It is reasonable, however, to assume that what makes them unrepresented beliefs (more specifically, propositions to which we are disposed to assent) is that they are inferable from other beliefs which *are* mentally represented. What we need to add for this to the belief box is some inferential device allowing subjects to accept as theirs these unrepresented beliefs on the basis of the actually represented ones. The inferences in question are not made consciously, so the inferential device hooked up to the belief box must be distinct from, and need not resemble, human conscious reasoning abilities (see Sperber and Wilson 1986, ch. 2).

Besides accounting for unrepresented beliefs, hooking the belief box up to an inferential device introduces a factor of rationality in the construction of beliefs. Suppose that some of the representations in our belief box come from perception (broadly understood to include the "perception" of one's own mental states), and that all other beliefs are directly or indirectly inferred from the perceptually based ones. This will already ensure areas of consistency among our beliefs. Suppose, furthermore, that the inferential device recognizes an inconsistency when it meets one, and corrects it. Then you get a tendency to enlarge areas of consistency (even though contradictory beliefs may still be held, provided they are never used as joint premises in an inference).

While perception plus unconscious inference might be the whole story for the beliefs of elephants, it could not be for the beliefs of humans. There are two interconnected reasons for this: first, many—possibly most—human beliefs are grounded not in the perception of the things the beliefs are about, but in communication about these things. Second, humans have a meta-representational, or *interpretive,* ability. That is, they can construct not only *descriptions*—that is, representations of states of affairs—but also *interpretations*—that is, representations of representations. Now, humans use this interpretive ability to understand what is communicated to them and, more generally, to represent meanings, intentions, beliefs, opinions, theories and so on, whether or not they share them. In particular, they can represent a belief and take a favorable attitude to it, and therefore express it, assent to it, and generally show behaviors symptomatic of belief, on a basis quite different from belief box inclusion.

Young Lisa is told by her teacher: "There are male and female plants." She understands "male" and "female" with respect to animals as more or less an extension of the distinction between men and women: females have children, males fight more easily, and so on. She does not see in plants anything resembling this distinction, and so she does not quite understand what her teacher is telling the class. On the other hand, she understands it in part; she understands that in some species there are two types of plants, and guesses that this difference has to do with reproduction, and so on. She trusts her teacher, and if he says that there are male and female plants, then she is willing to say so herself, to say that she believes it, and to exhibit various behaviors symptomatic of that belief.

Behind Lisa's belief behavior, do we have a genuine belief? Not of the belief box kind, certainly, since such a half-understood idea (what I called a "semi-propositional representation" in Sperber 1985, ch. 2) could not have emerged from perception or from inference from perception: it is a typical outcome, rather, of not totally successful communication. Remember, too, that the inferential device must be able to operate freely on beliefs in the belief box so as to yield more mutually consistent beliefs; but in that case half-understood ideas should not be allowed directly in the box, since their consistency with other representations and their implications are largely indeterminate.

But how, then, might Lisa's half-understood idea of there being male and female plants be represented in her mind? Well, she might have in her belief box the following representations:

What the teacher says is true.
The teacher says that there are male and female plants.

Lisa's partial understanding of "there are male and female plants" is now embedded in a belief box belief about what her teacher said. This belief, together with the other belief that "what the teacher says is true," provides a validating context for the embedded representation of the teacher's words. This gives Lisa rational grounds for exhibiting many of the behaviors symptomatic of belief—but grounds quite different from plain belief box inclusion.

What this example suggests is that the beliefs we attribute to people on the evidence provided by their behavior do not belong to a single psychological kind; in other words, quite different types of mental states can bring about identical belief behavior.

I maintain that there are two fundamental kinds of beliefs represented in the mind. There are descriptions of states of affairs directly stored in the belief box; let us call this first kind *intuitive beliefs*. Such beliefs are intuitive in the sense that they are typically the product of spontaneous and unconscious perceptual and inferential processes; in order to hold these intuitive beliefs, one need not be aware of the fact that one holds them, and even less of reasons for holding them. Then there are interpretations of representations embedded in the validating context of an intuitive belief, as in the above example; let us call this second kind *reflective beliefs*. These beliefs are reflective in the sense that they are believed in virtue of second-order beliefs about them.

Intuitive beliefs are derived, or derivable, from perception by means of the inferential device. The mental vocabulary of intuitive beliefs is probably limited to *basic concepts*: that is, concepts referring to perceptually identifiable phenomena and innately pre-formed, unanalyzed abstract concepts (of, say, norm, cause, substance, species, function, number, or truth). Intuitive beliefs are on the whole concrete and reliable in ordinary circumstances. Together they paint a kind of common-sense picture of the world. Their limits are those of common sense: they are fairly superficial, more descriptive than explanatory, and rather rigidly held.

Unlike intuitive beliefs, reflective beliefs do not form a well-defined category. What they have in common is their mode of occurrence: they come embedded in intuitive beliefs (or, since there can be multiple embeddings, in other reflective beliefs). They cause belief behaviors because, one way or another, the belief in which they are embedded validates them. But they may differ in many ways: a reflective belief may be half-understood but fully understandable, as in the above example of the sex of plants; or, as I will shortly illustrate, it may remain half-understood for ever; or, on the contrary, it may be fully understood. The validating context may be an identification of the source of the reflective belief as a reliable authority (e.g. the teacher) or an explicit reasoning. Given the variety of possible contextual validations for reflective beliefs, commitment to these beliefs can widely vary, from loosely held opinions to fundamental creeds, from mere hunches to carefully thought-out convictions. Reflective beliefs play different roles in human cognition, as I will very briefly illustrate.

For Lisa, forming and storing the half-understood reflective belief that there are male and female plants may be a step towards a more adequate understanding of the male–female distinction. It provides her with an incomplete piece of information which further encounters with relevant evidence may help complete. After she achieves an adequate understanding of the matter, her reflective belief that there are male and female plants may well be transferred to, or duplicated in, her belief box as an intuitive belief. So, one role of reflective belief is to serve as a "hold" format for information that needs to be completed before it can constitute an intuitive belief.

Now, consider the following case. Young Bobby has in his belief box the two representations:

What Mom says is true.
Mom says that God is everywhere.

Bobby does not fully understand how somebody, be it God or anyone else, can be everywhere. However, his mother saying so gives him sufficient ground to exhibit all the behaviors symptomatic of belief: he will readily state that God is everywhere, will assent when the same statement is made by others, and may even refrain from sinning in places where (apparently) nobody can see him. That God is everywhere is for Bobby a reflective belief. As he grows older, he may keep this belief and enrich it in many ways, but, if anything, its exact meaning will become even more mysterious than it was at first. Here is a belief which, like most religious beliefs, does not lend itself to a final, clear interpretation, and which therefore will never become an intuitive belief. Part of the interest of religious beliefs for those who hold them comes precisely from this element of mystery, from the fact that you are never through interpreting them. While the cognitive usefulness of religious and other mysterious beliefs may be limited (but see Sperber 1975), it is not too difficult to see how their very mysteriousness makes them "addictive."

In the two examples considered so far—Lisa and the sex of plants, Bobby and divine omnipresence—what made the reflective representation a belief was the authority granted to the source of the representation: the teacher and the mother respectively. Laymen accept scientific beliefs on authority too. For instance, most of us believe that $e = mc^2$ with only a very limited understanding of what this formula means, and no understanding of the arguments that led to its adoption. Our belief, then, is a reflective belief of mysterious content, justified by our trust in the community of physicists. It is not very different, in this respect, from Bobby's belief that God is everywhere.

There is a difference, though. Even for theologians, that God is everywhere is a mystery, and they too accept it on authority. For physicists, on the other hand, the theory of relativity is not a mystery, and they have reasons to accept it which have nothing to do with trust. Well-understood reflective beliefs, such as the scientific beliefs of scientists, include an explicit account of rational grounds to hold them. Their mutual consistency and their consistency with intuitive beliefs can be ascertained, and plays an important, though quite complex, role in their acceptance or rejection. Still, even for physicists, the theory of relativity is a reflective belief; it is a theory, a representation kept under scrutiny and open to revision and challenge, rather than a fact that could be perceived or unconsciously inferred from perception.

Half-understood or mysterious reflective beliefs are much more frequent and culturally important than scientific ones. Because they are only half-understood and therefore open to reinterpretation, their consistency or inconsistency with other beliefs, intuitive or reflective, is never self-evident, and does not provide a robust criterion for acceptance or rejection. Their content, because of its indeterminacy, cannot be sufficiently evidenced or argued for to warrant their rational acceptance. But that does not make these beliefs irrational: they are rationally held if there are rational grounds to trust the source of the belief (e.g. the parent, the teacher, or the scientist).

This, then, is my answer to those who see, in the great diversity and frequent apparent inconsistency of human beliefs, an argument in favor of cultural relativism: there are two classes of beliefs and they achieve rationality in different ways. Intuitive beliefs owe their rationality to essentially innate, hence universal, perceptual and inferential mechanisms; as a result, they do not vary dramatically, and are essentially mutually consistent or reconcilable across cultures. Those beliefs which vary across cultures to the extent of seeming irrational from another culture's point of view are typically reflective beliefs with a content that is partly mysterious to the believers themselves. Such beliefs are rationally held, not in virtue of their content, but in virtue of their source. That different people should trust different sources of beliefs—I, my educators, you, yours—is exactly what you would expect if they are all rational in the same way and in the same world, and merely located in different parts in this world.

Different Types of Beliefs, Different Mechanisms of Distributions

Let us now bring together the anthropological and psychological speculations developed so far. If there are different kinds of beliefs, then we might expect them to be distributed by different mechanisms. More precisely, we might expect the distribution of intuitive beliefs, which are a relatively homogeneous kind, to proceed along roughly common lines, and the distribution of reflective beliefs, which are much more diverse, to take place in many different ways. In this concluding section, I would like to suggest that such is indeed the case.

In all human societies, traditional or modern, with or without writing, with or without pedagogic institutions, all normal individuals acquire a rich body of intuitive beliefs about themselves and their natural and social environment. These include beliefs about the movement of physical bodies, the behavior of one's own body, the effects of various body-environment interactions, the behavior of many living kinds, the behavior of fellow humans. These beliefs are acquired in the course of ordinary interaction with the environment and with others. They need no conscious learning effort on the part of the learner and no conscious teaching effort on the part of others (see Atran and Sperber 1991). Even without teaching, these beliefs are easily acquired by everybody. The more fundamental ones are acquired quite early, suggesting a very strong innate predisposition (see Keil 1979; Carey 1982, 1985; Gelman and Spelke 1981; Hirschfeld 1984, 1994).

Some intuitive beliefs are about particulars (particular locations, personal events, individual animals or people), and are idiosyncratic or are only shared very locally; others are general (or about widely known particulars such as historical events and characters), and are widespread throughout a society. General intuitive beliefs vary across cultures, but they do not seem to vary greatly. To mention just one piece of anecdotal evidence, one has yet to find a culture in which intuitive beliefs about space and movement are so differ-ent from modern Western ones that the natives have inordinate problems in learning to drive a car. Much recent work in ethno-science shows, too, that cross-cultural differences in zoological, botanical, or color classification are rather superficial, and that for each of these domains (and presumably for other domains, e.g. artifacts or mental states), there are underlying universal structures (see Berlin and Kay 1969; Berlin et al. 1973; Berlin 1978; Atran 1985, 1986, 1987).

What role does communication play in the construction of intuitive beliefs? The answer is not simple. Intuitive beliefs are (or are treated as) the output of perception and unconscious inference, either the subject's own perceptions and inferences or those of others in the case of intuitive beliefs acquired through communication. Even when an intuitive belief is derived from the subject's own perceptions, the conceptual resources and the background assumptions which combine with the sensory input to yield the actual belief have, in part, been acquired through communication. So, it seems, both per-ception and communication are always involved in the construction of intu-itive beliefs. Perception is involved either as the direct source of the belief or as its assumed indirect source (which puts a strong constraint on the possible contents of intuitive beliefs). Communication is involved either as a direct source or, at the very least, a source of concepts and background.

What, now, is the relationship between the relative shares of perception and communication in the construction of an intuitive belief, on the one hand, and its social distribution, on the other? Is it the case that the greater the share of communication, the wider the distribution? Again, the answer is not that simple. A great number of very widespread beliefs owe their dis-tribution to the fact that all members of a society, or in some cases all humans, have similar perceptual experiences. However, as already suggested, the resources for perception are themselves partly derived from communi-cation.

Take the widespread intuitive belief that coal is black: were you told it, or did you infer it from your own perception? Hard to know. But even if you inferred it from perception, in doing so, you used the concepts of black and of coal, and how did you acquire those? Regarding "black," it seems that the category is innately prewired, so that, when you learned the word "black," you merely acquired a way to express verbally a concept you already possessed (see Berlin and Kay 1969; Carey 1982). Regarding "coal," no one would claim that the concept is innate; but what might well be innate is the structure of substance-concepts with the expectation of regular phenomenal features—in particular, color. So, while you probably acquired the *concept* of coal in the process of learning the *word* "coal," acquiring the concept meant no more than picking the right innate conceptual schema and fleshing it out. In the process of fleshing it out, either you were told, or you inferred from what you saw, that coal is black.

It does not make much difference, then, whether an individual's belief that coal is black is derived from perception or from communication: once the concept of coal is communicated, the belief that coal is black will follow one way or the other. This is generally true of widespread intuitive beliefs. These beliefs conform to cognitive expectations based on culturally enriched innate dispositions, and are richly evidenced by the environment. As a result, different direct perceptual experiences and different vicarious experiences acquired through communication converge on the same general intuitive beliefs.

Widespread intuitive beliefs, even exotic ones, are rarely surprising. They are not the kind of beliefs that generally excite the curiosity of social scientists, with the exception of cognitive anthropologists. Among psychologists, only developmental psychologists have started studying them in some detail. Yet intuitive beliefs not only determine much of human behavior; they also provide a common background for communication and for the development of reflective beliefs.

Whereas widespread intuitive beliefs owe their distribution both to common perceptual experiences and to communication, widespread reflective beliefs owe theirs almost exclusively to communication. The distribution of reflective beliefs takes place, so to speak, in the open: reflective beliefs are not only consciously held; they are also often deliberately spread. For instance, religious believers, political ideologists, and scientists, however they may differ otherwise, see it as incumbent upon them to cause others to share their beliefs. Precisely because the distribution of reflective beliefs is a highly visible social process, it should be obvious that different types of reflective beliefs reach a cultural level of distribution in very different ways. To illustrate this, let us consider very briefly three examples: a myth in a non-literate society, the belief that all men are born equal, and Gödel's proof.

A myth is an orally transmitted story which is taken to represent actual events, including "supernatural" events incompatible with intuitive beliefs. Therefore, for a myth to be accepted without inconsistency, it has to be insulated from intuitive beliefs: that is, held as a reflective belief. A myth is a cultural representation; this means that the story is told (given public versions) often enough to cause a large enough proportion of a human group to know it (have mental versions of it). For this, two conditions must be met. First the story must be easily enough and accurately enough remembered on the basis of oral inputs alone. Some themes and some narrative structures seem in this respect to do much better cross-culturally than others. The changing cultural background affects memorability, too, so that the content of a myth tends to drift over time so as to maintain maximal memorability.

Second, there must be enough incentives to actually recall and tell the story on enough occasions to cause it to be transmitted. These incentives may be institutional (e.g. ritual occasions where telling the story is mandatory); but the surest incentive comes from the attractiveness of the story for the audience and the success the story-teller can therefore expect. Interestingly, though not too surprisingly, the very same themes and structures which help one remember a story seem to make it particularly attractive.

If the psychological conditions of memorability and attractiveness are met, the story is likely to be well distributed; but in order for it to be a myth, rather than, say, a mere tale recognized and enjoyed as such, it must be given credence. What rational grounds do people have to accept such a story as true? Their confidence in those who tell it to them: typically, their confidence in elders whom they have many good reasons to trust and who themselves claim no other authority than that derived from *their* elders. The originator of the chain might be a religious innovator who claimed divine authority for a distinctly different version of older myths. Reference to elders provides a self-perpetuating authority structure for a story which already has a self-perpetuating transmission structure. Still, the authority structure is more fragile than the transmission structure, and many myths lose their credibility, though neither their memorability nor their attractiveness, and end up as tales.

The belief that all men are born equal is a typically reflective belief: it is not produced by perception or by unconscious inference from perception. Rather, except for a few philosophers who originated the belief, all those who have held it came to it through communication. Such a belief does not put any significant weight on memory, but it does present a challenge for understanding, and indeed it is understood differently by different people. As already suggested, the fact that it lends itself to several interpretations probably contributed to its cultural success.

Still, the most important factor in the success of the belief that all men are born equal is its extreme relevance—that is, the wealth of its contextual implications (see Sperber and Wilson 1986)—in a society organized around differences in birthrights. People who accepted, and indeed desired, the implications of this belief found there grounds to accept the belief itself and to try to spread it. However, there was a risk, not to holding the belief, but to spreading it, and so the belief spread only where and when there were enough people willing to take this risk. In other words, unlike a myth, which seems to have a life of its own and to survive and spread, as myth or as tale, in a great variety of historical and cultural conditions, the cultural destiny of a political belief is tied to that of institutions. Ecological factors (more particularly, the institutional environment) play a more important role in explaining the distribution of a political belief than cognitive factors.

Consider now a mathematical belief, such as Gödel's proof. Again, all those who hold it, except Gödel himself, arrived at it through communication. However, the communication, and hence the diffusion, of such a belief meets extraordinary cognitive difficulties. Only people with a high enough level of education in mathematical logic can begin to work at understanding it. Outside scholarly institutions, both the means and the motivation to do that work are generally lacking. On the other hand, once the difficulties of communication are overcome, acceptance is no problem at all: to understand Gödel's proof is to believe it.

The human cognitive organization is such that we cannot understand such a belief and not hold it. To some significant extent, and with obvious qualifications, this is the case with all successful theories in the modern natural sciences. Their cognitive robustness compensates, so to speak, for their abstruseness in explaining their cultural success. The fact that successful scientific theories impose themselves on most of those who understand them is manifest to people who don't understand them. This leads, quite rationally, to lay persons believing that these theories are true and expressing as beliefs whatever they can quote or paraphrase from them. Thus Gödel's proof, and scientific theories generally, become cultural beliefs of a different tenor, accepted on different grounds by the scientists themselves and by the community at large.

We might contrast our three examples in the following way. The distribution of a myth is determined strongly by cognitive factors, and weakly by ecological factors; the distribution of political beliefs is determined weakly by cognitive factors, and strongly by ecological factors; and the distribution of scientific beliefs is determined strongly by both cognitive and ecological factors. However, even this exaggerates the similarities between the three cases: the cognitive factors involved in myth and in science, and the ecological factors involved in politics and in science, are very different. The very structure of reflective beliefs, the fact that they are attitudes to a representation, rather than directly to a real or assumed state of affairs, allows endless diversity.

Notwithstanding their diversity, explaining cultural beliefs, whether intuitive or reflective, and if reflective, whether half-understood or fully understood, involves looking at two things: how they are cognized by individuals and how they are communicated within a group; or to put it in the form of a slogan: *Culture is the precipitate of cognition and communication in a human population.*

Note

* This article was originally published in *Explaining Culture: A Materialist Approach* (Blackwell, 1996).

References

Atran, S. 1985. The Nature of Folk-botanical Life-forms. *American Anthropologist* 87: 298–315.

—1986. *Fondements de l'histore naturelle*. Brussels: Complexe.

—1987. Constraints on the Ordinary Semantics of Living Kinds. *Mind and Language* 2(1): 27–63.

Atran, S., and D. Sperber. 1991. Learning without Teaching: Its Place in Culture. In *Culture, Schooling and Psychological Development*, ed. L. Landsman, 39–55. Norwood, NJ: Ablex.

Berlin, B. 1978. Ethnobiological Classification. In *Cognition and Categorization*, ed. E. Rosch and B. Lloyd, 9–26. Hillsdale, NJ: Lawrence Erlbaum Associates.

Berlin, B., and P. Kay. 1969. *Basic Color Terms*. Berkeley: University of California Press.

Burge, T. 1979. Individualism and the Mental. *Midwest Studies in Philosophy* 5: 73–122.

Carey, S. 1982. *Semantic Development: The State of the Art*. Cambridge: Cambridge University Press.

—1985. *Conceptual Change in Childhood*. Cambridge, MA: MIT Press.

Dretske, F. 1981. *Knowledge and the Flow of Information*. Cambridge, MA: MIT Press.

Fodor, J. 1975. *The Language of Thought*. New York: Crowell.

—1987. *Psychosemantics*. Cambridge, MA: MIT Press.

Geertz, C. 1973. *The Interpretation of Cultures*. New York: Basic Books.

Gelman, R. and E. Spelke. 1981. The Development of Thoughts about Animate and Inanimate Objects. In *Social Cognitive Development*, ed. J. Flavell and L. Ross, 43–66. Cambridge: Cambridge University Press.

Hirschfeld, L. 1984. Kinship and Cognition. *Current Anthropology* 27(3): 217–42.

—1994. The Acquisition of Social Categories. In *Mapping the Mind: Domain Specificity in Cognition and Culture*, ed. L. A. Hirschfeld and S. A. Gelman, 201–33. New York: Cambridge University Press.

Keil, F. C. 1979. *Semantic and Conceptual Development*. Cambridge, MA: Bradford Book/ MIT Press.

Millikan, R. G. 1984. *Language, Thought and Other Biological Categories*. Cambridge, MA: MIT Press.

Ryle, G. 1949. *The Concept of Mind*. London: Hutchinson.

Sperber, D. 1975. *Rethinking Symbolism*. Cambridge: Cambridge University Press.

—1985. *On Anthropological Knowledge*. Cambridge: Cambridge University Press.

Sperber, D., and D. Wilson. 1986. *Relevance: Communication and Cognition*. 2nd ed. Oxford: Blackwell, 1995.

Tarde, G. 1895. *Les Lois de l'imitation*. Paris: Félix Alcan.

—1898. *Les Loissociales*. Paris: Félix Alcan.

Vygotsky, L. 1965. *Thought and Language*. Cambridge, MA: MIT Press.

Wittgenstein, L. 1953. *Philosophical Investigations*. Oxford: Blackwell.

3

Toward a Topography of Mind: An Introduction to Domain Specificity*

Lawrence A. Hirschfeld and Susan A. Gelman

Over the past decades, a major challenge to a widely accepted view of the human mind has developed across several disciplines. According to a long predominant view, human beings are endowed with a general set of reasoning abilities that they bring to bear on any cognitive task, whatever its specific content. Thus, many have argued, a common set of processes apply to all thought, whether it involves solving mathematical problems, learning natural languages, calculating the meaning of kinship terms, or categorizing disease concepts. In contrast to this view, a growing number of researchers have concluded that many cognitive abilities are specialized to handle specific types of information. In short, much of human cognition is domain-specific.

The notion of domain specificity is not new. Indeed, intriguing (although brief) hints of domain specificity emerge in the epistemologies of Descartes and Kant and in the psychologies of Thorndike, Vygotsky, and de Groot. For example, in *Mind in Society*, Vygotsky argues that

> the mind is not a complex network of general capabilities such as observation, attention, memory, judgment, and so forth, but a set of specific capabilities, each of which is, to some extent, independent of others and is developed independently. Learning is more than the acquisition of the ability to think; it is the acquisition of many specialized abilities for thinking about a variety of things. Learning does not alter our overall ability to focus attention but rather develops various abilities to focus attention on a variety of things. (1978, 83)

Still, in recent years, increased and detailed attention has turned toward the question of domain specificity. Psychologists with concerns ranging from animal learning to emergent theories of mind and body, cognitivists exploring problem solving and expertise, anthropologists working with color terms and folk taxonomies, psycholinguists investigating auditory perception, and philosophers and others examining reasoning schemata have concluded—often independently—that humans simply could not come to know what they do know in a purely domain-neutral fashion.

This chapter will orient readers to a domain specificity perspective. It is divided into three sections. In the first section, we examine work antecedent to the domain perspective drawn from a number of fields. By doing so we hope to give a broad sense of the intellectual traditions from which domain specificity has emerged. Throughout we will highlight the conclusion that the mind is less an all-purpose problem solver than a collection of enduring and independent subsystems designed to perform circumscribed tasks. This common conviction aside, it is important to keep in mind that a domain perspective is not the achievement of a coordinated body of research, unified in a common challenge. Domain researchers have reached some shared conclusions while asking quite diverse questions. In the second section we draw from this multidisciplinary work a common notion of what a domain is. It is important to stress that our intention in this section is to characterize rather than define what a domain is. Finally, in the third section we consider questions that arise by looking at ways in which domain researchers differ in their approaches and conclusions.

It is essential to note, given the diversity of interests and backgrounds of researchers in domain specificity, that conclusions about the nature and scope of the domain specificity approach are not reducible to differences in the traditions from which researchers have engaged the question. Rather, both the major lines of contention and commonality evident in these chapters are largely independent of academic discipline or research methodology. We believe that this is one of the most encouraging aspects of domain research, one that provides broad and exciting possibilities for future research directions.

The Roots of Domain Specificity

In this section we review the intellectual antecedents of the contemporary domain perspective. Our goal is twofold. First, we want to indicate the research and theory that have been crucial to the evolution of a domain approach. Although the authors of some of this work may well not be advocates of a domain-specific perspective, their work has nonetheless been critically important to the development of the approach. Second, we review this work with an eye toward building a characterization, if not a definition, of what a domain is and what a domain is not.

Several traditions have converged on a domain perspective. All attempt to solve the central problem of domain specificity, namely, how do humans come to have the wealth of knowledge that they do? These traditions have their roots in the following: (1) Chomsky's theory of natural language grammar; (2) modular approaches to knowledge (particularly vision and auditory speech processing); (3) constraints on induction; (4) philosophical insights into the most intricate knowledge structures created by humans (theories); (5) the learning, memory, and problem solving of our best learners (experts); and (6) the wisdom gained from a comparative perspective (animal, evolutionary, and cross-cultural studies).

Chomsky's Theory of Natural Language Grammar

We start with Chomsky's theory of language for two reasons. First, it has special historical interest: Virtually all subsequent domain-specific accounts bear the imprint of Chomsky's arguments about cognitive architecture. Although previous researchers recognized the need for conceiving thought in terms of discrete mental functions, Chomsky elaborated the first modern, sustained, and general account of domain specificity. It would be hard to overestimate the importance that his views have had in forming a broad-ranging domain-specific perspective. Although none of this volume's contributions directly treats natural language grammar, all grapple with issues raised in Chomsky's work.

The second reason for beginning with this theory is the clarity of its claims. Perhaps because it remains controversial, the notion that the language faculty represents a unique mental organ is probably the most widely known domain-specific argument. This attention is well deserved: The study of natural language processing is the arena in which the domain challenge has most continuously and explicitly unfolded. Although not all scholars are convinced that syntax must be described in domain-specific terms, the research from which this claim is derived provides an apt and excellent illustration of one domain perspective.

Current Chomskian linguistic theory distinguishes the principles of language structure at the core of the language faculty from language-specific rules derived from these principles. According to this model, (1) understanding a sentence involves assigning it a structural description in terms of abstract categories; (2) operations on sentences necessarily involve interpreting sentences in terms of this abstract phrase structure; (3) this abstract phrase structure cannot be inferred from surface properties of utterances (such as the linear order of words in the sentence).

For example, consider how a grammatically well-formed question is derived from the following two sentences (the example is drawn from Chomsky 1980a, see also 1988):

(1) The man is here.—Is the man here?
     The man will leave.—Will the man leave?

Chomsky suggests that two hypotheses fit these data. The first hypothesis for forming an interrogative from a declarative sentence is the *structure independent hypothesis* (H$_1$). According to this hypothesis, the speaker processes the sentence from beginning to end, word by word. When the speaker reaches the first occurrence of a class of words, say a verb such as *is* or *will*, he or she transposes this word to the beginning of the sentence. The alternative, *structure dependent hypothesis* (H$_2$), is the same as the first "but select[s] the first occurrence of *is, will*, etc., following the *first noun phrase of the declarative*" (Chomsky 1980a, emphasis added).

The (first structure independent) hypothesis is less complex in that it relies on superficial features of sequential order rather than requiring speakers to interpret utterances with respect to components of their constituent phrase structure, that is, "the first noun phrase." If the mind prefers "simpler" solutions—that is, is guided by a sensitivity to mental economy—we would expect to find language organized by principles captured with the structure independent hypothesis rather than the more abstract and language-specific structure dependent hypothesis.

The issue is resolved, Chomsky argues, by looking at the different predictions the two hypotheses make for similar sentences and their associated questions. First, on the structure dependent hypothesis the following movements are predicted:

(2) The man who is here is tall.—Is the man who is here tall?
     The man who is tall will leave.—Will the man who is tall leave?

In contrast, the structure independent hypothesis, in which movements are calculated over surface properties of the sentence (such as word order), predicts a pattern that is not only ungrammatical, but also never encountered:

(3) Is the man who here is tall?
     Is the man who tall will leave?

The structure dependent claim, accordingly, more adequately captures the linguistic facts.

The crucial question, Chomsky observes, is how children come to know that structure dependence governs such operations but structure independence does not. It is not, he contends, that the language learner accepts the first hypothesis and then is forced to reject it on the basis of data such as (2). No child is taught the relevant facts. Children make many errors in language learning, but none such as (3), prior to appropriate training or evidence. A person might go through much or all of his life without ever having been exposed to relevant evidence, but he will nevertheless unerringly employ H_2, never H_1, on the first relevant occasions.... We cannot, it seems, explain the preference for H, on grounds of communicative efficiency or the like. Nor do there appear to be relevant analogies of other than the most superficial and uninformative sort in other cognitive domains. If humans were differently designed, they would acquire a grammar that incorporates H_1, and would be none the worse for that (Chomsky 1980a, 40).

Chomsky concludes that the mind is *modular*—"consisting of separate systems [i.e., the language faculty, visual system, facial recognition module, etc.] with their own properties" (Chomsky 1988, 161). The modular claim has three components: First, the principles that determine the properties of the language faculty are unlike the principles that determine the properties of other domains of thought. Second, these principles reflect our unique biological endowment. Third, these peculiar properties of language cannot be attributed to the operation of a general learning mechanism. Linguistic principles such as structure dependence cannot be inferred from the general language environment alone. Yet children's language development is guided by these principles.

As we observed above, this claim is not uncontroversial. For example, a number of researchers have suggested that the young child's task of inferring the structural properties of language is made easier because adults simplify the language that learners are presented with (Snow 1972; Furrow and Nelson 1984, 1986). Cross-cultural work, however, indicates that such simplifications are not a universal feature of the language learning environment (Ochs and Schieffelin 1984; Pye 1986). Other studies find that properties of child directed speech do not correlate with the ease of language learning (e.g. Gleitman, Newport, and Gleitman 1984; Hoff-Ginsberg and Shatz 1982). Nonetheless, language acquisition appears to be quite stable and regular across diverse cultural and linguistic environments (Slobin 1985). The conclusion Chomsky and others have reached is that the child has an innate capacity to learn languages, thus filtering "the input data through an emerging system of rules of grammar" (Gleitman 1986, 7).

Other evidence lends support to Chomsky's theory. For instance, language learning appears to be stable and regular across significant variation in language *learners* as well as language *learning environments*. Curtiss (1982) has shown that severe disturbances in cognitive capacity do not necessarily result in disrupted language capacity (see also Cromer 1988). Language development continues to unfold in the typical, predictable sequence for learners who are blind (Landau and Gleitman 1985) and so have very different sensory experience from sighted children, and for those who are deaf and acquiring language in a different sensory modality (see studies of sign language, such as American sign language (ASL); Klima and Bellugi 1979; Newport and Meier 1985; Petitto 1988). Even deaf children who, in their first few years of life, have had little exposure to spoken language and no exposure to sign language, invent "words" and two- or three-word "sentences" (Goldin-Meadow 1982). These results do not imply that the environment has no effect. For example, delaying exposure to language until later in life can have consequences ranging from moderate to severe (Newport 1991; Curtiss 1977). Nonetheless, it is striking that learners manage to construct language systems across a wide array of circumstances.

Modular Approaches to Cognition

As we observed, Chomsky and others maintain that these findings provide compelling evidence for the claim that the mind is modular, comprising a number of distinct (though interacting) systems (the language faculty, the visual system, a module for facial recognition), each of which is characterized by its own structural principles (1980b, 1988). Clearly this claim is related to the notion that thought is domain-specific, the idea that many cognitive abilities are specialized to handle specific types of information.

Chomsky, however, has also suggested that the mind is modular in a somewhat different way, giving rise to a set of proposals about cognitive architecture stressing the organization and contribution of each of the system's subcomponents rather than the system's overall characteristics. Thus, in other more technical writings, Chomsky has described "modules of grammar" (e.g., the lexicon, syntax, bounding theory, government theory, case theory, etc.) (1988, 135). Here the notion of modularity appears to be tied to specific subcomponents or subsystems of the language faculty rather than to the modular uniqueness of the language faculty itself. The grammar, in the traditional sense, is located at the intersection of these distinct modules.

It is not clear whether these two notions of modularity are to be distinguished, and if so how to interpret the relationship between them. One possibility is that modules are nested, that is, the language faculty is a separate module that in turn consists of distinct component operations or modules. Another interpretation—supported indirectly by the fact that Chomsky speaks of the language faculty as a module to nonlinguists but speaks of the language faculty as consisting of modules to linguists—is that the mind is, strictly speaking, modular with respect only to these second-level component modules. The language faculty itself would accordingly be a more vaguely defined construct resulting from the operation of these modules, but one that in itself is not modular in the sense of being defined in terms of a distinct set of principles.[1]

Modular accounts of other cognitive competencies more often resemble the second modular interpretation of Chomsky's position than the first. Thus, for example, although the visual and auditory systems are often compared with the language faculty as contrasting modules (Chomsky 1988, 1980b;

Fodor 1983), detailed accounts of these systems typically analyze their structure in terms of a set of component modular operations, each of which accounts for only part of the overall system's functional output. Thus, descriptions of such systems adhere to what Marr (1982) called the principle of modular design, "the idea that a large computation [such as vision] can be split up and implemented as a collection of parts that are as nearly independent of one another as the overall task allows" (p. 102).

Marr's own theory of vision is a clearly elaborated example of this sort of modular explanation. The theory's principal goal is to understand how it is that we see stable and identifiable images in spite of great variation and "noise" in the input. For example, although we perceive colors, shapes, and sizes as constant, the stimulus information available to the visual system is not sufficiently constrained to permit us to infer constancy without additional interpretation. Areas of unequal shading (which makes some areas of a single color appear darker than others), the possibility of object movement (which makes the same object appear smaller or larger depending on whether it is moving toward or away from the viewer), or partial occlusion (which obscures large parts of objects that are nonetheless perceived as a single whole) mean that visual information alone often underdetermines our perception of color, shape, and size constancy.

To explain such judgments, Marr puts forward a computational theory of vision that analyzes the perception of shape, size, and motion into representations constructed from a set of specific algorithms. These algorithms transform representations by means of modular devices that detect edges, apparent motion, surface texture, and the like. Vision, the process of seeing, involves the coordination of these atomic visual modules into a coherent whole.

Other modular devices seem to control auditory processing. A considerable body of research emerging from the Haskins Laboratory under Alvin Liberman provides a computational theory of auditory processing. Central to this work is the demonstration that the phonetic analysis of speech involves mechanisms different from those that affect the perceptual analysis of auditory nonspeech (Mattingly, Liberman, Syrdal, and Halwes 1971; Liberman and Mattingly 1989).

Drawing on this empirical work in vision and speech processing, in *Modularity of Mind*, Fodor (1983) offers the first general discussion of the implications of modularity for a wide set of domains. Fodor lists a number of candidate modules, including color perception, analysis of shape, analysis of three-dimensional spatial relations, recognition of faces, and recognition of voices.

Fodor's model involves a functional cognitive taxonomy that distinguishes between input systems or modules (which produce knowledge about the world, such as edge detectors) and transducers (which compile information *from* the world, such as perceptual organs). Input systems, in turn, are distinguished from central processors that take information from the input systems, in a format appropriate for the central processors, and use this information to mediate higher functions, such as the fixation of belief.

Thus, according to Fodor's modular view, knowledge of the different aspects of the world is mentally represented in distinct formats. Perception accordingly involves not only interpretation, but an interpretation that is constrained by the format under which particular world knowledge is represented. In other words, input systems are not simply conduits for perceptual encodings of information; they are mental modules that "deliver representations that are most naturally interpreted as characterizing the arrangement of *things in the world*. Input analyzers are thus inference-performing systems" (1983, 42, original emphasis).

Modular views of cognition represent a major challenge to predominant, domain-general approaches found in psychology, linguistics, philosophy, and anthropology. As such, they have important implications for any domain-specific perspective. Yet modular and domain-specific approaches also contrast in significant ways. The principal difference is the former's emphasis on specificity in functional cognitive architecture and the latter's focus on specialization for specific types of knowledge. In the following three sections we consider the direct intellectual antecedents to domain specificity. The work we examine, rather than focusing on cognitive architecture (a modular issue), is concerned with the mental activities that operate on that architecture. We turn first to the issue of constraints on representations.

Constraints

An appeal to constraints begins with the problem of induction. As Rochel Gelman phrased it (1990), "How is it that our young attend to inputs that will support the development of concepts they share with their elders?" She raises two significant difficulties with developing the appropriate concepts: Experience is inadequate in that many of the critical concepts children need to learn never appear: it is "pluripotential" in that it is logically open to many alternative construals. As R. Gelman (1990) points out, "the indeterminacy or inadequacy of experience and the pluripotentiality of experience ... are central to current discussions of the acquisition of syntax (Landau and Gleitman 1985; Wexler and Culicover 1980), visual perception (Marr 1982; Ullman 1980), the nature of concepts (Armstrong, Gleitman, and Gleitman 1983; Medin and Wattenmaker 1987), and the learning of word meaning (Macnamara 1982; Quine 1960)."

The inadequacy and pluripotentiality of experience are implicit in many accounts of learning, including Quine's treatment of word meaning acquisition (1960) and Peirce's discussion of hypothesis generation in science

(1960). For the child to learn word meanings without constraints is akin to an alien trying to discover the laws of nature by examining the facts listed in the Census Report. Both would be doomed to positing thousands upon thousands of meaningless hypotheses. The child might wonder whether "rabbit" refers to a certain patch of color, or the positioning of a limb; the alien may wonder whether there is a meaningful causal relation between the number of babies born in Cancun and the height of women in Brazil whose names start with "Z." If left unconstrained, induction would yield meaningful knowledge only rarely (if at all), and even then only by chance.

One promising response to the induction puzzle is to suggest that there are constraints on the form development takes. Constraints are restrictions on the kinds of knowledge structures that the learner typically uses (Keil 1981, 198). With constraints, the induction problem is simplified because the learner need not consider every possible reading of the input. For example, regarding the acquisition of word meanings, Markman (1989) suggests that children first assume that nouns refer to whole objects that are taxonomically related (the *taxonomic* and *whole object* constraints). These constraints would exclude from consideration meanings for *rabbit* such as "white fur" or "things that hop [including pogo sticks and wallabees]." Keil (1981) also proposes domain-specific constraints on number concepts, deductive reasoning, ontological knowledge, and natural language syntax.

All theorists acknowledge the need for constraints of some sort. Even traditional learning theorists propose constraints on learning (e.g., perceptual constraints; contiguity). Disagreement remains as to the importance of constraints, how much focus they deserve, and on how best to characterize their nature (see Behrend 1990; Nelson 1988).

Keil points out that constraints could be in the learner or outside the learner. Even focusing just on those in the learner, Keil observes that there are still strong disagreements about whether they are innate or acquired, probabilistic or absolute, regarding process or structure, domain-specific or domain-general, and so forth. Thus, a constraints view need not be domain-specific. For example, in an ingenious argument, Newport (1990) suggests that there are domain-general information-processing constraints on attention that help children acquire language. Other theorists are agnostic as to whether the constraints they propose are domain-specific (e.g., Markman 1989).

However, in the present context, the suggestion of domain-specific constraints is of particular interest. Indeed, there may be a natural affinity between constraints and domain specificity. If constraints are appealing because they make the induction problem easier, then domain-specific constraints are all the more appealing because they make the induction problem all the more easy (Keil 1981). The argument is that

> it is necessary to grant infants and/or young children domain-specific organizing structures that direct attention to the data that bear on the

concepts and facts relevant to a particular cognitive domain. The thesis is that the mind brings domain-specific organizing principles to bear on the assimilation and structuring of facts and concepts, that learners can narrow the range of possible interpretations of the environment because they have implicit assumptions that guide their search for relevant data. (R. Gelman 1990)

There appears to be a rich array of such constraints. Spelke (1990) proposes a variety of constraints on object perception that seem to be operating from early infancy. R. Gelman (1990) provides support for constraints on early numeric understanding (specifically, principles for counting) and causal understanding of animate and inanimate movement. She refers to these constraints as "skeletal principles" because they are the framework on which developing knowledge depends and grows. Brown (1990) shows evidence for constraints on interpretations of causal relations, and argues that such constraints guide the kinds of analogical transfer subjects find easy or difficult.

The flourishing of a constraints perspective and the wealth of evidence being amassed on domain-specific constraints do not lead to convergence on what is meant by "domain." As Keil points out (1990, 139):

The notion of domain varies considerably across researchers. In some cases.... the domains cover very broad areas of cognitive competency such as the representation of space or physical objects. In other cases, the domains may be locally circumscribed bodies of expertise. The critical common factor in all cases is that domain specific constraints are predicated on specific sorts of knowledge types and do not blindly constrain any possible input to learning.

Theories

Another sense of domain specificity arises from considering everyday knowledge as falling into folk or commonsense theories. Theories are by nature domain-specific. A theory of biology cannot be applied to the phenomena of physics. Theories make different ontological commitments (biologists appeal to species and DNA; physicists appeal to quarks and masses). They put forth domain-specific causal laws (e.g., gravity does not affect mental states; biological processes such as growth or respiration cannot be applied to force dynamics). So, if human thought is in important ways analogous to scientific theories, then it should be organized separately for distinct domains.

The claim that there are theories is a controversial and substantive one. Theories are not in principle required for getting around the world. It is possible to form biological categories without the benefit of theories, as when pigeons classify birds and trees (Herrnstein 1979) or humans form groupings of the biological world (Atran 1990). It is possible to respond to others' mental states by simply reflecting on one's own (Harris 1994).

Moreover, at first blush the claim that everyday knowledge is theory laden may seem implausible. If "theory" means "scientific theory," then it is certainly not the case that everyday knowledge is organized into theories. It is clear that few of us have the detailed, explicit, formal understanding that PhD biologists or physicists have. We rarely, if ever, conduct scientific experiments to test our everyday hypotheses. We often lack conscious awareness of those principles that we do understand implicitly. Consider, for example, how subjects reason about physical laws regarding motion and velocity. Kaiser, Proffitt, and Anderson (1985) found that subjects implicitly know the correct natural trajectory of an object in motion, but perform badly when asked to judge the naturalness of static representations of the same events.

However, a commonsense or folk theory is not the same as a scientific theory. This point has been made by Karmiloff-Smith and Inhelder (1975), Murphy and Medin (1985), Carey (1985), Keil (1994), Gopnik and Wellman (this volume), and others. Instead, everyday thought may be theory-like in its resistance to counterevidence, ontological commitments, attention to domain-specific causal principles, and coherence of beliefs. We sketch out some examples of these properties in the following sections.

The argument that ordinary knowledge can be likened to commonsense theories is rooted in several distinct strands of research. Karmiloff-Smith and Inhelder (1975), in an important demonstrational study, showed that children construct hypotheses (akin to miniature theories-in-action) that are resistant to counterevidence. They gave children a series of blocks to balance on a fulcrum. Some were symmetrical and thus balanced in the center, but others were asymmetrical, either visibly so (e.g., having an extra, visible weight at one end) or invisibly so (e.g., having a hidden weight at one end). Many of the children at first used trial and error to balance the blocks. They were fairly successful at the task, because they were approaching the task strictly as empiricists. However, as the session continued some children formed the explicit hypothesis that the blocks balanced in the middle, and so started making errors that they did not make previously. Children had particular difficulty with the invisibly asymmetric blocks. Some of the children, after repeated attempts, finally abandoned the blocks that would not balance in the middle, reporting that they were impossible to balance. This demonstration suggests the importance of theoretical beliefs in organizing input.

Another set of demonstrations of theory-like beliefs in ordinary thought emerges from examining semantics and categorization. Murphy and Medin (1985) propose that theories are needed to account for the insufficiencies of similarity as a construct. On a similarity view, word meanings and categories are constructed on the basis of similarity of members to one another, whether these similarities are computed in terms of prototypes, feature lists, or similarity to exemplars (Smith and Medin 1981). However, Murphy and Medin

(1985) note (following Goodman 1972) the problems with a pure similarity view.

To give an intuitive example, if you see someone jump into a swimming pool with all his clothes on, you may classify him as a "drunk" even though nothing about him or his actions specifically resembles drunks you have seen in the past. Rather, your interpretation of his behavior in that context leads to a series of inferences about the likely causes of his actions, and so yields the classification. More generally, as Goodman points out, similarity is insufficiently constrained to solve the problem of classification or induction. Depending on what counts as a feature, any two objects could have indefinitely many features in common (e.g., a lawnmower and hummingbird both weigh less than 200 pounds, less than 201 pounds, less than 202 pounds ...). Thus, we need constraints on what counts as a feature and how to weight features, and these constraints come from our theories.

Three examples here suffice. One is taken from a series of items constructed by Rips (1989). Subjects were told about hypothetical circular objects three inches in diameter, and were asked to rate them on four dimensions: similarity to pizzas, similarity to quarters, likelihood of being a pizza, likelihood of being a quarter. Rips discovered that similarity judgments and categorization judgments diverged. The object was judged more similar to a quarter than a pizza, but more likely to be a pizza than a quarter. Theoretical beliefs about the possible features of pizzas and quarters yielded the classification but a general similarity metric did not (see also Medin and Shoben 1988).

The second example is from Keil (1989). He told children stories, for example about a skunk that was surgically altered to resemble a raccoon but still had the parents and internal structure of a skunk. By approximately the second grade, children reported that the animal was still a skunk, despite its outward appearances. They did not do so for artifacts, such as a coffeepot altered to resemble a birdfeeder. Again, a theoretical grasp of species seems to be driving children's answers. It is striking that this understanding emerges so early. Gelman and Wellman (1991) have similar findings with children as young as preschool age.

The third example is from Putnam (1970) (see also Kripke 1972, and Schwartz 1979, for related arguments). He proposes a series of thought experiments. For example, what is required for something to be a lemon? Is it the yellow color, tart taste, thick peel, etc.? He argues that, in the final analysis, none of these features is critical. We treat all the properties associated with lemons as corrigible—that is, potentially disconfirmable. We appeal to experts to know for certain which are the lemons and which are not—and even the experts may ultimately prove to be wrong. This example differs somewhat from the other two. In particular, it emphasizes the corrigibility of "theoretical" properties. Nevertheless, the point again is that semantics are tied into theories, which themselves are open to change.

These examples illustrate some of the benefits of proposing folk theories. However, many questions remain. How many theories are there? Is there a small and manageable set, or can their number be multiplied endlessly? How coherent are everyday beliefs, and do they cohere enough to constitute a theory? How do new theories grow out of old ones? Why posit theories instead of other, related structures (such as constraints)? The characterization is far from settled, and more substantive issues continue to be discussed.

Expertise

The claim that expertise carves out domains begins with the following observation. With enough practice at a task, whether that task is the game of chess or the gathering of factual knowledge about dinosaurs, an ordinary person begins to look extraordinary. With sufficient experience, a person attains amazing feats of memory (Chase and Ericsson 1981), reorganizes knowledge into complex hierarchical systems and develops rich networks of causally related information (Chi, Hutchinson, and Robin 1989), and can hold in mind an impressive array of possibilities (e.g., expert chess players considering many more chess pieces than novices) (Chase and Simon 1973). These abilities are so striking that they can even erase the usual developmental finding of adults outperforming children. Chi has found that children who are chess experts have better memory for the positioning of chessboard pieces than adults who are chess novices.

Just as important, these abilities cannot be explained as individual differences in the starting point of the experts, nor as generalized, cross-domain effects. The same individual who is remarkable on the chessboard shows mundane performance on tasks outside the skill domain. For example, the chess expert's memory for a string of digits is quite ordinary, even though the expert's memory for positions of chess pieces on a chessboard is far above what the novice can do. The expertise is so focused in scope that it does not even extend to memory for chess pieces placed randomly on the board. It seems, then, that these abilities are domain-specific, at least in some sense of "domain."

The notion of skill domains identified by expertise is distinct from any of the other senses of domain we have reviewed. There has been no appeal to innate modular structures, innate constraints, or the importance of evolutionary forces. In part this is because it is unlikely that we have innate structures dedicated to the acquisition of chess or go. It may be that skill domains such as chess or go, though themselves artificial and invented, draw on other kinds of cognitive abilities that can be explained in terms of modules or evolutionary constraints. For example, aspects of visual pattern recognition are presumably hardwired into our visual perceptual system, and appear to be an important component of these kinds of board games. Thus, it may be impossible to be an expert in chess if you do not have excellent visual memory. Nonetheless, the abilities honed for chess do not generalize to other tasks relying on visual pattern recognition. Thus, it seems unlikely that the domains here can be reconceptualized as broader than what they appear to be. In other words, a chess expert really does seem to be an expert in chess, not an expert in visual pattern recognition.

Expertise effects are unlikely to result from innate evolutionary constraints, for the same reasons discussed above. They also cannot always be explained in terms of causal belief systems, as in naive theories (again, consider that chess, although a rule-governed system, is not a theory and is not corrigible). Rather, these domains appear to result from hours of intensive practice.

Consideration of expertise-driven skill domains poses an interesting challenge to other notions of domain specificity. First, it challenges us to consider what can count as a domain. From the perspective of Chomsky, Fodor, and their followers, it has been assumed that domains constitute large and important chunks of cognition—language, perception, mathematics, music. Yet from the expertise literature it is clear that at least in one sense domains can include invented and small corners of experience. Even if we were to reconcile these perspectives by saying that different theorists are dealing with very different senses of domain, we are left with the reminder that the notion of domain needs some constraints if it is to be meaningful. In other words, how can chess be excluded as a domain, excluded from the perspective of theorists who would like to claim that it is not? The challenge, then, is to decide what is not a domain, and why.

A second point is that the effects of expertise demonstrate the far-reaching influences of intensive experience. It reminds us to take seriously the nature of experience, and not to dismiss its potential influence. It becomes all the more important to explicate and understand how experience interacts with more internal mechanisms at the focus of attention (such as constraints).

Comparative Perspectives

Animal Studies

It is apparent from the work already reviewed that much research relevant to the domain-specificity perspective is comparative in the sense that it contrasts children's states of understanding with adult ones. A particularly critical issue is the extent to which the external world underdetermines children's knowledge. Human children, of course, are not the only animals that learn, and therefore are not the only animals to encounter the problem of how to limit inductions. Like those working on human conceptual development, researchers in animal learning have also framed this question in terms of *constraints*. Constraints, however, are often interpreted as limitations on general abilities, in the sense that constraints modify and sharpen a unitary learning device.

An emphasis on constraints, thus, may seem appropriate when viewed from a human developmental perspective, where children can be seen as having a (less developed) subset of capacities that adults have. From a broader comparative perspective—say, a cross-species or cross-cultural one—constraints make less sense as a way of characterizing domain specificity (Gallistel et al. 1991). A species-specific adaptation, for example, is not a "constrained" version of an adaptation made by another species. Thus, it does not make sense to say that bats have a subset of human sensory equipment; the sonar-based mental images of the world that bats construct may produce representations of equivalent richness to those humans build through vision, but they are fundamentally different in terms of the capacities employed (Dawkins 1987).

The claim that much of conceptual development is best understood as a succession of theories about the world raises a similar issue. Rozin and Schull point out that the notion of constraint is unfortunate not only because it overly emphasizes the idea of limitation, but because it has come to "stand for the study of specialized psychological processes" (1988, 506). Thus, unlike studies of human conceptual development, where the differences between a domain-specific and domain-general interpretation may be more difficult to document, research in animal learning has increasingly stressed that learning may be possible only in the context of species-specific mechanisms.

This point is dramatically evident from Garcia's work on animal aversion training. According to the domain-general view that has long predominated in comparative psychology, inferential skills are homogeneous. Problem solving across tasks in different content areas involves the same principles. From a stimulus-response framework this translates into the principle of equipotentiality, the prediction that differences in strength of association between a stimulus and a response are attributable to conditions of pairing (contiguity, duration, etc.) and independent of the nature of the reinforcer. Garcia and Koelling (1966) conducted a study that confronted this prediction directly.

They showed that when rats were given electric shocks and these shocks paired with either a visual or taste stimulus, the rats subsequently avoided only the visual stimulus. In contrast, when the experimenters poisoned the rats and paired the poisoning with the same visual and taste stimuli, the rats avoided the flavored water but not the visual stimulus. How rats paired stimulus with response thus depended on the nature of the relation between stimulus and response, undermining the equipotentiality assumption.

Furthermore, the poisoned rats developed an aversion to the new taste stimulus in spite of the fact that there was a delay between ingesting the poison and its effects. This finding also challenges the contiguity assumption. Thus, rats' pairing of stimuli seems to be governed by a constraint: If poisoned, seek the cause in something ingested. From the perspective of stimulus-response psychology this sort of guided hypothesis was unthinkable. From the perspective of contemporary research on the evolution of domain-specific mechanisms, however, such a pairing is both sensible and predictable. It makes good evolutionary sense to select for a cognitive mechanism that teaches the species to avoid poisonous, spoiled, or unripe foods, even if they are eaten considerably before the onset of symptoms.

Students of animal cognition and evolution have stressed the need to interpret cognitive and other adaptive mechanisms in domain-specific terms (Rozin and Schull 1988; Cosmides and Tooby 1989). The range of behaviors covered by this approach is quite broad. Cosmides (1989), for example, suggests that conditions of social exchange have selected for certain reasoning schemata, including the one underlying the selection task. Symons (1979) and Langlois and Roggman (1990) have argued that notions of physical attractiveness may be governed by innate mechanisms. Gallistel (1990) reviews the considerable literature on animal systems of navigation, dead reckoning, and temporality, arguing that they reflect similarly specialized, domain-specific mechanisms.

Researchers in animal and evolutionary studies have detailed the importance of viewing learning (specifically what Marler [1991], has called "an instinct to learn") in domain-specific terms. Several researchers have argued that learning could hardly proceed without domain-specific devices (Cosmides and Tooby 1989; Gallistel et al. 1991; Symons 1979). The reason, as Symons notes (1979, 20), is that learning is not a general ability to modify behavior. Rather it is a set of predispositions that a species has developed to resolve specific problems encountered during the course of evolutionary history. Garcia's demonstration that rats will adopt certain aversions and not others showed that some things are more easily learned, and evolutionary constraints help explicate what those things are.

Cross-cultural Studies

The cognitive perspective that emerged in anthropology at the end of the 1950s put forward a program of research aimed at describing cultural competencies on the model of rules of grammar. It was widely agreed that all word meanings in all languages and in all conceptual domains would involve semantic representations in a single general format, namely, one in which elementary semantic features were simply combined: no domain-specific structural idiosyncrasies were envisaged. But as with animal learning studies, the cultural comparative perspective in fact uncovered empirical regularities that proved particularly difficult to interpret in a domain-general light. Moreover, these regularities would almost undoubtedly have escaped discovery in the absence of cross-cultural work.

Color terms. It had long been noted that different languages segment the color spectrum in dramatically different ways. Some languages, for example, appear to have only two color terms, linguistically distinguishing only light from dark chroma. Other languages, like English, have a rich and varied color vocabulary. Given the prevailing doctrine of linguistic relativity, the almost universally accepted interpretation of these data was that language differences reflected differences in the way color was experienced as well as named.

In 1969, Berlin and Kay directly confronted this view of color classification. By analyzing color terms in 98 languages, Berlin and Kay computed that there are 11 basic color terms.[2] There are 2,048 possible ways to combine these 11 basic terms into sets of two or more (black/white, red/blue, white/green/yellow, ...). Strikingly, Berlin and Kay found that only 22 combinations were actually used. Moreover, the order in which basic color words enter a language is also patterned. If a language has only two terms they are invariably black or white; if three terms they are black, white, and red; if five they are black, white, red, green, and yellow, etc.

[white black] > [red] > [green yellow] > [blue] > [brown] > [purple pink orange gray]

They and subsequent researchers also found that although the boundaries of color terms vary, the focal point of each basic color (that point, e.g., in the array of reds that is the reddest of red) is largely the same across languages. Heider and Oliver (1972), working with Dani tribesmen in New Guinea whose language has only two basic color terms, provided experimental cross-cultural evidence that memory for color as well as the naming of colors is also largely independent of color vocabulary.[3]

Reviewing these and other cross-cultural data, Sperber (1974) proposed a domain-specific approach in semantics and in anthropology. He speculated that the organization of the color lexicon (which Kay and McDaniel [1978], later argued was tied to specific properties of the visual pathway) was unlikely to be duplicated in other conceptual domains. He evoked the case of kinship terminology where Lounsbury (1964) had proposed a semantic formalism whose application was clearly limited to kinship, and he concluded that there must be "specific devices linked to particular semantic domains" (1974, 502).[4] In an extension of this work, Hirschfeld (1986; 1989) reanalyzed studies of both children and adults' kinship semantics in terms of a domain-specific device for understanding the social world.

Folk biology. A similar pattern, of cross-cultural uniformity in a content area that previously had been assumed to vary widely, was uncovered by Berlin's work on systems of folk biological classification. In a series of studies, Berlin and his associates (1972, 1978; Berlin, Breedlove, and Raven 1966,

1973, 1974) showed that in spite of significant variation in the plants and animals that any local population encounters, and in spite of the fact that many of these plants and animals lack any cultural salience for any given local population, there is striking consistency in the way humans everywhere classify the world of living things. The basic principles of classification of biological kinds are extremely stable over significant differences in learning environment and exposure. In several publications, including this volume, Atran proposes that these principles must be understood in terms of a domain-specific device for categorizing the biological sphere. He argues that folk biology is uniquely organized in at least two ways: first, that a presumption of underlying essence applies to all living things, and second, that a strict taxonomic hierarchy spans all and only living kinds (1990). Although Atran draws on evidence from a number of disciplines, his cognitive interpretation of the history of natural science is a particularly interesting contribution that has prompted anthropologists to review conclusions about the nature of folk taxonomies (Brown 1992).

Symbolic representations. Knowledge of biological diversity is a cultural domain closely linked with survival. Not surprisingly, anthropologists working with preliterate populations living in small-scale communities report that biological classifications are the focus of a great deal of attention and interest (Berlin 1978). But anthropologists have also observed that the biological world is often as much the object of symbolic attention as pragmatic interest (Bulmer 1967; Rosaldo 1972; Tambiah 1969). The impetus to interpret the world symbolically, in fact, is an ubiquitous cultural feature. The predominant view in anthropology has been that symbolism is a kind of language provided by the culture and that symbols get their meanings by metonymic and metaphorical associations. The underlying psychology, usually left implicit, is a mixture of associationism and content-neutral learning mechanisms that allow the internalization of whatever the culture provides.

In a major rethinking of the anthropology of symbolism, Sperber (1975a) argued that symbols are not signs in that they do not figure in codelike structures and do not have paraphrasable meanings. Rather, Sperber proposes that the true cognitive role of symbolic beliefs is to focus attention and to evoke representations from memory. He depicted symbolic representations as metarepresentations of hard-to-process beliefs (such as the not-fully- interpretable notion of the Trinity, in which three is one). Sperber stresses the role such metarepresentations play in communication and culture. He further links such representations with the relative availability of domain-specific competencies. Thus he attempted to explain the rich symbolism of smells by the discrepancy between a powerful perceptual module and the poverty of conceptual tools for the domain. He also argued that the cultural symbolic exploitation of animal representations, a much discussed topic in cultural anthropology, was based more on the domain-specific character of zoological taxonomies than on the symbolic "codes" in terms of which such beliefs have typically been interpreted (Sperber 1975b). Boyer (1990) extends this insight by examining how religious representations may also be shaped by domain-specific principles even if there is no domain of religious beliefs. Hirschfeld (1994) also explores the extent that domain-specific competence for living kind classification shapes beliefs about the human realm.

Domains, a Characterization

Is it possible, given this survey, to extract what researchers mean when they talk of domain specificity? In spite of the wealth of research, curiously we lack an explicit and well-articulated account of what a domain is. It is easier to think of examples of a domain than to give a definition of one. Physical entities and processes, substances, living kinds, numbers, artifacts, mental states, social types, and supernatural phenomena are all candidate domains. Which of these, if any, are cognitive domains is a question not for general science but for anthropology and psychology: The supernatural may be a domain for human minds though it is not one for science; the cognitive domain of physical phenomena may be quite different from that of physics.

Are there features common to all domains? Our review, though brief, allows us to identify areas of accord, often implicit, in much domain-relevant research. The following we take to be a fairly uncontroversial characterization:

> A domain is a body of knowledge that identifies and interprets a class of phenomena assumed to share certain properties and to be of a distinct and general type. A domain functions as a stable response to a set of recurring and complex problems faced by the organism. This response involves difficult-to-access perceptual, encoding, retrieval, and inferential processes dedicated to that solution.

Let us consider each part of this characterization in turn.

Domains as Guides to Partitioning the World

Most accounts converge on a view that domains function conceptually to identify phenomena belonging to a single general kind, even when these phenomena fall under several concepts. For example, living kinds can be classified in a number of different ways, ranging from foodstuffs to zoo animals. The psychological correlates of competing classifications and their internal structures have significant effects on the way many common categories for living things are sorted, recalled, and recognized (Rosch et al.

1976). Yet in spite of these competing ways of classifying living things, some beliefs about living kinds are typically early emerging, consistent, and effortlessly acquired. Domain competency facilitates this by focusing attention on a specific domain rather than general knowledge (Chi et al. 1989).

Domains as Explanatory Frames

Most researchers would also accept that a domain competence systematically links recognized kinds to restricted classes of properties. Thus a cognitive domain is a class of phenomena that share among themselves, but not with other kinds, a number of relevant properties. Though virtually all domains seem to make reference to causal or otherwise model-derived connections, there is considerable variation across domains as to how flexible these connections are.[5]

It is not necessary, for example, that all and only members of a given domain share a property. It is a recognized property of humans—recognized through the agency of a naive psychology—that human beings behave in association with their beliefs, whereas artifacts do not. Still, we have little trouble accepting that there are humans who do not have beliefs (e.g., people in deep comas) or humans who do not recognize that others have beliefs (e.g., autistic individuals) or artifacts that are most sensibly dealt with as if they had beliefs (e.g., a chess-playing computer). In other domains (say, auditory processing of speech), there may be substantially less flexibility in the degree to which domain properties (say, categorical perception of speech) span domain members.

Domains as Functional and Widely Distributed Devices

It is generally accepted among domain researchers that domain competencies are a restricted set of the cognitive skills the organism may develop. Domains of knowledge represent widely shared adaptations targeting recurring problems that an organism faces. Cases where the adaptive aspect of the domain has been challenged, as with the language faculty, have been much debated recently (Pinker and Bloom 1990). Domains are also generally seen as highly (though not universally) shared among members of a species, not idiosyncratic solutions to individual problems.

Even if a domain skill is unevenly distributed within a population, it must be a solution to a repeatedly encountered problem. To the extent that chess is a domain, the development of perceptual strategies for analyzing chess positions arises *because* chess masters frequently encounter chess problems. Nonmasters do not have a less developed domain of chess; they lack such a domain skill. This relationship between frequency of encounter and domain skill, however, is complex. Some domain skills may appear to be closely tied to differences in the learning environment even if the *underlying domain competence* does *not* depend on environmental conditions.

> The ability to develop and understand mathematics may be rooted in some fairly specific cognitive mechanisms, which human beings are innately endowed with. But if so, many cultures do not require that people use this ability. Nor is it occasioned by every environment. Mathematics does not spontaneously arise irrespective of social context, but seems to require a richer and more sustained sequence of experience and instruction in order to flourish than, say, basic grammatical knowledge, color perception or appreciation of living kinds. (Atran 1988, 8)

Such mathematical skills, involving a formal language of mathematics, are distinct from other, universally emerging arithmetic competencies such as those principles underlying counting and cardinal enumeration (R. Gelman and Brenneman, this volume; R. Gelman and Gallistel 1978).

Domains as Dedicated Mechanisms

Domain-specific processing is typically seen as independent of will and accessible to consciousness only with difficulty (if at all). This property is easily evident in domains such as color perception or phonetic interpretation, cases in which some innate mechanism is difficult to doubt. But it is also apparent when an innate mechanism seems less likely, as, for instance, in what some consider a marginal case of domain specificity, like chess. Chess masters differ from chess novices in their visual-perception processing of chess information, not in logical-deductive thinking or memory processes (Chase and Simon 1973). Accordingly, domain operations generally involve focused, constrained, and involuntary perceptual, conceptual, or inferential processes.

What Domains are Not

Domains can be characterized by what they are not as well as what they are. In this regard it is useful to contrast domains with other mental structures with which they are potentially confuseable. These include semantic fields, schemata and scripts, prototypes, and analogies. What all of these structures (including domains) share is that they are ways of achieving conceptual interconnectedness and mental economy. However, domains differ from each in important respects as well. Unlike *semantic fields*, domains are not contingent on language (cf. Wierzbicka 1994). In fact, evidence of the robustness of a domain phenomenon is sometimes supplied by the fact that the effects of domain-specific knowledge organization occur in the absence of lexical indices (as, e.g., in the case of focal color categories [Heider 1972] or covert folk biological taxa [Berlin 1974]). In contrast to *scripts* and *schema*, domain structures involve expectations about the model-derived connections between domain elements. In a restaurant script, payment follows service by a convention that the script itself cannot account for. Another way in which conceptual interconnectedness is achieved is via prototypes. According to a widely held position, categories are not built around defining features but around central members or *prototypes*. Because prototypes are described as consisting of collections of correlated attributes, they contribute to underlying conceptual interconnectedness. The particular category structure found in prototypes, however, applies to a wide range of phenomena; hence, domain competencies cross-cut them. Thus, prototypes could apply to any domain. (Conversely, they may not truly characterize any domain. Lakoff [1987] suggests that prototypes are effects, reflecting other kinds of conceptual structure.) Finally, *analogical transfers* contribute to conceptual interconnectedness and mental economy. Analogical transfer may in fact represent a means for integrating domain knowledge across domains (Brown 1989; Hirschfeld 1994). But unlike domain structures, transfers can be both idiosyncratic and not functional.

In addition to these ways of producing conceptual interconnectedness that are clearly not domainlike, there are several means for accomplishing conceptual interconnectedness that domains may not be. These include the notions of *category* and *motoric competencies*. Our characterization of domain stressed the expectation that there is some specific "formal" or "syntactic" property of the mental representations pertaining to a given domain that accounts for their distinctive cognitive role. Unfortunately, this does not exclude arrays that we would hesitate to call domains. For example, single concepts have distinctive semantic and formal properties, yet we would not call single concepts domains. Similarly, pairs of concepts like male or female, key and lock, or hot and cold are too narrow to be domains although they fit most of our criteria. Note also that our characterization does not exclude strictly motoric competencies such as riding a bicycle, which many may not find a compelling example of domain-specific skills.

Domain Differences

Clearly, a principled way of defining what a domain is continues to elude us. For this reason, in the present chapter we have tried to *characterize* rather than *define* domains. We have highlighted several qualities of domains, particularly their functional and semantic features. In the rest of this chapter we explore four suggestions for more closely defining domains and their consequences. These are: domains (1) as innate mechanisms, (2) as distinct ways of acquiring knowledge, (3) as reflections of specific relations between the world and our knowledge of it, and (4) as the product of a distinct research orientation.

Are All Domains Innate Modules?

One proposal for defining domains is to restrict candidate domains to sets of computationally relevant concepts that are the product of innate mechanisms or innately guided learning systems. Even if this proposal is adopted, significant issues remain unresolved. For example, Fodor's modular hypothesis sees domains in terms of discrete subsystems, each tied to a specific perceptual channel. Other biologically oriented approaches, including Atran's claims about biological beliefs (1994) or Leslie's contention about theory of mind (1994), construe domains in terms of much larger competencies implicating numerous perceptual modalities. It is thus not evident that their positions and Fodor's would pick out the same candidate domains. Chomsky (1986) similarly argues that viewing the language module as an input system is too narrow.

Can Domains be Defined by their Mode of Acquisition?

Domains may be defined in terms of the specific pattern of learning associated with them. Keil (1990) and Atran and Sperber (1991) argue that candidate domains may be identifiable with respect to their mode of acquisition. Many domain skills are acquired with ease by virtually all members of the species. A broad consensus has emerged that the language faculty is a universally distributed and rapidly acquired cognitive system whose acquisition depends on an innately guided learning device. Other domains seem to be considerably less widely distributed, acquired only with great effort, and appear to be outside the scope of any innately dedicated program of learning. Chess mastery, for example, is an unevenly distributed cognitive ability that requires determined and often formal training to acquire. Even within a single domain there may be considerable variation. Many aspects of naive biology emerge spontaneously across quite different learning environments (Boster 1988). Yet, some biological knowledge appears to be sensitive to differences in expertise, such as the degree to which elements within a content area are seen as causally interconnected (Chi et al. 1989). Inagaki (1990b) suggests that familiarity with a domain increases not only the amount of factual knowledge children have but also their conceptual organization of the domain.

To What Extent can Domains be Defined by their Relationship to the External World?

Some domains appear to carve the world at its joints. When we think of domains, we think of ranges of phenomena comparable to the ranges of facts that are the subject matter of the different sciences. Naive linguistics, biology, psychology, physics, mathematics, cosmology, and so forth, have all been proposed as domains. It is tempting to go from this observation to a view that some causal link exists between the structure of empirical sciences and domain competencies (Carey 1985). Domains, on this view, would *necessarily* be comparable in size to the subject matter of the different sciences. Is there reason to believe that we are unduly influenced by the way scientific disciplines partition the universe?

Yes. For example, some domains not so much carve nature at its joints as they create such joints. Color terminology and perception, for example, reflect discrete categories of the mind imposed on a continuous natural phenomenon. In processing speech we automatically ignore variations between the representations of what we take to be the same sounds across speakers and within the utterances a single speaker produces. Yet, when attending to the same human voice singing we just as automatically are sensitive to variations in pitch. In short, color and speech perception are less discoveries about nature than interpretations of it. By the same token, a fairly extensive literature documents domainlike competencies that span contrived phenomena not typically associated with a unique science or discipline—ranging from chess to chicken sexing (Biederman and Shiffrar 1987) to reading x-rays (Lesgold et al. 1988)—whereas others encompass phenomena that lack scientific validity or correspondence (for example, race, magic, or the supernatural).

The degree to which a domain is dependent on the world is complex and variable. Some domains (e.g., naive biology and physics) may be less closely linked to our scientific understandings of the world than is sometimes appreciated. Some changes in scientific understanding quite rapidly become part of commonsense. Thus, whales are widely understood to be mammals, not fish, even by children. Examples of this sort prompted Putnam (1975) to speak of a linguistic division of labor, in which science is seen as determining the meaning of natural kind terms. But changes in the validity of a given scientific or formal description do not always alter our commitment to the commonsense conceptualization of that phenomenon (see Resnick 1994; Strauss and Shilony 1994). Anthropologists, for example, have shown that the notion *tree* is central to our understanding of the plant world (Witkowski, Brown, and Chase 1981). Nonetheless, tree does not represent an interesting evolutionary line and is therefore not a concept in modern systematics. But unlike instances where our commonsense knowledge is altered by scientific discovery (e.g., in the reclassification of whales as mammals), the concept of tree maintains its conceptual salience in the face of scientific challenge. This appears to be true even for experts. Botanists in everyday contexts continue to hold the commonsense notion of tree (Atran 1990).

Interestingly, discovering the incorrigibility of some commonsense concepts may be less an inference from new data than a function of having adopted a domain perspective. For example, the regularity in systems of folk biological classification, and particularly the close correspondence between these systems and formal systematics in biology, is not a new discovery. Ernst Mayr (1949) documented close parallels between nonliterate Papuan folk biology and formal systematics. However, these parallels were interpreted as evidence for the scientific validity of the species concept rather than as evidence of a shared cognitive mechanism for conceptualizing living kinds (Diamond 1966). In other words, it was assumed that a close correspondence between common sense and science reflected regularities in the world external to cognition, rather than indicating a set of shared cognitive dispositions. As several of the chapters in this volume suggest, the empirical and structural parallels between folk beliefs and science are indeed informative; but from the perspective of understanding mental domains, these parallels are more pertinent to the cognitive than the other sciences.

Does the Question Asked Make a Difference?

It is possible that the research question posed may have a profound impact on the candidate domains we discover. It may not, in short, be possible to distinguish between the research interest that prompted a set of data and what those data can be interpreted as supporting. A case in point may be the relation between a competence associated with a given domain and the knowledge represented in that domain. Keil (1981) makes a similar point regarding approaches to developmental change, when he distinguishes between theories that are knowledge based from those that are competence based. Keil's concern is with constraints, but his observation can be extended to a discussion of how to approach domains. In broad terms, knowledge-based research sees domains as being derived from knowledge structures, whereas competence-based research focuses more on how differing states of knowledge are derived from distinct competencies. The strongest versions of each of these are, respectively, expertise studies and modular approaches.

The competence-based view lays emphasis on the domain-specific principles of organization that shape the sorts of knowledge to which the organism attends and the kinds of knowledge structures the organism develops (see Gallistel et al. 1991). A central concern of the competence-based researcher is how attention is guided toward a circumscribed set of observations, not only during development but also during mature processing. Knowledge-based studies, in contrast, focus more on the consequences of holding domain knowledge than on the principles that underlie its acquisition (see Shantz 1989; Chase and Simon 1973; de Groot 1966). The principal question posed in this work is what impact does domain knowledge have on subsequent processing? Given a certain level of knowledge integration, what are the implications for thought?

Accordingly, the two viewpoints could be seen simply as different perspectives on the same phenomenon, in which somewhat distinct emphases are applied. Knowledge- and competence-based approaches would accordingly be slightly different points of view on a single issue, namely, the relationship between knowledge of something and the competence underlying that knowledge. The two orientations, however, can also be seen as different levels of analysis, yielding quite different kinds of generalizations. Keil, for example, argues that the knowledge-based approach does not provide a principled way of "distinguishing what is merely a change in a knowledge base from what is a change in computational and representational machinery" (1981, 204). Knowing that a cognitive skill changes with experience thus does not permit us to decide whether that change is best described in knowledge or competence-based terms. By the same token, knowing that a knowledge-based hypothesis accounts for a set of observations does not permit us to conclude that a competence-based vantage would construe the observations as coming from a bounded type.

Consider, for example, the problem of deciding whether a change in the way knowledge is represented reflects a change in domain competence. There appears to be a domain of dinosaur knowledge for which some children develop a special expertise. Thus Chi and her associates (1989) have shown that increased knowledge about dinosaurs leads to an enriched network of causally linked beliefs. Generally, the conceptual effects of such causal networks appear to be quite limited, in the sense that they do not readily transfer to closely allied content areas (Inagaki 1990). From a competence-based perspective, however, dinosaur knowledge is not so much a domain as a subset of another domain, namely, living things. What are the implications of this?

One implication is that knowledge-based claims may not commit the researcher to a particular opinion on questions like "What is a domain?" "What are domain boundaries?" or "How are domains implicated in the learning process?" Discovering the relationship between domain-specific and other sorts of knowledge is presumably dependent on determining what is and what is not domain knowledge, and by extension what is and what is not a domain. Thus, like the contrast between domain-general and domain-specific perspectives, knowledge-based and competence-based views may differ in terms of the kinds of generalizations that each can enlist, particularly about domains.

Conclusion

In this chapter we have sketched out several distinct intellectual traditions that have contributed to the view that human cognition can be fruitfully considered domain-specific. Clearly, the approach seems to us extremely promising. Still, a series of difficult questions remain: What is a domain? How many domains are there? Do they concern processes, representations, or both? Do we have conscious access to domains? Can domains change over time, and if so, how? Do the changes that occur in childhood differ in important ways from those changes in domain knowledge that take place after maturity? Does conceptual change occur because of or in spite of domains? Do domains "communicate" among themselves, and if so, how? We leave these issues for the reader to consider.

Notes

* This article was originally published in *Mapping the Mind: Domain Specificity in Cognition and Culture* (Cambridge: Cambridge University Press, 1994).

1. In a manner analogous to the way language as a social phenomenon ("a shared property of a community" defined in terms of "obscure sociopolitical and normative factors") is built out of language as an individual phenomenon ("a system represented in the mind/brain of a particular individual") (Chomsky 1988, 36–37).

2. Berlin and Kay (1969, 5–6) defined as basic those color terms that (among other properties): (1) are monolexemic (so that the meaning of the term is not predictable from the meaning of its parts), (2) apply to a broad range of phenomena (thus excluding blond, a term that applies only to hair), and (3) are psychologically salient for all speakers (thus excluding the color of something with which only a few individuals are familiar).

3. The domain of color remains a contested one. Berlin and Kay's conclusions regarding linguistic relativity have been tempered by Kay and Kempton (1984) and challenged by Lucy and Shweder (1988) and Lakoff (1987). Yet even if there is significant cross-linguistic relativity in basic color terms, the principles organizing the color lexicon are everywhere specific to the conceptual and perceptual domain of color.

4. Specifically, Lounsbury's proposal argued that the kinship lexicon must be analyzed in terms of core or focal meanings and reduction rules from which other meanings could be derived.

5. As we pointed out, in many domains these connections are clearly seen as causal (Leslie, this volume). Members of a particular living kind, for example, are assumed to share an underlying essence that causes the regularities in outward appearance that help us identify category members (Atran 1990; Keil, this volume). But the outward appearance is not the shared property since modifying that appearance (by painting out the spots on a leopard) does not change category membership. In other domains these implications are less clearly causal, but nonetheless not arbitrary. Current linguistic theory proposes that links between the abstract categories of phrase structure grammars are controlled by a few principles (Projection Principle, Bounding Principle, Binding Theory, Case Theory, etc.) that "explain" the surface features of utterances in the way underlying essences (on folk theories) or DNA (on scientific ones) explain the outward appearance of living things, namely, in terms of model-derived connections.

References

Armstrong, S. L., L. R. Gleitman, and H. Gleitman. 1983. What Some Concepts Might Not Be. *Cognition* 13: 263–308.

Atran, S. 1988. Basic Conceptual Domains. *Mind and Language* 3: 7–16.

—1990. *Cognitive Foundations of Natural History*. New York: Cambridge University Press.

—1994. Core Domains Versus Scientific Theories: Evidence from Systematics and Itza-Maya Folkbiology. In *Mapping the Mind: Domain Specificity in Cognition and Culture*, ed. L. Hirschfeld and S. Gelman, 316–40. Cambridge: Cambridge University Press.

Atran, S., and D. Sperber. 1991. Learning Without Teaching: Its Place in Culture. In *Culture, Schooling, and Psychological Development*, ed. L. Landsmann, 39–55. Norwood, NJ: Ablex Publishing.

Behrend, D. A. 1990. Constraints and Development: A Reply to Nelson (1988). *Cognitive Development* 5: 313–30.

Berlin, B. 1972. Speculations on the Growth of Ethnobotanical Nomenclature. *Language and Society* 1: 63–98.

—1974. Further Notes on Covert Categories. *American Anthropologist* 76: 327–31.

—1978. Ethnobiological Classification. In *Cognition and Categorization*, ed. E. Rosch and B. Lloyd. Hillsdale, NJ: Erlbaum.

Berlin, B., D. Breedlove, and P. Raven. 1966. Folk Taxonomies and Biological Classification. *Science* 154: 273–75.

—1973. General Principles of Classification and Nomenclature in Folk Biology. *American Anthropologist* 75: 214–42.

—1974. *Principles of Tzeltal Plant Classification*. New York: Academic Press.

Berlin, B., and P. Kay. 1969. *Basic Color Terms: Their Universality and Growth*. Berkeley: University of California Press.

Biederman, I., and M. M. Shiffrar. 1987. Sexing Day-old Chicks: A Case Study and Expert Systems Analysis of a Difficult Perceptual-learning Task. *Journal of Experimental Psychology: Learning, Memory, and Cognition* 13: 640–45.

Boster, J. 1988. Natural Sources of Internal Category Structure: Typicality, Familiarity, and Similarity of Birds. *Memory and Cognition* 16(3): 258–70.

Boyer, P. 1990. *Tradition as Truth and Communication*. New York: Cambridge University Press.

Brown, A. 1989. Analogical Learning and Transfer: What Develops? In *Similarity and Analogical Reasoning*, ed. S. Vosniadou and A. Ortony, 369–412. New York: Cambridge University Press.

Brown, A. L. 1990. Domain-specific Principles Affect Learning and Transfer in Children. *Cognitive Science* 14: 107–33.

Brown, C. 1992. Cognition and Common Sense. *American Ethnologist* 19: 367–74.

Bulmer, R. 1967. Why is the Cassowary not a Bird? *Man* 2: 5–25.

Carey, S. 1985. *Conceptual Change in Childhood*. Cambridge, MA: MIT Press.

Chase, W., and H. Simon. 1973. The Mind's Eye in Chess. In *Visual Information Processing*, ed. W. Chase. New York: Academic Press.

Chase, W. G., and K. A. Ericsson. 1981. Skilled Memory. In *Cognitive Skills and their Acquisition*, ed. J. R. Anderson. Hillsdale, NJ: Erlbaum.

Chi, M., J. Hutchinson, and A. Robin. 1989. How Inferences about Novel Domain Related Concepts can be Constrained by Structured Knowledge. *Merrill-Palmer Quarterly* 35: 27–62.

Chomsky, N. 1980a. On Cognitive Structures and their Development: A Reply to Piaget. In *Language and Learning: The Debate between Jean Piaget and Noam Chomsky*, ed. M. Piattelli-Palmarini, 35–54. Cambridge: Harvard University Press.

—1980b. *Rules and Representations.* New York: Columbia University Press.

—1986. *Knowledge of Language: Its Nature, Origin, and Use.* New York: Praeger.

—1988. *Language and Problems of Knowledge.* Cambridge, MA: MIT Press.

Cosmides, L. 1989. The Logic of Social Exchange: Has Natural Selection Shaped how Humans Reason? Studies with the Wason Selection Task. *Cognition* 31: 187–276.

Cosmides, L., and J. Tooby. 1989. Evolutionary Psychology and the Generation of Culture. Part II: A Computational Theory of Social Exchange. *Ethology and Sociobiology* 10: 51–97.

Cromer, R. F. 1988. The Cognition Hypothesis Revisited. In *The Development of Language and Language Researchers: Essays in Honor of Roger Brown*, ed. R. S. Kessel, 223–48. Hillsdale, NJ: Erlbaum.

Curtiss, S. 1977. *Genie: A Psycholinguistic Study of a Modern-day "Wild Child."* New York: Academic Press.

—1982. Developmental Dissociation of Language and Cognition. In *Exceptional Language and Linguistics*, ed. L. K. Obler and L. Menn, 285–312. New York: Academic Press.

Dawkins, R. 1987. *The Blind Watchmaker.* New York: Norton.

de Groot, A. 1966. Perception and Memory Versus Thought: Some Old Ideas and Recent Findings. In *Problem Solving: Research, Method, and Theory*, ed. B. Kleinmuntz, 19–51. New York: John Wiley.

Diamond, J. 1966. Zoological Classification System of a Primitive People. *Science* 151: 1102–1104.

Fodor, J. 1983. *Modularity of Mind.* Cambridge, MA: MIT Press.

Furrow, D., and K. Nelson. 1984. Environmental Correlates of Individual Differences in Language Acquisition. *Journal of Child Language* 11: 523–34.

—1986. A Further Look at the Motherese Hypothesis: A Reply to Gleitman, Newport, and Gleitman. *Journal of Child Language* 13: 163–76.

Gallistel, C. 1990. *The Organization of Learning.* Cambridge, MA: MIT Press.

Gallistel, C., A. Brown, S. Carey, R. Gelman, and F. Keil. 1991. Lessons from Animal Learning for the Study of Human Development. In *The Epigenesis of Mind: Essays on Biology and Cognition*, ed. S. Carey and R. Gelman. Hillsdale, NJ: Erlbaum.

Garcia, J., and R. Koelling. 1966. Relation of Cue to Consequence in Avoidance Learning. *Psychonomics Science* 4: 123–24.

Gelman, R. 1990. First Principles Organize Attention to and Learning about Relevant Data: Number and the Animate-Inanimate Distinction as Examples. *Cognitive Science* 14: 79–106.

Gelman, R., and C. Gallistel. 1978. *The Child's Understanding of Number.* Cambridge: Harvard University Press.

Gelman, S. A., and H. M. Wellman. 1991. Insides and Essences: Early Understandings of the Nonobvious. *Cognition* 38: 213–44.

Gleitman, L. 1986. Biological Disposition to Learn Language. In *Language Learning and Concept Acquisition: Foundational Issues*, ed. W. Demopoulos and A. Marras, 3–28. Norwood, NJ: Ablex Publishing.

Gleitman, L., E. Newport, and H. Gleitman. 1984. The Current Status of the Motherese Hypothesis. *Journal of Child Language* 11: 43–79.

Goldin-Meadow, S. 1982. The Resilience of Recursion: A Study of a Communication System Developed Without a Conventional Language Model. In *Language Acquisition: The State of the Art*, ed. E. Wanner and L. R. Gleitman, 51–77. Cambridge: Cambridge University Press.

Goodman, N. 1972. Seven Strictures on Similarity. In *Problems and Projects*, ed. N. Goodman, 437–47. Indianapolis: Bobbs-Merrill.

Harris, P. 1994. Thinking by Children and Scientists: False Analogies and Neglected Similarities. In *Mapping the Mind: Domain Specificity in Cognition and Culture*, ed. L. Hirschfeld and S. Gelman, 294–315. Cambridge: Cambridge University Press.

Heider, E. 1972. Universals in Color Naming and Memory. *Journal of Experimental Psychology* 93: 10–20.

Heider, E., and D. Oliver. 1972. The Structure of the Color Space in Naming and Memory for Two Languages. *Cognitive Psychology* 3: 337–54.

Herrnstein, R. J. 1979. Acquisition, Generalization, and Discrimination Reversal of a Natural Concept. *Journal of Experimental Psychology: Animal Behavior Processes* 5: 116–29.

Hirschfeld, L. 1986. Kinship and Cognition: Genealogy and the Meaning of Kinship Terms. *Current Anthropology* 27: 217–42.

—1989. Rethinking the Acquisition of Kinship Terms. *International Journal of Behavioral Development* 12(4): 541–68.

—1994. Is the Acquisition of Social Categories Based on Domain-specific Competence or on Knoweldge Transfer? In *Mapping the Mind: Domain Specificity in Cognition and Culture*, ed. L. Hirschfeld and S. Gelman, 201–33. Cambridge: Cambridge University Press.

Hoff-Ginsberg, E., and M. Shatz. 1982. Linguistic Input and the Child's Acquisition of Language. *Psychological Bulletin* 92: 2–26.

Inagaki, K. 1990. The Effects of Raising Animals on Children's Biological Knowledge. *British Journal of Developmental Psychology* 8: 119–29.

Kaiser, M. K., D. R. Proffitt, and K. Anderson. 1985. Judgments of Natural and Anomalous Trajectories in the Presence and Absence of Motion. *Journal of Experimental Psychology: Learning, Memory, and Cognition* 11(1–4): 795–803.

Karmiloff-Smith, A., and B. Inhelder. 1975. If You Want to Get Ahead, Get a Theory. *Cognition* 3: 195–211.

Kay, P., and W. Kempton. 1984. What is the Sapir-Whorf Hypothesis? *American Anthropologist* 86: 65–79.

Kay, P., and C. McDaniel. 1978. The Linguistic Significance of the Meanings of Basic Color Terms. *Language* 54: 610–46.

Keil, F. 1981. Constraints on Knowledge and Cognitive Development. *Psychological Review* 88(3): 197–227.

—1989. *Concepts, Kinds, and Cognitive Development*. Cambridge, MA: MIT Press.

—1990. Constraints on Constraints: Surveying the Epigenetic Landscape. *Cognitive Science* 14: 135–68.

—1994. The Birth and Nurturance of Concepts by Domains: The Origins of Concepts of Living Things. In *Mapping the Mind: Domain Specificity in Cognition and Culture*, ed. L. Hirschfeld and S. Gelman, 234–54. Cambridge: Cambridge University Press.

Klima, E. and U. Bellugi. 1979. *The Signs of Language*. Cambridge, MA: Harvard University Press.

Kripke, S. 1972. *Naming and Necessity*. Cambridge, MA: Harvard University Press.

Lakoff, G. 1987. *Women, Fire, and Dangerous Things*. Chicago: University of Chicago Press.

Landau, B., and L. Gleitman. 1985. *Language and Experience*. Cambridge, MA: Harvard University Press.

Langlois, J., and L. Roggman. 1990. Attractive Faces are Only Average. *Psychological Science* 1(2): 115–21.

Lesgold, A. M., H. Rubinson, P. Feltovich, R. Glaser, D. Klopfer, and Y. Wang. 1988. Expertise in a Complex Skill: Diagnosing X-ray Pictures. In *The Nature of Expertise*, ed. M. Chi, R. Glaser, and M. Farr. Hillsdale, NJ: Erlbaum.

Leslie, A. M. 1994. ToMM, ToBY, and Agency: Core Architecture and Domain Specificity. In *Mapping the Mind: Domain Specificity in Cognition and Culture*, ed. L. Hirschfeld and S. Gelman, 119–48. Cambridge: Cambridge University Press.

Liberman, A., and I. Mattingly. 1989. A Specialization for Speech Perception. *Science* 243: 489–94.

Lounsbury, F. 1964. A Formal Account of the Crow and Omaha-type Kinship Terminologies. In *Explorations in Cultural Anthropology*, ed. W. Goodenough. New York: McGraw-Hill.

Lucy, J., and R. Shweder. 1988. The Effect of Incidental Conversation on Memory for Focal Colors. *American Anthropologist* 90: 923–31.

Macnamara, J. 1982. *Names for Things: A Study of Human Learning*. Cambridge, MA: MIT Press/Bradford Books.

Markman, E. M. 1989. *Categorization and Naming in Children: Problems of Induction*. Cambridge, MA: MIT Press.

Marler, P. 1991. The Instinct to Learn. In *The Epigenesis of Mind: Essays on Biology, and Cognition*, ed. S. Carey and R. Gelman. Hillsdale, NJ: Erlbaum.

Marr, D. 1982. *Vision*. New York: W. H. Freeman.

Mattingly, I., A. Liberman, A. Syrdal, and T. Halwes. 1971. Discrimination in Speech and Nonspeech Modes. *Cognitive Psychology* 2: 131–57.

Mayr, E. 1949. *List of New Guinea Birds*. New York: American Museum of Natural History.

Medin, D. L., and E. J. Shoben. 1988. Context and Structure in Conceptual Combination. *Cognitive Psychology* 20: 158–90.

Medin, D. L., and W. D. Wattenmaker. 1987. Category Cohesiveness, Theories, and Cognitive Archeology. In *Concepts and Conceptual Development: Ecological and Intellectual Factors in Categorization*, ed. U. Neisser, 25–62. New York: Cambridge University Press.

Murphy, G. L., and D. L. Medin. 1985. The Role of Theories in Conceptual Coherence. *Psychological Review* 92: 289–316.

Nelson, K. 1988. Constraints on Word Learning? *Cognitive Development* 3: 221–46.

Newport, E. L. 1990. Maturational Constraints on Language Learning. *Cognitive Science* 14: 11–28.

—1991. Contrasting Concepts of the Critical Period for Language. In *The Epigenesis of Mind: Essays on Biology, and Cognition*, ed. S. Carey and R. Gelman, 111–30. Hillsdale, NJ: Erlbaum.

Newport, E. L., and R. P. Meier. 1985. Acquisition of American Sign Language. In *The Cross-linguistic Study of Language Acquisition*, ed. D. I. Slobin, Vol. 1, 881–938. Hillsdale, NJ: Erlbaum.

Ochs, E., and B. Schieffelin. 1984. Language Acquisition and Socialization: Three Developmental Stories and their Implications. In *Culture Theory: Essays on Mind, Self, and Emotion*, ed. R. Shweder and R. LeVine, 276–320. New York: Cambridge University Press.

Peirce, C. S. 1960. *Collected Papers of Charles Sanders Peirce*, ed. Hartshorne and P. Weiss, 4th edn, Vols. 1 and 2. Cambridge, MA: Harvard University Press.

Pettito, L. A. 1988. "Language" in the Prelinguistic Child. In *The Development of Language and Language Researchers: Essays in Honor of Roger Brown*, ed. R. S. Kessel, 187–221. Hillsdale, NJ: Erlbaum.

Pinker, S., and P. Bloom. 1990. Natural Language and Natural Selection. *Behavioral and Brain Sciences* 13: 707–84.

Putnam, H. 1970. Is Semantics Possible? In *Language, Belief, and Metaphysics*, ed. H. E. Kiefer and M. K. Munitz, 50–63. Albany, NY: State University of New York Press.

—1975. The Meaning of "Meaning." In *Mind, Language, and Reality: Philosophical Papers*, Vol. 2, ed. H. Putnam. New York: Cambridge University Press.

Pye, C. 1986. Quiche Mayan Speech to Children. *Journal of Child Language* 13: 85–100.

Quine, W. V. O. 1960. *Word and Object*. Cambridge, MA: MIT Press.

Resnick, L. B. 1994. Situated Rationalism: Biological and Social Preparation for Learning. In *Mapping the Mind: Domain Specificity in Cognition and Culture*, ed. L. Hirschfeld and S. Gelman, 474–94. Cambridge: Cambridge University Press.

Rips, L. J. 1989. Similarity, Typicality, and Categorization. In *Similarity and Analogical Reasoning*, ed. S. Vosniadou and A. Ortony, 21–59. New York: Cambridge University Press.

Rosaldo, M. 1972. Metaphor and Folk Classification. *Southwestern Journal of Anthropology* 28: 83–99.

Rosch, E., C. Mervis, W. Gray, D. Johnson, and P. Boyes-Braem. 1976. Basic Objects in Natural Categories. *Cognitive Psychology* 8: 382–439.

Rozin, P., and J. Schull. 1988. The Adaptive-Evolutionary Point of View in Experimental Psychology. In *Steven's Handbook of Experimental Psychology*, ed. R. Atkinson, R. Herrnstein, G. Lindzey, and R. Luce. New York: John Wiley and Sons.

Schwartz, S. P. 1979. Natural Kind Terms. *Cognition* 7: 301–15.

Shantz, C., ed. 1989. *Merrill-Palmer Quarterly* 35(7).

Slobin, D. 1985. *The Crosslinguistic Study of Language Acquisition*. Hillsdale, NJ: Erlbaum.

Smith, E. E., and D. L. Medin. 1981. *Categories and Concepts*. Cambridge, MA: Harvard University Press.

Snow, C. 1972. Mothers' Speech to Children Learning Language. *Child Development* 43: 549–65.

Spelke, E. S. 1990. Principles of Object Perception. *Cognitive Science* 14: 29–56.

Sperber, D. 1974. Contre certains a priori anthropologiques. In *L'Unite de l'homme*, ed. E. Morin and M. Piatelli-Palmarini, 491–512. Paris: Le Seuil.

—1975a. Pourquoi les animaux parfaits, les hybrides et les monstres sont ils bon a penser symboliquement? *L'Homme* 15(2): 5–24.

—1975b. *Rethinking Symbolism*. New York: Cambridge University Press.

Strauss, S., and T. Shilony. 1994. Teachers' Models of Children's Minds and Learning. In *Mapping the Mind: Domain Specificity in Cognition and Culture*, ed. L. Hirschfeld and S. Gelman, 455–73. Cambridge: Cambridge University Press.

Symons, D. 1979. *The Evolution of Human Sexuality*. New York: Oxford University Press.

Tambiah. S. 1969. Animals are Good to Think and Good to Prohibit. *Ethnology* 8(4): 422–59.

Ullman, S. 1980. Against Direct Perception. *Behavioral and Brain Sciences* 3: 373–415.

Vygotsky, L. 1978. *Mind in Society*. Cambridge: Harvard University Press.

Wexler, K., and P. W. Culicover. 1980. *Formal Principles of Language Acquisition*. Cambridge, MA: MIT Press.

Wierzbicka, A. 1994. Cognitive Domains and the Structure of the Lexicon: The Case of the Emotions. In *Mapping the Mind: Domain Specificity in Cognition and Culture*, ed. L. Hirschfeld and S. Gelman, 431–52. Cambridge: Cambridge University Press.

Witkowski. S., C. Brown, and P. Chase. 1981. Where Do Trees Come From? *Man* 16: 1–14.

4

EXPLORING THE NATURAL FOUNDATIONS OF RELIGION*

Justin L. Barrett

Abstract

A new cognitive approach to religion is bringing fresh insights to our understanding of how religious concepts are maintained, acquired and used to motivate and direct actions. This approach suggests that seemingly extraordinary thoughts and behaviours can be supported by quite ordinary cognition and may thus be termed "natural." Simultaneously, this research is expanding the domain of concepts and causal reasoning in general. This review examines recent research into religious rituals, communication and transmission of religious knowledge, the development of god-concepts in children, and the origins and character of religious concepts in adults. Together, these studies consistently emphasize and support the notion that the cultural phenomena typically labeled as "religion" may be understood as the product of aggregated ordinary cognition. The new cognitive science of religion should eventually provide a fuller account of the distinctive and apparently extraordinary properties of religion.

ॐ ॐ

Are god-concepts much different from gorilla-concepts? Is performing a religious ritual a profoundly different action from sending a greeting card to a friend? Perhaps not. When considering the kind of cognitive resources required for representing and acquiring these concepts and actions, the sacred and the profane may be less discriminable than is commonly assumed.

The scientific study of religion has historically focused on what might distinguish religion from ordinary life: special ecstatic experiences, peculiar brain states, uncommon emotional commitments, and beliefs in supernatural agents. What has been largely ignored until recently are the natural foundations of religion. Regardless of metaphysical claims, what we observe as religion is still a constellation of human phenomena communicated and regulated by natural human perception and cognition.

The new cognitive science of religion was motivated by a dissatisfaction with the vagueness of previous theories of religion, and thus their inability to be empirically tested, as well as by a desire to extend the psychological scholarship concerning concepts and causation. It differs from previous approaches to the study of religion by insisting that much of what is typically called "religion" may be understood as the natural product of aggregated ordinary cognitive processes. This perspective may be called the "naturalness-of-religion thesis." Much as language is naturally acquired as a result of cognitive preparedness plus exposure to a typical sociolinguistic environment, ordinary cognition plus exposure to an ordinary environment goes a long way towards explaining religion. Of course, this observation does not imply that any particular religion is independent of cultural considerations any more than particular languages are independent of culturally variable inputs.

Anticipated by Sperber (1975), this subfield is only about ten years old and still consists of a small number of religionists, anthropologists, philosophers and psychologists. Neuroscientists, linguists and computer scientists are yet to contribute to the discussion.

In this review, the emerging story about the natural origins of religion is summarized, and theoretical and empirical gaps that exist in this young enterprise are noted. The naturalness-of-religion thesis is currently focused on three main issues: (1) how people represent concepts of supernatural agents; (2) how people acquire these concepts; and (3) how they respond to these concepts through religious action such as ritual. The review concludes by suggesting areas that might be fruitful for future research. For the purpose of discussion here, "religion" designates a shared system of beliefs and actions concerning superhuman agency.

This review does not concern the more sensational faces of religion, such as bizarre experiences, visions, or altered states of consciousness. Consequently, neurological studies that address religious topics such as possible connections between epilepsy and mystical experiences (Shaver and Rabin

1997), and the suggestion that religious visions reflect the activity of temporal lobe structures (Persinger 1993), are not discussed. The study of religion from the perspective of personality and social psychology is also outside the scope of the present review.

Representing Supernatural Concepts

Religious concepts may be more "natural" than they seem. Though theologies around the world include enormously complex concepts, these are not the concepts that typically occupy the working minds of religious people. Much as folk science differs from true science, religious concepts often differ from theological ones in their relative conceptual simplicity (Barrett 1999; McCauley 2000). For example, even in a theological system that posits a non-temporal god, believers will represent the god as experiencing time much like any human does, when they are engaging in real-time problem solving or casual reasoning (Barrett, in press, a). This tendency to entertain religious concepts that are simpler than their theological counterparts is not merely an issue of expertise. The complexity of the concept used appears to vary based largely on the cognitive demands of the context in which it is used (Barrett, in press, a). For example, theologians might fully appreciate that the god Shiva knows their every thought before it is conceived, but will still intuitively feel it necessary to make Shiva aware of their thoughts through prayer. The simplification of concepts from the theological to the religious level appears to consist of a systematic distortion of features such that they more closely resemble intuitive ontological assumptions, and is not simply a matter of shedding superfluous features.

Over the past 20 years, researchers in the area of concepts, categorization, and cognitive development have amassed considerable evidence supporting the idea that people have a large number of often tacit, intuitive assumptions about the sorts of properties different things possess, based on ontological category membership (Keil 1989). For example, when encountering a completely novel animal, even six-year-old children make a host of assumptions about unobserved characteristics; for example, because it is a bounded physical object, it cannot pass directly through other solid objects and cannot occupy more than one location at a time. By virtue of being a living thing, it is automatically assumed to have nutritional needs and is composed of natural materials with parts designed for particular functions. As an animal it can move itself in purposeful ways to satisfy its desires (Sperber, Premack and Premack 1995). These intuitive assumptions appear to be largely invariant across cultures, and allow rapid categorization of novel things, as well as generation of predictions and explanations (Avis and Harris 1991; Sperber 1996; Walker 1992a and b).

If this characterization of conceptual structures is accurate, much as they constrain creativity (Ward 1994; 1995), these categorical intuitions also limit the sorts of religious concepts that may be successfully used to generate inferences during on-line processing. As an illustration of this constraint, Barrett and Keil found that when adults in India and the United States reflected on their theological ideas about supreme beings, they generated abstract, theologically correct, descriptions of gods that have no physical or spatial properties, are able to know and attend to everything at once, and have no need to rely on sensory inputs to acquire information. However, when comprehending narratives about the same deities, the same adults mistakenly remembered the god of the narratives as having a single location in space, as being unable to attend to multiple events at once, and as needing to see and hear in order to complete otherwise fallible knowledge. In other words, the gods of theological reflection contained many violations of intuitive assumptions for intentional agents, but the god-concepts used in the narrative comprehension task appeared to be very similar to an ordinary intentional agent—a person (Barrett 1998; Barrett and Keil 1996; Barrett and VanOrman 1996). Tacit assumptions about the ontological category of intentional agents constrained the way gods were represented in both cultural groups tested.

One consequence of this cognitive constraint is that people might only represent religious concepts that have a limited number of features that violate intuitive assumptions. That is, despite sophisticated theology, religious concepts might only be minimally counterintuitive (Bryer 1996a and b; 1998).

Acquiring Supernatural Concepts

The idea that religious concepts are minimally counterintuitive in the sense of violating few intuitive assumptions for their ontological categories underlies a second sense in which religion might be deemed natural. People seem to be naturally receptive to religious concepts, and concepts for which people are more receptive are more likely to become widespread and part of shared cultural concepts (Sperber 1996). Thus, as Boyer argues, the finding that people are receptive to religious concepts can help to explain why these concepts are so prevalent (Boyer 1993; 1994; 1995). The following sections explore the evidence for the contention that people are naturally receptive to religious concepts.

Religious Concepts in Childhood

Researchers in child development frequently note that children easily adopt ideas about gods, ghosts, Santa Claus and other agents possessing supernatural properties, and use ordinary conceptual resources for reasoning with these concepts (Harris 2000). Furthermore, many of the properties that set religious entities apart from natural agents might actually be easily accommodated by children's less developed conceptual systems. Recent developmental work using false-belief and perspective-taking tasks suggests that four- and five-year-olds can understand that, unlike people, God does not have false beliefs (Barrett 2001). Regarding God's creative power, preschoolers appear to be capable of understanding that God creates natural things but not artifacts, whereas humans create artifacts but not natural things (Petrovich 1997). Although available data is still limited, it appears that many concepts central to major religious traditions are not as opaque to young children as often thought.

Memorability and Transmission of Cultural Concepts

Natural receptivity to religious concepts is not limited to children. Adults appear to find minimally counterintuitive concepts, of which religious concepts are a subset, both easily represented (as discussed above) and highly memorable.

Adults from various cultures have been tested for the recall of concepts, and the sorts of concepts that are more likely to be remembered and transmitted successfully to others have been noted (Boyer 2000). The results showed that concepts that violate one of a number of category-level assumptions (e.g. a dog that passes through solid objects) are better remembered and transmitted than concepts that either satisfy assumptions (e.g. a brown dog) or that violate basic-level assumptions (e.g. a dog weighing five tons). That is, concepts with a counterintuitive feature are more memorable than either mundane or bizarre concepts that do not challenge categorical assumptions. Together with the finding that concepts that have too many counterintuitive features will be reduced to more intuitive forms in on-line processing (Barrett 1998; Barrett and Keil 1996), it appears that minimally counterintuitive concepts have a transmission advantage. Minimally counterintuitive concepts attain a "conceptual optimum" such that they are understood and represented without allocating too many cognitive resources, but are also challenging enough to require extra attention to assimilate into conceptual schemes (Sperber 1994). As a class of minimally counterintuitive concepts, religious concepts are likely to enjoy this advantage as well (Boyer 1994; 1995).

However, counterintuitive concepts such as invisible sofas rarely occupy important (if any) roles in religious systems.

Counterintuitive beings or objects of commitment in religious belief systems are most often intentional agents. They may be people with unusual physical or biological properties (such as an invisible person), or non-humans with humanlike abilities (such as a statue that can listen) (see Boyer 2000; Box 1). Perhaps counterintuitive agent concepts are more common because they enjoy additional selective advantages by being remembered and transmitted. But why might agent concepts have such advantages?

Box 1. Boyer's conceptual catalog of the supernatural

In the face of apparent enormous diversity in religious concepts, Boyer (Ref a) has argued that supernatural concepts typically share five representational similarities:

[1] A lexical label.

[2] Implicit classification in an intuitive ontological category.

[3] Explicit representation of a violation of intuitive expectations for that category, either: (3a) a breach of relevant expectations for that category, or (3b) a transfer of expectations associated with another category.

[4] Implicit default expectations for the category.

[5] Additional encyclopaedic information.

For example a 'ghost' [1] is categorized [2] as a person that can violate [3] intuitive physics for solid objects by passing through walls, but meets intuitive psychological assumptions for persons [4], and might be understood as likely to return to where it once lived [5]. What separates supernatural concepts from natural concepts is a violation of intuitive expectations for a given ontological category [3]. Supernatural concepts, therefore, are not wholly novel or determined by cultural instruction but exist as minor aberrations of natural concepts.

These violations of expectations may be in one of three intuitive knowledge domains: intuitive psychology, intuitive biology, or intuitive physics. For categories that assume a domain (e.g. 'Plant' assumes intuitive biology and intuitive physics), violations will consist of breaches of expectations for the domain (as in an invisible fern, a breach of intuitive physics for a Plant). However for categories that do not assume a domain (e.g. Plant does not assume intuitive psychology), violations may consist of transfers of expectations from another domain (as in a pensive shrub, a Plant having intuitive psychological properties).

Given three domains of knowledge and five primary ontological categories from which supernatural concepts are drawn, the vast majority of supernatural concepts that become part of cultural knowledge can be categorized in a 3 × 5 matrix. Table 1 gives examples of each of the 15 possible types of supernatural concepts.

Reference

a. Boyer, P. Evolution of a Modern Mind and the Origins of Culture: Religious Concepts as a Limiting Case. In *Evolution and the Human Mind: Modularity, Language and the Meta-Cognition*, ed. P. Carruthers and A. Chamberlain. Cambridge University Press (2000).

Table 1. Categories of supernatural concepts

Ontological categories	Intuitive-knowledge-domain violations		
	Psychology	Biology	Physics
Person	A person who knows everything	A person requiring no food to live	A person who is invisible
Animal	A snail that uses language	A dog that is immortal	A bear that can be in two places at once
Plant	A flower that listens to people's requests	A shrub composed of metal	A tree that is weightless
Artifact	A hammer that feels neglected	A shoe that sprouts roots	A car that can drip through a sieve
Natural, non-living	An icicle that enjoys music	A diamond that was born	A rock that passes through solid objects

Adapted from Ref. a

Hyperactive Agent-Detection Device (HADD)

On the basis of ethnographic data and psychological research, Guthrie argues that people have a bias towards detecting human-like agency in their environment that might not actually exist (Guthrie 1980; 1993; Lawson and McCauley 1990). Thus, people are particularly sensitive to the presence of intentional agency and seem biased to over attribute intentional action as the cause of a given state of affairs when data is ambiguous or sketchy (Heider and Simmel 1944; Rochart et al. 1997)). These observations suggest that whatever cognitive mechanism people have for detecting agency might be extremely sensitive; in other words, people can be said to possess hyperactive agent detection devices (HADD). According to Guthrie, such a biased perceptual device would have been quite adaptive in our evolutionary past, for the consequences of failing to detect an agent are potentially much graver than mistakenly detecting an agent that is not there.

The implication for religion is that the HADD might lead people to posit agents, perhaps of a counterintuitive sort, that are then well-transmitted because of their easy fit within intuitive conceptual systems. Similarly, counterintuitive-agent concepts would be more likely to receive attention and be transmitted than non-agent concepts, because agent concepts are more likely to resonate with agents posited by the HADD. For example, someone might be told that an invisible person lives in the forest and trips intruders. This story could become salient because it reminds the person of having tripped in the forest and wondering, "Who did that?" (because of the HADD). Alternatively, a story about an invisible rock is less likely to be spread because the hypothesis, "Did I trip over an invisible rock?" is unlikely to be expressed, albeit a more testable hypothesis. Because of the human tendency to seek intentional explanations for a given state of affairs, counterintuitive agents provide ready explanations in ways that nonagents do not. In this way, selective pressure of the HADD might contribute to the prevalence of religious-agent concepts over other counterintuitive concepts. Furthermore, when individuals talk about these agents they may cite empirical evidence consistent with the agents' existence.

Acting on Supernatural Concepts

Religions are not merely collections of shared concepts, but also include action in response to those concepts. Indeed, religious practice often more than religious belief strikes outside observers as peculiar and in need of explanation. Furthermore, people spread religious concepts in the context of shared religious actions. Religious actions such as rituals seem quite unnatural in many respects. Nevertheless, cognitive scientists of religion argue that, here too, ordinary cognition both structures religious practices and underlies the representation (and thus the execution) of religious actions in participants' and observers' minds.

Cognitive Contributions to Religious Events

Whitehouse has argued that many aspects of a given religious event might be, in part, a consequence of mnemonic and other cognitive dynamics (Whitehouse 1992; 1995; 1996a; 2000). These include the frequency of performance, the degree of sensory and emotional intensity (or "sensory pageantry" hereafter), the potential for producing group solidarity, the potential for encouraging spontaneous exegetical reflection, and the potential for transmitting theology. For an event to become part of a religious system, its procedures must be repeatedly performed in such a way that various instances are identifiable as the same event. Procedures without mnemonic aids that are infrequently performed are unlikely to be remembered. In oral traditions, a primary mnemonic aid is sensory pageantry. Use of elaborate sights, sounds, smells, tastes and feelings set an event apart from mundane life as something special and worthy of memory resources. Additionally, intensely arousing events, such as initiation rites that serve to "terrorize" initiates through physical and emotional torment, may elicit "flashbulb" memories for the participants (Brown and Kulik 1977). Such dramatic and traumatic events are unlikely to be easily forgotten (Whitehouse 1996b). However, as flashbulb memory research has indicated, only certain components of such an event are likely to be remembered well (Brown and Kulik 1977). Participants in highly dramatic events tend to form strong imagistic and episodic memories regarding the sequence of events (thus enabling repeat performances after long delays), who was a co-participant (increasing likelihood of group cohesion), and salient visual features of the event (providing symbolic materials for later reflection) (Neisser 1996). However, long theological (i.e. conceptually complex) treatises are unlikely to be remembered accurately. Consequently, events with a high degree of sensory pageantry typically include little sophisticated theological communication to justify or explain the event, and so participants are left to speculate why the event, in all its drama, was performed. In contrast, frequently repeated events need not require such resource-intensive, high sensory pageantry, and may include more complicated theological communication including an explicit rationale for the event.

The Case of Religious Rituals

In contrast to Whitehouse's analysis, which applies to religious events generally, the most developed cognitive theory of religious rituals in particular is that put forward by Lawson and McCauley (1990; Lawson 1993). Rituals may be regarded as a subclass within religious events, and are distinguished by being represented as an agent acting upon someone or something (a "patient") to bring about some state of affairs, by virtue of invoking supernatural causation. For example, for most Catholics, baptism is a religious ritual because an agent (the priest) acts (sprinkles water) upon a patient (an infant) for God to accept the child as part of the Church. In contrast, while possibly including rituals, Protestant worship services are religious events but not rituals.

Rather than cultural inputs wholly determining knowledge about rituals, their structures, and their potential effectiveness, Lawson and McCauley observe that the representation of religious ritual actions depends upon cognitive mechanisms for the representation of actions generally. In their view, religious rituals are distinguished from ordinary actions by the presence of supernatural agency represented in the action structure. A baptism is only a man wetting an infant except that the man is understood to be acting in the place of a superhuman agent. Because ordinary cognitive resources are drawn upon to make sense of religious rituals, little cultural knowledge is necessary for groups of people to have converging ideas about what are the important features of a ritual structure, or what makes a ritual "well-formed" and likely to be successful.

Indeed, as predicted by this account, Barrett and Lawson demonstrated that ritually naive adults have converging intuitions that the most important components for a religious ritual to be successful in bringing about the intended consequences are, first, that superhuman agency is represented in the action structure; and second, that an appropriate agent, capable of the right intentions, initiates the action (Lawson 1999). Unlike popular conceptions of magic, having the right agent is more important than performing precisely the correct action. Note that the priority of agent over action is not characteristic of natural mechanistic causation (e.g., it does not matter who strikes a window with a hammer, the action will have the same result). It is, however, characteristic of social causation: being the right person with the right intentions might make more difference in the consequence of an action than the particular action. For example, a woman who receives flowers to which she is allergic is likely to respond very differently if they were sent by a bitter ex-lover who knows of her allergies than by an innocent and adoring new suitor. What these findings suggest is that the ordinary cognitive structures that religious rituals draw upon may be those of social causal cognition. (For further discussion, see Box 2.)

Future Directions

Cognitive scientists of religion are making large strides in demonstrating that much of religious cognition, including the representation of god-concepts, successful transmission of religious concepts, and the development of practices based on religious concepts, is largely reliant on ordinary cognition. No special domain for religious thought need be postulated.

Box 2. Lawson and McCauley's theory of ritual competence

Lawson and Mccauley's theory of religious ritual (Ref. a) begins by observing that on one level of representation, rituals are merely actions of the form: An agent acts upon a patient by means of an instrument to produce a consequence. This basic action may be represented as shown in Fig. Ia.

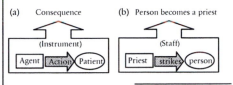

(a) Consequence (b) Person becomes a priest

trends in Cognitive Sciences

Fig.1. Lawson and McCauley's theory of religious ritual. (a) Representation of the basic action. (b) The surface representation of the ritual.

What distinguishes religious rituals from ordinary actions, and is essential for a well-formed ritual, is superhuman agency being represented somewhere in the action structure. Either the agent, instrument, or patient must have special properties by virtue of a represented relationship with a deity. For example, a priest is a special agent by virtue of having been given special power of authority by a god. This specialness may be designated by an S-marker in the action structure.

Thus, the surface representation of the ritual 'A priest strikes a person with a staff and the person becomes a priest' may be illustrated as shown in Fig. Ib.

This surface representation is likely to presume the effectiveness of previous rituals, most probably the ritual that resulted in the officiating priest becoming a priest. Commonly, S-markers are endowed on the basis of previous rituals. For example, a complete representation of the ritual above might be that in Fig. II.

The succession of embedded rituals in this example ends with the third action because it is represented as having been performed by a divine being who has an S-marker by virtue of ontological essence and not previous action. Similar series of previous rituals may be represented as having precipitated the use of a sacred object as an instrument or patient of a ritual, all ending with a god acting.

Lawson and McCauley argue that the structural considerations are sufficient for religious ritual observers or participants to generate at least four specific predictions about particular rituals. Deliberate inculturation is not needed. The first prediction depends upon the number of embedded rituals implicitly represented. Religious rituals vary in their degree of centrality or importance for a particular tradition (e.g., the Lord's Supper is generally considered more central than the marriage ritual). Lawson and McCauley argue that judgments of relative centrality are directly related to the number of embedded predecessor rituals. The longer the chain of assumed rituals, the less central the ritual will be to a tradition. Put another way, rituals that have more direct connections to a god will be more central.

The remaining three predictions are tied to the location of S-markers in the immediate, surface representation, whether an S-marker occurs in the agent position or not, and are depicted in Table 1. These predictions are based not on enculturation but on consideration of ritual form.

Reference
a Lawson, E.T., and R.N. McCauley (1990) *Rethinking Religion: Connecting Cognition and Culture*. Cambridge University Press.

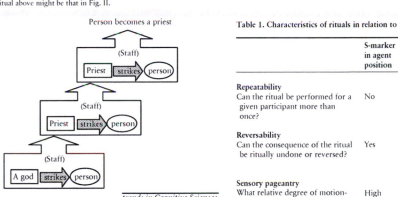

Person becomes a priest

trends in Cognitive Sciences

Fig. II. A complete implicit representation of the same ritual, with the addition of S-markers (see text for explanation).

Table 1. Characteristics of rituals in relation to S-marker position

	S-marker in agent position	S-marker not in agent position
Repeatability Can the ritual be performed for a given participant more than once?	No	Yes
Reversability Can the consequence of the ritual be ritually undone or reversed?	Yes	No
Sensory pageantry What relative degree of motion-evoking spectacle and adornment is there likely to be in performing the ritual?	High	Low

Religion is, in some ways, quite natural. However, the current story is not complete in either its coverage of issues or in its empirical support.

Cross-cultural investigations of many of the claims discussed above are still needed. For example, while it's plausible, the claim that people sometimes spontaneously account for events by reference to unseen agents needs systematic examination, as do many of the claims regarding ritual intuitions made by Lawson and McCauley. While receiving some ethnographic support, Whitehouse's claims about how sensory pageantry and memory dynamics interact to produce different sorts of religious events have not been examined in a controlled fashion.

Outstanding Questions

- How do truth-claims interact with the representation and transmission of religious concepts and practices? Are minimally counterintuitive concepts easier or harder to believe than other concepts? How is the success of rituals evaluated and how does this evaluation feed into whether or not the ritual is repeated?
- If religious concepts are so naturally accommodated by cognitive structures, why do they sometimes seem difficult to entertain? (For some preliminary thoughts on this issue, see McCauley 2000)
- How does cognition constrain and inform other classes of religious phenomena, such as petitionary prayer, worship and conversion?
- If children easily represent properties of superhuman agents, why do adults seem to have great difficulty in many contexts?
- From a cognitive perspective, does religious ritual differ (cognitively) from superstitious observances or from magic?
- Could recent advances in understanding social kinds bear upon how religious roles and special religious people such as priests, prophets, and shamans are represented?

Conclusion

The new cognitive approach to religion has begun to demonstrate that religion is not a wholly different, intractable domain of human experience but one that may be productively explored using the tools of the cognitive sciences. Rather than being seen as extraordinary, the area of religious phenomena may be seen as grounded in quite ordinary forms of cognition. Although the youth of this field of research precludes a full account at present of the cognitive processes underlying religious belief, it is hoped that further experimental and ethnographic work will provide rigorous empirical data to support the claims of this new science of religion. Research in this area is also extending what is known about conceptual systems in general to include non-natural concepts and intentional explanations of natural events.

Acknowledgments

The author thanks Pascal Boyer, Tom Lawson, Brian Malley, Bob McCauley, Keith Vander Linden, and Harvey Whitehouse for comments and suggestions.

Note

* This article was originally published in *Trends in Cognitive Science* 4(1) (2000): 29–34.

References

Avis, J., and P. L. Harris. 1991. Belief–Desire Reasoning among Baka Children: Evidence for a Universal Conception of Mind. *Child Development* 62: 460–67.

Barrett, J. L. 1998. Cognitive Constraints on Hindu Concepts of the Divine. *Journal for Scientific Study of Religion* 37: 608–19.

—1999. Theological Correctness: Cognitive Constraint and the Study of Religion. *Method and Theory in the Study of Religion* 11(4): 325–39.

—2001. Do Children Experience God Like Adults? Retracing the Development of God Concepts. In *Religion in Mind: Cognitive Perspectives on Religious Experience*, ed. J. Andresen, 173–91. Cambridge: Cambridge University Press.

Barrett, J. L., and F. C. Keil. 1996. Anthopomorphism and God Concepts: Conceptualizing a Non-natural Entity. *Cognitive Psychology* 3: 219–47.

Barrett, J. L., and B. VanOrman. 1996. The Effects of Image Use in Worship on God Concepts. *Journal of Psychology and Christianity* 15: 38–45.

Boyer, P. 1993. Pseudo-natural Kinds. In *Cognitive Aspects of Religious Symbolism*, ed. P. Boyer, 121–41. Cambridge: Cambridge University Press.

—1994. *The Naturalness of Religious Ideas: A Cognitive Theory of Religion*. Berkeley: University of California Press.

—1995. Causal Understandings in Cultural Representations: Cognitive Constraints on Inferences from Cultural Input. In *Causal Cognition: A Multidisciplinary Debate*, ed. D. Sperber et al., 615–49. Oxford: Oxford University Press.

—1996a. Cognitive Limits to Conceptual Relativity: The Limiting Case of Religious Categories. In *Rethinking Linguistic Relativity*, ed. J. Gumperz and S. Levinson, 203–31. Cambridge: Cambridge University Press.

—1996b. What Makes Anthropomorphism Natural: Intuitive Ontology and Cultural Representations. *Journal of the Royal Anthropological Institute* 2: 1–15.

—1998. Cognitive Aspects of Religious Ontologies: How Brain Processes Constrain Religious Concepts. In *Theory and Method in the Study of Religion*, ed. T. Alhbäck, 134–57. Stockholm: Donner Institute.

—2000. Evolution of a Modern Mind and the Origins of Culture: Religious Concepts as a Limiting Case. In *Evolution and the Human Mind: Modularity, Language and Meta-Cognition*, ed. P. Carruthers and A. Chamberlain. Cambridge: Cambridge University Press.

Brown, R., and J. Kulik. 1977. Flashbulb Memories. *Cognition* 5: 73–99.

Guthrie, S. 1980. A Cognitive Theory of Religion. *Current Anthropology* 21: 181–203.

—1993. *Faces in the Clouds: A New Theory of Religion*. Oxford: Oxford University Press.

Harris, P. L. 2000. On Not Falling Down to Earth: Children's Metaphysical Questions. In

Imagining the Impossible: The Development of Magical, Scientific, and Religious Thinking in Contemporary Society, ed. K. Rosengren et al. Cambridge: Cambridge University Press.

Heider, F., and M. Simmel. 1944. An Experimental Study of Apparent Behavior. *American Journal of Psychology* 57: 243–59.

Keil, F. C. 1989. *Concepts, Kinds, and Cognitive Development*. Cambridge, MA: MIT Press.

Lawson, E. T. 1993. Cognitive Categories, Cultural Forms, and Ritual Structures. In *Cognitive Aspects of Religious Symbolism*, ed. P. Boyer, 188–206. Cambridge: Cambridge University Press.

—1999. Religious Ideas and Practices. In *MIT Encyclopedia for Cognitive Science*, ed. R. Wilson and F. C. Keil, 720–22. Cambridge, MA: MIT Press.

Lawson, E. T., and R. N. McCauley. 1990. *Rethinking Religion: Connecting Cognition and Culture*. Cambridge: Cambridge University Press.

McCauley, R. N. 2000. The Naturalness of Religion and the Unnaturalness of Science. In *Explanation and Cognition*, ed. F. C. Keil and R. Wilson. Cambridge, MA: MIT Press.

Neisser, U. 1996. Remembering the Earthquake: Direct Experience Versus Hearing the News. *Memory* 4: 337–57.

Persinger, M. A. 1993. Paranormal and Religious Beliefs May be Mediated Differentially by Subcortical and Cortical Phenomenological Processes of the Temporal (Limbic) Lobes. *Perceptual and Motor Skills* 76: 247–51.

Petrovich, O. 1997. Understanding of Non-natural Causality in Children and Adults: A Case Against Artificialism. *Psyche en Geloof* 8: 151–65.

Rochat, P., R. Morgan, and M. Carpenter. 1997. Young Infants' Sensitivity to Movement Information Specifying Social Causality. *Cognitive Development* 12(4): 441–65.

Shaver, J. L., and J. Rabin. 1997. The Neural Substrates of Religious Experience. *Journal of Neuropsychiatry and Clinical Neurosciences* 9: 498–510.

Sperber, D. 1975. *Rethinking Symbolism*. Cambridge: Cambridge University Press.

—1994. The Modularity of Thought and the Epidemiology of Representations. In *Mapping the Mind: Domain Specificity in Cognition and Culture*, ed. L. A. Hirschfeld and S. A. Gelman, 39–67. Cambridge: Cambridge University Press.

—1996. *Explaining Culture: A Naturalistic Approach*. Oxford: Blackwell.

Sperber, D., D. Premack, and A. J. Premack, eds. 1995. *Causal Cognition: A Multidisciplinary Debate*. Oxford: Clarendon Press.

Walker [Jeyifous], S. 1992a. Developmental Changes in the Representation of Word-meaning: Cross-cultural Findings. *British Journal of Developmental Psychology* 10: 285–99.

—1992b. Supernatural Beliefs, Natural Kinds and Conceptual Structure. *Memory and Cognition* 20: 655–62.

Ward, T. B. 1994. Structured Imagination: The Role of Category Structure in Exemplar Generation. *Cognitive Psychology* 27: 1–40.

—1995. What's Old about New Ideas? In *The Creative Cognition Approach*, ed. S. M. Smith et al., 157–78. Cambridge, MA: MIT Press.

Whitehouse, H. 1992. Memorable Religions: Transmission, Codification, and Change in Divergent Melanesian Contexts. *Man* 27: 777–97.

—1995. *Inside the Cult: Religious Innovation and Transmission in Papua New Guinea*. Oxford: Oxford University Press.

—1996a. Jungles and Computers: Neuronal Group Selection and the Epidemiology of Representations. *Journal of the Royal Anthropological Institute* 2: 99–116.

—1996b. Rites of Terror: Emotion, Metaphor, and Memory in Melanesian Initiation Cults. *Journal of the Royal Anthropological Institute* 2: 703–15.

—2000. *Arguments and Icons: The Cognitive, Social, and Historical Implications of Divergent Modes of Religiosity*. Oxford: Oxford University Press.

5

Are Children "Intuitive Theists"?: Reasoning about Purpose and Design in Nature[*]

Deborah Kelemen

Abstract

Separate bodies of research suggest that young children have a broad tendency to reason about natural phenomena in terms of a purpose and an orientation towards intention-based accounts of the origins of natural entities. This article explores these results further by drawing together recent findings from various areas of cognitive developmental research to address the following question: Rather than being "artificialists" in Piagetian terms, are children "intuitive theists"—disposed to view natural phenomena as resulting from non-human design? A review of research on children's concepts of agency, imaginary companions and understanding of artifacts suggests that, by the time children are around 5 years of age, this description of them may have explanatory value and practical relevance.

಄ ಄

Piaget's (1929) claim that children are "artificialists" who draw on their subjective intentional experience to conclude that all things are made by people for a purpose has encountered substantial skepticism in the past few decades of cognitive developmental research. This is because, at core, Piaget's proposal embodied not just the suggestion that children misunderstand the limits of human creative power but a stronger claim about the profound incommensurability of children's and adults' conceptual systems. Specifically, Piaget believed that young children indiscriminately generate artificialist explanations because they are psychologically incapable of conceiving of physical causes, a shortcoming that he argued rendered them insensitive to the fundamental distinction between natural kinds and artifacts.

Research since Piaget has challenged these assumptions. Not only can children reason in physical-causal terms from infancy (e.g., Baillargeon 1993) but they also recognize that people make artifacts not natural entities (e.g., Gelman and Kremer 1991). But although these results may put aspects of Piaget's interpretation to rest, recent research has raised the specter of Piaget's findings once more. Consistent with Piaget's results, contemporary studies have found that, although children are not entirely indiscriminate, they do indeed evidence a general bias to treat objects and behaviors as existing for a purpose (Kelemen 1999a, 1999b, 2003; but see Keil 1992) and are also broadly inclined to view natural phenomena as intentionally created, albeit by a non-human agent (Evans 2000a, 2001; Gelman and Kremer 1991). This articles explores these findings further by drawing them together with other recent cognitive developmental research to address the following question: Even if children are not artificialists, as Piaget conceived of the term, are they perhaps "intuitive theists"—predisposed to construe natural objects as though they are non-human artifacts; the products of non-human design?

Promiscuous Teleology and "Creationism" in Children

Contemporary research on teleological reasoning—the tendency to reason about entities and events in terms of purpose—was initiated in context of the debate on the origins of biological understanding. Consistent with the view that children's reasoning about living things is constrained by teleological assumptions from a very early age, studies have found that young children attend to shared functional adaptation rather than shared overall appearance (or category membership) when generalizing behaviors to novel animals (Kelemen et al. 2003a), judge whether biological properties are heritable based on their functional consequences rather than their origin (Springer and Keil 1989) and explain body properties by reference to their self-serving functions not their physical-mechanical cause (Keil 1992; Kelemen 2003).

Results like these lend support to the idea that a "purpose-based" teleological stance might, therefore, be humans' innate adaptation for biological reasoning (Atran 1995; Keil 1992). This conclusion has been complicated, however, by findings that children see not only the biological but also the non-biological natural world in teleological terms. For example, when asked to identify unanswerable questions, American 4- and 5-year-olds differ from adults by finding the question "what's this for?" appropriate not only to artifacts and body parts, but also whole living things like lions ("to go in the zoo"), and non-living natural kinds like clouds ("for raining"). Additionally, when asked whether they agree that, for example, raining is really just what a cloud "does" rather than what it is "made for," preschoolers demur, endorsing the view that natural entities are "made for something" and that is why they are here (Kelemen 1999a).

These kinds of promiscuous teleological intuitions persist into elementary school, particularly in relation to object properties. For instance, when asked to conduct a "science" task and decide whether prehistoric rocks were pointy because of a physical process (e.g., "bits of stuff piled up for a long period of time") or because they performed a function, American 7- and 8-year-olds, unlike adults, prefer teleological explanations whether they invoke "self-survival" functions (e.g., "so that animals wouldn't sit on them and smash them") or "artifact" functions (e.g., "so that animals could scratch on them when they got itchy") (Kelemen 1999b, but see Keil 1992). This bias in favor of teleological explanation for properties of both living and non-living natural objects occurs even when children are told that adults apply physical kinds of explanation to non-living natural entities (Kelemen 2003). In American children, the bias begins to moderate around 9- to 10-years of age, and this pattern now has been found with British children for both object properties and, slightly less markedly, natural object wholes. These British findings are relevant because they weigh against interpretations that promiscuous teleological intuitions are a simple reflection of the relatively pronounced cultural religiosity or religious exceptionalism (in post-industrial, international context) of the United States (see Kelemen 2003 for discussion of religiosity differences).

So, if ambient cultural religiosity is not the obvious explanation, what does cause this "promiscuous teleology"? A study of responses young children receive when asking questions about nature indicates parents generally favor causal rather than teleological explanation, so current evidence suggests the answer does not lie there, at least not in any straightforward sense (Kelemen et al. 2002b). Another hypothesis being explored in my lab is, therefore, as follows (e.g., Kelemen 1999a, 1999b). Perhaps children's generalized attributions of purpose are, essentially, side-effects of a socially intelligent mind that is naturally inclined to privilege intentional explanation and is, therefore, oriented towards explanations characterizing nature as an intentionally-designed artifact—an orientation given further support by the artifact-saturated context of human cultures. Specifically, the proposal is that the human tendency to attribute purpose to objects develops from infants' core, and precociously developing, ability to attribute goals to agents (as discussed later). Initially, on the basis of observing agents' object-directed behavior, children understand objects as means to agents' goals, then as embodiments of agent goals (thus "for" specific purposes in a teleological sense), and, subsequently—as a result of a growing understanding of artifacts and the creative abilities of agents—as intentionally caused by agents' goals. A bias to explain, plus a human predilection for intentional explanation, may then be what leads children, in the absence of knowledge, to a generalized, default view of entities as intentionally caused by someone for a purpose.

Details aside, the basic idea that children are disposed to view entities in terms of intentional design, or as "quasi-artifacts," is similar to one independently developed by Evans in her work on origins beliefs (Evans 2000a, 2000b, 2001). Evans has found that, regardless of the religiosity of their home background, children show a bias to endorse intentional accounts of how species originate. Thus, when asked questions like "how do you think the very first sun bear got here on earth?" 8- to 10-year-olds from both fundamentalist and nonfundamentalist American homes favored "creationist" accounts whether generating their own answers or rating agreement to (a) God made it, (b) a person made it, (c) it changed from a different kind of animal that used to live on earth, or (d) it appeared (Evans 2001). This preference was also found in 5- to 7-year-old children's agreement ratings for animate and inanimate entities. Indeed, it was only among 11- to 13-year-old nonfundamentalist children that divergence from the theist position emerged. Evans' results do not stand in isolation. Gelman and Kremer (1991) found that, while American preschoolers recognize that artifacts rather than natural entities are human-made, they favor God as the explanation of remote natural items (e.g., oceans). Petrovich (1997) found similar results with British preschoolers (although see Mead 1932 on Manus children's disinclination to use supernatural explanation).[1]

Considered together, current data on children's promiscuous teleology and explanations of origins might therefore suggest an obvious affirmative answer to the question of whether children are intuitive theists: Children view natural phenomena as intentionally designed by a god. Non-coincidentally, they therefore view natural objects as existing for a purpose. But before embracing, or even entertaining, this conclusion, we must look first at whether it is actually defensible? What evidence is there that children possess any of the conceptual prerequisites that intuitive theism might entail? What evidence is there that their intuitions display any coherence at all?

Conceptual Prerequisites to Intuitive Theism

Piaget (1929) found that when asked how natural objects originated, children frequently identified "God" as the cause. Piaget argued that these statements were simply further cases of artificialism: Unable to entertain an abstraction such as God, and egocentrically focused, children use "God" to refer to a person who is fundamentally similar to the dominant authority in children's own lives—their parent.

Once again, however, Piaget's assumptions about the concreteness of children's concepts have been challenged. Research now suggests that rather than being anthropomorphic, children's earliest concept of agency is abstract, and is invoked by a range of non-human entities from the time when overt signs of children's sensitivity to mental states are becoming increasingly robust. Thus, 12-month-old infants will follow the gaze of faceless blobs as long as they have engaged in contingent interaction with them (Johnson et al. 2001) and will attribute goal-directedness to computer-generated shapes (e.g., Csibra and Gergely 1998). By 15-months, infants will complete the incomplete actions of a non-human agent by inferring its goals (Johnson et al. 2001). From infancy, we are, then, excellent "agency-detectors" (Barrett 2000; Guthrie 2002).

But, while relevant, these indications that children attribute mental states to perceivable non-human agents while watching them are still non-evidential with respect to young children's ability to reason about the creative intentions of intangible, non-natural agents like gods. Presumably several capacities are minimally prerequisite in order to reason about such special causal agents: First, the capacity to maintain a mental representation of such an agent despite its intangibility; second, the ability to attribute to that special agent mental states distinguishing it from more commonplace agents; and third—and particularly pertinent to the question of non-natural artifice—the basic ability to attribute design intentions to agents and understand an object's purpose as deriving from such intentions.

Conceptions of Intangible Agents

Several lines of research are suggestive of young children's abilities regarding the first two prerequisites. First, Taylor's (1999) research on children's propensity to maintain social relationships with imaginary companions suggests that by 3- to 4-years, children are already conceptually equipped to vividly mentally represent the wants, opinions, actions and personalities of intangible agents on a sustained basis. Like supernatural agents, such companions are found cross-culturally and are often distinguished from more commonplace agents by special biological, psychological, and physical traits beyond invisibility. Examples are animals that talk and individuals who understand gibberish, hear wishes, or live on stars (Taylor 1999). Interestingly, ideas about imaginary companions, such as ideas about gods, can be culturally transmitted, at least within families.[2]

Imaginary companions, then, provide some indications of young children's ability to symbolically represent and reason about immaterial individuals. But research explicitly focused on children's understanding of God has also found that by 5-years of age, children can make quite sophisticated predictions as to how a more widely-recognized nonnatural agent's mental states are distinguished from those of more earthly individuals. Specifically, Barrett, Richert, and Driesenga (2001) cleverly capitalized on the well-documented 3- to 5-year-old shift in children's ability to pass "false-belief" tasks—tests that putatively measure children's "theory of mind" understanding that beliefs are mental representations and, as such, can mismatch with physical reality. In their study, Barrett et al. used a standard form of the task: Children were shown a cracker box, asked what they believed it contained, allowed to peek inside and see the actual contents (pebbles), and then asked the test question, What would someone (who had not been shown) believe was inside the container? As is typical in such studies, Barrett et al. found that 3-year-olds failed the test, giving an answer that, in some sense, assumes that people are all-knowing; that is, 3-year-olds answered, "pebbles." In contrast, an increasing percentage of 4- and 5-year-olds passed, saying "crackers"—an answer recognizing the fallibility of beliefs. Interestingly, however, a different pattern emerged when these Protestant-raised children were asked what God would believe. At all ages tested, children treated God as all-knowing even when they clearly understood that earthly agents would have a false belief. This developmental pattern led Barrett et al. (2001) to provocatively suggest that children may be innately attuned to "god-like" non-human agency but need to acquire an understanding of the limitations of human minds. Similar results have now also been obtained with Yukatek Mayan children, who not only discriminated the Christian God but other supernatural agents as less susceptible to false belief than people (Knight et al. 2003; also Atran 2002 for description).

In sum, then, these findings suggest that around 5 years of age, children possess the prerequisites to make advanced, distinctive, attributions of mental states to non-natural agents. But are children truly conceptually distinguishing these agents from people or just representing these agents as humans augmented with culturally-prescribed, superhuman properties inferred from adults' religious talk? The answer to this question is unclear. Certainly children's supernatural concepts, like those of adults, are likely to be influenced by culturally-prescribed, systematically counterintuitive properties (Atran 2002; Boyer 2001) and may also be anthropomorphic in many ways. But, even if children's concepts of non-natural agency do have human features, this does not undermine the claim that children conceive of such agents as distinct: We do not question adults' capacity to conceive of supernatural agents and yet research indicates that even when adults explicitly attribute gods with properties like omnipresence, they assume, in their implicit reasoning, that gods act in accordance with human temporal, psychological, and physical constraints (Barrett 2000).

Even so, perhaps applying the phrase "intuitive theists" to children—given all that the term "theism" implies to adults—might seem misplaced, if not irreverent. After all, while young children might conceive of non-natural agents and hypothesize about their mental states, presumably they do not contemplate the metaphysical "truth" of which such agents can be part, or experience emotions concomitant with endorsing a particular metaphysical religious system. Intuitively, these assumptions seem correct although, again, there are reasons to equivocate. This is not only because research suggests adult religious belief systems are often not particularly coherent or contemplated (e.g., Boyer 2001) but also because the question of when children begin to develop metaphysical understanding in the adult self-reflective sense is debated (e.g., Evans and Mull 2002; Harris 2000; Johnson 2000). Specifically, although children might not explicitly demarcate their musings as special, it has been found that even from very young ages, children pose questions about the nature of things that echo adult metaphysical themes (Harris 2000; Piaget 1929). Furthermore, we actually know little about young children's emotions concerning self-generated or culturally derived concepts of non-natural agency, outside of their emotional relationships with imaginary companions. Gaps in our knowledge therefore preclude general conclusions as to children's capacity to entertain adult-like religious feeling.

However, for the present purpose, such issues are, to a large extent, irrelevant because in the current context the term "intuitive theist" embodies no claims regarding children's emotional or metaphysical commitments. All that is under question is whether children make sense of the world in a manner superficially approximating adult theism, by forming a working hypothesis that natural phenomena derive from a non-human "somebody" who designed them for a purpose—intuitions which may be elaborated by a particular religious culture but are proposed to derive primarily from cognitive predispositions and artifact knowledge.[3] This point circles us back to the third conceptual prerequisite for intuitive theism—children's ability to understand that object purposes derive from designer's goals.

Children's Understanding of Artifacts and Design

Adult reasoning about artifacts is anchored by intuitions about the designer's intended function (e.g., Keil 1989; Rips 1989) but although behavioral measures suggest that from around 3-years of age children will teleologically treat artifacts as "for" a single privileged function (Casler and Kelemen 2003a; Markson 2001), the question of when children adopt an adult-like teleological construal based on reasoning about the creator's intent (the "design stance") is debated (Kelemen and Carey 2003b).

One reason for the lack of consensus is studies suggesting that, until they are quite old, children apply category labels to artifacts on the basis of shared shape, not shared function (e.g., Gentner 1978; Graham, Williams, and Huber 1999; Landau et al. 1998). Such studies have found that until around 6 years of age, children will judge that if an object looks similar to an artifact called "a wug," it is also "a wug" even though it doesn't do the same thing. Children's apparent indifference to what artifacts did in these categorization studies seemed to render it unlikely that the deeper principle of intended function could play much of a role in their concepts of artifacts. However, recent findings suggest that the stimuli in earlier studies may have significantly contributed to children's categorization failures in that experimenters unnaturally dissociated artifact form from artifact function, an approach leading to uncompelling "functions" equivalent to general object properties (e.g., capacities to rattle, roll, absorb). In current research using artifacts that look designed, in that their structural properties clearly relate to their functional affordances, children from around the age of 2-years have generalized labels on the basis of function rather than shape similarity (e.g., Kemler Nelson et al. 2000a, 2000b). Furthermore, evidence also suggests that even when children categorize artifacts by shape, rather than being a superficial perceptual strategy, this approach reflects the valid conceptual assumption that shape predicts the creator's intent. Thus, Diesendruck, Markson, and Bloom (2003) found that if 3-year-olds have the shape similarity between two artifacts pointed out to them but then hear that the objects have different intended functions, they eschew classifying them as the same kind of artifact, instead forming categories based on shared function and perceptual dissimilarity. Importantly, this shift from a shape to a function strategy happens only if children hear about intended functions—information about possible function is not sufficient.

These findings provide suggestive evidence that young children have a sensitivity to intended function from around the age of 3 years. They are particularly interesting when considered alongside research explicitly focused on when children weigh overt information about intended design. In studies in my own lab, this tendency is increasingly evident between the ages of 4 and 5 years. For example, in one study, 4- and 5-year-old children were told stories about depicted novel artifacts that were intentionally designed for one purpose (e.g., squeezing lemons), given away, and then accidentally or intentionally used for another activity (e.g., picking up snails). When asked what each object was "for," the children, like adults, favored the intended function, even in experimental conditions where the alternative use occurred

frequently rather than just once (Kelemen 1999b). A subsequent study replicated this effect using manipulable, novel artifacts. In contrast to 3-year-
olds, groups of 4- and 5-year-olds not only judged the objects as "for" their
designed function rather than their everyday intentional use, but also favored
intended function when judging where items belonged in a house (Kelemen,
Sumutka and Grobman 2001).

Research by Matan and Carey (2001) also reveals some early sensitivity
to intended function. In their study, children were told about artifacts that
were made for one purpose (e.g., to water flowers) but used for something
else (to make tea in). When asked which familiar artifact category the object
belonged to (e.g., watering can or teapot), 4- and 6-year-olds, like adults,
had a preference for the design category. However, 4-year-olds' tendency to
be influenced by the order of forced-choice response options on some trials
led Matan and Carey to conclude that an understanding of designer intent
does not organize children's artifact concepts until around 6 years of age.[4]

According to German and Johnson (2002), however, even the design bias
that Matan and Carey's (2001) results did reveal offers no real indication of
children's understanding of the designer's role in designating function. Instead, German and Johnson argued that naming results such as these reveal
little more than children's more shallow knowledge that the designer has
the right to designate an object's category name and membership ("baptism
rights").

Although it is not clear that this explanation accounts for Matan and
Carey's (2001) results,[5] German and Johnson's (2002) results were consistent with the notion that this is the limit of children's understanding. Using
function-judgment methods similar to those used in my lab, they found that
although 5-year-olds weigh designer intent over another agent's intentional
action when determining what a novel artifact's category name is, they do
not reliably use designer intent when judging what a novel object is "really
for"—a lack of design-based construal that is also reflected, German and
Defeyter (2000) argue, in 5-year-olds' relative success at function-based insight problem-solving: Specifically, employing methods classically used to
explore functional fixedness, German and Defeyter found that although 6-
and 7-year-olds find it difficult to disregard an artifact's design function when
asked to solve a problem creatively with it, 5-year-olds do not have this difficulty, more readily seeing how an artifact can be used unconventionally to
achieve a goal (seeing a box as a platform not a container; also Defeyter and
German 2003). Such a lack of design stance in 5-year-olds is, in fact, no
surprise, suggest German and Johnson, when the computations involved in
reasoning about design intentions are actually considered; that is, design
attributions require recursive reasoning about second order mental states—
"maker intends (that user intends) that X will perform Y"—something
acknowledged as difficult for children.

However, this explanation of 5-year-olds' lack of design sensitivity in German and Johnson's (2002) tasks is challengeable: Design intentions may not require second order computation (they may reduce to "maker intends that user does X with Y" or "maker intends that X does Y") and reasoning about mental state content of a more complex form than the goal states of design intentions has been documented among 3- and 4-year-olds (e.g., Chandler, Fritz, and Hala 1989; Siegal and Beattie 1991). Furthermore, although, in combination, their findings might suggest that a design-based grasp of artifact function is not present until 6- or 7-years, some patterns across their various studies raise questions: For example, in German and Johnson's function-judgment task, even adults' tendency to judge that the novel artifacts were "really for" the designed function rather than an intended use was weak—more than half of adult subjects made design-based judgments 50% or less of the time. Perhaps, then, unintended qualities of the stimuli had a particular impact on children's judgments across all the German and Johnson studies. Additionally, studies directly exploring whether there is a relationship between 3- to 5-year-olds' susceptibility to functional fixedness and their tendency to construe artifacts in terms of original design have found no correlation between the two abilities, suggesting that other factors (e.g., age- or education-related changes in conventionality) might account for 5-year-olds' advantage in German and Defeyter's (2000) insight tasks (Kelemen 2001).

These disparities aside, an underlying developmental pattern does emerge across all of these studies. With some reliability, the findings suggest that beginning some time around the kindergarten period, children adopt a design-based teleological view of objects with increasing consistency. In light of this work, and the earlier-described research on children's reasoning about nonnatural agents' mental states, the proposal that children might be intuitive theists becomes increasingly viable. However, an issue still remains: Just because children can consider objects as products of design does not mean this ability has any actual connection to children's attributions of purpose to nature. It is possible, after all, that, like some adults, children view supernatural agents as originators of nature but consider the functionality of many natural phenomena as deriving from an entirely different, nonintentional cause (e.g., evolution). Thus, although children may invoke God in their explanations of origins (e.g., Evans 2001) and view natural phenomena as existing for a purpose (e.g., Kelemen 1999b), the two sets of intuitions may have no systematic relation.

A recent study addressing this question suggests that this is not the case. Six- to 10-year-old British children were first asked to generate ideas about why various animals, natural objects, and events exist, and then consider other people's explanations, indicating their preference between teleological and physical explanations for each item. Subsequently, the children were also asked questions probing their ideas about intentional origins and whether they thought the earlier items originated because they "just hap-pened" or because they were "made by someone/something." The design of the study precluded children from tracking their answers and aligning their answers to earlier and later questions in the absence of intuitions of their own. Nevertheless, the results revealed correlations between children's teleo-logical ideas about nature and their endorsements of intentional design. Furthermore, no artificialism was found: Children identified people as the designing agents of artifacts (control items), distinguishing God as the design-ing agent of nature (Kelemen and DiYanni 2002).

Summary

This article began by posing a question: Given findings regarding children's beliefs about purpose and their ideas about the intentional origins of nature, is it possible that children are intuitive theists insofar as they are predis-posed to develop a view of nature as an artifact of nonhuman design?

A review of recent cognitive developmental research reveals that by around 5 years of age, children understand natural objects as not humanly caused, can reason about nonnatural agents' mental states, and demonstrate the capacity to view objects in terms of design. Finally, evidence from 6- to 10-year-olds suggests that children's assignments of purpose to nature relate to their ideas concerning intentional nonhuman causation. Together, these research findings tentatively suggest that children's explanatory approach may be accurately characterized as intuitive theism—a characterization that has broad relevance not only to cognitivists or the growing interdisciplinary community studying the underpinnings of religion (Barrett 2000), but also, at an applied level, to science educators because the implication is that chil-dren's science failures may, in part, result from inherent conflicts between intuitive ideas and the basic tenets of contemporary scientific thought.

Further research is required, of course, to clarify how well the description really holds across individuals and cultures (reliable, empirical cross-cultural research is limited), how robust the orientation to purpose and design is, and how it interacts with education over time. A significant theoretical goal is to empirically discriminate the present hypothesis that children are inher-ently predisposed to invoke intention-based teleological explanations of nature and find them satisfying (see Bering 2002, for a related stance) from the milder hypothesis that children's teleological orientation arises primarily from their possession of the kind of cognitive machinery (e.g., agency detec-tion) that renders them susceptible to the religious representations of their adult culture—a position that predicts children would not independently generate explanations in terms of designing nonnatural agency without adult cultural influence.

A proper discussion of the pros and cons of each position, along with how to empirically distinguish them, is beyond the scope of this short article. However, it is worth emphasizing that the kind of research program proposed here is one that involves focusing on adults as much as children because although the question "are children intuitive theists?" implies a dichotomy between child and adult thought, the current proposal tacitly assumes that the idea of such a fundamental dichotomy is false: If, as suggested here, the tendency to think in teleological quasi-artifact terms is a side effect of human mental design (and pan-cultural experience with artifacts) rather than socialization, it is likely to remain as a default explanatory strategy throughout life, even as other explanations are elaborated. This idea contrasts with the notion that through conceptual change (e.g., Carey 1985), such an explanatory approach is revised and replaced by a physical-reductionist view of nature in cultures endorsing such ideas.

Several factors provide support for this suggestion of developmental continuity. First, reasoning about all aspects of nature in nonteleological physical-reductionist terms is a relatively recent development in the history of human thought (see Kelemen 1999a, for a brief history of the "design argument"), and contemporary adults are still surprisingly bad at it. For example, evolution is generally misconstrued as a quasi-intentional needs-responsive designing force, indicating that even when adults elaborate alternative scientific explanations, signs of intention-based reasoning about nature are still in evidence (see Evans 2000a, for review). Second, recent research with American college undergraduates has found that although such populations endorse teleological explanation in a selective, scientifically appropriate way in the evaluative context of a forced-choice "scientific" experiment, in a less evaluative environment they will more promiscuously generate teleological explanations of why animals and inanimate natural objects exist. These results suggest that even in a post-Darwinian culture, continuity rather than conceptual change may be at play in educated individuals' preference for teleological explanation (Kelemen 2003). Finally, and significant to the conjecture that scientific educations suppress rather than replace teleological explanatory tendencies, research with scientifically uneducated Romanian Gypsy adults has found that they have promiscuous teleological intuitions much like scientifically naive British and American elementary-school children (Casler and Kelemen 2003b). In conclusion, the question of whether children and adults are intuitive theists provides fertile ground for future research.

Notes

* This article was originally published in *Psychological Science* V.15(5) (2004): 295–301.

1. Mead explored attributions of consciousness to inanimates by children from a small-scale animist society. However, the nature of Mead's data (e.g., drawings, queries about inanimate malintentions) make children's non-reference to supernatural agency difficult to interpret. Furthermore, while her data suggest the children were not animists, they don't rule out possible "intuitive theism."

2. This discussion is not to suggest that children's relationships with imaginary companions are akin to adults' relationships with gods. Importantly, the latter are experienced as real (Boyer 2001) while evidence suggests that (American) children's imaginary companions are experienced as fictions (Taylor 1999).

3. Some form of folk religion appears existent in all human cultures but not all religions are theist (e.g., animism), raising the interesting possibility that children's intuitions may sometimes mismap with the dominant adult culture's religious ideas. However, since all known folk religions involve non-natural agents and intentional causation—the substrate of intuitive theism—such mismappings need not represent an ongoing conceptual conflict but instead leave children's intuitions open to co-exist with and be influenced by cultural religious ideas.

4. Matan and Carey's children made fewer design-based judgments when the design category name was presented second rather than first—an effect perhaps inadvertently caused by pretrial familiarization of the familiar artifact stimuli which may have prompted pre-potent responding to the first function information heard, reducing design-based reasoning overall.

5. Half of Matan and Carey's stimuli had names encoding intended function, rendering it unlikely that participants only processed intended category membership.

References

Atran, S. 1995. Causal Constraints on Categories. In *Causal Cognition: A Multi-disciplinary Debate*, ed. D. Sperber, D. Premack, and A. J. Premack, 263–65. Oxford: Clarendon Press.

—2002. *In Gods We Trust: The Evolutionary Landscape of Religion*. New York: Oxford University Press.

Baillargeon, R. 1993. The Object Concept Revisited: New Directions in the Investigation of Infants' Physical Knowledge. In *Visual Perception and Cognition in Infancy, Carnegie Mellon Symposia on Cognition*, Vol. 23, ed. C. E. Granrud. Hillsdale, NJ: Erlbaum.

Barrett, J. L. 2000. Exploring the Natural Foundations of Religion. *Trends in Cognitive Sciences* 4: 29–34.

Barrett, J. L., R. Richert, and A. Driesenga. 2001. God's Beliefs Versus Mother's: The Development of Non-Human Agent Concepts. *Child Development* 72: 50–65.

Bering, J. 2002. Intuitive Conceptions of Dead Agents' Minds: The Natural Foundations of Afterlife Beliefs as a Phenomenological Boundary. *Journal of Cognition and Culture* 2: 263–308.

Boyer, P. 2001. *Religion Explained: The Evolutionary Origins of Religious Thought*. New York: Basic Books.

Carey, S. 1985. *Conceptual Change in Childhood*. Cambridge, MA: MIT Press.

Casler, K., and D. Kelemen. 2003a. *Teleological Explanations of Nature among Romanian Roma (Gypsy) Adults*. Unpublished manuscript. Boston, MA.

Casler, K., and D. Kelemen. 2003b. *Tool Use and Children's Understanding of Artifact Function*. Unpublished manuscript. Boston, MA.

Chandler, M., A. S. Fritz, and S. Hala. 1989. Small-scale Deceit: Deception as a Marker of Two-, Three-, and Four-year-olds' Early Theories of Mind. *Child Development* 60: 1263–77.

Csibra, G., and G. Gergely. 1998. The Teleological Origins of Mentalistic Action Explanations: A Developmental Hypothesis. *Developmental Science* 1: 255–59.

Defeyter, M., and T. German. 2003. Acquiring an Understanding of Design: Evidence from Children's Insight Problem-solving. *Cognition* 89(2): 133–55.

Diesendruck, G., L. M. Markson, and P. Bloom. 2003. Children's Reliance on Creator's Intent in Extending Names for Artifacts. *Psychological Science* 14: 164–68.

Evans, E. M. 2000a. The Emergence of Beliefs about the Origin of Species in School-age Children. *Merrill Palmer Quarterly* 46: 221–54.

—2000b. Beyond Scopes: Why Creationism is Here to Stay. In *Imagining the Impossible: The Development of Magical, Scientific and Religious Thinking in Contemporary Society*, ed. K. Rosengren, C. Johnson, and P. Harris, 305–33. Cambridge: Cambridge University Press.

—2001. Cognitive and Contextual Factors in the Emergence of Diverse Belief Systems: Creation Versus Evolution. *Cognitive Psychology* 42: 217–66.

Evans, E. M., and M. Mull. 2002. *Magic can Happen in that World (But Not this One): Constructing a Naïve Metaphysics*. Manuscript submitted for publication.

Gelman, S. A., and K. E. Kremer. 1991. Understanding Natural Cause: Children's Explanations of How Objects and their Properties Originate. *Child Development* 62: 396–414.

Gentner, D. 1978. What Looks Like a Jiggy but Acts Like a Zimbo? A Study of Early Word Meaning Using Artificial Objects. *Papers and Reports on Child Language Development* 15: 1–6.

German, T., and M. Defeyter. 2000. Immunity to Functional Fixedness in Young Children. *Psychonomic Bulletin and Review* 7: 707–12.

German, T., and S. A. Johnson. 2002. Function and the Origins of the Design Stance. *Journal of Cognition and Development* 3: 279–300.

Graham, S. A., L. D. Williams, and J. F. Huber. 1999. Preschoolers' and Adults' Reliance on Object Shape and Object Function for Lexical Extension. *Journal of Experimental Child Psychology* 74: 128–51.

Guthrie, S. 2002. Animal Animism: Evolutionary Roots of Religious Cognition. In *Current Approaches in the Cognitive Science of Religion*, ed. I. Pyysiainen and V. Anttonen, 38–67. London: Continuum.

Harris, P. 2000. On Not Falling Down to Earth: Children's Metaphysical Questions. In *Imagining the Impossible: The Development of Magical, Scientific and Religious Thinking in Contemporary Society*, ed. K. Rosengren, C. Johnson, and P. Harris, 157–78. Cambridge: Cambridge University Press.

Johnson, C. N. 2000. Putting Different Things Together: The Development of Metaphysical Thinking. In K. S. Rosengren, C. N. Johnson, and P. L. Harris, *Imagining the Impossible: The Development of Magical, Scientific and Religious Thinking in Children*, 179–211. Cambridge: Cambridge University Press.

Johnson, S. C., A. Booth, and K. O'Hearn. 2001. Inferring the Goals of a Nonhuman Agent. *Cognitive Development* 16: 637–56.

Keil, F. C. 1989. *Concepts, Kinds, and Cognitive Development*. Cambridge, MA: MIT Press.

—1992. The Origins of an Autonomous Biology. In *Minnesota Symposia on Child Psychology: Vol. 25. Modularity and Constraints in Language and Cognition*, ed. M. R. Gunnar and M. Maratsos, 103–37. Hillsdale, NJ: Erlbaum.

—1999a. Beliefs about Purpose: On the Origins of Teleological Thought. In *The Descent of Mind: Psychological Perspectives on Hominid Evolution*, ed. M. Corballis and S. Lea, 278–94. Oxford: Oxford University Press.

—1999b. The Scope of Teleological Thinking in Preschool Children. *Cognition* 70: 241–72.

—1999c. Why are Rocks Pointy? Children's Preference for Teleological Explanations of the Natural World. *Developmental Psychology* 35: 1440–53.

—2003. British and American Children's Preferences for Teleo-functional Explanations of the Natural World. *Cognition* 88: 201–21.

Kelemen, D. April, 2001. *Intention in Children's Understanding of Artifact Function*. Paper presented at the Biennial Meeting of the Society for Research in Child Development, Minnesota, MN. (Also manuscript in preparation).

Kelemen, D., M. Callanan, K. Casler, and D. Pérez-Granados. 2002b. *"Why Things Happen": Teleological Explanation in Parent-Child Conversations*. Manuscript submitted for publication.

Kelemen, D., and S. Carey. 2003b. The Essence of Artifacts: Developing the Design Stance. In *Creations of the Mind: Theories of Artifacts and their Representation*, ed. S. Laurence. and E. Margolis. Oxford: Oxford University Press.

Kelemen, D., and C. DiYanni. 2002. *Children's Ideas About Nature: The Role of Purpose and Intelligent Design*. Manuscript in submission.

Kelemen, D., D. Widdowson, T. Posner, A. Brown, and K. Casler. 2003a. Teleofunctional Constraints on Preschool Children's Reasoning about Living Things. *Developmental Science* 6: 329–45.

Kemler Nelson, D. G., R. Russell, N. Duke, and K. Jones. 2000a. Two-year-olds will Name Artifacts by their Functions. *Child Development* 71: 1271–88.

Kemler Nelson, D., A. Frankenfield, C. Morris, E. Blair. 2000b. Young Children's Use of Functional Information to Categorize Artifacts: Three Factors that Matter. *Cognition* 77: 133–68.

Knight, N., P. Sousa, and J. L. Barrett, and S. Atram. 2004. Children's Attributions of Beliefs to Humans and God: Cross-Cultural Evidence. *Cognitive Science* 28: 117–26.

Landau, B., L. B. Smith, and S. S. Jones. 1998. Object Shape, Object Function, and Object Name. *Journal of Memory and Language* 38: 1–27.

Markson, L. M. April 2001. *Developing Understanding of Artifact Function*. Paper presented at the Biennial Meeting of the Society for Research in Child Development, Minnesota, MN.

Matan, A., and S. Carey. 2001. Developmental Changes within the Core of Artifact Concepts. *Cognition* 78: 1–26.

Mead, M. 1932. An Investigation of the Thought of Primitive Children with Special Reference to Animism. *Journal of the Royal Anthropological Institute of Great Britain and Ireland* 62: 173–90.

Petrovich, O. 1997. Understanding of Non-natural Causality in Children and Adults: A Case Against Artificialism. *Psyche and Geloof* 8: 151–65.

Piaget, J. 1929. *The Child's Conception of the World*. London: Routledge and Kegan Paul.

Rips, L. J. 1989. Similarity, Typicality and Categorization. In *Similarity and Analogical Reasoning*, ed. S. Vosniadou and A. Ortony, 21–59. Cambridge: Cambridge University Press.

Siegal, M., and K. Beattie. 1991. Where to Look First for Children's Knowledge of False Beliefs. *Cognition* 38: 1–12.

Springer, K., and F. C. Keil. 1989. On the Development of Biologically Specific Beliefs: The Case of Inheritance. *Child Development* 60: 637–48.

Taylor, M. 1999. *Imaginary Companions and the Children who Create them*. New York: Oxford University Press.

Part II

6

Conceptualizing a Nonnatural Entity: Anthropomorphism in God Concepts[*]

Justin L. Barrett and Frank C. Keil

Abstract

We investigate the problem of how nonnatural entities are represented by examining university students' concepts of God, both professed theological beliefs and concepts used in comprehension of narratives. In three story processing tasks, subjects often used an anthropomorphic God concept that is inconsistent with stated theological beliefs; and drastically distorted the narratives without any awareness of doing so. By heightening subjects' awareness of their theological beliefs, we were able to manipulate the degree of anthropomorphization. This tendency to anthropomorphize may be generalizable to other agents. God (and possibly other agents) is unintentionally anthropomorphized in some contexts, perhaps as a means of representing poorly understood nonnatural entities.

ဆ ෬

There has been increasing interest in uncovering how we represent the categories of existence. Our notions of what sorts of things there are, that is, our ontological knowledge, may undergird in largely implicit ways much of how we categorize and make sense of the world (Sommers 1963; Keil 1979). The nature of ontological knowledge and its degree of distinctiveness from other forms of knowledge remains an active area of inquiry (Chi 1992); but one critical question rarely addressed asks how entities that do not conform to existing ontological knowledge are conceived by adults. Developmentally, it is often assumed that children learn how to incorporate such new entities by restructuring their ontological knowledge (ibid.); but there is much less consensus on how adults might conceive of a widely discussed entity that is nonetheless apparently not conforming to any other ontological kind. No entity poses the problem more clearly than God.

In contrast to the ancient Greeks, contemporary Western theologies suggest the existence of a gaping ontological chasm between God and humans: "On this view, God and the world are two distinct realities. The difference is not merely quantitative but qualitative. God is not simply more of what we are. There is an essential discontinuity ..." (Spykman 1992, 64). One way to appreciate this "essential discontinuity" is to consider the descriptions of God offered by the three monotheisms that have most influenced Western thought about God.

Catholic and Protestant teachings describe God as being: infinite, limitless, all-perfect, all-powerful, unchanging, nonmaterial, all-knowing, and perfectly simple (Smith 1955). Similarly, Judaism speaks of God as omnipotent, omniscient, omnipresent, and eternal (Kohler 1918). God is neither bound nor limited by space or physical laws. Within Islamic theology the same essential themes are repeated: human existence is entirely different than God's (Allah's). Indeed, Islamic theologian Mohammad Zia Ullah discusses the distinction in terms of its psychological consequences: "God is infinite, pervasive, and man finite and limited to a locality. Man cannot comprehend God as he can other things ... God is without limits, without dimensions ... How can a limitless, infinite being be contained in the mind of a limited being like man?" (1984, 19).

If these religions, which have had a profound impact on Western theological concepts, attribute to God a vastly different type of existence than our own, how do we cross this ontological gap and understand God? Theologically this problem may be addressed by what in Christianity is called revelation: God allows self-disclosure in terms that people can understand and appreciate. The specifics of this doctrine are an interesting study for theologians, but the general notion of revelation raises particular questions for psychologists as well.

If God is revealed through naturalistic means and in naturalistic terms, how then do we make sense of this revelation? How do we incorporate natural features into our representation of a nonnatural[1] entity? An analogous problem might be to consider what it would be like to be a bat (Nagel 1974). The other state of being is so different that the task seems impossible. However, we know many things about bats, and so this problem is trivial when compared to comprehension of a being that is invisible, immaterial, atemporal, and so on. As natural creatures, we can only draw upon natural experiences in our attempts to characterize God.

Unfortunately, the canonical texts of Western religions do not simplify matters much. Information about God in these texts takes the form of either proclamations of God's vast ontological differences from us, or characterizations of God in natural and often anthropomorphic terms. The implication of the ontological gap is that this second class of canonical data is metaphorical to a great extent. In order to understand these metaphors we must have some basis for application. For example, understanding the statement "God is loving" requires us to make some preliminary assumptions about what type of being God is in order for that statement to be useful. If we cannot agree that God is the type of thing that can be referred to—an ontological assumption—then "God" would be meaningless in this context, and so "God is loving" would also be meaningless. Apparently "able to be referred to" is one property that is nearly universally attributed to God. Surely there must be others. The words we choose to describe God or the activities of God are not random or arbitrary, suggesting some basic, commonly held conceptions of God.

The problem of understanding God can now be recast as the problem of finding these basic underlying assumptions and where they come from. One possible solution suggested by an examination of religious language and the psychological literature is anthropomorphism: making God in the image of ourselves.

God is often spoken about in very naturalistic, human-like terms, as if God is a super-human. Sometimes God-talk is blatantly anthropomorphic as in "the hand of God," and sometimes it is subtle as in "God sees." Even more subtle are instances of assigning natural properties to God in our discourse, as in "Then God." Simply prefacing a phrase about God with "then" places an atemporal being in a temporal framework. Although this language is generally considered metaphorical, it could be the case that this language actually expresses the underlying conception of God. The needed basic assumptions for understanding discourse about God are supplied by ignoring the ontological distance.

Psychologists have long assumed that anthropomorphic language reflects underlying cognitive anthropomorphism. Freud initiated this line of thought most dramatically with the suggestion that God concepts are projections of one's father and that the start of religion is the "humanization of nature" (Freud 1961, 20). Since Freud, other authors have suggested similarities between God concepts and images of a parent (Argyle 1975), both parents in conjunction (Justice and Lambert 1986; Briky and Ball 1988), or of the self (Jolley and Taulbee 1986).

Other psychologists of religion have assumed that the adjectives used to describe God are more than metaphorical. Benson and Spilka (1973) reported a positive correlation between self-esteem and loving images of God. Others suggest a relationship between loneliness and the concept of a "wrathful God" (Schwab and Petersen 1990), while locus of control may be positively correlated with a "loving God" (deJonge 1993). Subjects attribute particular personality dispositions to God—not merely dispositions analogous to particular human traits. Congruence between human personality and God's "personality" is implicit.

It may seem easy enough to accept that God is anthropomorphized when it comes to personality traits and dispositions, but these studies suggest that our anthropomorphism goes much farther. Perhaps anthropomorphism, as Guthrie argues (1980; 1993) is an integral part of religious thought. If people anthropomorphize God's "personality," then more fundamental anthropomorphism may be needed to form God concepts. If we think of God's existence as wholly different from our own, how do we even think of God as loving? The thought is somewhat analogous to calling a quark "charming" or a pile of sand "treacherous." Are we committing a category mistake by suggesting cross-ontological properties? If we do assign personality to different ontological groups while fully comprehending the incongruency, this practice would still represent a bizarre cognitive activity worthy of further investigation. Alternatively, we may not perceive the incongruency.

Cognitive accounts of religious ideas argue that God concepts must be comprised of naturalistic and nonnaturalistic properties and cannot only include one or the other. Sperber (1994) has emphasized the role counter-intuitive characteristics play in contributing to the "cultural robustness" of religious ideas. Boyer has expanded this observation into a well-developed cognitive theory of religion (1994).

In short, Boyer argues that religious ideas are propagated if they (1) violate some cognitive intuitions regarding characteristics of members of their particular ontological categories, while (2) adhering to the bulk of these intuitions. If religious ideas do not fit with a large number of common intuitions, they will be difficult to hold coherently and use to generate predictions and inferences.

Too many violations of cognitive intuitions would cause an enormous processing strain. However, as Sperber (1994) has pointed out, some violations are necessary to make the ideas extraordinary and attention-demanding; otherwise they would not be interesting enough to pass on as "religious" ideas.

Although Boyer (1994) has applied this theory to explain supernatural agents of the Fang people (Cameroon), the theory has some difficulty accounting for the Abrahamic God of the Western world. The main difficulty is that the cognitive inductions that are to be maintained or violated are based on an ontological category membership. In the case of the bekong (ghosts/ancestors) of the Fang, they are classified as sentient beings, the ontological category humans occupy. As has been suggested above, it is common in the Abrahamic religions to assign God to a different ontological category than people. This category does share some properties in common with sentient beings (e.g., intention), but it is no more in the same category with humans than dogs are with rocks, even though those categories also share some properties (e.g., physical structure). Since God occupies a different ontological category, it is unclear what cognitive intuitions apply to God's ontology. God concepts held by common people might actually characterize God as a sentient being. If so, Boyer's theory would predict that they would take the specific form of a prototypical "sentient being" with some unusual or counterintuitive properties, probably a super human.

A different cognition-based account of religious thought has been advanced by Guthrie (1993), who stresses the centrality of anthropomorphism. The tendency to anthropomorphize is seen as a fundamental cognitive bias in which novel or ambiguous stimuli are processed as anthropomorphic until other evidence is made available to prove this bias wrong. This strategy is generalized to natural concepts and processes and, consequently, becomes a foundation for all religious thought. All religious ideas, including the Western God, are anthropomorphic by nature under this model.

Despite theological descriptions, people seem to incorporate anthropomorphic and naturalistic characterizations into their intuitive God concepts. This study asks whether anthropomorphic and naturalistic language about God is more than a simple literary device. Perhaps conceptions of God must be anthropomorphic, even while theological beliefs maintain otherwise. It may be that the "theological God" is radically different from the "intuitive God" normally described in everyday discourse. Even individuals who explicitly endorse the theological version of God might nonetheless implicitly embrace a very different version in most of their daily thoughts.

The first study described in this paper uses a variation of a well-known story comprehension paradigm (Bransford and McCarrell 1974). With this method Bransford and McCarrell showed that information expressed by a sentence cannot always be equated with what is comprehended. Subjects' prior beliefs can distort their recall of the information actually provided in sentences and resolve ambiguities. In the present study, subjects were read a battery of short stories in which God was an agent. After each story, subjects were asked to recall if particular pieces of information had been included in the story. Prior assumptions and beliefs were examined by considering errors in subjects' memory for the stories and how potentially ambiguous information was interpreted.

We chose this indirect method for getting at subjects' God concepts because it avoided the problem of "theological correctness." If subjects were asked directly what they believed about God, responses would tend to fit into an abstract theology. Even if people use an anthropomorphic God concept in daily life, they would be hesitant to articulate this as their personal theology because it might appear juvenile. By using stories, we hoped to tap into the God concepts that subjects use in their daily lives to make judgments in real time, rather than into their theological knowledge. Moreover, in day-to-day life, the vast majority of thoughts about God seem to be framed in casual, story-like discourse rather than in abstracted theological discourse.

Barrett and VanOrman (1996) have successfully used this method to detect differences in degree of anthropomorphism between Christians who use images of God for worship and those who do not. Image users were found to anthropomorphize to a greater extent than nonimage users. Consequently, we were hopeful that this method would also be sensitive to differences between theological concepts and everyday concepts of God used in real time.

Study 1A evaluates differences between theological expressions about God and everyday God concepts by examining differences between professed theological characterizations of God as measured by a questionnaire and concepts revealed by a story-recall task. Study 1B looks to see if these differences are peculiar to God concepts or if similar differences are found with other nonhuman, super agents. In this condition, God was replaced by a super-computer called "Uncomp." Because Uncomp was completely novel for the subjects, entirely different from existing supercomputers, they could not bring any preexisting concept of Uncomp to bear on the task. Consequently, if the results of Study 1A were due to an artifact of the task, the language of the stories should prompt subjects to anthropomorphize Uncomp to the same degree that they anthropomorphized God in that condition. Study 1C is an attempt to make subjects' theological concepts more salient to see if performance in the story-recall task can be manipulated in this way. If so, this is strong evidence that concepts of God are what is important in determining subjects' performance and not some artifact of the task.

Study 2 investigates the importance of memory and potential bias in Study 1 by allowing subjects in five different conditions to perform the story-recall task with transcripts of the stories right in front of them. To demonstrate how spontaneous use of anthropomorphic concepts might be, subjects in Study 3 were asked to write paraphrased versions of some of the narratives used in Study 1.

Study 1

If theological God concepts are used in everyday activities, then subjects' reported theological concepts regarding God's properties should match the God concept revealed by how subjects remember short narratives. Alternatively, subjects' theological God concepts may place few if any physical or psychological constraints on God, but in the processing of stories, limitations on God similar to those experienced by people and other natural entities might be imposed. To illustrate this distinction, one story reads:

> A boy was swimming alone in a swift and rocky river. The boy got his left leg caught between two large, gray rocks and couldn't get out. Branches of trees kept bumping into him as they hurried past. He thought he was going to drown and so he began to struggle and pray. Though God was answering another prayer in another part of the world when the boy started praying, before long God responded by pushing one of the rocks so the boy could get his leg out. The boy struggled to the river bank and fell over exhausted.

Subjects whose everyday God concept is anthropomorphic may infer that God finished answering one prayer before attending to the boy. If so, they would tend to misreport that this is actually what the story said. Subjects who employ a God concept in which God performs many tasks simultaneously would be unlikely to report that the story said God finished answering one prayer before saving the boy. It is just as likely that God rescued the boy while answering the other prayer.

Method: 1A

Subjects

Subjects for the first three studies were 52 volunteer graduate and undergraduate university students of various majors, ranging in age from 17 to 28 with a mean age of 20.0 years. Sixty percent of the subjects were female. Subjects represented many different religious affiliations including Bahaism, Buddhism, Christianity (Catholic and Protestant), Hinduism, and Judaism. Many subjects reported being atheist or agnostic. Subjects were randomly assigned to one of the first three studies: 22 to the first (1A), and 15 each to Studies 1B and 1C.[2]

Materials

A questionnaire of beliefs about God was composed and given to 18 subjects. The questionnaire included ratings of self-religiosity and religious affiliation, and a number of multiple choice and yes–no questions targeted at specific properties God might possess. The written instructions asked subjects to answer the questions using their own concepts of God assuming that God exists. Freedom to use one's own concept of God was also included on the subjects' consent form. Although the questionnaire included a number of questions, the ones of interest for this study were those that asked whether or not (a) God can read minds; (b) God knows everything; (c) God can do multiple mental activities simultaneously; (d) God needs to be near something to see, hear, smell, taste, or feel it; (e) God is spatial (in a particular place or places) or nonspatial (nowhere at all); and (f) God can occupy space with another object without in any way distorting it.

Eight short narratives (approximately 100 words each) in which God was an agent were composed and recorded on audio cassette. Recall items for each story were also recorded with brief pauses following each item. For example, a recall item for the story given above included "The boy was swimming alone," followed by a pause. The pauses were intentionally brief (approximately 2 seconds) so that subjects would be forced to answer whether or not the information of the given item was included in the story based on their conceptual representation of the story. Six of the eight stories were followed by eight recall items and the remaining two stories had nine, for a total of 66 recall items: 44 "base" items that were concerned with the basic facts of the story including God's activities (see example above), and 22 "God" items that were concerned with how God was conceptualized. For 21 of the 44 base items, the correct answer was "yes."

Because this protocol relies on mistaken comprehension, all God items included information not in the stories but suggesting particular dimensions of an anthropomorphic concept (e.g., sequential agency as in the God item given above). A "yes" answer on any of these items was considered evidence for the attribution of particular property to God that was not expressed in the story, even if an omnipotent God could exhibit some of these properties. The possibility of behaving in a certain way does not entail that the behavior or particular property was exhibited in the story. These properties included God moving, being in a particular place, requiring sensory input to gather information, performing only one task at a time, having a single focus of attention, having sensory limitations, and being unable to process competing sensory stimuli distinctly. To illustrate, it is an anthropomorphic assumption to infer that when the sound of a jet makes it impossible for two birds to hear each other, God cannot hear the birds over the sound of the jet either.

The stories and corresponding recall items were played on a standard audio cassette player in the same random order for all subjects. Subjects were asked to circle "Yes" when the subject thought the information conveyed by the recall sentence was included in the story, and "No" when it was not.

Procedure

It was intended for questionnaire–story task presentation to be counterbalanced across subjects. However, after running seven subjects each in the two presentation orders, it appeared that answering the questionnaire first was improving performance on the God items of the story task. Perhaps this is due to priming subjects' theological concepts (see Study 1C). Consequently, the remaining subjects completed the story task first. Four of these subjects left before completing the questionnaire. Analyses for Study 1A were performed on the 18 subjects who participated in both tasks. The 15 subjects who completed the story task before the questionnaire (including the four who did not complete the questionnaire) were used as the control group for comparisons with Studies 1B and 1C.

Subjects were encouraged to think of "God" in any way they wished for the duration of the task. The stories were then played. After each story, the experimenter asked three questions, pausing for subjects to write answers: (1) Who or what do you think was the main character in the story? (2) Do you think the author of the story was female or male? (3) Do you think the author of the story was older than 30 or younger than 30? The function of these questions was twofold. They were intended to increase the delay between the telling of the story and its recall and to give subjects reason to reflect on the story on a conceptual level. Pilot work suggested that if there were no such delay, some subjects would remember specific words and phrases better than the general narrative content.

After the filler questions, the experimenter said, "Now I would like you to tell me which of the following pieces of information were included in the story," and then played the recording of the recall items for the preceding narrative. This process was repeated for all eight stories. Subjects were then asked to fill out the questionnaire at their leisure.

Method: 1B

Materials

There were only a few differences between this task and the first condition. Most importantly, "God" was replaced by "Uncomp" in all the stories and recall items, and subjects were not told that the study was about God concepts. Additionally, a few minor changes in the stories had to be made to accommodate the change in character. Wherever a form of "pray" appeared in the original stories, it was replaced by a form of "call." One story also includes God helping an angel work on a crossword puzzle. This was replaced with Uncomp helping a UN delegate work on a crossword puzzle.

Procedure

Before the stories were played, Uncomp was described to the subjects. As much as possible with a physical entity, Uncomp was attributed properties that the questionnaires suggested are commonly attributed to God. However, two God recall items had to be omitted from the analysis. Both items asked if the story included information about the location of Uncomp (God). For the God stories, no information about location was included but for the Uncomp stories, the information is implicitly included. Subjects were read the following description of Uncomp twice:

124

The year is 4093 AD. Uncomp is a super-computer which was built by the United Nations to help keep peace and do good in the world. Uncomp is a system of pairs of microscopic disks: one a sensor and one an effector. The sensor disk of each pair gives Uncomp abilities roughly similar to hearing, seeing, smelling, tasting, and feeling even when an object is not in direct contact with the sensors. The sensors also perceive heat, electric, and chemical activity with great sensitivity. Uncomp can use these capabilities to understand what a person does even without seeing or hearing them. Uncomp can even track the electric activity of the brain and thus read minds. The effector disks make use of electromagnetic and antigravity emissions to act on the world. These effectors enable Uncomp to move anything without touching it or being near it. Uncomp can even effect how people think and feel. These pairs of disks cover every square centimeter of the earth and so no information escapes processing. The disks do not move. Uncomp has no other components. The disks are electrically linked with any other part of the system at any time. Uncomp has no central processor and so is not anywhere in particular. Uncomp has been given a program for ethics and a program for emotions as well which run in the entire network at once. Uncomp runs independently all the time and can perform many different functions in many different places at the same time. Uncomp can retrieve information from many different places simultaneously.

After hearing the description of Uncomp, subjects were given a short, seven-item multiple-choice quiz testing whether they understood the description. Only one of the 15 subjects missed any items and this subject only missed one. The correct answer was given in this case. Subjects then listened to and responded to the questions as in 1A.

Method: 1C

Materials and Procedure
Subjects in the salience condition were given the story-recall task after completing a questionnaire concerning relevant characteristics of God. The questionnaire included five free-form thought questions intended to encourage subjects to reflect on their beliefs about God, thereby making more salient their theological beliefs. Again, subjects were encouraged to answer based on their own concept of God assuming that God exists. The questions were: (1) Can it be said (using your concept of God) that God can be in two places at the same time? Why or why not? (2) Can it be said (using your concept of God) that God can do more than one thing at a time, like prevent a flood, work on a crossword puzzle, and listen to 1000 people's prayers at the same time? Why or why not? (3) Can it be said (using your concept of God) that God can act on objects or perceive things without being near them? Why or why not? (4) Can it be said (using your concept of God) that God can see,

feel, taste, smell, or hear more than one thing at a time? (5) Can it be said (using your concept of God) that God does not need to use senses to gather information? Why or why not?

Subjects were given 10 minutes to complete the questionnaire. They then participated in the story task as in the first condition.

Results and Discussion: 1A

As predicted, answers to the questionnaires showed substantial inter-subject agreement, suggesting theological concepts in which God is subject to few if any physical and psychological constraints. However, in the story task, there was a strong tendency for subjects to think of God exhibiting human limitations. Subjects showed an overwhelming tendency to agree that God can read minds, knows everything, can perform multiple mental activities at the same time, does not need to be near something to receive sensory information about it, and has nonnatural spatial properties. Table 1 lists the results of the questionnaire.

Characteristic of god implied by question		*Percent agreed*
Can read minds		94.4[a]
Knows everything		94.4[a]
Performs multiple mental activities		94.4[a]
Nearness is *not* important for	Vision	100.0[a]
	Hearing	100.0
	Smell	93.3
	Taste	93.3
	Touch	93.3
Is everywhere		75.0
Is many places at once		6.3
Is nowhere		18.7
Is at one place at a time		0.0
Does not occupy space		68.7
Occupies space with another object		31.3
Does not occupy space with another object		0.0

[a] Eighteen subjects answered these items. Sixteen responded to the remaining items.

Table 1. *Answers to questionnaire items regarding characteristics of God*

In striking contrast to the results of the questionnaire, the results of the story-recall items suggest an anthropomorphic everyday God concept. For the God items, subjects incorrectly reported that the information was included in the story 61.2% of the time on average, a mean accuracy of 38.8%. This compares to an average accuracy of 86.2% on the base items.

This difference was shown to be significant using a Mann-Whitney U test, $z = 5.139$, $p \leq .00001$, indicating that most of the time subjects falsely remembered particular anthropomorphic characteristics of God being mentioned in the story.

In the implausible case that subjects had no God concept available to understand and remember the stories, or the information was completely ambiguous, we would expect the God item accuracy to be at the 50% chance level. Using this extremely conservative criterion and assuming a roughly normal distribution, a Student's t gives 47.9% as the upper boundary of the 95% confidence interval for God item accuracy ($M = 38.8\%$). Therefore, God item accuracy was significantly poorer than base item accuracy and also less than 50%.

One interpretation of the difference in performance on the God items and the base items is that God items were simply more difficult. The God items may just be more subtle, not because of the presence of an anthropomorphic God concept, but because the items emphasize very slight distinctions. Although this explanation may account for some of the difference in performance, it is unlikely that it explains the bulk of the difference. If the God items were conceptually no different than the base items, then it would be expected that those subjects who perform well on the base items would also perform well on the God items. In fact, a Pearson's correlation shows that performance on the two types of items was not correlated, $r = 0.092$, supporting the conclusion that the two types of items are qualitatively rather than just quantitatively different.

In this task, subjects apparently used anthropomorphic God concepts to process and remember the stories, even though these concepts did not agree with the "theological" characterizations of God implied by the questionnaire. Specifically, subjects seemed to characterize God as having to be near something to receive sensory information from it, not being able to attend differentially to competing sensory stimuli, performing tasks sequentially and not in parallel, having a single or limited focus of attention, moving from place to place, and sometimes standing or walking. God was not conceptualized as completely free of constraints. However, it is unclear if subjects brought this anthropomorphic God concept to the task or if this concept is artifactual. Perhaps the language of the stories offers enough anthropomorphic suggestion (e.g., "God watched ...") that subjects discard their actual everyday God concept in favor of one they think better fits the story context. Under this interpretation, the stories do not draw on any preconceived anthropomorphic ideas about God, but apply only to the character in the stories who happens to be called "God." The context of the story would prompt subjects to anthropomorphize any character. This does not contradict theological characterizations of God at all.

Results and Discussion: 1B

As hypothesized, subjects made fewer errors in recalling the Uncomp (God) items in this condition than in the previous condition.[3] Mean accuracy on these items was 49.1% for the Uncomp group, compared to only 38.8% in the control condition. After adjusting each subject's God item accuracy to account for base item performance,[4] the mean accuracy of the control group was 45.1%, compared to 59.9% for the Uncomp group. The difference between the groups was significant as measured by a Tukey–Duckworth test, $T = 7$, $p \leq .025$ (Tukey 1959; Gans 1981).[5] This difference in subject performance was also manifest across the majority of the individual God items. The Uncomp group had higher average accuracy on 15 of the 20 God items. On four items, the first group was more accurate and there was one tie. This difference is significant as measured by a Wilcoxon Signed Rank test, $z = 1.977$, $p = .024$.

It is not the case that the Uncomp variation was simply more attention demanding, resulting in enhanced performance. The accuracy on base items was slightly, but not significantly, worse for the Uncomp condition. The mean accuracy on base items was 81.5% for the Uncomp group, compared to 86.2% for the control group. Taken together, these findings suggest that the language of the stories is not the only factor contributing to the anthropomorphic God concept revealed in the first study.

Although the results for God and Uncomp are markedly different, it is still the case that subjects anthropomorphized Uncomp. Subjects' mean accuracy on the Uncomp items was 49.1%, which is much poorer than would be expected, based on the description of Uncomp and the mean accuracy on the base items (M = 81.5%). Some subjects misremembered that the stories described Uncomp as moving, even though it is explicitly stated in the description of Uncomp, and all subjects (except for one who was immediately corrected) answered correctly on the preliminary quiz that Uncomp cannot move.

These curious findings could have many different explanations. It could be that because Uncomp was a novel concept (unlike God), it had no stability or resilience. Through the course of hearing the stories and being asked if they remember Uncomp doing things that are anthropomorphic, subjects modified their concept of Uncomp into a human-like agent. The data do not speak to this possibility.

A more likely possibility is that, even though subjects could correctly answer a multiple-choice test about Uncomp immediately after hearing the information, the concept was too new and complicated for most subjects to accurately apply to the story task context. Subjects may have anthropomorphized Uncomp as a default mechanism because processing Uncomp as such is easier. A third possible explanation of why subjects used an anthropomorphic concept of Uncomp is that, on some level, subjects found it difficult to digest the Uncomp cover story because Uncomp is a natural entity, albeit a super-human one. Had Uncomp been a nonnatural entity without the constraints of explicit mechanisms and spatial properties, subjects might have been able to process Uncomp without using a human-like representation.

All three explanations follow from Uncomp not being comparable to God in an important sense: God is nonnatural. Consequently, Uncomp cannot be a proper substitute for God in this paradigm. The results of this study can only suggest that anthropomorphic concepts play a larger role for stories about God than stories about Uncomp. That is, the story context cannot account for all of the anthropomorphism in the control group.

Results and Discussion: 1C

Subjects in the salience manipulation group showed less evidence for anthropomorphic everyday God concepts than did the subjects in the first study. Mean accuracy on each God item was 47.3% as compared to 38.8% in the first group. A Tukey–Duckworth test detected a significant difference between the adjusted scores of each group, $T = 7$, $p \leq .025$. This difference in performance can be seen in the differences between items as well. Of the 22 items, the salience manipulation group performed more accurately on 15 items, the control group was more accurate on five items, and there were two ties. This difference was significant by a Wilcoxon Signed Rank test, $z = 2.409$, $p = .008$. No differences were found on base item accuracy between the two groups; denying the difference can be accounted for by the questionnaire somehow making subjects generally more attentive to the stories.

Although the Uncomp study suggests that the anthropomorphism revealed in the first study is not merely artifactual, the differences between God and Uncomp make it unclear if the existence of anthropomorphic concepts in both conditions is due to the same underlying processes. Two conflicting explanations must still be distinguished. It could be that the subject's theological and everyday God concepts are actually distinct, context-dependent concepts: one that is engaged when discussing God in abstract, theological terms (as in the questionnaire task) and one that is active when processing informal, real-time discourse (as in the story task). Subjects then bring these two God concepts, and any connections they have with each other, to the task. Alternatively, there may be some properties of the story task that, when paired with a super-agent that is nonnatural (like God), yield an anthropomorphic concept. That is, the tendency to anthropomorphize is a product of the task and the agent's ontological category membership and independent of actual concepts of God.

The results of the salience manipulation contradict this second explanation. Under this account, it would be expected that no manipulation of God concepts before entering the task should have an effect on the results. Alternatively, assuming that subjects' theological God concepts are not anthropomorphic, priming of these concepts would encourage subjects to rely less on their anthropomorphic everyday God concepts in processing the stories, thereby making fewer recall errors on God items, which is what happened. This demonstrated link between subjects' theological concepts and their performance on the story task is also strong evidence that the results are a measure of the subjects' own concept rather than the stories' author's concept.

As in the Uncomp study, subjects as a group still exhibited poorer accuracy than expected, based on theological beliefs as measured by the questionnaire in Study 1 and base item accuracy. This implies the persistence of an anthropomorphic concept in many of these subjects. Inability to wholly remove the effect is not surprising. It is likely that for a large number of subjects, the questionnaire did not succeed in making a theological God concept more salient. The answers to the salience questionnaire suggest that some subjects did not have a clear, preexisting God concept on which to draw, so the salience manipulation provided no competition for an anthropomorphic concept. Assuming that people often do hold at least two parallel God concepts, one for use in formal settings and one used in informal discourse, the connections between these two concepts might have been weak and strongly context-driven. For some subjects it is possible that the questionnaire only made the theological concept salient while yielding no effect on the everyday concept. A third possibility is that some subjects simply did not take the questionnaire seriously and it therefore failed to make their theological God concepts salient.[6]

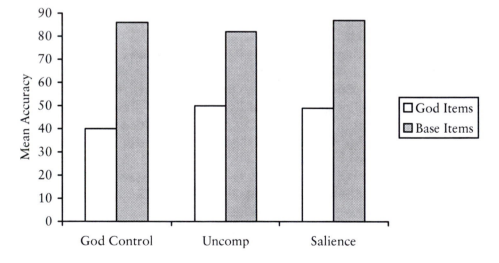

Figure 1. *Mean subject accuracy on God items and base items for Study 1.* All three groups performed significantly better on base items than on God items.

Furthermore, some subjects admitted to having a very anthropomorphic theological God concept. This being the case, the salience manipulation may have actually made the everyday concept more anthropomorphic in these subjects, resulting in more mistakes in the recall of God items. Perhaps this explains why the salience manipulation group showed greater variance (using a normal approximation) in God item accuracy (SD = 20.6%) than the subjects in the first group (SD = 14.9%). Despite these problems with the salience manipulation, the two groups were clearly different.

A summary of the results of Study 1 can be found in Fig. 1.

Study 2

In an attempt to establish more firmly during what process anthropomorphism takes place and to more directly address whether or not subjects anthropomorphize due to biases in the stories, subjects in Study 2 were asked to perform the story-recall task using printed transcripts. Subjects were allowed to answer the recall items at their own pace, with the narratives right in front of them. If anthropomorphism in the first task were due to the stories introducing an anthropomorphic God concept that subjects then adopted for the task, subjects would be expected to anthropomorphize in this task as well, regardless of whether the agent was God or novel fictitious super-agents. If the findings of Study 1 were a result of memory distortion, subjects would not be expected to anthropomorphize in this task.

To address these possibilities, five different conditions of the task were performed: (1) "God"—a simple replication of the original task: Similar results as in Study 1 with God as the main character would suggest that the anthropomorphism is not just a form of memory distortion. (2) "Nonhuman God"—a version of this task in which subjects are asked to think of God as very different from humans: If the anthropomorphism is profoundly reduced, this would suggest the presence of general bias to think of God in human-like terms in the original task. (3) "Super-agents"—God replaced by super-agents with relevant properties similar to God's: If the stories are constructed such that subjects are compelled to treat God anthropomorphically, regardless of their own theological beliefs, then replacing God with super-human agents assigned relevant God-like properties should not change the level of anthropomorphism. If God is only anthropomorphized because of bias in the text, then these agents should also be anthropomorphized. If God is anthropomorphized because subjects' concepts of God are anthropomorphic, then new agents should be treated differently. (4) "Survey God"— a version in which the God stories were preceded by a rating of particular properties: In the case that the explicit descriptions required to introduce new agents in group 3 unfairly primed subjects to be mindful of particular properties, the same descriptions offered as applicable to God should provide the same priming. Consequently, performance of conditions 3 and 4 should not be different. (5) "Superman"—Superman as the main character: For the sake of seeing if God is even treated as different from highly anthropomorphic super-agents, a version of the task with Superman as the main character was also performed.

Method

Subjects
Eighty-one college students were recruited to participate in this study. They were randomly assigned to one of five groups, four with 16 subjects and one with 17 subjects due to a miscount.[7]

Materials
Transcripts of the stories and recall items from Study 1 were prepared in three different ways: with God as the main character, with Superman as the main character and necessary adjustments to the text made, and with three fictitious characters (Mog, Beebo, and Swek) endowed with relevant properties commonly attributed to God. Mog occupied the "God" role in three of the eight stories, Beebo was in three, and Swek was in two stories. Three agents were used to help subjects keep clear the God-like properties of each one. Although this makes the task slightly different, if anthropomorphism is due to biased language in the story, it would persist in this condition as well.

For the Super-agents condition, descriptions of the three fictitious characters were also prepared. These descriptions explicitly endowed Mog, Beebo, and Swek with properties that would lead to nonanthropomorphic responses in the recall task. These descriptions appear in Appendix B.

For one variation using the original "God" stories, a short questionnaire was created using the same properties that were attributed to Mog, Beebo, and Swek. These properties were made into agree–disagree Likert scales. Because a theologically correct answering of the questions would lead to mostly "agree" answers, a few distracter items that would be more likely to receive "disagree" responses were included.

Procedure
Subjects in the "God" group each received a transcript of the story-recall task and were asked to read the stories and answer the recall items construing God in any way they wished. Subjects in the "Nonhuman God" condition were asked to complete the task construing God as "radically different from a human," in an attempt to bias subjects away from using an anthropomorphic concept. Subjects in the "Survey God" group completed the questionnaire of God's properties and then performed the story-recall

task. They were assured that they could use the ratings from the questionnaire to perform the task if they wished. "Superman" subjects simply performed the recall task using that variation of the narratives. In the final condition, subjects read the Super-agents descriptions and then performed the recall task using that version of the narratives. They were allowed to refer to the descriptions whenever they wished. Subjects in all five conditions were allowed as much time as needed to complete the task, and could check over or change answers as they deemed fit.

Results

As in Study 1, the measure of anthropomorphism used was the percentage of accurate God items for each subject, adjusted for base item accuracy. These data roughly fit parametric assumptions and so each group's performance was compared to every other, using multiple t-tests. A Bonferroni correction for multiple tests was then performed. The p-values reported below are the precorrection values for tests that remained significant after correction. The results of these tests are illustrated in Fig. 2.

The Super-agents group's mean performance (M = .925, SD = .134) was significantly better than each of the other four groups: Superman, M = .461, SD = .28, t(31) = 6.14, p ≤ .00001; God, M = .622, SD = .198, t(31) = 5.181, p ≤ .00001; Nonhuman God, M = .559, SD = .248, t(31) = 5.319, p ≤ .00001; and Survey God, M = .766, SD = .154, t(29) = 3.07, p =.0046.[8]

The Survey God group performed significantly better than only the Superman group, t(28) = 3.63, p = .0011. The Superman, God, and Nonhuman God groups showed no significant differences from each other. Incidentally, only the Survey God and Super-agents groups showed significantly better performance than the "God" condition in Study 1A, t(27) = 4.403, p =.0002; t(30) = 7.645, p ≤ .00001; respectively.

These differences do not seem to be the result of base item accuracy differences. A one-way, five-factor analysis of variance (ANOVA) detected no significant differences between the groups, F(4,74) = .584, p = .6754. Consistent with the results of Study 1, for all of the groups God item accuracy was poorer than their base item accuracy. The Super-agents group's mean base accuracy was 92.6%, compared to its God item accuracy of 85.6%, t(16) = .408, p = .0284.

Discussion

These results support the conclusion that anthropomorphism in Study 1 takes place with the reading or hearing of the stories and not as a consequence of recall error. Even though all five conditions of Study 2 are reading tasks

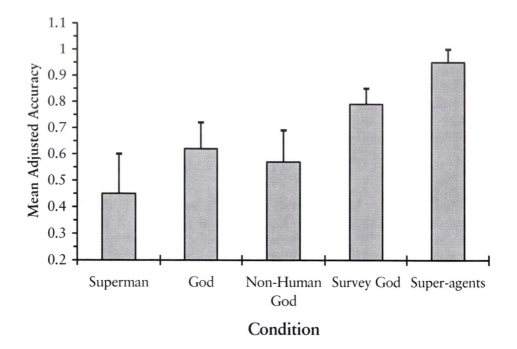

Figure 2. *Mean adjusted God item accuracy and 95% confidence limit error bars for Study 2.* The Super-agents group performed significantly better than the other four groups. The Survey group performed better than Superman. No other differences were significant.

in which subjects have the stories right in front of them, subjects still provided evidence of anthropomorphizing the main character. In fact, God was treated no differently than Superman in this task except when subjects were primed to think of God nonanthropomorphically by the survey manipulation. Even when subjects were encouraged to think of God as "radically different than a human" the anthropomorphism persisted at the same levels.

The influence of the stories' biasing subjects seems very small at best, given these results. An active attempt to bias subjects against thinking of God anthropomorphically (Nonhuman God condition) was unsuccessful. In fact, the results tended in the opposite direction.

Subjects are not compelled by the stories to make anthropomorphic errors. The Super-agents group demonstrated that if subjects can keep in mind the relevant nonanthropomorphic properties of a nonnatural agent, anthropomorphism can be nearly erased. If subjects really have theologically correct concepts of God, these nonanthropomorphic properties are available. The small difference between the God item performance of Super-agents subjects and their base item accuracy (approximately 7%, or 1.5 God items) may be due to a combination of subtlety in the items and anthropomorphic bias, but this remaining difference to be explained is negligible, compared to the massive differences in all of the God conditions. Super-agents is the only condition in which some subjects had no God item errors but did have base item errors.

The inability of the Survey God group to have the same effect as the Super-agents group is strong evidence that the results are due to subjects' applying their own anthropomorphic God concepts to the task. It does not appear to be the case that the differences between these two groups were due to subjects' rejection of God's nonanthropomorphic properties. Of the seven important properties included in the Super-agents' descriptions and the Survey God scales, Survey God subjects expressed agreement (a score of 1 or 2) 80% of the time on average. Reminiscent of the questionnaire in Study 1, 10 of the 15 subjects agreed with six or all seven items, and only one subject expressed agreement less than half the time. A simple regression relating these scores to anthropomorphism scores was not significant, $r = .131$, $F = .211$, $p = .6542$.

These studies should not be taken as evidence that with training people can easily process narratives involving nonnatural entities in real-time. Study 2 was a slowed-down reading task allowing subjects time for reflection and modification of intuitive responses. What Study 2, and the Super-agents group in particular, does demonstrate is that (1) it is very difficult to keep from anthropomorphizing nonnatural agents, but (2) it is possible in some contexts. The story-recall task does seem to be one context in which it is possible to avoid anthropomorphizing. Regardless, subjects persist in anthropomorphizing God.

Study 3

Because Studies 1 and 2 relied on recall items as a measure of anthropomorphism, it is not clear how spontaneous or automatic the tendency to anthropomorphize God is. Also of interest is the quality of the anthropomorphic inferences and how they affect the character of the narratives. Study 3 is a preliminary attempt to address these issues and to amplify the findings of the first two studies by asking subjects to paraphrase stories involving God.

If subjects in Study 1 anthropomorphized in response to the prompting of recall items, because of demand characteristics, or a "Yes"-answer bias, subjects would not be expected to use anthropomorphic language when paraphrasing the narratives. Additionally, spontaneous use of anthropomorphic language in paraphrasing would suggest the anthropomorphic concept is used at the stage of initial processing and not in recall, supporting the interpretation that subjects bring the concept to the task.

Method

Materials

Four of the eight stories from Study 1 were selected on the basis of general dissimilarity from each other. Transcripts of these stories were presented on a page alternated with space enough for subjects' paraphrases.

Procedure

Thirteen new subjects were instructed to rewrite each of the narratives in their own words, adding or omitting details as they deemed fit to clarify and preserve the meaning of the original. Subjects were allowed as much time as needed. Again, subjects were encouraged to construe God in any way they wished.

Results and Discussion

Two scorers familiar with the concepts of anthropomorphism and theologically correct God concepts were independently asked to check each subjects' paraphrased stories for (1) the inclusion of language not in the original story that suggested anthropomorphic inferences, (2) the inclusion of language not in the original story that seemed to clarify God's theologically correct properties, and (3) general errors in preserving the facts of the narratives. Interscorer agreement was 94.9%. Disagreements were resolved through discussion.

Most of the time subjects gave almost exact restatements of the original narratives with only slight modifications. However, when subjects did provide information not in the original stories, it was almost exclusively anthropomorphic in nature. Twelve of the 13 subjects retold at least one of the stories using anthropomorphic language quite similar to the God items of the previous studies. This compares to only one subject adding details to make clear God's nonanthropomorphic properties. For example, it was common for subjects to write something like "The noise was so loud God couldn't hear the birds," for the first story. Table 2 lists some of these responses.

Summing across subjects, of the 52 paraphrases, 26 showed anthropomorphic intrusions. Two paraphrases included details to clarify God's non-anthropomorphic properties, and four others had factual errors. Overall, subjects showed evidence of treating God as a being that requires the use of sensory information, has a limited focus of attention, performs tasks serially, has a particular location, and cannot always differentiate competing sensory information.

One subject even transformed God into a person in his paraphrases, referring to God as "a homeless man," "the president of a major corporation," and "a local aborigine" in different stories. However, in one story this subject referred to God as "an unthinkable force."

It was a clear, sunny day. Two birds were singing back and forth to each other. They were perched in a large oak tree next to an airport. God was listening to the birds. One would sing and then the other would sing. One bird had blue, white and silver feathers. The other bird had dull gray feathers. While God was listening to the birds, a large jet landed. It was extremely loud: the birds couldn't even hear each other. The air was full of fumes. God listened to the jet until it turned off its engines. God finished listening to the birds.

"God was listening to two birds singing in a tall tree next to an airport. When a large jet landed, God listened to it because he could no longer hear the birds. Then he listened to the birds again."

". . . A jet came and began destroying the beauty and even took God's attention away . . ."

". . . The noise was so loud God couldn't hear the birds. . ."

". . . God could only hear the jet until it turned off its engines . . ."

A boy was swimming alone in a swift and rocky river. The boy got his left leg caught between two large, gray rocks and couldn't get out. Branches of trees kept bumping into him as they hurried past. He thought he was going to drown and so he began to struggle and pray. Though God was answering another prayer in another part of the world when the boy started praying, before long God responded by pushing one of the rocks so the boy could get his leg out. The boy struggled to the river bank and fell over exhausted.

"This story suggests that God cannot listen to more than one prayer at a time; however, he will get to each prayer and answer it in time. Much like Santa Claus delivers toys to all houses in one night."

Somewhere in Asia, a master chef was preparing a gourmet dinner at a fancy restaurant. There was a waterfall coming through the roof in the middle of the restaurant and small groves of tropical plants in each corner. The kitchen was alongside one of the walls. The chef seasoned the meal wonderfully and the aroma filled the place. God enjoyed the smell. Then a sewer line broke beside the restaurant filling the air with a horrible and powerful stench. The chef complained that he could no longer smell his masterpiece. God appreciated the chef's disappointment. A boy in London began praying to God so God answered the prayer by helping the boy find his way home.

"In a fancy restaurant in Asia with tropical plants and a waterfall, a master chef was preparing a spectacular meal. It smells fantastic, and God liked the smell. Then, to his dismay and the dismay of the chef, a sewer line broke, giving off an awful smell, so bad that they could no longer enjoy the meal. . ."

On a dry, dirt road in Australia was a beautiful and interesting rock. One day, God was looking at the rock. It was green with blue, red, and gold flakes. While God was looking at the rock, a stampede of brown long-horned cattle came charging down the road over where the rock was. God watched them go. They were kicking up dust and bellowing. The noise was thunderous. God finished looking at the rock which was then dust covered and had hoof prints all around it.

"On a dirt road in Australia lay a beautiful rock. God looked down and admired the rock. Suddenly a herd of cattle came along, stirring up the dirt and trampling where the rock lay. God admired the herd as they went, and after they passed, God once again looked at the now dust covered rock and thought it was beautiful."

"God looked down from heaven admiring a green rock with blue, red, and gold flakes. As he admired this rock, a stampede of long-horned cattle ran by and obscured the rock. . ."

Note. The paragraphs in bold type are the original stories.

Table 2. *Excerpts from subjects' paraphrased narratives*

Interestingly, subjects expressed these anthropomorphic properties without being prompted or cued. These appear to be specific, subject-generated applications of an anthropomorphic God concept.

This study suggests that at least some of the anthropomorphism takes place with the reading of the stories and not just as a result of memory errors or at the prompting of the recall items. Evidence from this study is consistent with the hypothesis that subjects engage the story processing tasks with their own anthropomorphic concepts of God, concepts that can be explicitly elaborated without cuing.

General Discussion

These three studies reveal that subjects do use anthropomorphic concepts of God in understanding stories even though they may profess a theological position that rejects anthropomorphic constraints on God and God's activities. It appears that people have at least two parallel God concepts that are used in different contexts, and these concepts may be fundamentally incompatible.

Although this set of studies offers some insights into how people conceive of God, the conclusions have several restrictions due to the design of the studies. The stories were designed to fit with an agent-God who interacts with the natural world and people. People or contexts that do not assume such a basic property may not exhibit the same phenomenon. Further restrictions include problems with the sample. Because the sample was relatively small and heterogeneous with regard to religious affiliation, the questions raised by Barrett and VanOrman (1996) regarding differences among religious groups cannot be addressed, except that there is no obvious difference between theists and nontheists. Finally, the design of the task does not allow us to make any firm conclusions regarding specific properties that are attributed to God. We may only report that the corpus of characteristics are more consistent with an anthropomorphic concept than with a strictly theological concept from the traditions best represented. Questions about specific properties must be left for future studies.

Keeping in mind these restrictions, at least five general conclusions can be drawn from the data. First, it appears that the concept of God used in the context of listening to and remembering stories is not the same as the concept of God that is claimed in a more abstract, theological setting. The "God" condition of the first study showed a great disparity between the theological beliefs about God and the properties attributed to God in the course of processing stories.

Second, the effects demonstrated are not merely artifacts of the task. The Uncomp study and the Mog, Beebo, and Swek task showed that novel characters placed in the same task will not necessarily evoke the same anthropomorphic representation. There is something specific to subjects' representation of God that is instrumental in this anthropomorphic characterization.

The salience study and the Survey God condition of Study 2 demonstrated that performance on this task is manipulable through priming subjects' theology, implying that the way one thinks of God when approaching the task is important in determining the God concept used to process the stories. The concept used in the story context is not independent of one's personal theology. A natural extension of this finding is that people seem to possess and use more than one concept of God in real-life activities, and these parallel concepts have some markedly different properties.

A stronger form of this conclusion may also be argued. It may be that some subjects actually have only an anthropomorphic concept of God, and in response to the social demands of a formal context, the vocabulary of theological correctness is employed to mask this concept. That is, the "theological" concept is actually hollow, lacking any power to facilitate meaningful representations. Perhaps the tendency to anthropomorphize God cannot be resisted because it inevitably follows from a human necessity to conceive of deity in terms of natural categories (Brandon 1970).

Third, as the overwhelming majority of subjects in all five studies used anthropomorphic concepts to process stories about God, Uncomp, Superman, or Mog, Beebo, and Swek, the demands of story processing seems to make it difficult to avoid anthropomorphization. This is not just an uninteresting problem with the method. The characteristics of these stories that facilitate use of an anthropomorphic God concept are likely to be present in other real-time, real-life discourse about God and other agents. If a person's theological God concept shows no resilience in this task, how would it do so in the face of real-life situations similar to this? To take an example from a specific religious tradition, if people are inclined to use anthropomorphic processing in a story context, then do those in the Judeo–Christian tradition read stories about God in the Bible this same way, despite the contradictions with their professed theology?

A final conclusion that may be drawn from these studies is that anthropomorphization in discourse processing contexts is not restricted to God. As Uncomp demonstrated, other agents may be treated in a similar way, regardless of previous exposure to the agent. These studies have shown that God and a fictitious super-computer are anthropomorphized during story processing, but is this effect limited to super-agents? One problem for future research is to find what properties are necessary for an anthropomorphic representation to be used. Perhaps it is the case that any intentional agent is conceptualized using an agent-concept based on people, thus yielding an anthropomorphic representation. Another possibility is that only vaguely understood agents are treated in this way (Caporael 1986), since well understood agents have firm enough representations to make the use of an anthropomorphic concept as a default schema unnecessary. It is also unknown in what contexts agents are anthropomorphized.

It has been suggested that two of the most fundamental ontological kinds are simple mechanical physical objects and psychological agents. So fundamental are they, that infants may have intuitive physics and psychologies for grasping them (Carey and Spelke 1994). If so, folk psychology may offer a highly constrained view of the mind as a serial processor, with single focused window of attention. Similarly, intuitive physics may suggest that entities are normally bounded objects in one place at a time and move on spatio-temporally continuous paths (ibid.). Concepts of God may be strongly pressured to fit into these two ontologies, as other alternatives are too cognitively laborious to employ in real-time discourse.

It may be that the pressure to fit into these ontologies is a form of cognitive constraint even prior to those constraints suggested by Boyer's theory of religious ideas (1994). Boyer's theory begins with the assumption that when a particular entity fits into a natural ontological category such as "sentient beings," it is then constrained by the intuitive cognitive expectations of this category. Theological treatments of God generally assert that God does not fit into one of these natural ontological categories, and consequently the concept cannot be constrained by cognitive intuitions. However, it may be that intuitive physics and psychology encourage the processing of any entity as part of the natural ontological category which most closely matches the entity's perceived properties.

Usually represented as a being with a mind, desires, and the ability to communicate, God seems to best fit in the category of sentient beings. Once this is established, Boyer's balance of satisfying most intuitive expectations while violating a small number seems to fit the results of the present studies. God is treated as meeting many of the expectations of folk psychology and intuitive physics while possessing a few unusual properties such as being able to receive sensory information at an enormous distance and move from place to place very quickly.

In these ways Boyer's theory can be modified to offer an explanation of the two parallel God concepts: (1) The theory applies to the real-time concept and not the theological concept. (2) A prior source of cognitive constraint, perhaps intuitive physics and psychology, pressure the theological concept to conform to one natural ontological category. This gives rise to a sentient being which looks very much like a human being, the most salient example of this specific ontology.

Similarly, the results of these studies could be understood as a case of structured imagination (Ward 1994; 1995). If there exists some pressure to fit God into the ontological category of sentient beings, under the theory of structured imagination, specific properties of God would then be generated based on properties of known sentient beings. With humans as the most out-standing exemplar of this category, it would be expected that God would share many properties in common with humans.

Alternatively, it may not be necessary for God to be classified into a specific ontological category before anthropomorphism takes place. It has been suggested that anthropomorphic God concepts illustrate analogical reasoning (Holyoak and Thagard 1995). God's unknown properties can be understood through analogy with human properties. Under this interpretation, the data presented would suggest that analogical reasoning can be so internalized and automatic that it can generate understandings of God used in online processing that are inconsistent with theology and are difficult to inhibit.

The interpretations by way of analogical reasoning, structured imagination, and Boyer's theory of religion all require some a priori reason for pairing God with human properties as opposed to properties from some other ontology. Such a reason is not necessary to explain these findings in terms of Guthrie's theory (1993). Under Guthrie's model, novel or ambiguous objects are first processed as human unless there is sufficient counterevidence. Therefore, in a real-time task, God (or even the novel agent Uncomp) is automatically treated anthropomorphically; and it is only through conscious effort or priming that this is avoided, as in the salience condition, Super-agents, and the Survey God condition of Study 2. Furthermore, because God is of a different ontological category and surrounded by a great deal of mystery, the necessary counterevidence to disengage the tendency to anthropomorphize may not be very powerful. Perhaps this is why it was more difficult for subjects to avoid anthropomorphizing in the Survey God condition than in the Super-agents condition. Unfortunately, the very premise of Guthrie's theory, that anthropomorphism is a general and fundamental cognitive bias, is in need of empirical support before any confident conclusions may be drawn.

These studies also raise some questions specifically for the study of God concepts. The data suggest that subjects possess and use at least two different parallel God concepts depending on the context (although one may actually be an empty concept), but there is no obvious reason why these two concepts exist. Perhaps stories involving an atemporal and omnipotent agent create processing difficulties, and an efficient way to deal with the problem is to use a simpler God concept to understand stories. Whether or not this is the case, the relationship between the two concepts needs further investigation. The salience manipulation suggested that there are some points of contact between the two concepts. Making the theological God concept more salient seemed to inhibit use of the anthropomorphic everyday God concept in at least some of the subjects. It may just as well be the case that it was not inhibition but modification of the everyday concept that occurred.

These studies challenge previous work in the psychological study of God concepts or "images" in two ways. First, it seems important when making claims about God concepts to differentiate between the theological concept and the concept used in everyday life. Research methods are likely to probe different concepts depending on the nature of the task. This is not a commonly made distinction.

Second, the cognitive development literature has almost unanimously supported the notion that God concepts undergo a concrete to abstract shift from early childhood to adolescence (Gorsuch 1988). One study has even noted a shift from anthropomorphic to symbolic representations of God depending upon the level of mental impairment (Bassett et al. 1994). The present studies raise some doubts about these purported shifts. At least concepts of God used in processing narratives appear to be concrete and anthropomorphic even in young adult college students. Rather than practical concepts of God becoming more abstract with age, perhaps children learn better skills for inhibiting this concept in favor of a more theologically correct one.

Although many questions remain, these studies provide a first step in answering the question of how it is we understand God, and by implication, how we understand some nonnatural beings. At least on one level, the problem created by the ontological chasm between humans and the supernatural is solved by ignoring the difference. It appears we accept information about God quite literally. No longer is God a wholly different being, inexplicable and unpredictable. God is understood as a super-human and likely to behave as we do. The problem is addressed by creating God in the image of ourselves, and using the constraints of nature and humanity as our basic assumptions for understanding God. So it appears that the God of many people today is not quite so different from Zeus as it might at first seem.

Appendix A:
Narratives and Recall Items

These are examples of the narratives and corresponding recall items as presented to subjects. "God items" are in bold. Four additional stories appear in Table 2.

(2) One day while God was helping an angel work on a crossword puzzle, a woman in South America got lost in a large, dense forest. It was hot and humid with insects buzzing about wildly. Only thin rays of light trickled to the fungus-covered forest floor. She was terribly afraid that she would not get out and so she prayed to God for help. God comforted her and showed her a path which led between two hills, around a small lake, and out of the forest. God helped the angel finish the crossword puzzle.

2. No a. The woman was in a jungle.
   Yes b. The path led between two hills.
   No c. God was working on a crossword puzzle.
   No d. The woman was a South American.
   No e. There were insects hopping around.
   Yes f. The woman prayed because she was afraid.
   No g. **God stopped helping an angel work on a crossword puzzle to help the woman.**
   No h. **After answering the woman's prayer, God finished helping the angel work on the crossword puzzle.**

(3) A young girl was playing in a forest of birches and oaks when she came across a baby bird. It was chirping loudly because it had fallen from its nest. The girl carefully picked up the bird using some strips of birch bark so that she would not leave her scent on the bird. She climbed the old oak tree where the nest was. She placed the bird in the small gray nest. She climbed down and went on her way. God was aware of the girl's deed and was pleased by it so God gave her a happy feeling.

3. Yes a. The bird's nest was in an oak tree.
   No b. **God was pleased by seeing the girl put the bird in its nest.**
   No c. There were only oaks in the forest.
   No d. The bird chirped quietly.
   No e. The bird was a robin.
   No f. The girl picked up the bird with her hands.
   Yes g. God gave the girl a happy feeling.
   No h. The girl was playing in a jungle.

(5) A woman was exploring a cave when she got lost. The woman was terrified. She was alone in a dark, small, damp cave. There was not even enough room for her to stand upright. The walls had a bumpy texture with patches of fungus. Out of fear she started praying aloud for someone to come help her. As she prayed, her voice echoed mockingly in the cave. She then fell asleep. God responded by pushing a large stone from behind the woman to reveal a tunnel out of the cave. When she awoke, she saw no one, but the rock had been moved. She left the cave.

5. No a. The woman fell asleep while praying.
   Yes b. There was fungus on the walls of the cave.
   No c. The woman cried when she discovered she was lost.
   Yes d. God responded to the woman's prayer by moving a rock.
   Yes e. The cave was dark, damp, and small.
   Yes f. The woman got lost in a cave.
   No g. **God heard the woman's prayer and helped her.**
   No h. **When the woman awoke, God had already left but the rock was moved.**

Appendix B:
Descriptions of Mog, Beebo, and Swek

Mog, Beebo, and Swek are beings from another dimension of existence that can have some contact with our world. They have some fairly unusual characteristics that you should try to keep in mind when reading the stories about them:

Mog. Mog is not spatial which means that Mog has no location. It doesn't make sense to say Mog is at any particular place, or moves from place to place. Mog also has no sensory limitations. This means that there is never a situation in which Mog cannot see, hear, taste, touch, or smell something. Furthermore, Mog can process sensory information from more than one source without the info blending or competing with the other info. Finally, Mog has no limits on attention. Therefore, Mog can pay attention to any number of things at the same time without them competing with each other.

Beebo. Beebo, like Mog, is not spatial and cannot be said to move or be in a particular location. Also like Mog, Beebo has no attention limits and so can pay attention to and do any number of tasks at the same time. Beebo can affect people's thoughts and emotions and can also affect the physical world (e.g., move things).

Swek. Like Beebo, Swek can affect people's emotions. Also like Beebo and Mog, Swek has no limits on attention and so is never distracted. Swek can process sensory information (see-watch, hear-listen) but does not have to. Swek can read minds and electromagnetic waves and other forms of energy, so Swek can know what is going on at any moment without using sensory information (like seeing, hearing, tasting). Unlike Beebo and Mog, Swek can have a location if it wishes, though Swek does not have a solid, physical body that is subject to gravity and other physical forces.

Notes

* This article was originally published in *Cognitive Psychology* 31(3) (1996): 219–47.
1. God is termed a "nonnatural" rather than a "super-natural" entity to emphasize the theological claim that God has a completely different state of being. God is not a part of nature or simply "above" nature. "Nonnatural" is also chosen because of the potential family resemblance concepts of God might have with other attempts to conceptualize entities of unusual but perhaps not "super" ontological categories.
2. The first three studies were conducted simultaneously with subjects selected from a common sample. Consequently, they can be understood as one three-group experiment. For the sake of clarity they are presented as separate studies. For the God items, the correct answer was always "no" due to the nature of the items. An example of a God item is "God had just finished answering another prayer when God helped the boy." A representative set of stories and recall items are shown in Appendix A.
3. Two of the God items were dropped from the Uncomp analysis because they had to do with Uncomp's particular location, and unlike God, Uncomp was stipulated as being everywhere at the same time.
4. For comparisons of God item accuracy between groups, God item accuracy was adjusted to account for subjects' base line accuracy. The assumption is that a subject's accuracy on base items is the highest we can expect performance on God items to be. To take this information into consideration, subjects' God item accuracy was expressed as a proportion of their own base accuracy. Therefore, a score of 100% would indicate that the subject answered all of the God items correctly that would be expected given that subject's particular recall error rate. The computation is simply God item accuracy divided by base item accuracy.
5. These data did not fit parametric assumptions. This nonparametric test was chosen for its power with relatively small sample sizes.
6. The differences between various classes of subjects can be illustrated by looking at three different subjects' answers to question 5, "Can it be said that God does not need to use senses to gather information?" One subject answered, "I wouldn't limit God to our 5 senses, so I guess it doesn't need to "see" anything. But, I suppose I've imagined God as all-seeing, -tasting, -smelling, -hearing, and -feeling, so I guess it doesn't really have the option of not seeing something." This is the type of thoughtful answer it was hoped the questions would elicit. This subject had a God item accuracy of 90.9%. An example of a subject who did not seem to have any clear God concept to draw upon answered, "Perhaps. These issues have never been foremost in my thoughts." A subject who did not seem to take the task seriously simply answered, "See above question/answer." These subjects had God item accuracies of 54.5% and 27.3%, respectively.
7. One subject did not complete the task and was dropped from the analysis, leaving one condition with 15 subjects.
8. One subject's confusion over directions forced removal from these analyses. This is reflected in the degrees of freedom for tests involving the "Survey God" group.

References

Argyle, M. 1975. *Bodily Communication*. London: Methuen.

Barrett, J. L., and B. VanOrman. 1996. The Effects of the Use of Images in Worship on God Concepts. *Journal of Psychology and Christianity* 15(1): 38–45.

Bassett, R. L., K. Perry, R. Repaso, E. Silver, and T. Welch. 1994. Perceptions of God among Persons with Mental Retardation: A Research Note. *Journal of Psychology and Theology* 22(1): 45–49.

Benson, P. L., and B. Spilka. 1973. God Image as a Function of Self-esteem and Locus of Control. *Journal for the Scientific Study of Religion* 12(3): 297–310.

Boyer, P. 1994. *The Naturalness of Religious Ideas: A Cognitive Theory of Religion*. Berkeley: University of California Press.

Brandon, S. G. F. 1970. Anthropomorphism. In *Dictionary of Comparative Religion*, ed. S. G. F. Brandon. Ithaca: Cornell University Press.

Bransford, J. D., and N. S. McCarrell. 1974. A Sketch of a Cognitive Approach to Comprehension: Some Thoughts about Understanding What it Means to Comprehend. In *Cognition and the Symbolic Processes*, ed. W. B. Weimer and D. S. Palermo, 189–229. Hillsdale, NJ: Erlbaum.

Briky, I. T., and S. Ball. 1988. Parental Trait Influence on God as an Object Representation. *Journal of Psychology* 122(2): 133–37.

Caporael, L. A. 1986. Anthropomorphism and Mechanomorphism: Two Faces of the Human Machine. *Computers in Human Behavior* 2(3): 215–34.

Carey, S., and E. Spelke. 1994. Domain-specific Knowledge and Conceptual Change. In *Mapping the Mind: Domain Specificity in Cognition and Culture*, ed. L. A. Hirschfeld and S. A. Gelman, 169–200. Cambridge: Cambridge University Press.

Chi, M. T. H. 1992. Conceptual Change Within and Across Ontological Categories: Examples from Learning and Discovery Science. In *Cognitive Models of Science: Minnesota Studies in the Philosophy of Science*, Vol. 15, ed. R. N. Giere, 129–86. Minneapolis: University of Minnesota Press.

deJonge, J. J. 1993. Personality Constructs and Related God Concepts. *The Analyst* 2: 22–29.

Freud, S. 1961. *The Future of an Illusion*. Trans. J. Strachey. New York: Norton. (Original work published 1927.)

Gans, D. J. 1981. Corrected and Extended Tables for Tukey's Quick Test. *Technometrics* 23: 193–95.

Gorsuch, R. L. 1988. Psychology of Religion. *Annual Review of Psychology* 39: 201–21.

Guthrie, S. 1980. A Cognitive Theory of Religion. *Current Anthropology* 21(2): 181–94.

—1993. *Faces in the Clouds: A New Theory of Religion*. New York: Oxford University Press.

Holyoak, K. J., and P. Thagard. 1995. *Mental Leaps: Analogy in Creative Thought*. Cambridge, MA: MIT Press.

Jolley, J. C., and S. T. Taulbee. 1986. Assessing Perceptions of Self and God: Comparison of Prisoners and Normals. *Psychological Reports* 59(3): 1139–46.

Justice, W. G., and W. Lambert. 1986. A Comparative Study of the Language People Use to Describe the Personalities of God and Earthly Parents. *Journal of Pastoral Care* 40(2): 166–72.

Keil, F. C. 1979. *Semantic and Conceptual Development*. Cambridge, MA: Harvard University Press.

Kohler, K. 1918. *Jewish Theology: Systematically and Historically Considered*. New York: Macmillan.

Nagel, T. 1974. What is it Like to be a Bat? *The Philosophical Review* 83(4): 435–50.

Schwab, R., and K. U. Petersen. 1990. Religiousness: Its Relation to Loneliness, Neuroticism and Subjective Well-being. *Journal for the Scientific Study of Religion* 29(3): 335–45.

Smith, G. D., ed. 1955. *The Teaching of the Catholic Church*. Vol. 1. New York: Macmillan.

Sommers, F. 1963. Types and Ontology. *Philosophical Review* 72: 327–63.

Sperber, D. 1994. The Modularity of Thought and the Epidemiology of Representations. In *Mapping the Mind: Domain Specificity in Cognition and Culture*, ed. L. A. Hirschfeld and S. A. Gelman, 39–67. Cambridge: Cambridge University Press.

Spykman, G. J. 1992. *Reformational Theology: A New Paradigm for Doing Dogmatics*. Grand Rapids: Eerdmans.

Tukey, J. W. 1959. A Quick, Compact, Two-sample Test to Duckworth's Specifications. *Technometrics* 1: 31–48.

Ullah, M. Z. 1984. *Islamic Concept of God*. London: Kegan Paul International.

Ward, T. B. 1994. Structured Imagination: The Role of Category Structure in Exemplar Generation. *Cognitive Psychology* 27: 1–40.

—1995. What's Old about New Ideas? In *The Creative Cognition Approach*, ed. S. M. Smith, T. B. Ward, and R. A. Finke, 157–78. Cambridge, MA: MIT Press.

7

Spreading Non-natural Concepts: The Role of Intuitive Conceptual Structures in Memory and Transmission in Culture[*]

Justin L. Barrett and Melanie A. Nyhof

Abstract

The four experiments presented support Boyer's theory that counterintuitive concepts have transmission advantages that account for the commonness and ease of communicating many non-natural cultural concepts. In Experiment 1, 48 American college students recalled expectation-violating items from culturally unfamiliar folk stories better than more mundane items in the stories. In Experiment 2, 52 American college students in a modified serial reproduction task transmitted expectation-violating items in a written narrative more successfully than bizarre or common items. In Experiments 3 and 4, these findings were replicated with orally presented and transmitted stimuli, and found to persist even after three months. To summarize, concepts with single expectation-violating features were more successfully transmitted than concepts that were entirely congruent with category-level expectations, even if they were highly unusual or bizarre. This transmission advantage for counterintuitive concepts may explain, in part, why such concepts are so prevalent across cultures and so readily spread.

80 03

Around a large citrus ranch in California, the locals all know about the Chivo Man who roams the "haunted dairy." Presumed by some to have been invented a generation ago by a mother trying to keep her children away from crumbling buildings, the story of the elusive and dangerous part-goat Chivo Man is now part of local cultural knowledge and regarded by many as true. Around the world and throughout the centuries people have shared stories and tales about animals that talk, artifacts that have feelings, and people with superhuman powers. These non-natural concepts spread with ease within and between cultures. Unlike natural concepts such as "water" and "food" that have definite and repeatedly verified real-world instantiations, these less mundane cultural concepts typically lack regular reinforcement through experience. Rarely does anyone actually report an encounter with the Chivo Man. Why then do concepts such as these occur across cultures and spread so well?

One way to account for the prevalence of types of concepts is how well they are remembered and transmitted (Boyer 1994; Sperber 1996). For a concept to become a part of a cultural system, somehow it must be represented in individual minds and passed on or transmitted. Sperber has even argued that "Culture is the precipitate of cognition and communication in a human population" (p. 97), and proposed an epidemiological program in the study of cultural representations: "To explain culture, then, is to explain what and how some ideas happen to be contagious" (p. 1). All else being equal, a concept that is easily remembered, with rich conceptual structure grounding it, will be transmitted more successfully and thus be more common than concepts that are difficult to remember or represent. To explain cross-cultural regularities or how a new concept could spread within and between cultures, what is needed is a set of conceptual mechanisms that is pan-cultural: essentially inevitable given innately specified cognitive biases plus ordinary interaction with the world in any cultural setting.

The two most prevalently discussed classes of conceptual structures are schemas and scripts, both of which are sets of culturally informed expectations used to interpret and remember stimuli that have been built up over past experiences (Bartlett 1932; Brewer and Nakamura 1984; Rubin 1995; Schank and Abelson 1977). Both facilitate efficient communication by allowing speakers of a common culture or set of relevant experiences to make assumptions about what others already know. Because schemas and scripts are used to fill in ambiguous or missing information, they often serve a conservative effect in the transmission of ideas: unless stated otherwise, ordinary properties, events, or relations are assumed (Rubin 1995; Rumelhart 1977; Thorndyke 1977; van Dijk and Kintsch 1978).

Additionally, in some contexts, concepts or features of an account that do not fit with the anticipated script or schema are difficult to integrate and thus remember accurately (Harris, Schoen, and Hensley 1992). Using the wrong schema or script to interpret and encode a narrative or situation has also been shown to cause distortions or omissions in what is recalled (Bransford and McCarrell 1974).

In some tasks (e.g., when using recognition measures instead of recall, or after very short delays), script inconsistent information is frequently remembered better than elements that meet the expectations for that scenario (Gaesser et al. 1980). However, the inconsistent items in these previous studies disrupted the script structure or were irrelevant, rather than integrated into a structure such as a narrative as occurs in real folk tales. Whereas research on schemas emphasizes their typically conservative function in the transmission of cultural materials, some memory research using within-subject designs also demonstrates that, much like perceptually distinctive stimuli are recalled better than nondistinctive stimuli, semantically or conceptually incongruous material is recalled more than surrounding mundane material (Schmidt 1991; Waddill and McDaniel 1998; Imai and Richman 1991).

Although research on schemas and scripts suggests the possibility that incongruent concepts may be better remembered thus contributing to their transmission, these conceptual structures are culturally variable to a large extent and will not provide an explanation for cross-culturally prevalent classes of concepts. The best developed account of how such conceptual systems might help explain cultural systems and religious systems in particular is Boyer's (1994) treatment of "counterintuitive" concepts. Drawing heavily on the work of developmental and cognitive psychologists studying concepts, conceptual structure, and ontologies, Boyer's theory contends that for any category, such as animal or artifact, people regardless of culture, hold a host of intuitive assumptions about its member's properties. These assumptions, in turn, are the consequence of a host of intuitive theories (Keil 1989; Gelman and Markman 1986). For example, because a cat is an animal, our intuitive or folk biology applies to cats and we tacitly assume that cats have nutritional needs and will eventually die. These are two properties of "cat" that need not be explicitly represented or communicated. Further, we expect cats to move purposely to fulfill their needs. These intuitive expectations provide the basic structure to concepts.

What distinguishes many "religious" and some cultural concepts from other concepts is that religious concepts typically possess a small number of features that violate category-level expectations (Barrett 2000; Boyer 1994, 1995, 2000). For example, a person who can pass through solid objects (a ghost) is counterintuitive, satisfying the bulk of intuitive expectations for the category of intentional agents but possessing one category violation concerning physical properties. Concepts of these sorts are common in religious systems and folk tales from around the world. As has been argued elsewhere (Sperber 1994), it is these counterintuitive properties that make religious concepts salient. Increased salience, in turn, enhances the likelihood that the concept will be remembered and passed on.[1]

Expectation-incongruent or "counterintuitive" does not necessarily mean unusual, surprising, or difficult to think about. A theologian may find it very easy and common to reason about God's omniscience but that does not mean that an intentional agent who knows everything does not violate expectations at the category level. Counterintuitive in this technical sense means that a member of a particular category (e.g., animal, artifact) possesses a feature that violates intuitive expectations that are regularly acquired by children in any cultural setting for a given category.

Previous research on conceptual structures and memory dynamics is encouraging, but was not intended to test if counterintuitive concepts have a mnemonic advantage (see Boyer and Ramble 2001, as a notable exception). The following four experiments begin to address the hypothesis that, all else being equal, concepts that have a property that violates intuitive assumptions for that thing's category membership will be better remembered and *transmitted* than other concepts.

Experiment 1

To test the hypothesis that expectation-incongruent concepts are more memorable than standard concepts, an experiment was constructed and results analyzed along the lines of Bartlett's serial reproduction studies. Using an American Indian story, "The War of the Ghosts" (1932), Bartlett had subjects read the story and then retell the tale in writing.

These retellings were then read and retold by other subjects. Over several generations of retellings, Bartlett reported that culturally unfamiliar concepts became distorted to better fit cultural schema, while other nonschematic concepts were forgotten. Most strikingly, Bartlett observed that although the story's title suggests that the story features ghosts, the concept of ghost had been eliminated over the course of ten retellings. In trying to capture both omissions and distortions in a single explanation, Bartlett argued that culturally unfamiliar, non-schematic concepts such as ghosts and canoes are more difficult to represent and thus less likely to be remembered and transmitted faithfully. In addition to Bartlett's study, other cross-cultural studies have repeatedly demonstrated that stories from one's own cultural setting are better remembered and retold than stories from other cultures (e.g., Kintsch and Greene 1978; Steffensen and Colker 1992), and that the tendency to distort a story from another culture fit one's own cultural knowledge increases with length of delay before recall (Harris, Schoen, and Hensley 1992).

Despite this supporting research, if expectation-violating concepts are more salient than standard ones and thus have a transmission advantage as Boyer's theory suggests, then Bartlett's finding is problematic. Several methodological issues make his conclusion suspect. In his explanation of his findings, Bartlett fails to distinguish between omissions and distortions of concepts, leaving unanswered the question of why the concept of "canoe" was remembered while that of "ghost" was forgotten. Furthermore, Bartlett relied on only one story whose idiosyncrasies might have contributed to the eventual omission of the "supernatural" features of the story. In addition, Bartlett's experiment was set up in such a way that the recall rate of the culturally exotic, expectation-violating items was not compared to that of culturally familiar items, so the rate of omission might not be above chance.

Experiment 1 involves a reexamination of Bartlett's findings with similar stimuli, American Indian folktales. Since American Indian stories are generally unfamiliar to non-American Indian North American university students, and historic American Indian culture is likewise unfamiliar, the use of such stories should limit the effect of culture-based schema on memory, allowing non-cultural ontological assumptions to surface. Native American stories are also appropriate to this study since they are the products of oral tradition involving many generations of retellings and are thus representative of most simple cultural narratives around the world.

Method

Participants
Participants were 48 university students, 21 female, ranging in age from 18 years to 21 years, with a mean age of 18.7 years. None of the participants were American Indian. Half of the participants read and retold one set of three stories, and half the other three stories.

Materials and Procedure
In hopes of avoiding the problem of using an unrepresentative story, ten stories of 500 words or less were randomly selected from a collection of 166 American Indian stories (Erodes and Ortiz 1984). To maximize thematic and stylistic differences in the sample, one story from each of the ten thematic divisions of the collection (e.g., creation stories, trickster stories, end times, etc.) was randomly selected. Of these ten stories, four did not contain any counterintuitive characters or events and so were not used in the experiment. The remaining six stories were randomly ordered and divided into groups of three. Six stories were used rather than one to help control for any idiosyncrasies of any particular story.

To illustrate, one story told of two children waiting by a fire while their grandmother climbed to the top of a mountain to fetch a special plant. The grandmother diligently struggles to the top only to roll down the mountain to her death when the plant pulls out of the ground in her grasp. The grandmother's bones then walk home singing. The children hear the singing and know that their grandmother has been transformed. Thus, they run inside their dwelling, covering the opening. The children then transform themselves, one turning into a burning stick and one into a blue stone.

Participants in the experiment were read one group of three stories all the way through, one time slowly. After participants completed an unrelated questionnaire requiring approximately 15 minutes, the experimenter instructed participants to retell the stories in the same order they had heard them, recording the retelling in writing on lined notebook paper.

We hypothesized that concepts or events with counterintuitive features would be remembered and retold more accurately than concepts with only common features.

Results and Discussion

The stories participants generated were coded simply for recall of expectation-violating concepts and ordinary concepts. For example, in the story about the transformed grandmother, there are two basic expectation-violating concepts: the events of the grandmother's dead bones coming back to life, and of the grandchildren turning themselves into a blue stone and a stick burning at one end. The ordinary concepts in the story were a mountain, a plant, rocks, a house, and a mine (blanket). Expectation-violating concepts were relatively easy to identify because they are almost always a single event or property. However, ordinary concepts can be demarcated in many ways. To keep from inflating the number of ordinary concepts (and thereby increase the chance of them being forgotten), any reference to an explicitly mentioned object, person, or activity was coded as remembering the general concept. For example, in the transformed grandmother story, the plant that the grandmother climbs the mountain to retrieve is described as "a plant which the Indians use for food," participants were not required to recall "Indians" and "food" in addition to the concept "plant;" the mention of "plant" alone was sufficient.[2]

Averaging across both sets of stories, the 20 counterintuitive concepts (8 in one set and 12 in the other) were recalled 60.4 percent of the time (SD = 20.7 percent), whereas the 46 control concepts (18 in one set and 28 in the other) were recalled 43.3 percent of the time (SD = 18.1 percent). This difference was significant, t (23) = 8.08, p < 0.001.

As with Bartlett's studies, the retellings demonstrated several types of changes from the original stories. In his studies of serial reproduction, Bartlett noted three main classifications of change: omission, in which concepts are completely forgotten; rationalization, in which participants forge explanatory links and provide reasons for occurrences; and transformation of detail, in which unfamiliar concepts are transformed into more familiar concepts. All three types of change were evident in the retellings.

Transformation of detail occurred with culturally unfamiliar concepts in many of the retellings: a buffalo chip was remembered as a cow chip and a wood chip, the Salt Lake was remembered as the Great Lakes, and a man fishing from the shore was remembered as a man fishing from a boat. Some of the changes involved the simplification of a more complex concept rather than a complete transformation of detail: specific listings of plants were remembered as crops and plants, the pinon tree remembered as just a tree, and the old man's decree that if the wood chip floats people will die and after four days come back to life was remembered simply as if it floats then people will live forever.

Rationalization was exhibited in a number of participant's recollections of the stories. For example, in the story of the "Greedy Father," the wife and children turn into a bear lily, a hazel bush, and a pine tree and are now said to "line up in front of rich people, baskets in the deerskin dance" (Erodes and Ortiz 1984, 321). One participant retold this section of the story in a more rational, cohesive way, explaining that "trees and bushes are used to make baskets." Another participant demonstrated rationalization by interpreting the story, "Woman Chooses Death," as "the Garden of Eden with a bit of a twist." In retellings of the story, "The Transformed Grandmother," two participants rationalized the part of the story in which the grandmother "pulled too hard, and away she rolled down the mountainside," by inferring that she fell because "a rock slipped" or "she lost her balance."

A small number of concepts suffered omission in most of the retellings. Proper names were often omitted, and sometimes distorted: the town of Cochiti was remembered as a pueblo called Chiripaw; the pinon tree remembered as chimperon tree and perapah tree. Contrary to Bartlett's findings conclusions, omissions in Experiment 1 mainly involved common concepts. Moreover, this study revealed no evidence that counterintuitives were omitted more often than other concepts. If anything, counterintuitive concepts were remembered better than other concepts.[3]

Although the rate of successful transmission in this experiment is suggestive, the design prohibits strong conclusions. Since the narrative format used did not allow for control of the importance, frequency, and development of concepts in the story, any number of factors might account for the results. In addition, the stories used were traditional tales that had been retold countless times and so the printed editions are likely the product of cognitive selective pressures that might have already tailored the stories to be maximally transmittable.

Despite the possible interference of factors due to design, this experiment challenges the assumption that culturally unfamiliar and expectation-violating concepts always present transmission difficulties. At least in the context of these stories representative of actual folktales, the concepts which violated intuitive assumptions were remembered and retold better than more common concepts that concur with assumptions, setting the stage for more controlled studies.

Experiment 2

To retest the suggestion that a concept with a limited number of properties that violate categorical expectations might be remembered and transmitted more faithfully than a concept which meets expectations, a story was constructed that allowed for a controlled number of both concepts with expectation-violating properties and concepts with mundane, control properties. The story described an inter-galactic ambassador's visit to a Museum on another world (see Appendix A). This museum had 18 exhibits: six that illustrated various types of physical objects, six that illustrated various types of living things, and six that illustrated various types of intentional agents. As in Bartlett's serial reproduction, the first "generation" of participants were asked to read the story and then retell it from memory. The second generation read those retellings and retold them. The measure of central interest was how well the 18 exhibits were remembered and transmitted from generation to generation.

Method

The experimental manipulation was the version of the 18 exhibits with which participants were presented. Each exhibit had ontological information (living thing, physical object, or intentional agent), plus a sentence description of a property. These properties were one of three types: expectation-violating items possessed a feature that violates intuitive assumptions for the object's category membership (e.g., a living thing that never dies violates assumptions about all living things); bizarre items possessed a highly unusual feature that violates no category-level assumptions but may violate basic-level regularities (e.g., a living thing that weighs 5000 kilograms may be unusual for a dog, but weighing 5000 kilograms does not violate assumptions about living things in general); and common items possessed an ordinary feature for their category membership (e.g., a living thing that requires nutrients to survive). Table 1 lists examples from the story used.[4]

Intentional Agent

Counterintuitive	"a being that can see or hear things no matter where they are. For example, it could make out the letters on a page in a book hundreds of miles away and the line of sight is completely obstructed."
Bizarre	"a being that can see or hear things that are far away. For example, it could make out the letters on a page in a book if it is as much as 50 feet away, provided the line of sight is not obstructed."
Common	"a being that can see or hear things that are not too far away. For example, it could make out the letters on a page in a book if it is no more than eight feet away, provided the line of sight is not obstructed."

Living Things

Counterintuitive	"a species that will never die of natural causes and cannot be killed. No matter what physical damage is inflicted it will survive and repair itself."
Bizarre	"a species that does not die easily of natural causes and is hard to kill. If any of its principal parts are severed it will still live with the remaining parts."
Common	"a species that will die if it doesn't get enough nourishment or if it is severely damaged. If any of its principal parts are severed it will surely die."

Physical Objects

Counterintuitive	"an object that is completely invisible under any viewing conditions."
Bizarre	"an object that is difficult to see under normal lighting conditions even with the aid of a microscope."
Common	An object that is easy to see under normal lighting conditions from within 50 feet away."

Table 1. *Selected items from Experiment 2 representing all three item types and all three levels*[5]

Materials

All three versions of each of the 18 items were generated and written such that they were as similar as possible. Each of the three different versions of the story had six expectation-violating items, six bizarre items, and six common items. Similarly, for each ontological grouping (living things, physical objects, intentional agents), each level appeared twice in a given story. Each of these three story versions also had three different orders to control for any order effects. Consequently, in all there were nine different versions of the story with each item and level appearing the same number of times.

The stories were structured to ensure maximum control over complicated variables such as the role of objects in the narrative structure and amount of repeated exposure to a given concept. Though the story had a main character, a true beginning and a true ending, the appearance order of the test items was irrelevant for the narrative structure as was any particular item.

Participants
Eighteen college students participated in each of the three generations, two for each of the nine versions of the story, for a total of 54 participants ranging in age from 16 to 25, with a mean age of 18.8 years. Thirty-four were female.

Procedure
In the first generation, participants read their story once through "carefully" and then one more time through. After a delay of approximately two minutes (the time it took for each to move to a computer terminal and type in a story number, age, and sex, and receive instructions) participants typed out the story as best they could from memory.

This generated two retellings of each of the nine story versions. Participants in the second generation then read both retellings for one of the nine original stories one time carefully. For example, one would read the two retellings of story version #1, another would read the two retellings of version #2, and so forth. Before reading, the experimenter told participants that they were reading two versions of the same story. The second generation participants were then asked to retell the two retellings they read as one story. Again, this produced two retellings of each of the nine stories. The procedure followed by Generation 2 was repeated for Generation 3.

Participants in Generations 2 and 3 read both retellings from the previous generation to maximize the chance for all information to be preserved. One problem with a serial reproduction design is that once information is omitted from a series, it is gone for good. One forgetful person at the beginning of the chain would permanently lose a concept.

Another reason for cross-fertilizing the transmission process was to better approximate what happens when stories are passed down in a real cultural setting. Rarely is information disseminated in a completely linear manner.

In this task, Boyer's theory leads to the prediction that assumption-violating items should be remembered and transmitted more successfully than common items. Bizarre items were included just to see if noncounterintuitive properties, if salient, would be transmitted just as well or better, as suggested by previous research.

Results and Discussion

Two hypothesis-blind, independent coders scored the produced stories for two things: (1) which of the original items (from the original story or the previous generation) were remembered and recorded in some identifiable form, and (2) whether the recorded items were described as counterintuitive, bizarre, or common.[6] With these two pieces of information, it was determined which items were best remembered in any form, and which item type was best represented by the end of transmission. Domains of items (agents, living things, and objects) were collapsed for these analyses.

Of the original items from the first stories, counterintuitive and bizarre items were remembered significantly more often than common items. By the time the third generation retold the stories, on average 5 of the original 18 items per story were left, 2.11 counterintuitive items (SD = 0.96), 1.89 bizarre items (SD = 1.41), and 0.89 common items (SD = 0.96). Paired t-tests comparing each type with each of the other two detected significant differences between both counterintuitive and common items, t (17) = 4.65, p < 0.001, and between bizarre and common items, t (17) = 2.64, p = 0.017. This pattern held across all three types of items (living things, intentional agents, and physical objects). So, just considering if an item was remembered at all, counterintuitive features do seem to provide some advantage over common features. However, this advantage might have nothing to do with violating intuitive assumptions, but might simply be because these features are more interesting. Bizarre items, which do not have counterintuitive features but are also unusual and interesting, showed the same advantage over common items.

That common items were remembered so poorly relative to other items is particularly surprising given the reaction of some participants to these items. Since in normal discourse intuitive properties are assumed and not explicitly stated, some subjects reported that these items were particularly odd and memorable. In some instances of retelling these items, participants tried to make the common property sound exciting or unusual. For example, a physical object that could be moved at speeds of 100 miles per hour were said to move at amazingly fast speed (like 100 miles per hour), even though almost any physical object can be moved at this speed.

	Biological	Physical	Psychological	Total
Generation 1				
Counterintuitive	1.39	1.22	1.28	3.98
Bizarre	1.17	0.83	1.22	3.22
Common	0.72	0.78	0.78	2.28
Total	3.28	2.83	3.82	9.39
Generation 3				
Counterintuitive	0.56	1.39	0.78	2.72
Bizarre	0.33	0.50	0.56	1.29
Common	0.28	0.39	0.22	0.89
Total	1.17	2.28	1.56	5.00

Table 2. *Experiment 2 results: mean number of items recalled per subject as being a given type, by ontology*

In this task, concepts with minimal expectation-violating properties stood a better chance of surviving transmission than concepts that satisfied all intuitive assumptions. This facilitated transmission was due to two factors: counterintuitive concepts were simply more memorable, and unusual properties tended to be changed into counterintuitives.

Experiment 2 offered some evidence that expectation-violating concepts are better remembered and transmitted than merely bizarre concepts or mundane ones. However, Experiment 2 had some shortcomings. First, while fairly carefully controlled, the narrative used was artificial in style, using a setting (other world) commonly associated with counterintuitive concepts as found in science fiction, and only giving ontological information about objects (e.g., living thing) instead of basic level labels (e.g., dog).

Second, Experiment 2 used written stimuli while, traditionally, stories and cultural concepts are transmitted orally. Third, recall was only examined immediately following transmission, whereas in natural settings transmission of a concept may occur long after exposure to the concept. Finally, the style of transmission was only a modest approximation of how information is spread in a culture. Real world transmission involves actual face-to-face interactions, hearing different versions from multiple speakers, and the effects of telling stories multiple times. Experiments 3 and 4 were attempts to extend the findings to these other contexts.

Counterintuitive Items	A dog composing a symphony
	A rose jumping
	Shoes sprouting roots
	A carrot that speaks
	An iridescent blue horse
	A snowflake that burns clothing
Control Items	A slimy feeling earthworm
	Crumpled newspaper blowing in the wind
	Brittle, fallen leaves
	A bird with bright red feathers
	An aromatic shrub
	A red picket fence

Table 3. *Experiment 2 target items imbedded in the story*

In Experiments 3 and 4, a group of adults in a single room served as a small, mock village or cultural group. The experimenter told a subset of the group a story and then asked the subset to initiate a series of retellings within the greater group.

Experiment 3

Method

Participants

Thirteen male and ten female college students ranging in age from 18 to 20 (M = 18.7 years) from an introductory psychology class at a Midwestern American liberal arts college participated to fulfill part of their course requirements.

Materials

A story was composed by a student author about a boy and girl walking home from school. On the way home, they encounter twelve target items, six expectation-violating items and six control items. A list of ordinary objects including plants, animals, and inanimate objects was generated. Then a subset of these objects was selected randomly. Objects were randomly assigned to be either counterintuitive or control items with ontological category membership balanced across the two groups. That is, three of each item type were inanimate, two were animals, and one was a plant. Table 2 displays the twelve target items imbedded in the story. The complete text may be found in Appendix B.

Because the author constructed the story such that it sounded like a natural narrative rather than a formulaic listing of items, the protagonists (the boy and the girl) interacted with and reacted to the objects in different ways depending on the nature of the object. Consequently, not all items were mentioned the same number of times or interacted with the same number of times. To insure that this irregularity did not result in a bias for remembering the counterintuitives, two strategies were used. First, the author's narrative was modified slightly to make the number of mentions and interactions comparable. The six counterintuitive items were mentioned a total of 15 times (including pronouns) versus 14 times for the control items. Similarly, the children interact with the control items 10 times versus 7 times for the counterintuitive items. Additionally, post hoc linear regression analyses showed that neither the number of times an item was mentioned nor the number of times the children interacted with the items significantly predicted rate of item recall.

Procedure

The experimenter gathered participants in a single room and told them that they would be told a story that they should then tell to at least two other people. The experimenter placed no restriction on to whom the participants should choose to tell the story, but encouraged the participants to move about the room and tell anyone they liked. After giving these instructions, the experimenter extracted eight participants from the room and took them to an adjacent room. There, the experimenter told the eight participants the original story and then sent them back to the first room to retell the story. After all participants had been told the story, the experimenter asked them to each write their age, sex, and best account of the story on lined notebook paper. Then, without telling participants that they would be contacted again, the experimenter contacted students three months after initially participating and asked them to recall the story again.

Results

Two independent coders scored the stories produced by the participants for which of the original target items were recalled and if they were recalled accurately, i.e., having the original feature.[7] Paired t-tests were used to examine differences in recall rates between item type (control versus counterintuitive items). These results are illustrated in Figure 1.

Immediate Recall
Examining simply which items were recalled at higher frequency regardless of which features were remembered along with the item, counterintuitive items were recalled significantly more often than control items, t (22) = 7.36, p < 0.001. Participants recalled counterintuitive items 71.1 percent of the time on average (*SD* = 22.2) compared with 43.5 percent (*SD* = 24.5) for control items. Five of the six most frequently remembered items were counterintuitive items.

When using stricter criterion of accurate recall (i.e., recalling items with the same features as in the story), the same pattern emerged. Participants recalled counterintuitive items 57.2 percent of the time on average (*SD* = 26.5) compared with 21.0 percent (*SD* = 20.2) for control items, t (22) = 7.11, p < 0.001. The three most frequently accurately recalled items were counterintuitive, whereas the four least frequently accurately recalled items were control items.

Three-month Delayed Recall
Of the 23 original participants, only 17 were successfully contacted three months later. As with stories produced immediately following transmission, participants recalled counterintuitive items more frequently than control items when considering if items were recalled at all, t (16) = 3.38, p = 0.004, and when considering whether items were recalled accurately, t (16) = 2.89, p = 0.011. On average, participants recalled 35.3 percent (*SD* = 26.3) of the counterintuitive items in some form and 18.6 percent (*SD* = 26.3) accurately. Of the control items, 16.7 percent (*SD* = 20.4) were remembered in some form on average, and 2.9 percent (*SD* = 8.8) of them accurately. Figure 2 illustrates these results.

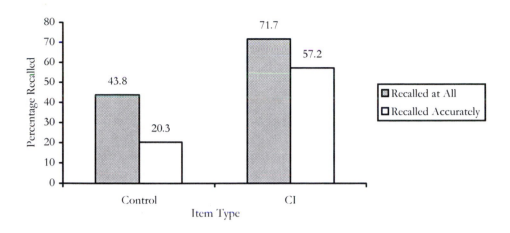

Figure 1. *Experiment 3 results for immediate recall.* Mean recall by coding criteria and item type. Differences between counterintuitive and control items are significant for both criteria.

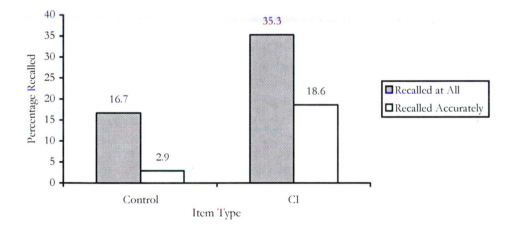

Figure 2. *Experiment 3 results for three-month delayed recall.* Mean recall by coding criteria and item type. Differences between counterintuitive and control items are significant for both criteria.

Discussion

As in Experiment 2, participants remembered and transmitted counterintuitive items better than control items. Unlike Experiment 2, the vehicle story for the concepts was more similar to natural narratives in setting, style, and descriptions of the items. Similarly, the oral, conversational style of the transmission, allowing participants to tell the story to whomever they wanted, was also more naturalistic. Finally, the recall advantage of counterintuitive items after a three-month delay suggests that the mnemonic advantage of these concepts may not be limited to immediate retellings.

Experiment 4

Whereas participants in Experiment 2 transmitted counterintuitive concepts more successfully than "bizarre" items, items were deemed "bizarre" a priori. Perhaps participants found counterintuitive items more bizarre than the "bizarre" items and remembered them better for this reason, not because of violations of expectations. Similarly, the transmission advantage of counterintuitive items in Experiment 3 could be because the control items appeared too mundane to be worthy of attention. Experiment 4 was an attempt to address these issues by replicating Experiment 3 with bizarre items replacing the control items, and asking subjects to rate the bizarreness or novelty of all the items for an independent measure of bizarreness.

Method

Participants
Eighteen female and nine male college students ranging in age from 17 to 19 years (M = 18.3) from an introductory psychology class at a Midwestern American liberal arts college, participated to fulfill part of their course requirements.

Materials and Procedure
The experimenter told participants the same story as in Experiment 3 with minor modifications. The control modifiers used in Experiment 3 were replaced with modifiers that would make the objects extremely unusual or bizarre without becoming counterintuitive or undermining category membership. For example, the crumpled newspaper from the original story became a bright pink newspaper—highly unusual for a newspaper, but still a newspaper. Other modifications include: a warm, fuzzy worm replaced a slimy-feeling worm, leaves as big as tables replaced brittle leaves, a bird swallowing nails replaced a bird with bright red feathers, a shrub that smells like laundry detergent replaced an aromatic shrub, and a rubber picket fence replaced a red picket fence. Consequently, the story contained six counterintuitive target items and six bizarre target items. Otherwise, the story and transmission process were identical to Experiment 3.

To examine more carefully if the previously demonstrated transmission advantage for counterintuitive items is another instance of the novelty effect often found in within-subjects designs (Waddill and McDaniel 1998), after writing the story following transmission, participants rated each of the twelve items for bizarreness or novelty. The experimenter gave each participant a sheet of ratings in which participants rated on a five-point scale "have you ever seen or encountered" each item in (1) "real life" or (2) "in movies, books, or anywhere else (other than this experiment)." The scale ranged from 1 = "yes, many times" to 5 = "no way, never." The two ratings for each item were combined to yield a "novelty" rating.

Results and Discussion

Two independent coders scored the stories produced by the participants for which of the original target items were recalled and if they were recalled accurately.[8] As in Experiment 3, paired t-tests were used to examine differences in recall rates between item type (bizarre versus counterintuitive items). These results are illustrated in Figure 3. As in previous experiments, counterintuitive items enjoyed a transmission advantage that appears independent of familiarity or novelty of the concepts.

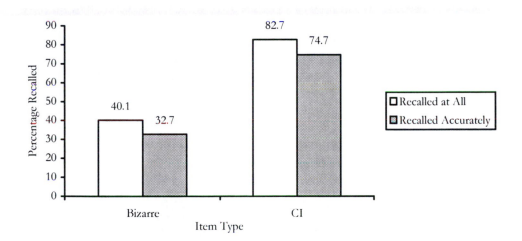

Figure 3. *Experiment 4 results for immediate recall.* Mean recall by coding criteria and item type. Differences between counterintuitive and bizarre items are significant for both criteria.

Immediate recall. Examining simply which items were recalled at higher frequency regardless of which features were remembered along with the item, counterintuitive items were recalled significantly more often than bizarre items, t (26) = 10.37, p < 0.001. Participants recalled counterintuitive items 82.7 percent of the time on average (SD = 12.6) compared with 40.1 percent

(SD = 17.5) for control items. Five of the six most frequently remembered items were counterintuitive items.

When using the stricter criterion of accurate recall (i.e., recalling items with the same features as in the story), the same pattern emerged. Participants recalled counterintuitive items 74.7 percent of the time on average (*SD* = 15.6) compared with 32.7 percent (*SD* = 19.9) for bizarre items, t (26) = 11.01, p < 0.001. Five of the six most frequently accurately recalled items were counterintuitive.

Interestingly, as in Experiment 2, some of the bizarre items transformed into counterintuitive items through transmission. The most common distortion of this kind was for the bright pink newspaper blown by the wind. Of the ten participants who remembered the newspaper, six recalled it as walking or running, not blowing in the wind. It is tempting to speculate that memory for the newspaper might have been even poorer if it had not been animated through retellings.

Three-month delayed recall. Twenty-one of the 27 original participants were successfully contacted and provided data. As with stories produced immediately following transmission, subjects recalled counterintuitive items more frequently than bizarre items when considering if items were recalled at all, t (20) = 2.74, p = 0.013, or recalled accurately, t (20) = 2.87, p = 0.009. On average, participants recalled 34.1 percent (SD = 25.0) of the counterintuitive items in some form and 23.0 percent (SD = 21.4) of them accurately. In contrast, participants only recalled 19.0 percent (SD = 15.2) of the bizarre items on average, and 11.9 percent (SD = 12.0) of them accurately. These results appear in Figure 4.

Novelty ratings. As expected, participants rated both counterintuitive items and bizarre items as extremely unusual or novel. However, participants rated bizarre items as more novel than counterintuitive items and novelty did not predict recall. On a five-point scale, bizarre items had a mean novelty rating of 4.47 (*SD* = 0.367) with counterintuitive items rated 4.36 (*SD* = 0.289) on average. This difference was significant, t (26) = 2.21, p = 0.036, with bizarre items considered slightly more novel or unusual. Consequently, a multiple linear regression predicting item recall from novelty ratings and item type (counterintuitive versus bizarre) detected no recall advantage related to higher novelty ratings once item type was statistically controlled. However, the partial relationship between item type (controlling for novelty) was a significant predictor for both general and recall rate, t (11) = 2.63, p = 0.027, and for accurate recall, t (11) = 2.92, p = 0.017.

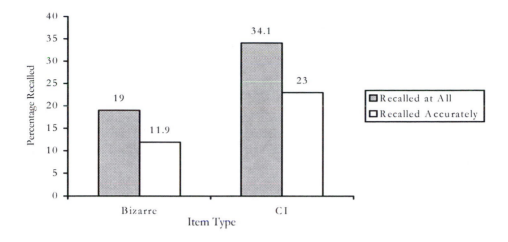

Figure 4. *Experiment 4 results for three-month delayed recall.* Mean recall by coding criteria and item type. Differences between counterintuitive and bizarre items are significant for both criteria.

General Discussion

The four experiments presented above support Boyer's theory that counterintuitive concepts have transmission advantages that account for the commonness and ease of communicating many nonnatural cultural concepts. In Experiment 1, participants recalled expectation-violating items from culturally unfamiliar folk stories better than more mundane items in the stories. In Experiment 2, participants in a modified serial reproduction task transmitted expectation-violating items in a written narrative more successfully than bizarre or common items. In Experiments 3 and 4, these findings were replicated with orally presented and transmitted stimuli, and found to persist even after three months. To sum, controlling for factors such as the role objects play in a story, the ecological relevance of the concepts, and motivational factors concerning the relaying of a concept, concepts with single expectation-violating features were more successfully transmitted than concepts that were entirely congruent with category-level expectations, even if they were highly unusual or bizarre. This transmission advantage for counterintuitive concepts may explain, in part, why such concepts are so prevalent across cultures and so readily spread.

The results converge with the findings of Boyer and Ramble's (2001) cross-cultural studies in which participants more accurately recalled items violating category-level expectations than items meeting expectations. Their research also demonstrated little difference between cultures in sensitivity to such violations.

The theory tested here does not claim that semantically- or script-incongruent concepts will be remembered better than congruent ones, but instead explores the pan-cultural mechanisms upon which scripts and schemas rely by testing the mnemonic advantage of concepts which contain violations of expectations at the category level (i.e., living things, physical objects, and intentional agents). Consequently, these findings do not challenge story comprehension theories that maintain that nonschematic or script-incongruent ideas, events, and concepts will not be well remembered but forgotten or distorted to fit schematic expectations (e.g., Rubin 1995), but involve a fundamentally different theory.

While the experiments presented do not directly address possible mnemonic advantages for concepts that evoke bizarre imagery (Einstein, McDaniel, and Lackey 1989), they do suggest that some bizarre images might be remembered better than other images because they represent an expectation-violating concept. However, as suggested above, not all expectation-violating concepts stimulate bizarre imagery and not all bizarre images are expectation-violating concepts.

The most striking thing about these data is that some intuitive but unusual properties were transformed into expectation-violating properties (Experiments 2 and 4), suggesting that some expectation-violating properties might be easier to represent. How could that be? Perhaps counterintuitive features that are mere negations of intuitive assumptions are easier to "tag," and therefore keep track of, than complicated, common features. For example, it could be easier to remember that some living thing will never die than that some living thing will die after its blood alcohol level reaches 0.4, provided its blood-sodium levels are less than 0.05. In the counterintuitive case, one need only put a negative tag on an intuitive assumption (that living things eventually die), but in the bizarre case, all of the conditions must be encoded.

Some support for this speculation can be found in Ward's (1994; 1995) work on "structured imagining." When adults were asked to draw and describe novel imaginary animals from a totally different world, it was found that they tended to structure the animals based on the intuitively assumed properties of the concept "animal." When participants did deviate from these intuitions, the deviations were almost always simple negations of an intuitive assumption. In this way the intuitive properties of the governing category still structured the novel concept.

Another bit of supporting evidence comes from Experiment 1. In one story, "Woman Chooses Death," Old Man proposes that to decide whether or not humans will experience death, he will throw a buffalo chip into a river. If the chip floats, humans will die but come back to life after four days. What would happen if the chip sinks is never stated in the story.

Several participants who retold this story remembered the bargain as being if the chip floats, people will live forever. This subtle distortion suggests that the simplified concept, "To live forever" is easier to represent than "to live for some time, die, and four days later come back to life." Note, however, that these may both be expectation-violating concepts.

If expectation-violating features facilitate transmission, why, then, are expectation-violating and "religious" concepts the minority of cultural concepts? Numerous other factors, such as frequency of concept exposure, attention paid to that exposure, motivation for communication, ease of concept reproduction, and conformism effects undoubtedly influence the production and transmission of concepts (Boyer and Ramble 2001). For example, a village might have a concept of "ghost" that is reinforced every time something mysterious happens such as an illness, a missing chicken, or a freak storm, but the concept "water" as something good for drinking is reinforced many times daily. Although ecological factors cannot be completely controlled, holding factors such as frequency of exposure constant, it appears that expectation-violating concepts might possess some advantages.

Does this suggest that the more counterintuitive features a concept has, the better? No. Too many counterintuitive features would undermine the structure of the concept. Its relations to relevant causal theories would be disrupted. A cat that can never die, has wings, is made of steel, experiences time backwards, lives underwater, and speaks Russian, would no longer be much of a cat. Consequently, the causal schemata would no longer generate sensible intuitive expectations, and so there would be no counterintuitive properties, but a list of disconnected features. What Boyer proposes is a cognitive optimum: a balance between satisfying ontologically driven intuitive expectations and violating enough of them to become salient (Boyer 1995). Concepts that meet this balance may be termed minimally counterintuitive.

If it is true, as Boyer argues, that many religious concepts are minimally counterintuitive and thus enjoy facilitated transmission, the data presented above corroborate the arguments of several scholars applying insights of cognitive science to the study of religion. Each of these scholars has maintained that religious beliefs and practices are "natural" or "intuitive" in the sense that they primarily enlist ordinary cognitive resources. Lawson and McCauley have shown how religious rituals are undergirded by garden-variety action and agent representations (1990). Guthrie (1993) maintains that gods are explained by an overactive agent detection device that cares little if a postulated agent has some non-human qualities such as invisibility since being able to reason about unseen agents would have had great survival value in our evolutionary past. Similarly, Barrett and colleagues (Barrett 2001; Barrett and Keil 1996; Barrett, Richert, and Driesenga 2001) have argued that concepts of religious agents, such as gods, are largely informed by intuitive assumptions governing all intentional agents, making these easy concepts to entertain and use in many contexts. Adding to these other cognitive perspectives on religious concepts, an explanation for how religious concepts might be so easily transmitted may build a cumulative, naturalistic explanation for much of religion in general.

The results presented here demonstrate the importance of intuitive conceptual structures in informing and constraining the spread of cultural materials that extend beyond mundane concepts or experiences. Many people know about ghosts, not because they have frequent interaction with them, or because knowledge about them is important for successful survival, but because they largely fit intuitive assumptions about agents while possessing a small number of expectation-violating features that make them interesting and memorable. Returning to the Chivo Man, he could have become such a widely known local character not because of any particular importance he holds in everyday life or because of any actual interaction with him. Rather, a part-animal, part-human creature violates one of our expectations for animals while maintaining rich inferential potential based on pan-cultural category-level knowledge.

Appendix A

One Version of Nine Used in Experiment 2

I was sent as a diplomat to the planet Ralyks. Because the decision was very sudden and I didn't have a lot of time to research Ralyks, I decided to take a visit to Ralyks' equivalent of the Smithsonian—a large network of museums and zoos intended to provide a representative sampling of all of the different kinds of things of this world.

The first building I entered was a huge cross with four wings, devoted to the various types of beings that initiate action in this world. They all act and behave in ways that are motivated by internal states. They don't just respond to their environment, they act on it as well. In the first one, perhaps the most telling wing, was a fine collection of restaurants and gift shops. All of them were outrageously overpriced, so I went on to the rest of the building.

The next wing I went into was painted blue and contained exhibits devoted to the various types of beings that initiate action in this world. In the first room was a type of being of which all members normally are able to reproduce. Each member of the species has two biological parents.

The second room illustrated a being that will never die of natural causes and cannot be killed. No matter what physical damage is inflicted it will survive and repair itself. Rounding a corner, I came upon an exhibit concerned with a being that is aware of its own existence and usually conscious of what it is doing. It knows when it is thinking and knows when it is trying to do something.

To the south of this room was one containing a being about the size of a young human that is impossible to move by any means.

The next room had in it a being about the size of an adult human that weighs about 150 pounds.

In the last room of the wing was a being that is easy to see under normal lighting conditions from within about 150 meters away.

The next wing I went into was painted red and contained exhibits devoted to the various types of beings that initiate action in this world. In the first room was a being that can see or hear things no matter where they are. For example, it could make out the letters on a page in a book hundreds of miles away and the line of sight is completely obstructed.

The next exhibit featured a being that has no desires that motivate what it does. It never wants something, it just goes after things for no reason. It never wants to do things, it just does things randomly.

I continued through the dimly lit hall and came to an exhibit about a being that is able to pass through solid objects. Being the size of an adult human, it can pass directly through solid objects.

Adjacent to this room was a display dedicated to a kind of being that requires nourishment and external sources of energy in order to survive. It consumes and metabolizes caloric materials to sustain itself.

After going up a few steps, I came to a room that displayed a being that can move quickly. It can move at speeds of about 20 miles per hour.

The next room I came to featured a being that can be completely in more than one place at a time. All of it can be in two or all four different corners of the room at the same time.

The next wing I went into was painted yellow and contained exhibits devoted to the various types of beings that initiate action in this world. The first exhibit I came to was about a being that never uses beliefs to guide its actions. For example, if it wants a banana, and it believes that a banana is in a box in the corner of the room, it will search randomly anyway as if it doesn't know the banana is there.

Then next exhibit concerned a being that can remember an unlimited number of events or pieces of information. For example, it could tell you, in precise detail, everything it had witnessed in the past, and if you read it a list of 10 billion words, it would remember them all flawlessly.

The third exhibit featured a being that can pay attention to any number of things all at the same time. For example, if ten people or ten billion people were talking to it at the same time, it would be able to keep track of what all of them were saying.

Near the end of the hall was another room featuring a being that is chiefly comprised of carbon-based molecules.

At the end of the hall were two more exhibits. One was a room devoted to a type of being that gives birth to and raises offspring that are the same type of being. Parents and offspring are always similar.

The final exhibit of this wing featured a being that grows and changes most of its life cycle. At birth it must grow considerably to reach maturity; and after reaching maturity, it then changes as it deteriorates.

I left the building and went to my new office to ponder all of the things that can be found on Ralyks.

Appendix B

Story Used in Experiment 3

A girl and a boy, sister and brother, were walking home from school on an ordinary day in an ordinary town. As they were walking towards home, they came upon a dog belonging to one of their friends. The dog crouched on the front lawn as it composed a symphony.

Since the dog was completely absorbed in its work, the two siblings continued on their way, chatting about what they had learned in school that day, until a beautiful rose jumped right in front of their path.

The children knew that they must be getting home, or else their mother would begin to worry, so they slipped away from the rose. They had hardly made any progress in their journey, when they noticed an earthworm crossing the sidewalk. The girl picked it up and felt its slimy texture and the squirm of its movement. She placed it on the grass on the other side of the pavement and they continued on their way.

As they were walking, the boy's shoes sprouted roots which broke up the pavement below and impaired his movement. He had had this trouble with these shoes several times before and always carried a pocket knife in order to cut the roots.

While the boy was engaged in the process of uprooting himself, a crumpled piece of newspaper blew past the girl in the cool breeze, brushing past her leg.

The children continued on their way. The leaves, which had fallen from the trees a while ago, were brittle and crackled under their feet. The children swished their way through the numerous leaves. The boy stopped to gather them in his arms and throw them at his sister.

They soon became hungry and so the boy reached into his backpack to retrieve a bag of carrots which he had not eaten during his lunch. She was just about to take a bite of one of the carrots when it screamed, "Stop!" The children then decided that perhaps they had better not eat any more carrots.

The children continued on their way until the girl paused to notice a bright red bird perched on the branch of a nearby tree. She explained to her brother that the red feathers of the bird signified that it was male. The boy moved towards the bird, but it sensed his approach and quickly flew away.

The boy's behavior angered the sister, and so she ran ahead of him. She crossed the road and walked along a rolling field, her brother trailing behind her. Soon a horse ran along the edge of the field to where the boy was standing. He called to his sister, and forgetting her anger, she ran to see what he wanted to show her. The horse was a dazzling iridescent, almost transparent blue. They had seen this horse galloping across the field many times before, but this was the first time that they had been able to examine it up close.

As the children stood gazing at the animal, they noticed a beautiful and aromatic shrub nearby. It had a very fragrant smell that reminded them of their garden at home.

The sky had become a little darker since they had left school and soon a few snowflakes fell from the sky. The boy caught one on the sleeve of his jacket. It burned a hole in his jacket.

The air had turned cold, but the children were almost home. They soon caught sight of the brown picket fence in their very own front yard. They ran towards it and easily swung upon the gate of the fence. Their mother was inside and greeted them with hot chocolate and cookies while the children told her about their day.

Notes

* This article was originally published in *Journal of Cognition and Culture* 1(1) (2001): 69–100.

1. The claim that intuitive ontology-violating properties of concepts make them salient and more likely to be remembered and transmitted should not be confused with the controversial claim that concepts that conjure bizarre imagery are more likely to be remembered (Einstein, McDaniel, and Lackey 1989). A concept may be bizarre or unusual (e.g., a 100-pound beetle) and not violate any intuitive assumptions. Likewise, a concept may clearly violate intuitive assumptions and not necessarily evoke bizarre imagery (e.g., a mountain with no mass). The two hypotheses are orthogonal. Boyer's claim is that, all else being equal, expectation-incongruent concepts will be better remembered and transmitted than mundane or merely bizarre concepts.

2. Since coders would have to first agree on what constituted a bit of information from the story, then which bits were remembered, and finally which bits were counter-intuitive, only a single coder was used. Consequently, the results are most helpful when combined with Experiments 2, 3 and 4.

3. Contrary to the overall results, one expectation-violating concept, that of the magic crystal in the story of the Salt Woman, was forgotten more than the other expectation-violating concepts in that story and in the other stories (only two subjects recalled the crystal at all and only one remembered that it was magic) and the omission was not straightforward, but involved a transfer of magic power from the crystal to Salt Woman.

4. To insure that the counterintuitive levels of each item were not easier to vividly imagine, thus potentially giving them a mnemonic advantage, an independent group of 14 participants (9 female; mean age, 20.8) rated each of the items "how easy it is for you to form a vivid mental image of them" on a seven-point scale with a low score representing ease. Counterintuitive versions were significantly rated as more difficult to imagine ($M = 5.01$, $SD = 1.08$) than either the bizarre items ($M = 3.69$, $SD = 0.82$), or the common items ($M = 2.19$, $SD = 1.11$), and so if anything there would be a bias against counterintuitives. The same precaution was taken for the stimuli used in Experiments 3 and 4, with a sample of 15 adults (9 female; mean age, 20.7 years). There was no evidence that counterintuitive items ($M = 3.99$, $SD = 1.04$) were easier to create a vivid image of than the bizarre items ($M = 4.37$, $SD = 1.06$), t (14) = 1.15, p = 0.267. However, counterintuitive items were significantly more difficult to imagine than common items, $M = 2.17$, $SD = 1.38$, t (14) = 3.51, p = 0.003.

5. A crossing error led to one set of physical objects being under-represented, appearing in only two instead of three versions of the story, and another set being over-represented, appearing four times. This did not change the overall number of counterintuitive, bizarre, or common items that were presented, and did not alter the results in any detectable way.

6. Inter-rater agreement was 85.0%. Disagreements were resolved through discussion.

   Considering *how* items were remembered provides more telling information. After three generations of retellings, along with many of the items being forgotten, many items were distorted. Some items that began as bizarre became common (12.5% of bizarres), and some common items became bizarre (22.2% of commons). But by far the largest type of shift was from bizarre to counterintuitive. While only 7.2% of counter-intuitive items that were transmitted degraded into bizarre items, 37.5% of bizarre items became counterintuitive items after repeated retellings. Consequently, on average, participants in Generation 3 remembered 2.72 items *as* counterintuitive items (*SD* = 1.49), as compared with 1.39 as bizarre (*SD* = 1.33), and 0.89 as common (*SD* =

0.96). The differences between counterintuitive and bizarre, t (17) = 5.62, p < 0.0001, are significant. The difference between bizarre and common recall is not significant, t (17) = 1.16, p = 0.261. Again, this pattern holds across the three item types and for all three generations. Table 2 shows these results. Results of Generation 2 are not reported because they are redundant with Generations 1 and 3.

7. For the stories produced immediately following transmission, raters agreed 96.4 percent of the time. For the stories produced after a three-month delay, raters agreed 92.2 percent of the time. Raters resolved disagreements through discussion.

8. For the stories produced immediately following transmission, raters agreed 96.0 percent of the time. For the stories produced after a three-month delay, raters agreed 95.2 percent of the time. Raters resolved disagreements through discussion.

References

Barrett, J. L. 2000. Exploring the Natural Foundations of Religion. *Trends in Cognitive Sciences* 4: 29–34.

—2001. Do Children Experience God Like Adults? Retracing the Development of God Concepts. In *Religion in Mind: Cognitive Perspectives on Religious Experience*, ed. J. Andresen. Cambridge: Cambridge University Press.

Barrett, J. L., and F. C. Keil, 1996. Conceptualizing a Non-natural Entity: Anthropomorphism in God Concepts. *Cognitive Psychology* 31: 219–47.

Barrett, J. L., R. A. Richert, and A. Driesenga. 2001. God's Beliefs Versus Mother's: The Development of Natural and Non-natural Agent Concepts. *Child Development* 72(1): 50.

Bartlett, F. C. 1932. *Remembering: A Study in Experimental and Social Psychology*. Cambridge: Cambridge University Press.

Boyer, P. 1994. *The Naturalness of Religious Ideas: A Cognitive Theory of Religion*. Berkeley, CA: University of California Press.

—1995. Causal Understandings in Cultural Representations: Cognitive Constraints on Inferences from Cultural Input. In *Causal Cognition: A Multidisciplinary Debate*, ed. D. Sperber, D. Premack, and A. J. Premack. New York: Oxford University Press.

—2000. Evolution of a Modern Mind and the Origins of Culture: Religious Concepts as a Limiting Case. In *Evolution and the Human Mind: Modularity, Language and Meta-Cognition*, ed. P. Carruthers and A. Chamberlain. Cambridge: Cambridge University Press.

Boyer, P., and C. Ramble. 2001. Cognitive Templates for Religious Concepts: Cross-Cultural Evidence for Recall of Counter-Intuitive Representations. *Cognitive Science* 25(4): 535–64.

Bransford, J. D., and N. S. McCarrell. 1974. A Sketch of a Cognitive Approach to Comprehension: Some Thoughts about Understanding What it Means to Comprehend. In *Cognition and the Symbolic Processes*, ed. W. B. Weimer and D. S. Palermo, 189–229. Hillsdale, NJ: Erlbaum.

Brewer, W. F., and G. V. Nakamura. 1984. The Nature and Functions of Schemas. In *Handbook of Social Cognition*, Vol. 1, ed. R. S. Wyer, Jr and T. K. Srull, 119–40. Hillsdale, NJ: Erlbaum.

Einstein, G. O., M. A. McDaniel, and S. Lackey. 1989. Bizarre Imagery, Interference, and Distinctiveness. *Journal of Experimental Psychology: Learning, Memory, and Cognition* 15: 137–46.

Erodes, R., and A. Ortiz, eds. 1984. *American Indian Myths and Legends*. New York: Pantheon Books.

Gelman, S., and E. Markman. 1986. Categories and Induction in Young Children. *Cognition* 23: 183–209.

Gaesser, A. C., S. B. Woll, D. J. Kowalski, and D. A. Smith. 1980. Memory for Typical and Atypical Actions in Scripted Activities. *Journal of Experimental Psychology: Human Learning and Memory* 6: 503–15.

Guthrie, S. 1993. *Faces in the Clouds: A New Theory of Religion*. New York: Oxford University Press.

Harris, R. J., L. M. Schoen, and D. L. Hensley. 1992. A Cross-cultural Study of Story Memory. *Journal of Cross-Cultural Psychology* 23: 133–47.

Imai, S., and C. L. Richman. 1991. Is the Bizarreness Effect a Special Case of Sentence Reorganization? *Bulletin of the Psychonomic Society* 29: 429–32.

Keil, F. C. 1989. *Concepts, Kinds and Conceptual Development*. Cambridge, MA: MIT Press.

Kintsch, W., and E. Greene. 1978 The Role of Culture-specific Schemata in the Comprehension and Recall of Stories. *Discourse Processes* 1: 1–13.

Lawson, E. T., and R. N. McCauley. 1990. *Rethinking Religion: Connecting Cognition and Culture*. Cambridge: Cambridge University Press.

Rubin, D. C. 1995. *Memory in Oral Traditions: The Cognitive Psychology of Epic, Ballads, and Counting-out Rhymes*. New York: Oxford University Press.

Rumelhart, D. E. 1977. Understanding and Summarizing Brief Stories. In *Basic Processes in Reading: Perception and Comprehension*, ed. D. LaBerge and S. J. Samuels. Hillsdale, NJ: Erlbaum.

Schank, R., and R. Abelson. 1977. *Scripts, Plans, Goals, and Understanding: An Inquiry into Human Knowledge Structures*. Hillsdale, NJ: Erlbaum.

Schmidt, S. R. 1991. Can We Have a Distinctive Theory of Memory? *Memory and Cognition* 19: 523–42.

Sperber, D. 1994. The Modularity of Thought and the Epidemiology of Representations. In *Mapping the Mind: Domain Specificity in Cognition and Culture*, ed. L. A. Hirschfeld and S. A. Gelman, 39–67. Cambridge: Cambridge University Press.

Sperber, D. 1996. *Explaining Culture: A Naturalistic Approach*. Cambridge, MA: Blackwell Publishers.

Steffensen, M. S., and L. Colker. 1982. Intercultural Misunderstandings about Health Care: Recall of Descriptions of Illness and Treatments. *Social Science and Medicine* 16: 1949–54.

Thorndyke, P. W. 1977. Cognitive Structures in Comprehension and Memory of Narrative Discourse. *Cognitive Psychology* 9: 77–110.

Van Dijk, T. A., and W. Kintsch. 1978. Cognitive Psychology and Discourse: Recalling and Summarizing Stories. In *Current Trends in Textlinguistics*, ed. W. U. Dressler. Berlin: Walter de Gruyter.

Waddill, P. J., and M. A. McDaniel. 1998. Distinctiveness Effects in Recall: Differential Processing or Privileged Retrieval? *Memory and Cognition* 26: 108–20.

Ward, T. B. 1994. Structured Imagination: The Role of Category Structure in Exemplar Generation. *Cognitive Psychology* 27: 1–40.

—1995. What's Old about New Ideas? In *The Creative Cognition Approach*, ed. S. M. Smith, T. B. Ward, and R. A. Finke, 157–78. Cambridge, MA: MIT Press.

8

COGNITIVE TEMPLATES FOR RELIGIOUS CONCEPTS: CROSS-CULTURAL EVIDENCE FOR RECALL OF COUNTER-INTUITIVE REPRESENTATIONS[*]

Pascal Boyer and Charles Ramble

Abstract

This article presents results of free-recall experiments conducted in France, Gabon and Nepal, to test predictions of a cognitive model of religious concepts. The world over, these concepts include violations of conceptual expectations at the level of domain knowledge (e.g., about "animal" or "artifact" or "person") rather than at the basic level. In five studies we used narratives to test the hypothesis that domain-level violations are recalled better than other conceptual associations. These studies used material constructed in the same way as religious concepts, but not used in religions familiar to the subjects. Experiments 1 and 2 confirmed a distinctiveness effect for such material. Experiment 3 shows that recall also depends on the possibility to generate inferences from violations of domain expectations. Replications in Gabon (Exp. 4) and Nepal (Exp. 5) showed that recall for domain-level violations is better than for violations of basic-level expectations. Overall sensitivity to violations is similar in different cultures and produces similar recall effects, despite differences in commitment to religious belief, in the range of local religious concepts or in their mode of transmission. However, differences between Gabon and Nepal results suggest that familiarity with some types of domain-level violations may paradoxically make other types more salient. These results suggest that recall effects may account for the recurrent features found in religious concepts from different cultures.

ഓ രു

Religious concepts label and describe supernatural agencies in ways that are specific to each culture. The concepts may describe a unique, omniscient and omnipotent God, as in Judaism, Christianity and Islam, or several gods with their particular features, or a variety of ghosts, spirits, ghouls, zombies, fairies, djinns, as well as specific artifacts (e.g., statues that listen to people's prayers), animals (e.g., jaguars that live in the sky) or parts of the natural environment (e.g., mountains that think, rivers that protect people, etc.) (see, e.g., Child and Child 1993). This variety might seem to suggest that "anything goes" in this domain. Anthropologists have long suspected that there were in fact limits to variability. However, there was no cognitive account of the processes that would make certain types of concepts more "culturally successful" than others.

Cognitive studies of religion start from the premise that religious concepts are governed by the same kind of constraints as other concepts and can be investigated in the same way (Goldman 1964; Watts and Williams 1988; Barrett 2000). A number of anthropologists have argued that religious concepts do not in fact constitute an autonomous "domain" (Spiro and D'Andrade 1958; Sperber 1985; Lawson and McCauley 1990; Bloch 1992; Whitehouse 1992; Guthrie 1993; Dulaney and Fiske 1994; Barrett and Keil 1996). Information derived from nonreligious conceptual schemata constrains religious ontology (Guthrie 1993; Barrett and Keil 1996), ritual taboos (Dulaney and Fiske 1994), concepts of ritual action (Lawson and McCauley 1990; Houseman and Severi 1998), the modes of transmission of religion (Whitehouse 1992) as well as some developmental aspects of religious belief (Boyer and Walker 1999).

The experiments presented here test the predictions of a particular cognitive account of religious concepts (Boyer 1992; 1994, see also Sperber 1996; Barrett 1996). This account is based on a distinction between information represented at the level of (roughly) "basic" kinds (henceforth "kind-concepts") and that associated with broader ontological categories ("domain-concepts"), such as person, artifact, animal, inanimate natural object, plant, and so forth (see Keil 1994 for a survey of these categories). Whenever an object is identified as belonging to one such domain, this triggers specific, principled expectations that go beyond the information given and establish causal links between observed features and underlying structure. Domain concepts are described by developmental psychologists as based on "skeletal principles" (Gelman 1990), more abstract "modes of construal" that emphasize particular forms of causation (Kelly and Keil 1985;

Keil 1994) or "foundational theories" that specify specific principles for each domain (Whitehouse 1992). This domain-level information produces expectations intuitively applied to new objects, however unfamiliar, if they are identified as members of a particular ontological domain (Keil 1979).[1]

The distinction between kind- and domain-concepts is relevant here because most religious notions imply a particular treatment of information associated with domain-concepts:

1. Religious concepts generally include explicit *violations of expectations* associated with domain-concepts. For instance, spirits and ghosts go through physical obstacles or move instantaneously, thereby violating early developed expectations about solid objects (Spelke 1988). Eternal gods, metamorphoses, chimeras and virgin birth go against entrenched expectations about living things (see, e.g., Carey 1985; Walker 1992; Keil 1994). Gods that perceive everything or predict the future violate early developed assumptions about intentional agency and about the causal links between events, perceptions and beliefs (Wellmann 1990; Perner 1991; Gopnik 1993). Anthropomorphic artifacts with a psychology, like for instance "listening statues" that hear and understand people's prayers, are construed as artifacts with nonstandard properties, intentional properties in this case (Guthrie 1993; Boyer 1996b; Barrett 2000).
2. Religious concepts invariably require that relevant *nonviolated assumptions are tacitly activated* by default. For instance, while people represent spirits as physically nonstandard agents, they also tacitly represent them as cognitively standard agents, spontaneously extending intuitive psychological expectations to supernatural agents (Barrett and Keil 1996). In a symmetrical way, "zombies" are construed as cognitively nonstandard, but "intuitive physics" is tacitly applied to them by default; their bodies are supposed to obey the same physical constraints as other solid objects (Boyer 1996b).

This model predicts that culturally successful religious concepts belong to a small number of recurrent types or *templates*. A template has the following entries:

[1] a pointer to a particular domain concept
[2] an explicit representation of a violation of intuitive expectations, either:
     [2a] a *breach* of relevant expectations for the category, or
     [2b] a *transfer* of expectations associated with another category;
[3] a link to (nonviolated) default expectations for the category.

For instance, most concepts of spirits, ghosts and ancestors correspond to a particular template, where [1] is a pointer to the category person, [2a] is the assumption that these special persons have counterintuitive physical properties (e.g., they can go through walls, violating "intuitive physics" for solid objects) and [3] specifies that these agents confirm all intuitive "theory of mind" expectations. These three features are found in most concepts of ghosts or spirits or gods, which is why we will say that they correspond to a single template. By contrast, concepts of statues that listen to people's prayers correspond to a different template, where [1] specifies the category artifact, [2b] mentions a transfer of intentional properties to these artifacts, and [3] confirms that ordinary physical properties of artifacts are still relevant.

Religious *concepts* are more specific than templates, in that they add to the template two other entries:

[4]   a slot for additional encyclopedic information;
[5]   a lexical label.

The Western concept of "ghost," for instance, implies the template described above, plus [4] information like "ghosts often come back to where they used to live" and [5] "ghost." The place-holder [4] is where all sorts of culturally specific information can be inserted, making the religious *concepts* of different places obviously different even though they may correspond to the same *templates*.

In this view, the reason why the "ghost" concept of a particular culture is easily transmitted lies not in the particulars of this concept but in the template it shares with other concepts of that type, found in many cultures. Anthropological evidence seems to support this prediction, in that limited violations of domain-level expectations constitute a narrow "catalogue" of templates that accounts for most kinds of supernatural concepts. The concepts found in the anthropological record generally include salient violations of intuitive expectations in their explicit characteristics; they also include tacit activation of nonviolated assumptions for the relevant domain-concepts (Boyer 1996a; Boyer 1996b).

The anthropological model suggests, first, that violations of intuitive expectations for domain-concepts are probably more salient than other types of cultural information, thereby leading to enhanced acquisition, representation and communication; second, that most inferences about religious concepts are driven by nonviolated, mostly tacit domain-level expectations, while explicit, consciously accessible, officially sanctioned theologies have little effect on representation and inference.

This latter point was illustrated by Barrett and Keil's work on God-concepts (Barrett and Keil 1996). This showed that even the most central aspects of a religious belief (e.g., for Christians, that God can attend to several events at once) are bypassed in favor of a more anthropomorphic concept (God like other agents attends to situations serially) when task demands require fast activation of an "on-line" God-concept. In story recall, participants produce inferences on the basis of their intuitive expectations about psychological functioning, even when these inferences contradict their official, reflective beliefs, an effect that was replicated in India (Barrett 1998). This would suggest that theologies have limited effects on concepts, compared with the inferential potential provided by domain-level expectations. This could explain a phenomenon familiar to most anthropologists: Although some theological systems do not correspond to the violation/default expectations model described above, their more widespread, "popular" interpretations generally distort the theological doctrine towards one of the templates described here (Boyer 1992).

The point of the present exploratory studies was to examine the effects of the violation part of the templates. We focused on the possible contribution of recall to the cultural fitness of "counterintuitive" concepts. Obviously, recall is only one of the conditions of cultural spread. Its effect interacts with the initial frequency of a particular cultural input, attention paid to that input, ease of reproduction, motivation for communication, conformism effects, and so forth to produce general cultural stability. We cannot limit what is represented to what is recalled. However, recall for particular input and distortions of cultural input created by individual recall are of prime interest because better recall is a condition of greater diffusion within a cultural environment (Sperber 1985; 1991). That is, considering opposite extremes for the sake of argument, we can expect, all else being equal, concepts that are very easy to recall to spread in a cultural environment and concepts that are intrinsically difficult to recall to spread less.

Surprisingly, there are few studies of recall for cultural material and their conclusions are ambiguous. On the basis of suggestive studies, Bartlett argued that recall is a "constructive" process that reframes exotic material in terms of familiar "schemata" (Bartlett 1932; Bergman and Roediger 1999). However, Bartlett's design made it difficult to set apart the contribution of "exotic" (nonculturally familiar) elements from that of expectation-violations. Higher recall for incongruous or surprising material is a familiar result from studies of story-recall (Hudson 1988; McCabe and Peterson 1990; Davidson 1994), of "memory for scripts" (Graesser et al. 1980; Brewer 1985), of naturally "scripted" situations (Nakamura et al. 1985), and of expectancy-incongruent material in the social domain (Stangor and McMillan 1992). However, in all these studies the elements that go against conceptual expectations also disrupt script-structure. In a typical religious narrative, by contrast, counterintuitive elements are neither peripheral nor disruptive. They constitute the focal points of the stories or events.

Semantic incongruity is also investigated in list designs, avoiding the possible confounds created by a narrative format. Such studies have generally shown classical "von Restorff" effects (von Restorff 1933; Hunt 1995). That is, in the same way as perceptually distinctive stimuli are recalled better than other ones, conceptually incongruous material is retrieved better than common conceptual associations in recall tasks (McDaniel and Einstein 1986; Schmidt 1991; Waddill and McDaniel 1998). The effect is probably not caused by differential encoding, since incongruous items that appear early in a list also produce the effect (Hunt 1995) and it does not always require the generation of bizarre mental imagery (Worthen 1997). Incongruous items enjoy an advantage at the representation or retrieval stage (Waddill and McDaniel 1998) which may depend upon two different processes: an intralist comparison that makes such items "distinctive" and a violation of expected associations with active schemas (Worthen 1997), although the specific process whereby incongruous information is compared to active schemata is not really elucidated (see Waddill and McDaniel 1998, 117–19). The empirical evidence accumulated over decades shows that intralist distinctiveness is a robust method for assessing the effects of incongruous conceptual associations. However, studies of distinctiveness have generally used violations of *kind-level* information, while religious concepts are mostly based on violations of *domain-level* information, which may engage different processes and lead to different recall effects.

To sum up, studies of memory effects on cultural material still leave open three questions. One is whether domain-level semantic incongruities of the type generally found in religious concepts trigger distinctive recall, which would help us understand why they are culturally widespread. A second question is whether these effects can over-ride culturally familiar, official theologies, as Barrett and Keil's results suggested. A third question is whether the recall effects of domain-level violations are found in different cultures, as suggested by the anthropological model described here.

To address these questions we used a series of free-recall tasks with essentially similar material in three different cultural settings, in France, Gabon and Nepal. We focused on the two categories that are most frequent in religious concepts, that of "person" and "artifact." Although religious systems include many other types of concepts (mountains, rivers, plants or clouds with supernatural properties) these two are by far the most frequent (Boyer 1996b). The stimuli consisted of quasi-stories, adapted from Barrett's studies of serial transmission (Barrett 1996), in which a narrative frame brackets a list of descriptions of various intuitive and counterintuitive situations (see Appendixes 1 and 2). Such narratives have a beginning and an end, there is a main character and something happens to him, thereby meeting minimal intuitive criteria for a "story" (Mandler et al. 1980; Brewer and Lichtenstein 1981; Ackerman et al. 1990). The format allowed us to produce a list of different situations none of which has any particular effect, disruptive or otherwise, on narrative structure. This quasi-story was suitably modified for other cultural settings, allowing us to use a task that made sense to non-Western participants.[2] We only used items that triggered no direct association with culturally familiar religious concepts.

Experiment 1

The first experiment contrasted standard situations with breaches of intuitive domain-level expectations: (i) nonstandard physical properties and (ii) non-standard psychological properties.

To evaluate the respective contributions of oddity and cultural familiarity, we also used two questionnaires to elicit (i) judgments of "oddity" for the situations described and (ii) judgments of familiarity, that is, whether participants thought they had previously encountered these situations in stories, films, cartoons, and so forth. We predicted a strong correlation between recall performance and the results of the first questionnaire (the distinctiveness literature suggests that items that are perceived to be odd are also recalled well) but no correlation with the second one (we conjectured that this effect would not be affected by how familiar the items were).

Method

Participants
Participants were recruited from humanities undergraduates (in various disciplines excluding psychology) at Université Lumière, Lyon. They took part in this experiment as the first part of a paid one-hour session. There were 18 participants (12 women, 6 men), aged 18 to 33 (M = 22, SD = 3).

Materials and Norming
The recall material consisted in a two-page story adapted from Barrett (1996). A diplomat is about to be sent as an ambassador to a distant galaxy. He goes to the local museum to get a better idea of what to expect over there. Between introduction (arrival at the museum) and end (return home), the main part of the text is a list of 24 short descriptions of exhibits in the museum. We used four versions of the stories, with identical items in different orders.

The story included 12 items for each of the Artifact and Person categories. In each category, six items described a breach of intuitive expectations ("Br" items) and the other six an expected association ("Sn" items). Person items consisted in colloquial descriptions of psychological features taken from the "theory of mind" literature, for example, "there were people who could see what was in front of them" (Sn) or "there were people who could see through a wall" (Br). The artifact items described physical features taken from the "intuitive physics" literature, for example, "pieces of furniture that you can move by pushing them" (Sn) and "pieces of furniture that float in the air if you drop them" (Br).[3] Order of presentation was counterbalanced.

All items were pre-tested with 18 students and staff of Université Lumière in three different conditions: asking them to rate the items as "normal vs. abnormal," "banal vs. surprising" and "familiar vs. unfamiliar." Items that reached less than 90% consensus were discarded. The remaining items were slightly modified to result in a similar sentence structure and roughly similar word-count. In the story, all items were described in two sentences, the second one being a straightforward paraphrase of the first.

A first questionnaire form (questionnaire 1–1) included all the items in the recall text, in a different order. Instructions read as follows: "The following sentences describe the different exhibits Mr. Wurg saw in the museum. For each sentence, indicate whether you find the object or person described similar or different from what we usually encounter in reality, by checking the appropriate box."

A second questionnaire (1–2) had the same list of items and different instructions: "The following sentences describe the different exhibits Mr. Wurg saw in the museum. Indicate whether each sentence describes an object or person that you have previously encountered, either in reality or in films, stories, cartoons, and so forth by checking the appropriate box."

Design and Procedure

This was a 2 (category) × 2 (level) design with both category (artifact vs. person) and level (standard items vs. breaches of expectations) as within-subject variables. The participants were all tested individually in an experimental booth. They were given the printed text of the story. The instructions were to read the story very carefully and try to imagine each situation described in the story. When they reached the end of the text they were instructed to hand back the text to the experimenter. As a distraction task, they were then asked to do some mental arithmetic and to multiply the number of vowels in various words. After this 5-minute distraction task, they were then given ruled sheets and instructed to write down as many of the exhibits in the museum as they could recall without regard for item order but with as much detail as they could recall. This part of the test was limited to ten minutes.

They were then given the two questionnaires and instructed to give spontaneous, literal responses and avoid metaphorical interpretations of the items. For the second questionnaire (1–2), the experimenter first asked the participant to explain the difference with questionnaire 1–1 and used two "training" questions to check that both fictional and real familiar items were assigned to the same category. The participants were then debriefed about the aims of the experiment and asked whether they saw any connection between the items and religious notions.

Results

Recall

The results are summarized in Fig. 1. Recall scores were raw number of items recalled by each participant in each cell. An item counted as recalled if the participants' version included (i) what made it a member of the stimulus categories and (ii) what made it different from other items.[4] Overall mean recall was 42.59% or 10.22 items out of 24 (SD = 3.56). A 2 (level) × 2 (category) analysis of variance (ANOVA) showed a significant effect of level (standard descriptions vs. breaches of expectations), $F(1, 17) = 26.5$, $p \leq 0.0001$, with better recall for Br items, a significant effect of category, $F(1, 17) = 22.22$, $p \leq 0.0001$, with better recall for Artifact items than Person items. There was no significant interaction between category and level, $F(1, 17) = 2.07$, $p = 0.167$.

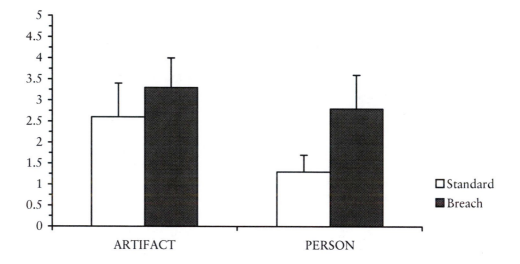

Figure 1. *Experiment 1. Mean number of Standard and Breach items recalled (max. 6) in the Artifact and Person categories, with 95% confidence intervals*

Questionnaire Results

They are summarized in Table 1. For questionnaire 1–1 (whether items are "different from what we find on Earth") a 2 (level) × 2 (category) ANOVA showed a significant effect of level, $F(1, 68) = 546$, $p \leq 0.0001$, a significant effect of category, $F(1, 68) = 8.05$, $p = 0.006$, as well as a significant interaction between level and category, $F(1, 68) = 4.6$, $p = 0.036$. For questionnaire 1–2 (whether items were "ever encountered before, either in fiction or in reality"), a 2 (level) × 2 (category) ANOVA showed a significant effect of level, $F(1, 68) = 128$, $p \leq 0.0001$, no effect of category, $F(1, 68) \leq 1$, and no interaction between category and level, $F(1, 68) \leq 1$.

		Standard	Breach
judged "different"	ARTIFACT	0.28 (0.826)	5.56 (0.97)
	PERSON	0.28 (0.461)	4.5 (1.09)
Judged "unfamiliar"	ARTIFACT	0 (-)	3 (1.75)
	PERSON	0.06 (0.24)	2.72 (1.18)

Table 1. *Experiment 1. Questionnaires 1-1 and 1-2. Mean number (and SD) of items judged "different from what is on Earth" and judged "not encountered before in fiction or reality" for Sn items (no breaches) and Br items (breaches) in two categories, Artifact and Person*

Correlation

There was a significant correlation between recall performance and the results of questionnaire 1–1 (items judged "different"), r = 0.474, p ≤ 0.0001, and a significant correlation between recall and items judged "unfamiliar," r = 0.373, p = 0.001.

Discussion

Recall results support the hypothesis that sentences that include a breach of expectations are recalled better than standard ones. Recall results also showed a category effect. Artifact items were recalled better than Person items in both Sn and Br item-types. This could be caused, either by an intrinsic advantage of artifact sentences or by an advantage of physical properties. In this design all the properties of artifacts were physical properties and all those associated with persons were psychological properties. Properties in a study of breaches cannot be fully crossed between categories, because artifacts do not include psychological or biological properties by default. Whether the effect was due to the properties or to the categories themselves is addressed in Experiment 2.

The results of Questionnaire 1–1 also showed both level and category were significant factors in judging that items are "different" from what is found on Earth. The level effect was expected, since the stimuli had been assigned to the Br or Sn cells on the basis of very similar pre-test questionnaires. The category effect showed that participants' judgments about the strangeness of breaches were less definite for psychological properties than for physical ones. This may help towards explaining the category effect in recall. If the participants found it easy to imagine counterintuitive psychological properties, these Br items would be less distinctive compared to Sn items than physical Br properties compared to Sn ones. There was an important divergence between the results of the two questionnaires, in the predicted direction. These results suggest a strong correlation between the fact that items are explicitly rated as "different" from what is found on Earth and the likelihood that they are remembered in the free recall task.

None of the participants saw any connection with religious concepts before the experimenter debriefed them.

Overall, these results support a "distinctiveness" interpretation of recall for semantically incongruous material. However, they also raise the question of what makes the Br items distinctive. It could be that the combinations of categories + properties were incongruous (our hypothesis) or that the properties by themselves were unfamiliar. Both interpretations are consistent with these results. This question is addressed in Experiment 2, where all properties are familiar ones.

Experiment 2

The point of Experiment 2 was to test the hypothesis that violations are recalled better than standard associations even if the properties themselves are familiar. This occurs in a transfer of properties across categories, a phenomenon that is common in religious representations (Boyer 1996b). An object or being is described as belonging to a particular category yet has properties usually excluded by membership in that category, for example, an artifact with cognitive capacities (e.g., a statue that listens to people) or a person with artifact properties (golems and other person-like beings assembled by someone). Such transfers do not require that one represents unfamiliar or impossible properties. In this way, Exp. 2 could test whether the results of Exp. 1 were caused by the incongruity of the situations described or by the oddity of the properties themselves. This experiment used similar properties for both artifact and person items, which should make it possible to evaluate the category differences observed in Exp. 1. The main hypothesis was that transfer items would be recalled better than no-transfer items. The story used was similar to that of Exp. 1, as were the two questionnaires following the recall test.

Method

Participants
Twenty-two Humanities, nonpsychologist majors (12 women, 10 men, aged 18 to 34, M = 21.6, SD = 3.73) at Université Lumière, Lyon were recruited as paid participants as part of a one-hour session.

Materials
The story frame was similar to that used in Exp. 1. The stories included items from two categories, Artifact and Person. For each category, there were six "Tr" items describing a transfer of expectations, that is, a category with a description of a feature that is usually expected for another category.

Six "Sn" items described properties that could be expected in members of that category. All sentences had been normed in the same way as in Experiment 1. There were four different versions of the stories with identical items in a different order.

For the Person category, Sn items described normal psychological properties. Tr items described the way the person had been made, for example, "people who are made of a rare metal," "people you can put together only with special tools," and so forth. For the Artifact category, psychological properties were Tr items and "manufacturing" properties were the Sn ones.

Design and Procedure
This was a 2 (category) × 2 (level) design with both category (artifact vs. person) and level (standard items vs. transfers of expectations) as within-subject variables. The procedure, as well as instructions for both questionnaires, were similar to those of Experiment 1.

Results

Recall
Mean recall rate was 49.43% or 11.86 items out of 24 (SD = 3.52). Results of the recall task were scored in the same way as for Exp. 1. Recall data are summarized in Fig. 2 below. A 2 (level) × 2 (category) ANOVA showed a significant effect of level (standard items vs. transfers of expectations), $F_{(1, 21)}$ = 4.84, $p = 0.039$, with higher recall rate for transfer items, a trend for category (person vs. artifact) below significance, $F_{(1, 21)}$ = 3.264, $p = 0.085$, and no significant interaction between level and category, $F_{(1, 21)} \leq 1$.

Questionnaire Results
They are summarized in Table 2 below. For 2–1, whether items were "different" or not from what is found on Earth, a 2 (level). 2 (category) ANOVA showed a significant effect of level, $F_{(1, 84)}$ = 359, $p = \leq 0.0001$, no significant effect of category, $F_{(1, 84)} \leq 1$, and no interaction between category and level, $F_{(1, 84)} \leq 1$. For questionnaire 2–2, where items were judged as "encountered before in fiction or reality" or not, a 2 (level) x 2 (category) ANOVA showed a significant effect of level, $F_{(1, 84)}$ = 39.8, $p = \leq 0.0001$, a trend but no significant effect for category, $F_{(1, 84)}$ = 3.47, $p = 0.066$, and a significant interaction between level and category, $F_{(1, 84)}$ = 10.88, $p = 0.0014$.

Correlation
There was a significant correlation between recall performance and the results of questionnaire 2–1 (items judged "different," $r = 0.255$, $p = 0.016$, but no significant correlation between recall and questionnaire 2–2 (items judged "unfamiliar"), $r = 0.035$, $p = 0.75$.

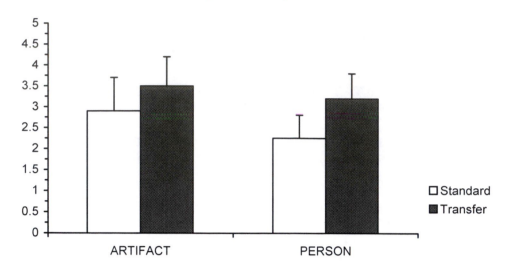

Figure 2. *Experiment 2. Mean number of standard and Transfer items recalled (max. 6) in the Artifact and Person categories, with 95% confidence intervals*

		Standard	Breach
judged "different"	ARTIFACT	0.273 (0.703)	5.14 (1.75)
	PERSON	0.045 (0.213)	5.05 (1.53)
Judged "unfamiliar"	ARTIFACT	0.455 (1.08)	1.409 (1.65)
	PERSON	0 (-)	3.05 (2.24)

Table 2. *Experiment 2. Questionnaires 2-1 and 2-2. Mean number (and SD) of items judged "different from what is on Earth" and judged "not encountered before in fiction or reality" for Sn items (no transfers) and Tr items (Transfers) in two categories, Artifact and Person*

Discussion

Recall results supported the hypothesis that items including a transfer of predicates from another category would be better recalled than items without such transfers. As expected, the results of questionnaire 2–1 correlate strongly with those of the recall task. The results of questionnaires 2–1 and 2–2 show that many items are judged both "nonstandard" and "encountered before," suggesting that recall is associated with distance from intuitive expectations more than with cultural familiarity.

Overall, Experiments 1 and 2 suggest that violating expectations or transferring them across categories produces a "distinctiveness effect" in a free recall task. In both studies we find that violations were recalled significantly better than standard items. This would be in keeping with the contention that "bizarreness" or "distinctiveness" effects are an effect of expectation-violation (Hirshman 1988). The items are compared with conceptual schemata and the discrepancy is sufficient to produce the effect. Waddill and McDaniel speculate that a comparison between target sentences and prior knowledge could occur very quickly during processing and tag atypical items with episodic information that boosts retrieval (Waddill and McDaniel 1998, 118). Such effects would support the anthropological conjecture, that recall effects may contribute to the cultural spread of violations of information at the domain level.

Experiment 3

Our results so far show that recall favors both breaches (properties that are appropriate for the category but violate expectations) and transfers (properties that are not appropriate for the category). This might suggest that combinations of these factors would trigger even stronger recall effects by presenting people with more obviously "supernatural" concepts. However, religious concepts rarely include such complex violations. In particular, combinations of breaches and transfers are virtually nonexistent in religious concepts, even in cultural settings where both breaches and transfers are common. For instance, many Catholics in Europe have representations of statues that listen (transfer), as well as a representation of a God who can hear sounds from anywhere in the world (breach). But they do not assume that listening statues can perceive distant sounds; people who pray to such statues generally stay within hearing distance, as it were, of the artifact.

That both breaches and transfers are common but not their combination cannot be a simple matter of conceptual overload, as the Christian God, for instance, combines many breaches (prescience, ubiquity, eternity, etc.). Our anthropological model would suggest that combinations are rare because they block inferences usually provided by the ontological category (in common conceptual associations) and preserved in the case of limited violations (breaches and transfers). If so, one would not expect the breach-transfer combinations to be recalled better than either breaches or transfers, although they are more distant from common associations.

Experiment 3 was designed to test whether recall also contributes to this other important feature of religious concepts. To do this, we tested free recall for items that combine the two factors studied so far. That is, they use properties that are intrinsically strange in their domain of application and apply it to an inappropriate domain. To allow comparisons with Experiments 1–2, we used essentially similar material and combined it to produce the following cells:

1. standard, no breach, no transfer ("Sn" items),
2. breach with no transfer ("Br" items),
3. transfer with no breach ("Tr" items),
4. breach with transfer ("BrTr" items).

A BrTr item includes a counterintuitive predicate and applies it to a category for which it is inappropriate. Consider for instance "only remembering what did not happen." This is a counterintuitive psychological property for any being or object that has a psychology: a person, but also an animal or an intelligent computer. If this kind of breach predicate is applied to categories of objects which do not normally have psychological processes (e.g., a piece of furniture), a transfer is added to the breach. Since we had some evidence from Experiments 1–2 that both transfer and breach contributed to better recall, this study could indicate how their effects are enhanced or cancelled when these factors are combined.

Method

Participants
Twenty-one undergraduate students at Université Lumière, Lyon (12 women and 9 men, aged 18 to 25, M = 21, SD = 2.1) participated as part of a paid one-hour session.

Materials
The narrative frame was the same as in Exp. 1 and 2. All the "exhibits" in the museum described properties of artifacts: standard physical properties (Sn), breaches of physical expectations (Br), standard psychological properties (Tr), breaches of psychological properties (BrTr). Some items were rephrased so that BrTr items were neither longer nor syntactically different from other item-types. We used four different versions to vary the order of presentation with identical items.

Design and Procedure
The main design was a 2 (breach) × 2 (transfer) design in which both category and level variables were manipulated within subjects. The procedure for recall tests as well as the questionnaire instructions were identical to those of Exp. 1-b.

Results

Recall
Overall mean recall was 40.01% or 9.62 items out of 24 (SD = 2.96). Fig. 3 breaks down recall rates by item-type.

A 2 (breach vs. no-breach) × 2 (transfer vs. no-transfer) ANOVA showed a significant effect of breach, F (1, 20) = 4.47, p = 0.0471, with higher recall for Breach items, no overall effect of transfer, F (1, 20) ≤ 1, and a significant interaction between breach and transfer, F (1, 20) = 10.28, p = 0.0044. Because of this interaction, we carried out a series of planned comparisons, summarized in Table 3.

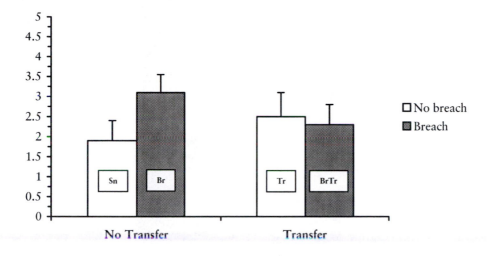

Figure 3. *Experiment 3. Mean number of No-Breach and Breach items recalled (max. 6) both No-Transfer and Transfer, with 95% confidence intervals*

These comparisons confirm that whether the property itself is counterintuitive (breach vs. no breach) has an effect only when the properties are appropriate for the category (no transfer). Whether the property is appropriate (Transfer × No-Transfers) has an effect on both intuitive and counterintuitive properties, but it goes in opposite directions. Transfer of a No-Breach property increases recall while transfer of Breach properties decreases recall.

	MS	F(1, 20)	p
1. No Transfer: Breach vs. No Breach	14.88	16.38	0.0006
2. With Transfer: Breach vs. No Breach	0.214	0.236	0.633
3. No Breach Items: Transfer vs. No-Transfer	4.02	4.43	0.0482
4. Breach items: Transfer vs. No-Transfer	5.37	5.898	0.0247

Table 3. *Experiment 3. Summary of planned comparisons*

Questionnaire Results
They are summarized in Table 4. For 3–1 (whether items were judged "different from what we find on Earth"), a 2 (breach vs. no-breach) 2 (transfer

× no-transfer) ANOVA showed a significant effect of breach, F (1, 80) = 80, p ≤ 0.0001, a significant effect of transfer, F (1, 80) = 152, p ≤ 0.0001, and a significant interaction, F (1, 80) = 76, p ≤ 0.0001. For questionnaire 3–2 (whether items were judged "encountered before, either in fiction or reality"), a 2 (breach vs. no-breach) × 2 (transfer vs. no-transfer) ANOVA showed a significant effect of breach, F (1, 80) = 51.41, p ≤ 0.0001, a significant effect of transfer, F (1, 80) = 41.5, p ≤ 0.0001, and no significant interaction, F (1, 80) ≤ 1.

		No breach	*With breach*
judged "different"	No transfer	.048 (.218) [Sn]	4 (1.095) [Br]
	With transfer	4.76 (1.09) [Tr]	4.81 (1.33) [BrTr]
Judged "not encountered"	No transfer	.143 (.478) [Sn]	1.952 (1.396) [Br]
	With transfer	1.762 (1.411) [Tr]	3.71 (1.271) [BrTr]

Table 4. *Experiment 3. Questionnaires 3-1 and 3-2. Mean number (and SD) of items judged "different from what is on Earth" and judged "not encountered before in fiction or reality" for four categories of items*

Correlation

There was a significant correlation between recall performance and the results of questionnaire 2–1 (items judged "different"), r = 0.341, p = 0.0014 but no correlation between recall and questionnaire 2–2 (items judged "unfamiliar"), r = 0.057, p = 0.61.

Discussion

The recall results showed an interaction between the two variables crossed to produce four categories of stimuli. As a result, properties that are intrinsically counterintuitive are recalled better if they are appropriate for the category, less if they are not. In contrast to possible extrapolations from the results of Experiments 1 and 2, combinations that represent the most salient departure from expected associations are not recalled better than simple breaches or transfers.

Decreased recall for material that is further removed from common schemata could be caused by the fact that BrTr items were (i) so strange they were "normalized" to Sn items by the subjects or (ii) misconstrued as Br or Tr items expressed in a complicated way or (iii) less clearly represented because of their inherent complexity. These explanations would predict confused renditions of BrTr items, which was not the case. In this as in Exp. 2, we found so few distorted items (or transfers to another cell, e.g., Sn items turned into Br) that their analysis was not possible. Besides, BrTr items were generally judged "different" from common representations and the most "unfamiliar" of all item-types. Compared to the other experiments, we find here a strong divergence between explicit judgment and recall. While BrTr items are rated "different" and "unfamiliar" more than any other item-types they are recalled less than either simple breaches or simple transfers.

That recall is optimal for limited violations and decreases with more bizarre material is a familiar result in memory research, and more generally illustrates Kagan's "stimulus-schema discrepancy" model, following which attention and recall are enhanced by limited departures from activated schemas but decrease as items are distorted beyond a certain limit (see, e.g., Zelazo and Shultz 1989; Bloom 1998). This effect was demonstrated in a variety of attentional and memory tasks for verbal and visual material. In this view, more bizarre material may result in decreased recall because it makes it less likely to activate the relevant schema. However, this operational understanding of "discrepancy" may denote very different phenomena, depending on the kind of "schema" activated. In the present case, what makes Breach + Transfer items different from other types is not that the relevant domain-level expectations were not activated, but that inferences on the basis of these expectations were blocked. An artifact that goes right through walls (Breach) still preserves some intuitive features of artifacts (it was made by people, for some purpose, etc.) and of physical objects (it has a location in space, a continuous trajectory, etc.). An artifact that thinks or has feelings (Transfer) still maintains intuitive features of solid objects and allows further inferences from psychological expectations (it has perception, memory, etc.). This latter domain of inferences is blocked in the case of BrTr items, described as having nonstandard psychological properties. One may speculate that this is one of the factors that lead to decreased recall as well as cultural rarity of such combinations of breaches and transfers.

Taken together, the results of Experiments 1–3 would seem to suggest that cultural familiarity is not a major factor in recall for limited violations of domain-level information. However, this last hypothesis was only supported by explicit judgments and these originated from a single cultural setting. To test this divergence between recall and cultural familiarity, one should test such material in different settings.

Experiment 4

To test the cross-cultural validity of the conclusions from Experiments 1–3, we chose to conduct a series of similar studies in a cultural setting where one of us had conducted anthropological fieldwork (Boyer 1990). This was a different context in terms not just of social and economic conditions but also of (i) people's everyday familiarity with religious concepts, (ii) the range of such concepts and (iii) their mode of transmission. By contrast to the secularized milieu in which our French participants live, most inhabitants of

Libreville, Gabon, are familiar with religious concepts and occurrences. That is, many events, either trivial or consequential, are readily construed as caused by supernatural agents. Second, concepts of such agents are much more diverse than in a Western context. Concepts from Christian denominations are completed with local witchcraft concepts and elaborate notions of ghosts and shadows (Boyer 1990). Third, information concerning such agents is acquired in the context of informal social interaction, not through literate sources or communication with specialized scholars.

Although the items were chosen from the same lists as in Exp. 1–3, this was not conducted as a straightforward replication, because of the special circumstances of this study. First, for this cultural setting we did not have a wealth of experimental results showing a recall effect for basic-level violations, as we did for Western subjects (see references to "distinctiveness" in the Introduction). We could not simply assume that such effects obtained with our Gabon participants, since one of our aims was precisely to test the cross-cultural validity of the schemata that make certain representations distinctive. We remedied this by adding a level of "basic-kind-level" violations to our lists. Our stories included items describing standard situations ("Standard" items, e.g., "a man who was slightly taller than a woman"), violations of kind-level information ("Kind-incongruous" items, e.g., "a man who could uproot a tree with his bare hands"), and category-level transfers or breaches ("Domain-incongruous" items, e.g., "a man who could walk right through a mountain"). Second, because of the increased number of items, we chose to manipulate category as a between-subject variable. Third, it proved impossible to use questionnaires to test the participants' judgments of cultural familiarity for the items, because of the sensitive nature of the topic.[5] We remedied this by pre-testing the items with assistants and eliminating all items that could evoke particular folk-tales or witchcraft themes.

Method

Participants

All participants were recruited informally at Libreville farmers' markets by a team of research assistants. Conditions for selection were (a) age (between 16 and 35), (b) French as first language and (c) educational level. We excluded participants who were either professionally engaged in literate work or deeply involved in religious activities. Participants were offered a small fee (a soft drink) for their participation. There were 81 participants (39 women, 42 men), age ranging from 16 to 37 (M = 24.3, SD = 4.59).

Materials

The stories were similar to those used in Exp. 1-b, with the exception of the narrative frame that bracketed the list of items. In the stories used here, an orphan leaves his village to seek fortune and returns empty-handed but with an account of all the villages he has visited. Stories of this kind are very common in Central Africa. There were two versions of the story, with Artifact and Person items respectively, each including six "Standard," six "Kind-incongruous" and six "Domain-Incongruous" items.

The items were taken from the lists used with the Lyon participants. They were pre-tested with a group of 10 undergraduate students at Libreville University, in the same way as in Exp. 1-b. We also asked subjects whether they could think of religious rituals or magical activities or folk-tales that included persons or artifacts described in the list and removed items that triggered such associations.

Design and Procedure

This was a mixed 2 (category) × 3 (level) design, with category (Artifact vs. Person) a between-subject variable and level (Standard, Kind-incongruous, Domain-incongruous) a within-subject variable. Pilots showed that it was not desirable to conduct the experiment in the special rooms available on campus. In this culture, being taken to a secluded place would be highly unnatural and suspicious. So a team of linguistics and anthropology students at the University of Libreville visited various markets and chose a quiet place where they could work in people's sight but without too much interference. Our assistants had been trained in interview techniques and the identification of first language.[6] They tested the participants one by one, asking them, first, various questions about occupation, educational level, age and first language. They then read the stories, presented as a test for text-comprehension. (Pilots showed that people explicitly tested for memory would generally refuse to take part.) After reading the stories, the experimenters asked them to perform elementary sums. They were then asked to relate what happened in the story in as much detail as possible. This was recorded by the experimenter. The subjects were then all debriefed about the purpose of the experiment.

Results

Recall was scored in the same "conservative" way as in Exp. 1-c and 2. We discarded confused renditions and distortions that included material from several items. Overall mean recall over both conditions was 31.62% or 6.075 items out of 18 (SD = 2.58). Mean recall was 6.43 items (SD = 2.86) in the Person condition and 5.69 items (SD = 2.2) in the Artifact condition.

A mixed 2 (category) × 3 (level) ANOVA on these results showed no effect of category, $F (1, 79) = 1.66$, $p = 0.201$, and a significant effect of level, $F (2, 79) = 8.39$, $p = 0.0003$. There was no interaction between category and level. However, there were some very low scores (one or two items recalled) that suggested that some participants had not grasped the point of the experiment, which was confirmed by subsequent interviews. To check whether these would produce spurious effects, we performed an additional ANOVA on recall performance exclusive of participants with low scores (participant's total number of items recalled $\leq$ (M -1 SD) in each condition). This produced similar results: no effect of category, F (1, 70) $\leq$ 0.41, a significant effect of level, F (2, 70) = 9.4, p = 0.0001, and no significant interaction between level and category, F (2, 70) = 0.23.

Fig. 4 illustrates these results, excluding very low scores.

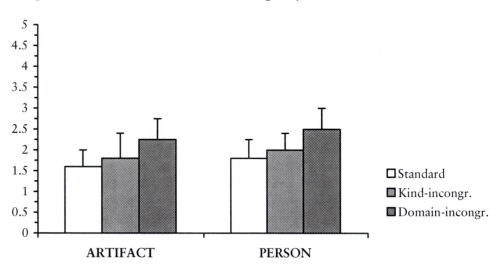

Figure 4. *Experiment 4. Mean number of items recalled, in two conditions (Artifact and Person) for three categories of items: Standard, Kind-incongruous and Domain-incongruous*

We also ran a series of related t tests to produce pairwise comparisons between conditions, summarized in Table 5.

		t (38)	p
	Standard vs. Kind-incongruity	0.407	0.6865
ARTIFACT	Kind- vs. Domain-incongruity	2.399	0.0225
	Standard vs. Domain-incongruity	2.639	0.0116
		t (32)	p
	Standard vs. Kind-incongruity	0.884	0.382
PERSON	Kind- vs. Domain-incongruity	2.44	0.019
	Standard vs. Domain-incongruity	2.588	0.0136

Table 5. *Experiment 4. Summary of comparisons between levels of recall for different item-types in the Artifact and Person conditions*

Discussion

These results support the main hypothesis, that violations of domain-level information trigger high recall for both artifact and person concepts. The main result was the significant difference between "Standard" and "Domain-incongruity" items, supporting the hypothesis that violations at the domain level trigger better recall than standard conceptual associations, in this cultural setting in the same way as with our French subjects.

Taken together, the results of Exp. 1–4 suggest that cultural differences have no noticeable effect on recall for category-level violations. Experiment 4 showed that neither everyday familiarity with concepts that include violations, nor a greater variety of such concepts, influence such effects, once the information that makes these violations familiar is removed. Finding similar recall effects across cultures suggests, first, that the links between the categories and the predicates used are represented in a similar fashion in these two cultures. This in itself is not too surprising, in the sense that pre-testing of the items revealed very few differences in judgment between French and Gabonese participants. We did not expect the person or artifact categories to be so different that such properties as "can see through walls" (for person) or "is sad when it is left alone" (for artifact) would be judged "normal" or "usual" in Gabon. More important, these results also show that such similar links between categories and properties result in similar recall performance for violations of those properties.

However, there might be a bias here. Despite cultural differences, our French and Gabonese groups were both taken from populations with minimal exposure to scholarly, literate religion. These were representative of both populations, though for different reasons (secularization in France, mainly oral transmission in Gabon). Now it could be argued that the cross-culturally similar sensitivity to violations observed here might be modified by the presence and cultural salience of scholarly religion, a question addressed in Experiment 5.

Experiment 5

This was conducted in a cultural setting where one of us had conducted anthropological fieldwork (Ramble 1984). The population from which we selected participants (Tibetan monks in Katmandu) offered several advantages for this study. First, this is a place where religious concepts are generally influenced by the canonical teachings of specialized Lamaist institutions. Second, the monks we worked with are experts in such concepts. They spend much of their time studying sacred texts that give explicit descriptions of the special characteristics of religious agents and situations. Their tradition (Bon) is broadly similar to Tibetan Buddhist tradition[7] in that it places great emphasis on ways to change one's cognitive and emotive processes in order to reach a higher form of consciousness. A whole range of exercises, for example, meditation, sensory deprivation, altered states of consciousness, and so forth, are used to effect such transformations (Ramble 1984). The texts monks read and study include many accounts of extraordinary feats performed as a result of such mental training.

This offered us an opportunity to test the relative validity of two interpretations of the cognitive effects of such literate theological versions of religious concepts. Most anthropological models, while noting the differences between official and popular theologies, assume that literacy has a profound influence on both "official" descriptions of religious concepts and their "popular" form (Goody 1977; 1986). By contrast, Barrett and Keil have presented suggestive evidence that the effects of official theologies are limited when task demands require fast, "on-line" inferences about religious agency (Barrett and Keil 1996; Barrett 1998). Our experiment was relevant to another aspect of this question, that of the relative salience of types of violations used in a theology. Since person violations are a privileged theme in this cultural setting, one could expect that items including such violations would be better recalled than artifact items, if familiarity with theological themes was an important factor driving recall. If, on the other hand, violations of intuitive expectations were the main factor, then artifact violations would be advantaged by the fact that they belong to less familiar templates.

Method

Participants
All participants were monks of the Triten Norbutse monastery in Katmandu. They were all native speakers of Tibetan. Participants were selected on grounds of age and literacy. There were 30 participants, all male, age ranging from 14 to 30 (M = 22.45, SD = 4.6). Although this spans a wide age-range, all participants were more or less at the same stage in their curriculum, that is, they were all novices or young monks with roughly equivalent experience of monastery teaching and the consequent familiarity with literacy (at least four years).

Materials
The recall materials, as in Exp. 1-c, consisted in a quasi-story with an embedded list of 18 two-sentence descriptions of different situations. The narrative frame from Exp. 1-c was modified to use a culturally familiar format. In this story, a trader returns to his village and tells his friends of all the things and people he has encountered. There were two versions of the story, one with descriptions of people with particular characteristics (PER

items) and the other one with artifacts (ART items) in all three levels. Item order was then counterbalanced to produce four different versions of each story.

Both stories were translated into Tibetan by C. Ramble with the help of Tenpa Yungdrung, vice-abbot of the Triten Norbutse monastery, to achieve a sufficiently idiomatic Tibetan rendition of the items. Items were modified (i) if they were made confusing by local idioms, (ii) if they happened to correspond too closely to some local story or belief, or (iii) if they were just unintelligible given the cultural context. The stories were back-translated to check that the items were still essentially similar to those of Experiment 4. They were printed in Tibetan script and Xeroxed to produce handouts for the participants.

Design and Procedure

This mixed design was similar to that of Experiment 4, with category (Artifact vs. Person) as a between-subject variable and level (Standard, Kind-incongruous, Domain-incongruous) as a within-subject variable.

The participants were gathered by the vice-abbot and informed that they would take part in an informal "test." They were not told that this would be a memory test. They were given the handouts and instructed to read them attentively. After about 15 minutes, they were asked to give the scripts back and to write down their name and age on a sheet of paper. As a distractor task, they were then asked to do sums and take down the results. They were then asked to write down all they could remember of the situations encountered by the hero in as much detail as possible, regardless of the order of items in the story. The experimenters then debriefed the participants about the purpose of the experiment.

Results

An item scored as positive if participant's version included the particular details that made it a member of the category and distinguished it from other items in the story. This excluded a number of cases for which the participants had mixed information from several items. Overall mean recall over both conditions was 38.52% or 6.93 items out of 18 (SD = 1.55). The mean number of items recalled was 6.06 items (SD = 2.9) in the Person condition and 8.08 items (SD = 2.69) in the Artifact condition. Recall data are summarized in Fig. 5 below, with results broken down by category and level.

A mixed 2 (category) × 3 (level) ANOVA showed a trend for category with a slightly higher recall rate for Artifact items, $F (1, 29) = 3.79$, $p = 0.061$. There was a significant effect of level, $F (2, 29) = 5.13$, $p = 0.012$, with Ontological items best recalled, followed by Basic and Standard items in both categories. There was no significant interaction between category and level.

As in the Libreville study and for similar reasons, we performed an additional ANOVA on recall performance exclusive of low scores (x ≤ (M −1SD) in each condition) to check for spurious effects induced by very low scores. This shows no effect or trend for category, $F (1, 21) ≤ 1$, a significant effect of level, $F (2, 21) = 5.7$, $p = 0.0065$ and a trend interaction, $F (2, 21) = 2.79$, $p = 0.078$.

Fig. 5 summarizes these results exclusive of very low scores.

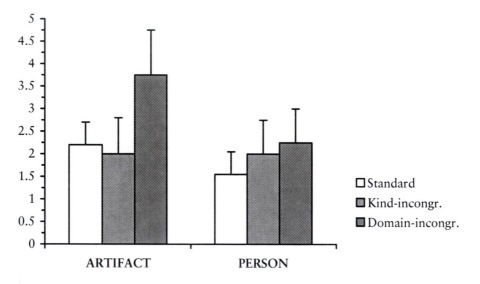

Figure 5. *Experiment 5. Mean number of items recalled, in two conditions (Artifact and Person) for three categories of items: Standard, Kind-incongruous and Domain-incongruous*

As in the Gabon experiment, we also ran a series of related t tests to produce pairwise comparisons between conditions, summarized in Table 6.

		$t (13)$	p
	Standard vs. Kind-incongruous	0.144	0.887
ARTIFACT	Kind incongr. vs. Domain-incongr.	3.33	0.0054
	Standard vs. Domain-incongr.	3.87	0.0019
	Standard vs. Kind-incongruous	1.33	0.205
PERSON	Kind incongr. vs. Domain-incongr.	0.467	0.648
	Standard vs. Domain-incongr.	1.75	0.102

Table 6. *Experiment 5. Summary of comparisons between levels of recall for different item-types in the Artifact and Person conditions*

Discussion

These results support the main hypothesis, that items including domain-level violations are generally recalled better than common conceptual associations, while violations of kind-level information do not produce such effects. However, finer-grained analysis shows that the contrast between levels of violation is only observed in the artifact category. Indeed, in that category Domain-level violations are recalled significantly better than Kind-violations. This did not result from a general advantage for all artifact cells or for all nonstandard artifact items. The category-difference was mainly driven by very high recall in the Domain-level violation artifact cell, in contrast to the Gabon results where there was little difference between the two categories.

This difference may be explained by the special cultural context of this study. Although person violations are common in the culture and in the specialized texts monks are familiar with, the participants recalled artifact violations much better than all other types of items. This suggests that cultural familiarity with a certain *type* of violations (what we called a "template" in Introduction) does not result in better recall. One could speculate that violations of a type that is *not* used in the participants' culture are more salient because they seem more "strange" or "novel" or "exotic." Note that this effect concerns the familiarity of *templates*, not *concepts*. In these studies, we took care to remove items that triggered direct associations with familiar concepts.

More generally, this specific result may add to the evidence provided by Barrett and Keil concerning the resilience of intuitive, on-line concepts in situations of literate, theologically informed religion (Barrett and Keil 1996). Although our subjects were trained to pay special attention to person-violations, this did not offset the novelty and intrinsic counterintuitive quality of artifact-violations.

Compared with the French and Gabonese studies, this experiment confirmed that overall recall performance was not much affected by the conditions of the test, as the rate of recall (M = 6.93 items out of 18) is quite similar to that of Gabon participants (M = 6.075). In comparison with the French results, this would tend to suggest that recall was affected more by the familiarity of the task (our French participants were used to academic tests) than by literacy in general or by the presence of literate religion (texts that describe violations) in the cultural environment.

General Discussion

The purpose of present studies was to examine the contribution of recall to the spread of religious concepts in different cultural settings. We used a familiar and robust method—differential recall in a within-list design—to test hypotheses concerning the structure of religious concepts. In particular, we tested recall for material that includes violations of domain-level information, since such violations are a common feature of religious concepts.

The results supported the hypothesis that violations (either breaches of relevant expectations for a domain or transfers of expectations from one domain to another) produce a retrieval advantage (Experiments 1, 2). This might have suggested that stimuli that combine such breaches and transfers, thereby producing material that is further removed from common conceptual associations than simple breaches and transfers, would be recalled better. The opposite is the case, which could explain why such combinations are not culturally widespread (Experiment 3). The fact that some items were identified as culturally familiar was not significantly correlated with recall (Experiments 1, 2, 3). This might indicate that sensitivity to violations of category-level information is not influenced by cultural familiarity.

Indeed, recall results show that the tendency to recall such material is stable across cultures (Experiments 4, 5). Differential recall for domain-level violations remains despite cultural differences in people's commitment to actual religious concepts, in the range of concepts (limited sources vs. various sources), or in the prevalent mode of transmission (literate vs. oral). This would suggest that some recurrent features of religious concepts may be explained to some extent by a specific sensitivity to violations of ontological category information. This sensitivity does not seem to be substantially modified by the participants' cultural background, their familiarity with or commitment to religious beliefs, the kind of religious concepts used in their cultures or their mode of transmission. The results also support the anthropological conjecture, that the reasons why some ways of representing supernatural agency are recurrent between cultures and stable in a culture are to be found, not in the specifics of cultural concepts but in the structure of more abstract templates. Each culture may or may not make use of a particular template. For instance, we find many notions of artifacts with intentional properties in modern European cultures but few concepts of artifacts with biological properties (apart from the occasional Madonna shedding tears on Good Friday).

One could have expected such cultural differences to boost recall for novel concepts that use familiar templates. However, we did not observe this effect. On the contrary, we found that Tibetan monks, who are familiar with many person-template concepts, recalled artifact items from templates that are not used in their culture (Experiment 5). Paradoxically, they were much less likely to recall person-domain violations. This suggests that cultural use of one kind of template does not hinder sensitivity to other ones, adding support to Barrett and Keil's studies of religious concepts (Barrett and Keil 1996). The protocols were different, as Barrett and Keil studied distortions in recall (not straight recall) for religious agents (in contrast with our non-religious items). However, the results converge in suggesting that a general sensitivity to certain types of supernatural concepts is only partly influenced by official and explicitly accessible theologies.

We did not observe differences related to the varying level of literacy (high in France and in this specific Tibetan population, low among our Gabonese participants). This is somewhat surprising given the well-established influence of literacy on many conceptual tasks, including recall. A possible interpretation would be that the present tasks are not really sensitive enough to reveal such differences (nor were they designed to test them). The massive effect of distinctiveness for domain-level violations might conceal some consequences of literacy. Also, the effects of literacy may be more important when participants are tested with the kind of material that they usually find in written sources (e.g., sacred texts for the Tibetan monks). (This was excluded here given our decision to use nonreligious material.) So the precise effects of literacy might be illuminated by running further studies with material that is much closer to familiar sources.

In Experiments 4 and 5 we also found a step-wise recall effect with kind-level violations recalled better than standard associations but less than domain-level violations. These results are far from conclusive, but they suggest that violations of expectations may have different cognitive effects, depending on the level of conceptual information that is affected. Indeed, violations of domain-level information trigger specific intuitions of sentence anomaly (Gerard and Mandler 1983) and specific event-related potential signatures (Polich 1985) that do not occur with syntactic anomalies (Ainsworth-Darnell, Shulman, and Boland 1998).

Why are *limited* violations optimal? Recall for violations illustrates familiar effects of incongruity. Bizarre items are recalled better both because they are "distinctive" in the stimuli-lists and because they violate expectations for the schemas activated (Hirshman 1988; Schmidt 1991; Hunt and Smith 1996; Waddill and McDaniel 1998). This might predict that increases in "bizarreness" would lead to better recall, which is not the case. Items that activate a particular domain-concept but block standard inferences from that concept are not recalled as well as those that maintain such default inferences.

The result suggests that representation of bizarre items does not necessarily end with a check-list in terms of compatibility with activated schemata, but also triggers inferences about possible scenarios that include the object described. The ease with which such inferences are generated may be an important factor in boosting retrieval.[8] This interpretation in terms of inferential potential may explain why most culturally successful religious concepts only use *limited* violations of domain-level information, as illustrated not just in the domain of religious concepts, but also in mythologies, where metamorphoses for instance typically occur between taxonomically close ontological categories (e.g., from person to animal) more often than between distant ones (e.g., from person to artifact) (Kelly and Keil 1985).

Our experiments focused on the role of recall and inference in cultural transmission. By contrast, cognitive anthropologists interested in religion have often stressed the fact that supernatural agency is "useful" in producing causal explanations of various unexplained events (Whitehouse 1992; Strauss and Quinn 1997; Bloch 1998). In the present view, these two interpretations are congruent. That cultural concepts can be used in causal explanations (and be selected by virtue of their potential for such use) requires that they trigger sufficiently rich inferences. Differential recall and explanatory "usefulness" might be two consequences of the connections established between particular cultural input and universal domain-level expectations.

Appendix 1:
Literal Translation of Sample Story from Experiment 2

Mr. Wurg was about to be sent as an ambassador to the Zenon 3 galaxy. He wanted to know what things are like over there before leaving. So he went to the Arts and Sciences Museum, where two halls contain exhibits about Zenon 3.

In the first hall, there were exhibits about the various kinds of furniture you can find in houses in the Zenon 3 galaxy. Some of these objects are like what you find here on Earth, and others are really different. There are objects that can be taken apart to be fixed. You can take a part out to change it. There are objects that are aware of what's around them. They know what's going on. There are objects that see what's in front of them. They can perceive what is opposite. There are objects made with parts from other objects. Someone took bits of other objects to make them. There are objects that hide away when they're scared. If something frightens them they run for cover. There are objects designed by engineers. These people made a blueprint of the objects before making them. There are objects that hear sounds around them. They can perceive sounds not too far from them. There are objects made by people as a hobby. They like spending a Sunday making them. There are objects that go where they want to go. If they plan to get somewhere they just go there. There are objects made of a special metal that's hard to melt. It is difficult to make objects in that metal. There are objects manufactured in small workshops. There are small places where people make them. There are objects that can notice people are staring at them. If someone looks at them they notice it.

In the second hall, there were exhibits about the various kinds of people who live in Zenon 3. Some of these people are very much like us and others are very different. There are people who remember the past. They can recall what happened to them. There are people who are sad when they are alone. They don't like being on their own. There are people you put together with a screwdriver. You screw the parts together to make them. There are people who try to do what they want. If they want to do something they try it. There are people who are made by machines. Special machines turn them out. There are people who can read books. If they open a book they can read it. There are people made of plaster. One uses plaster to make them. There are people who are manufactured when necessary. When you need more you make some. There are people who don't like being bossed around. If you bully them they don't like it. There are people who must be fine-tuned after installation. They must be adjusted after they are put into use. There are people you can fix yourself. If there is a breakdown you can fix them. There are people who understand jokes. They can get what is funny in a joke.

After he had seen all these exhibits, Mr. Wurg went back to the main lobby of the Museum of Arts and Sciences. He had a coffee at the museum cafeteria. He then went back home and cooked his dinner.

Appendix 2:
Literal Translation of Sample Story from Experiment 5, Person Condition

Nyima is a trader who has been to many places. One day, after he had come back from a journey to distant places, he told his friends about the people he had seen in those far-away countries. Some of those people are like you and me and others seem very different.

There was a person who was at two places at the same time. He was at one place and at another place at the same moment. There was another person who was visible if you put on the light. You could see him in daylight too. There was another person who could hear past conversations. He could hear the sounds of what people said in the past. There was another person who weighed more than an ox. It was terribly difficult to lift him. There was another person who could guess future events. He knew exactly what was going to happen. There was another person who was taller than a house. He was very tall and impressive. There was another person who could hear what people said. If people talked next to him he heard what they said. There was another person who ran faster than a horse. He went so fast that the horse could not catch up with him. There was another person who went through walls. If he wanted he could walk right through a wall. There was one person who had no shadow. Even in broad daylight, he did not have a shadow. There was another person who could understand jokes. If you told him a joke he laughed. There was another person who could see through a mountain. He could see what was on the other side of the mountain. There was another person who could remember thousands of different names. He recalled the names of thousands of people. There was another person who could see what was in front of him. If you placed an object next to him he saw it. There was another person who could see villages very far away. He could even see villages many miles away. There was another person who was five feet tall. His height was a little above that of a woman. There was another person who was at one place at a time. If he was somewhere you could see him there. There was another person who has read thousands of books. He has read huge collections of books.

Nyima had finished telling people what he had seen in these far-away places. He told them that after he had traveled to those places he had felt homesick, and that was why he had come back to be with his family.

Acknowledgments

Research for this paper was funded by a special grant (#AS41) from the "Cognisciences" Program of the Ministry for Scientific Research, France. The Lyons experiments were conducted at the Laboratoire d'Etude des Mécanismes Cognitifs, Université Lumière, Lyon, with assistance from Professor Nathalie Bedoin and Dr Hervé Bruni. The Gabon studies were conducted at the Ecole Normale Superieure de Libreville with generous support from its Director, Professor Auguste Moussirou-Mouyama as well as from Professor Patrick Mouguiama-Daouda, Université de Libreville. For help with the Katmandu experiments we are grateful to the Abbot of Triten Norbutse monastery, Katmandu for allowing us to run this study, to Vice-Abbot Tenpa Yungdrung for his generous help, and to the monks who participated. Thanks to Harvey Whitehouse, Sheila Walker, Carlo Severi, Michael Houseman, E. Thomas Lawson, Robert McCauley and especially Justin Barrett and Sandra Waxman for comments on a draft version of this paper.

Notes

* This article was originally published in *Cognitive Science* V.25 (4) (2001): 535–64.

1. It is still debated whether the development and adult representations of domain concepts requires prior principles or only abstraction from knowledge of kind-concepts (see Quinn and Johnson 1997 for an alternative to principle-based scenarios). However, the end-point of the developmental path is clear: specific information is stored in domain-concepts as opposed to kind or "entry-level" concepts (Jolicoeur et al. 1984; Chumbley 1986; Kosslyn et al. 1995). Also, some cognitive pathologies display a selective loss of information that affects a whole domain (e.g. living things) but only impairs kind-level in that domain (e.g., names for living things); see, for example, Warrington and Shallice 1984; Shallice 1987; Sartori et al. 1994; Moss, Tyler, and Jennings 1997; Kurbat and Farah 1998.

2. This kind of narrative format is found the world over, for example, in shamans' narratives or pilgrim's accounts, where narrative structure reduces to a list of distinctive places or situations with no causal connections between the episodes.

3. We used the term "pieces of furniture" rather than "objects," "machines" or "artifacts" because the former corresponds to a single, basic-level and frequent lexeme in French ("meuble"). This also blocked possible associations with intelligent machines, supercomputers, etc.

4. For instance, given the stimulus "there were pieces of furniture that could float in the air," neither "there were strange pieces of furniture" nor "there were people that flew around in a room" counted as recall. On the other hand, "there were funny pieces of furniture; they go up rather than down if you let go of them, and people are surprised" was scored as positive.

5. Formal questionnaires are awkward with nonschooled participants in the first place. Also, claiming in this cultural setting that one "knows about" a topic such as witchcraft implies that one is a practitioner.

6. Identifying (linguistically relevant) first language is not always easy in an urban African setting. About half of the population of Libreville have French as their first language, due to frequent marriages between members of different linguistic groups.

7. It is largely debated in Tibet and Nepal whether Bon is a variant of Buddhism or an altogether different doctrine. However, these debates (however politically charged) are academic in the present context. Like Buddhist traditions, Bon teaches that we are trapped like all other creatures, including gods, in a never-ending cycle of reincarnations as beings who desire and therefore suffer. It is possible to escape from this cycle by realizing how false or illusory "reality" is. On Bon-Po and Buddhist doctrines, the best source is Snellgrove (1959, especially 19–33; see also Ramble 1984).

8. However, it must be noted that spontaneous inferences in sentence-understanding and differences in richness between inferences are not necessarily mysterious phenomena. They are precisely described in pragmatic theories of utterance comprehension (Sperber and Wilson 1995) and some aspects of this "relevance" approach are experimentally testable (Jorgensen, Miller, and Sperber 1984; Sperber, Cara, and Girotto 1995).

References

Ackerman, B. P., K. Spiker, and I. Glickman. 1990. Children's Sensitivity to Topical Discontinuity in Judging Story Adequacy. *Developmental Psychology* 26: 837–44.

Ainsworth-Darnell, K., H. G. Shulman, and J. E. Boland. 1998. Dissociating Brain Responses to Syntactic and Semantic Anomalies: Evidence from Event-Related Potential. *Journal of Memory and Language* 38: 112–30.

Barrett, J. L. 1996. *Anthropomorphism, Intentional Agents, and Conceptualizing God*. Unpublished PhD dissertation, Cornell University.

—1998. Cognitive Constraints on Hindu Concepts of the Divine. *Journal for the Scientific Study of Religion* 37: 608–19.

—2000. Exploring the Natural Foundations of Religion. *Trends in Cognitive Science* 4(1): 29–34.

Barrett, J. L., and F. C. Keil. 1996. Conceptualizing a Non-natural Entity: Anthropomorphism in God Concepts. *Cognitive Psychology* 31: 219–47.

Bartlett, F. C. 1932. *Remembering: A Study in Experimental and Social Psychology*. Cambridge: Cambridge University Press.

Bergman, E. T., and H. L. I. Roediger. 1999. Can Bartlett's Repeated Reproduction Experiments be Replicated? *Memory and Cognition* 27: 937–47.

Bloch, M. 1992. *Prey into Hunter: The Politics of Religious Experience*. Cambridge: Cambridge University Press.

—1998. *How We Think They Think. Anthropological Approaches to Cognition, Memory And Literacy*. Boulder, CO: Westview Press.

Bloom, P. 1998. Theories of Artifact Categorization. *Cognition* 66: 87–93.

Boyer, P. 1990. *Tradition as Truth and Communication: A Cognitive Description of Traditional Discourse*. Cambridge: Cambridge University Press.

—1992. Explaining Religious Ideas: Outline of a Cognitive Approach. *Numen* 39: 27–57.

—1994. *The Naturalness of Religious Ideas: A Cognitive Theory of Religion*. Berkeley/Los Angeles: University of California Press.

—1996a. Cognitive Limits to Conceptual Relativity: The Limiting-case of Religious Categories. In *Rethinking Linguistic Relativity*, ed. J. Gumperz and S. Levinson. Cambridge: Cambridge University Press.

—1996b. What Makes Anthropomorphism Natural: Intuitive Ontology and Cultural Representations. *Journal of the Royal Anthropological Institute* (n.s.) 2: 1–15.

Boyer, P., and S. J. Walker. 1999. Intuitive Ontology and Cultural Input in the Acquisition of Religious Concepts. In *Imagining the Impossible: Magical, Scientific and Religious Thinking in Children*, ed. K. Rosengren, C. Johnson, and P. Harris. Cambridge: Cambridge University Press.

Brewer, W. F. 1985. The Story Schema: Universal and Culture-specific Properties. In *Literacy, Language and Learning*, ed. D. R. Olson, N. Torrance, and A. Hildyard. Cambridge: Cambridge University Press.

Brewer, W. F., and E. H. Lichtenstein. 1981. Event Schemas, Story Schemas and Story Grammars. In *Attention and Performance*, ed. J. Long and A. Baddeley. Hillsdale, NJ: Erlbaum.

Carey, S. 1985. *Conceptual Change in Childhood*. Cambridge, MA: MIT Press.

Child, A. B., and I. L. Child. 1993. *Religion and Magic in the Life of Traditional Peoples*. Englewood Cliffs, NJ: Prentice Hall.

Chumbley, J. I. 1986. The Roles of Typicality, Instance Dominance, and Category Dominance in Verifying Category Membership. *Journal of Experimental Psychology: Learning, Memory, and Cognition* 12: 257–67.

Davidson, D. 1994. Recognition and Recall of Irrelevant and Interruptive Atypical Actions in Script-based Stories. *Journal of Memory and Language* 33: 757–75.

Dulaney, S., and A. P. Fiske. 1994. Cultural Rituals and Obsessive Compulsive Disorder: Is there a Common Psychological Mechanism? *Ethos* 22: 243–83.

Gelman, R. 1990. Structural Constraints on Cognitive Development: Introduction. *Cognitive Science* 14: 3–9.

Gerard, A. B., and J. M. Mandler. 1983. Ontological Knowledge and Sentence Anomaly. *Journal of Verbal Learning and Verbal Behavior* 22: 105–20.

Goldman, R. 1964. *Religious Thinking from Childhood to Adolescence*. London: Routledge and Kegan Paul.

Goody, J. R. 1977. *The Domestication of the Savage Mind*. Cambridge: Cambridge University Press.

—1986. *The Logic of Writing and the Organization of Society*. Cambridge: Cambridge University Press.

Gopnik, A. 1993. How We Know our Minds: The Illusion of First-person Knowledge of Intentionality. *Brain and Behavioral Sciences* 16: 1–14.

Graesser, A. C., S. B. Woll, D. J. Kowalski, and D. A. Smith. 1980. Memory for Typical and Atypical Actions in Scripted Activities. *Journal of Experimental Psychology (Human Learning and Memory)* 6: 503–15.

Guthrie, S. E. 1993. *Faces in the Clouds: A New Theory of Religion*. New York: Oxford University Press.

Hirshman, E. 1988. The Expectation-violation Effect: Paradoxical Effects of Semantic Relatedness. *Journal of Memory and Language* 27: 40–58.

Houseman, M., and C. Severi. 1998. *Naven and Ritual*. Leiden: Brill.

Hudson, J. A. 1988. Children's Memory for Atypical Actions in Script-based Stories: Evidence for Disruption Effect. *Journal of Experimental Child Psychology* 46: 159–73.

Hunt, R. R. 1995. The Subtlety of Distinctiveness: What Von Restorff Really Did. *Psychonomic Bulletin and Review* 2: 105–12.

Hunt, R. R., and R. E. Smith. 1996. Accessing the Particular from the General: The Power of Distinctiveness in the Context of Organization. *Memory and Cognition* 24: 217–25.

Jolicoeur, P., M. Gluck, and S. M. Kosslyn. 1984. Pictures and Names: Making the Connection. *Cognitive Psychology* 16: 243–75.

Jorgensen, J., G. A. Miller, and D. S. Sperber. 1984. Test of the Mention Theory of Irony. *Journal of Experimental Psychology: General* 113: 112–20.

Keil, F. C. 1979. *Semantic and Conceptual Development: An Ontological Perspective*. Cambridge, MA: Harvard University Press.

——1994. The Birth and Nurturance of Concepts by Domains: The Origins of Concepts of Living Things. In *Mapping the Mind: Domain-specificity in Cognition and Culture*, ed. L. A. Hirschfeld and S. A. Gelman. New York: Cambridge University Press.

Kelly, M., and F. C. Keil. 1985. The More Things Change...Metamorphoses and Conceptual Structure. *Cognitive Science* 9: 403–6.

Kosslyn, S. M., M. Berhmann, and M. Jeannerod. 1995. The Cognitive Neuroscience of Mental Imagery. *Neuropsychologia* 33: 1335–44.

Kurbat, M. A., and M. J. Farah. 1998. Is the Category-Specific Deficit for Living Things Spurious? *The Journal of Cognitive Neuroscience* 10: 355–61.

Lawson, E. T., and R. McCauley. 1990. *Rethinking Religion: Connecting Culture and Cognition*. Cambridge: Cambridge University Press.

Mandler, J., S. Scribner, M. Cole, and M. DeForest. 1980. Cross-cultural Invariance in Story Recall. *Child Development* 51: 19–26.

McCabe, A., and C. Peterson. 1990. What Makes a Narrative Memorable? *Applied Psycholinguistics* 11: 73–82.

McDaniel, M. A., and G. O. Einstein. 1986. Bizarreness as an Effective Memory Aid: The Importance of Distinctiveness. *Journal of Experimental Psychology: Learning, Memory, and Cognition* 12: 54–65.

Moss, H. E., L. K. Tyler, and F. Jennings. 1997. When Leopards Lose their Spots: Knowledge of Visual Properties in Category-specific Deficits for Living Things. *Cognitive Neuropsychology* 14(6): 901–50.

Nakamura, G. V., A. C. Graesser, J. A. Zimmerman, and J. Riha. 1985. Script Processing in a Natural Situation. *Memory and Cognition* 13: 140–44.

Perner, J. 1991. *Understanding the Representational Mind*. Cambridge, MA: MIT Press.

Polich, J. 1985. Semantic Categorization and Event-related Potentials. *Brain and Language* 26: 304–21.

Quinn P, and M. Johnson. 1997. The Emergence of Perceptual Category Representations in Young Infants: A Connectionist Analysis. *Journal of Experimental Child Psychology* 66: 236–63.

Ramble, C. 1984. *The Lamas of Lubra: Tibetan Bonpo Householder-priests in Western Nepal*. D. Phil thesis, University of Oxford.

Sartori, G., M. Coltheart, M. Miozzo, and R. Job. 1994. Category Specificity and Informational Specificity in Neuropsychological Impairment of Semantic Memory. In *Attention and Performance: XV. Conscious and Non-conscious Information Processing*, ed. C. Umilta and M. Moscovitch, 537–50. Cambridge, MA: MIT Press.

Schmidt, S. R. 1991. Can We Have a Distinctive Theory of Memory? *Memory and Cognition* 19: 523–42.

Shallice, T. 1987. Impairments of Semantic Processing: Multiple Dissociations. In *The Cognitive Neuropsychology of Language*, ed. M. Coltheart, R. Job, and G. Sartori, 111–29. London: Lawrence Erlbaum Associates.

Snellgrove, D. 1959. *The Hevajra Tantra*. London: Oxford University Press.

Spelke, E. S. 1988. The Origins of Physical Knowledge. In *Thought Without Language*, ed. L. Weizkrantz. Oxford: Oxford University Press.

Sperber, D. 1985. Anthropology and Psychology: Towards an Epidemiology of Representations. *Man* 20: 73–89.

——1991. The Epidemiology of Beliefs. In *Psychological Studies of Widespread Beliefs*, ed. C. Fraser. Oxford: Oxford University Press.

—1996. *Explaining Culture: A Naturalistic Approach*. Oxford: Blackwell.

Sperber, D., F. Cara, and V. Girotto. 1995. Relevance Theory Explains the Selection Task. *Cognition* 57: 31–95.

Sperber, D., and D. Wilson. 1995. *Relevance, Communication and Cognition*. 2nd ed. Oxford: Blackwell.

Spiro, M., and R. G. D'Andrade. 1958. A Cross-cultural Study of some Supernatural Beliefs. *American Anthropologist* 60: 456–66.

Stangor, C., and D. McMillan. 1992. Memory for Expectancy-Congruent and Expectancy-Incongruent Information: A Review of the Social and Social-Developmental Literatures. *Psychological Bulletin* 111: 42–61.

Strauss, C., and N. Quinn. 1997. *A Cognitive Theory of Cultural Meaning*. New York: Cambridge University Press.

Von Restorff, H. 1933. Uber die wirkung von bereichsbildungen im spurenfeld. *Psychologische Forchung* 18: 299–342.

Waddill, P. J., and M. A. McDaniel. 1998. Distinctiveness Effects in Recall: Differential Processing or Privileged Retrieval? *Memory and Cognition* 26: 108–20.

Walker, S. J. 1992. Supernatural Beliefs, Natural Kinds, and Conceptual Structure. *Memory and Cognition* 20: 655–62.

Warrington, E. K., and T. Shallice. 1984. Category Specific Semantic Impairments. *Brain* 107: 829–53.

Watts, F., and M. Williams. 1988. *The Psychology of Religious Knowing*. Cambridge: Cambridge University Press.

Wellmann, H. 1990. *The Child's Theory of Mind*. Cambridge, MA: MIT Press.

Whitehouse, H. 1992. Memorable Religions: Transmission, Codification and Change in Divergent Melanesian Contexts. *Man* 27: 777–97.

Worthen, J. B. 1997. Resiliency of Bizarreness Effects under Varying Conditions of Verbal and Imaginal Elaboration and List Composition. *Journal of Mental Imagery* 21: 167–94.

Zelazo, P. D., and T. R. Shultz. 1989. Concepts of Potency and Resistance in Causal Prediction. *Child Development* 60: 1307–15.

9

Ritual Intuitions: Cognitive Contributions to Judgments of Ritual Efficacy[*]

Justin L. Barrett and E. Thomas Lawson

Abstract

Lawson and McCauley (1990) have argued that non-cultural regularities in how actions are conceptualized inform and constrain participants' understandings of religious rituals. This theory of ritual competence generates three predictions: (1) People with little or no knowledge of any given ritual system will have intuitions about the potential effectiveness of a ritual given minimal information about the structure of the ritual. (2) The representation of superhuman agency in the action structure will be considered the most important factor contributing to effectiveness. (3) Having an appropriate intentional agent initiate the action will be considered relatively more important than any specific action to be performed. These three predictions were tested in two experiments with 128 North American Protestant college students who rated the probability of various fictitious rituals to be effective in bringing about a specified consequence. Results support Lawson and McCauley's predictions and suggest that expectations regarding ordinary social actions apply to religious rituals.

෨ ෬

In many different cultures throughout history, people have tried to persuade gods to act in the natural world through the use of prayers and ritual actions. Much as in asking the boss for a raise or a parent for a favor, religious practitioners represent these activities as social actions. But how do practitioners decide on an appropriate interaction with the gods? How rituals should be performed? What knowledge is drawn upon?

Recent research in the study of religion from a cognitive perspective has emphasized that much as ordinary and imaginative thought is constrained and informed by conceptual structures (Ward 1995); so too religious concepts rely on ordinary cognition (Barrett 2000; Boyer 1994). For example, intuitive expectations about the properties of human-like intentional agents are applied to God when solving real-time problems, even when these expectations violate explicit theological convictions (Barrett 1999; Barrett and Keil 1996). Thus, god concepts may be largely informed by knowledge that is not culturally specific, nor needs to be explicitly transmitted (Boyer 1994, 1995).

Similarly, Lawson and McCauley (1990) have argued that religious ritual actions across cultures appear to have structural regularities under-explained by the reputed meanings of the actions. They note that ritual actions (despite their unusual qualities) are cognitively represented as actions. Whether a ritual action involves waving a wand to ward off witches, building a pyramid to facilitate the departure of a pharaoh to the realm of the gods, or lighting a fire to ensure the presence of a superhuman agent, it still requires using ordinary cognitive resources in its representation.

However, religious rituals are also a particular type of action. In such representations someone does something to someone or something in order to bring about some non-natural consequence. That is, rituals are actions that are performed to accomplish something that would not normally follow from this specific action. For example, a person who strikes a special pot in order to bring rain would be performing a ritual; whereas a person who strikes a special pot in order to create pottery fragments would not be performing a ritual.

Because this ritual action violates natural intuitive causal expectations, the difference in consequence must be justified in the minds of participants or observers. Even observers with little cultural knowledge of a particular religious system will still have intuitions that superhuman agency must be involved for the action to work. If a person smashes a pot with a staff in hopes of bringing rain, people will guess that not just any ordinary person smashing any ordinary pot with any ordinary staff will be successful at bringing rain. Some non-mechanistic, non-natural form of causation must be at play. The action must be cognitively tagged as more than it seems.

If the tag is some connection or appeal to superhuman agency, then the action qualifies as a religious ritual, say Lawson and McCauley.

Once an act is represented as appealing in some way to a superhuman intentional agent to account for the expected consequence, then the most fitting mode of causal cognition to use to generate inferences is social causation. Indeed, structurally, religious rituals mirror social actions: someone performs some kind of action in order to motivate another's action or change in disposition. It just so happens that the person being motivated to act is a god or other non-natural agent.

If people do apply ordinary representations of social actions to reason about religious rituals, one general and two specific empirical predictions follow:

1. Insofar as cross-cultural regularities in social cognition exist, individuals unfamiliar with a particular ritual, religious system, or any religious rituals at all, would have converging intuitions about whether or not a particular ritual is likely to be efficacious. Much as in making grammatical judgments about sentences apart from semantic considerations, judgments of ritual well-formedness may be made divorced from sophisticated understanding of the religious meaning. That is, ritually naïve subjects would have converging opinions about what makes a good, effective ritual a good, effective ritual.

2. Specifically, ritually naïve individuals would appreciate the central importance of superhuman agency being represented somewhere in the ritual structure to account for proposed non-natural consequences. A woman striking a sick man with a staff does not cure him unless the woman, the staff, the man, or some combination of them has some special connection to an agent (or agents) with special qualities. Otherwise, instead of a recovery you only get bruises. When judging if an unfamiliar ritual is effective, individuals will consider some connection to superhuman agency more important than any other aspect of the ritual including the choice of specific agent involved, of object, of action, or of instruments if any.

3. Finally, and most interestingly, because religious rituals are social actions and social actions require appropriate agents, having an appropriate agent for a given ritual will be the factor judged most important in its success or failure after connection to superhuman agency. Specifically, since rituals are intended events evoking superhuman intervention, an agent that can reasonably intend to achieve the specified consequence of the ritual must initiate the action. For example, a marriage ceremony must be performed by a person who, presumably, intends to see the participants married as a consequence. A talking parrot trained to say all the right words would not be an adequate replacement because of lack of intent. Consequently, individuals unfamiliar with a ritual (or any rituals) will judge the agent in a ritual to be relatively more important to the rituals' success than the particular action the agent performs.

Note that while this third prediction counters the folk notion of rituals as a set of highly specified actions that must be performed just so, it parallels a simple observation about social actions in general. Unlike when bringing about a physical or mechanistic consequence, such as breaking a window, in social interactions the actor's intentions are critical. Similarly, in religious rituals it is predicted that having an appropriate agent—one who can intend to act toward certain ends—will matter more to the success of the ritual than the specific action performed.

We tested these predictions using two experiments in which adult participants reasoned about the potential efficacy of fictitious rituals. If expectations regarding the potential efficacy of ritual form through learning arbitrary social conventions, then participants would have no converging intuitions about the success or failure of unfamiliar rituals such as those used in these experiments. In the first experiment, predictions regarding the importance of superhuman agency being represented in the action structure and the relative importance of having an appropriate agent over-performing a particular action were tested. Experiment 2 focused on the relative importance of particular agents over particular actions in rituals compared with non-ritual actions.

Experiment 1

Method

Subjects

Sixty-eight students recruited from introductory psychology courses at an American Midwest liberal arts college participated. They ranged in age from 17- to 22-years old, with a mean age of 18.6 years. Forty were female, 28 male. Participants were almost exclusively Protestant Christians with the majority identifying with the Christian Reformed Church, a denomination for which (at least theologically speaking) there are no religious rituals as operationalized above. Indeed, American Protestants in general have *at most* only five religious rituals: Communion, baptism, ordination, marriage and funerals. So that participants could not draw on their personal religious knowledge, none of the fictitious rituals used resembled any of these five observances.

Materials

A packet of twelve randomly ordered ritual sets was prepared. At the top of the first page of each packet, participants recorded age, sex, and religious affiliation, and then read these instructions: "For the following ratings 'special' means someone or something that has been given special properties or authority by the gods." The twelve sets of rituals followed.

For each of the twelve sets, a prototype ritual was followed by twelve variations including a reiteration of the prototype. In one-fourth of the prototypes, the agent was described as "special," in one-fourth the instrument was "special," in one-fourth both the agent and the instrument were "special," and in one-fourth nothing was labeled "special." These designations were counterbalanced so that each particular ritual appeared (across participants)in the same form the same number of times.

To systematically probe intuitions regarding the relative contributions of each element in the prototype to the success of the action, the theoretically relevant components of the prototypes were varied within subjects. The presence or absence of the term "special," the agent performing the action, the action itself, and the instrument used were manipulated independently. In total, the twelve variations following each prototype included: (1) a version of the prototype with both the agent and instrument designated "special," (2) a version with only the agent designated "special," (3) a version with only the instrument designated "special," (4) a version with nothing special but otherwise identical to the prototype, (5) a minor agent change (to an animal) with the agent labeled "special," (6) a minor agent change with no specialness, (7) a major agent change (to an inanimate object) with specialness, (8)a major agent change without specialness, (9 and 10) two action changes otherwise identical to the prototype, (11) an instrument change with specialness, and (12) an instrument change without specialness. Table 1 illustrates the various items.

a) A special person blew special dust on a field.	1	2	3	4	5	6	7
b) A special person blew ordinary dust on a field.	1	2	3	4	5	6	7
c) An ordinary person blew special dust on a field.	1	2	3	4	5	6	7
d) An ordinary person blew ordinary dust on a field.	1	2	3	4	5	6	7
e) A special rat blew ordinary dust on a field.	1	2	3	4	5	6	7
f) An ordinary rat blew ordinary dust on a field.	1	2	3	4	5	6	7
g) A special branch blew ordinary dust on a field.	1	2	3	4	5	6	7
h) An ordinary branch blew ordinary dust on a field.	1	2	3	4	5	6	7
i) A special person threw ordinary dust on a field.	1	2	3	4	5	6	7
j) A special person kicked ordinary dust on a field.	1	2	3	4	5	6	7
k) A special person blew special feathers on a field.	1	2	3	4	5	6	7
l) A special person blew ordinary feathers on a field.	1	2	3	4	5	6	7

Table 1. *Experiment 1 sample item. A successful religious action: A special person blew ordinary dust on a field and the field yielded good crops. How likely is each of the following actions to find favor with the gods and yield good crops? Please rate each action: 1 = extremely likely the action will work, 7 = extremely unlikely*

Each permutation was followed by a seven-point rating scale anchored as "1 = extremely likely the action will work" and "7 = extremely unlikely." The rituals were arbitrarily generated and not meant to be similar to any real religious rituals.

219

Procedure
Participants were told nothing about the purpose of the study, but simply recorded their age and sex on the response sheets and proceeded with the ratings.

Predictions
The social action hypothesis adapted from Lawson and McCauley predicts that the most important factor driving participants' ratings of the likelihood for the action variations to succeed would be having a "special" agent or instrument, and secondarily, having the same agent as the prototype. That is, given that these are unusual actions requiring something "special" in the action structure, social-causal expectations would be triggered and the same agent as the prototype would be considered more important to the success of the ritual than having the same action.

The social action hypothesis must be distinguished from a matching hypothesis. First, if participants had no intuitions regarding the importance of any particular element of the ritual, then a reasonable strategy for generating ratings would be to rate permutations that more closely matched the successful prototype as more likely to work. Consequently, for rituals in which no specialness was mentioned, the non-special replication would be rated as more likely to succeed than the other three versions with "special" labels. So, for example, if the prototype described "An ordinary person blew ordinary dust on a field and the field yielded good crops," then versions of the prototype that are most similar to the prototype—even having no "special" agents or instruments—would be rated as most likely to succeed. The version of the prototype "A special person blew special dust" should be rated as less likely to be successful than the reiteration of the prototype, the version with a special agent, or the version with a special instrument.

Likewise, since 50 percent of the prototypes had special agents and 50 percent had special instruments, but only 25 percent had "special" agents and instruments or neither, this matching hypothesis would predict that overall the one-"special" permutations would have lower ratings (i.e., are more likely to succeed) than either the two-"special" items or the no-"special" items, which should not differ from each other. Alternatively, the social action hypothesis would be that the items with two special elements should have scores at least as low as the one-"special" items followed by no marker items.

Results and Discussion

A single score was calculated for each of the change factors to be considered by averaging across the items from the 12 ritual sets. This produced scores for agent changes with the agent being special (e.g., items like e and g in

Table 1 for all 12 ritual sets), agent changes without the agent being special (e.g., items f and h), instrument changes (items k and l), action changes (items i and j); reiterations of the prototype with nothing special (e.g., item d), when two components were special (item a), when only the agent was special (item b), and when only the instrument was special (item c).

The theoretically relevant inferential comparisons were made between these scores using t-tests for paired samples. All contrasts were planned and, since essentially all of the tests performed were significant, this design does fit the conditions for multiple test corrections. However, all theoretically interesting differences do remain significant after application of Bonferroni corrections for multiple t-tests. Uncorrected values are reported. No omnibus ANOVA test is reported because only item-type differences are of interest.

If a particular change to the prototypes led to higher scores (less likely to succeed) than another change, then the changed component was regarded as relatively more important to the success of the ritual. Figure 1 displays the comparisons between the different specialness items. As predicted by the social action hypothesis and contrary to the matching hypothesis, the two-"special" items were rated significantly lower than the other marker items, $M = 2.00$, $SD = 1.22$, $t (67) = 7.15$, $p < .001$ (compared to the next closest type of item). The two-"special" items were even rated more likely to succeed than the no-"special" items when the prototype had no "special" label and so the no-"special" choices best matched the successful actions, $t (67) = 2.95$, $p = .004$. The two forms of one-"special" items did not differ significantly from each other ($t (67) = 1.29$, $p = .20$) but had significantly lower average ratings than the no-"special" items: $M = 3.06$, $SD = 1.20$ for the special instruments ($t (67) = 8.26$, $p < .001$ versus not special); $M = 2.91$, $SD = 1.30$ for the special agents ($t (67) = 9.75$, $p < .001$); $M = 4.65$, $SD = 1.32$ for the no-"special" items. The two one-"special" types did not differ significantly from no-marker items when the prototype had no "special" marker. It seems "special" labels did matter to subjects' judgments of the efficacy of rituals even if "special" labels were not included in a given ritual's prototype. That is, even if the ritual worked without any component being special, it would be still more likely to work when making an appeal to a superhuman agent.

The second prediction regarding "special" markers was that not having them would damage rituals' likelihood of success more than other changes in the action or instrument. Since some of the prototype rituals had nothing special, testing this hypothesis is muddied. By implicitly being told one-quarter of the time that specialness is unnecessary, subjects may have devalued specialness relative to other features. More importantly, in no-"special" prototypes, the no-"special" item does not constitute the removal of "special" but is a reiteration of the ritual that supposedly worked.

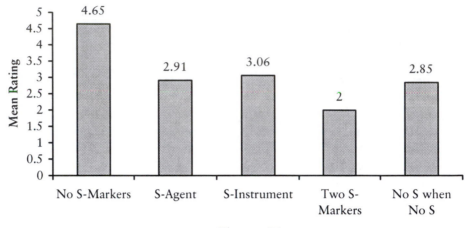

Figure 1. *Mean rating of ritual's likely effectiveness as a function of change type performed to the prototype for Experiment 1. "S-Agent" refers to items for which the only "special" was modifying the agent. "S-Instrument" refers to items for which the only "special" was modifying the instrument. The two "special"-marker items were rated as significantly more likely to succeed than all other types, even no "special" types when there were no "special" markers in the prototype (No s when No S). The no "special"-marker type is significantly greater than all other types.*

To eliminate these difficulties, the measure needed to represent the importance of "special"-markers in the ritual structure relative to other components was the average of no-"special" items only in cases when the prototype had at least one "special"-marker. In these cases, the no-special condition truly indicated the removal or absence of a 'special.' As predicted, this "special absent" score was greater than either the action or instrument scores, as illustrated in Figure 2. The mean special-absent score was 5.26, SD = 1.51, as compared with 3.60, SD = 1.07, for action changes (t (67) = 7.44, p < .001) and 4.39, SD = 1.15, for instrument changes (t (67) = 3.86, p < .001). Subject intuitions even converged on agent changes being less important for ritual success than the presence of "special"-markers. Agent change items had a mean rating of 4.71, SD = 1.35, t (67) = 2.36, p = .021.

Consistent with the social action predictions regarding agents, agent changes with and without "special"-markers were rated as more damaging to the possible success of the rituals than action changes. Agent changes with a "special"-marker ("special" agents) had a mean rating of 4.29, SD = 1.61, significantly greater than ratings for action changes, t (67) = 4.17, p < .001. Agent changes with "special"-markers were not rated significantly different than instrument changes. Agent changes without a "special" marker were judged as even more likely to ruin the rituals, M = 5.12, SD = 1.23; and were rated significantly different from both action changes (t (67) = 10.75, p < .001) and instrument changes (t (67) = 4.28, p < .001).

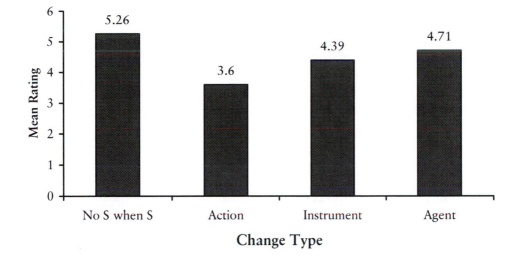

Figure 2. *Mean rating of rituals' likely effectiveness as a function of change type performed to the prototype for Experiment 1. "No S when S" indicates items in which at least one "special"-marker was present in the prototype but none in the test items. Removing "special"-markers was rated as significantly more disruptive than Action, Instrument, or Agent changes. Action changes were significantly rated as more likely to succeed than Agent changes*

Participants' ratings indicated that if a ritual has no indication that the agent or instrument involved has been endowed with special properties or authority by a divine source (no specialness), then it is unlikely to bring about the desired non-natural consequences. The representation of superhuman agency somewhere in the ritual structure was judged as more important for the success of the ritual than using the original instrument or performing the proper action. Participants' ratings also suggested intuitions that more than one indication of superhuman agency in the action structure, i.e., more than one "special"-marker is better than only one. Finally, in these religious actions, participants judged that having an agent capable of intending a particular outcome was more important than performing a particular action. Changing the action of the ritual was not as devastating to the intended consequences than changing the agent—even if the agent was performing the appropriate action.

The results of Experiment 1 are consistent with the social action hypothesis. Participants, having no familiarity with the rituals in question, had converging intuitions regarding which components were most important for the ritual success. Namely, having some connection to superhuman agency (via the "special"-markers) and having the appropriate agent. Note that having the right agent as more important than having the right action runs counter to our knowledge of real world physical/mechanistic causation. So, perhaps, rather than having intuitive theoretical knowledge to deal with actions such as religious rituals, participants simply countered their ordinary intuitions. That is, an alternative explanation is that because these were strange action sequences with "specialness" explicitly involved in 75% of them, participants were left trying to find a way to make their answers special as well. They tried to make relevant the specialness of the actions. The obvious solution is to take what comes naturally and turn it on its head. This relevance account is addressed in Experiment 2.

Experiment 2

In addition to the relevance account, two other potential problems might lurk in Experiment 1. Though somewhat improbable, one might suggest that the results of Experiment 1 could be explained as only demonstrating that there is something about the particular rituals and permutations used that biased participants to consider agents more important for success than actions. Or perhaps, this population of participants is of a cultural group that heavily stresses the importance of agents regardless of the type of action being described: results are the consequence of who agents are, more so than what they do.

Experiment 2 sought to address these counter-explanations using a between-subjects manipulation. One group of participants completed a task very similar to that used in Experiment 1, rating the likelihood of success of various actions with some connection to superhuman agents. For this first group, results were predicted to be comparable to Experiment 1 with the agent being regarded as relatively more important than the specific action.

A second group of participants rated the same actions described without any connection to superhuman agents. That is, nothing in the actions was described as "special."

Because the actions were still bizarre and set on another world, the relevance account would predict that participants in this condition would likewise answer counter to their natural inclinations and rate agents as more important. Likewise, if the results of Experiment 1 were due to bias in the items used or due to something about the population samples, participants in the second group would likewise be expected to rate agents as more important than actions. Alternatively, if the importance of agents over actions in Experiment 1 was due to participants having represented the special actions as social events as hypothesized, then participants in the non-special condition would rate actions as more important than agents, because the actions would no longer be social events but mere mechanistic ones.

Method

Participants

Sixty American Protestant liberal arts college students (32 female, 28 male, mean age 19.0 years) from introductory psychology courses participated.

Materials and Procedure

In both conditions, the "religious" condition and the "other-world" condition (detailed below), the experimenter presented each participant with a set of eight fictitious action sequences. Each of the eight successful sequences' descriptions was followed by seven variations of the sequence that participants rated for likelihood of success. Of the seven variations, two changed just the agent in the original sequence, two changed just the action, two changed just the instrument used in the original, and one was a restatement of the original. For example, one item from the "religious" condition read:

Given that: A special person cleans a trumpet with a special cloth and the village is protected from an epidemic. How likely is each of the following actions to protect the village from an epidemic? Please rate each action: 1 = extremely likely the action will work, 7 = extremely unlikely.

a) A special person cleans a trumpet with a special plant. 1 2 3 4 5 6 7
b) A special beetle cleans a trumpet with a special cloth. 1 2 3 4 5 6 7
c) A special person cleans a trumpet with a special paper. 1 2 3 4 5 6 7
d) A special dog cleans a trumpet with a special cloth. 1 2 3 4 5 6 7
e) A special person covers a trumpet with a special cloth. 1 2 3 4 5 6 7
f) A special person stuffs a trumpet with a special cloth. 1 2 3 4 5 6 7
g) A special person cleans a trumpet with a special cloth. 1 2 3 4 5 6 7

The order of presentation of each type of variation was randomized for each item.

In the "religious" condition, the packet of ritual ratings included an explanation of the term "special": "For the following ratings, 'special' means someone or something that has been given special properties or authority by the gods. All of the following are proposed religious actions. Try to use as much of the rating scales as is reasonable." To be sure any results from the religious condition were due to understanding the actions as appealing to superhuman agency and not merely a consequence of the particular actions, a second condition was conducted. In the "other-world" condition, the word "special" was dropped from all parts of the descriptions, and the packet included a different explanation: "All of the following are proposed actions on a world very much like ours. Try to use as much of the rating scales as is reasonable."

Results and Discussion

As in Experiment 1, participants in the religious condition rated the action sequences with changed agents as significantly less likely to be successful than sequences in which the action was changed, supporting the prediction that having a proper agent is more important than the particular action.

Participants gave agent-changed rituals a mean rating of 5.00 (SD = 1.70) compared with 3.99 (SD = 1.51) for the action-changed rituals, t (29) = 3.61, p = .001. In contrast, when participants rated the same action sequences in the other-world condition, the agent was no longer considered most important for success. Indeed, agent-changed rituals were rated as significantly more likely to succeed, M = 2.96, SD = 1.71, than action-changed rituals, M = 3.93, SD = 1.35, t (29) = 3.22, p = .003. Figure 3 illustrates these results.

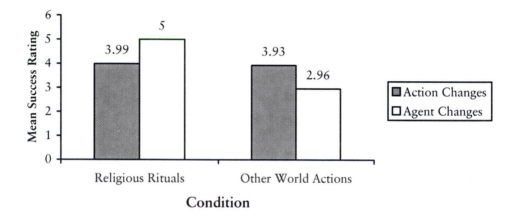

Figure 3. *Mean ratings of rituals' likely effectiveness as a function of change type in either a religious or "other-world" setting. Agent-changed sequences were rated as significantly less likely to be successful than action-changed sequences in the religious condition only. Agent-changed sequences were rated as significantly more likely to be successful than action-changed sequences in the "other-world" cognition*

Unsurprisingly, the reversal in relative importance between the two conditions was the result of a change in importance of having the right agent. In both the religious condition and the other-world condition changing the actions in the prototypes had comparable consequences on the likelihood of success ratings, t (58) = .17, p = .866. In contrast, changing the agent in the religious condition (M = 5.00) had a far more serious consequence than changing the agent in the other-world condition (M = 2.96), t (58) = 4.63, p < .001.

That relative judgments reversed as predicted between the two conditions strongly supports the interpretation that participants used different intuitive theories of causation to generate inferences about the efficacy of the actions. In the other-world condition, participants used ordinary mechanistic causal expectations—the action is more important to bring about a particular state of affairs than the agent. When the same actions were performed as appealing to superhuman agency, intuitions changed as they would in situations of social causation with agency acquiring a more substantive role in determining the outcome.

These results also support the contention that the relative importance of proper agent over proper action in Experiment 1 is not merely the consequence of bias in the particular items used or peculiar to the population sampled. After all, this second sample from the same population did not show an agent-bias in the other-world condition. Similar items in Experiment 2 produced comparable results in the "religious" condition, but intuitions in the "other-world" condition were just the opposite: action was understood as more important than the agent. Even though the actions were still peculiar and located on another world, participants demonstrated completely different intuitions regarding the efficacy of the actions between the two conditions. These results seem to speak against the relevance account.

General Discussion

These experiments tested three general predictions inspired by Lawson and McCauley (1990). First, if, as Lawson and McCauley argue, representation of religious rituals uses the same cognitive architecture used for representing any action, even people with no special knowledge of a religious system would have converging intuitions about whether or not a given ritual is likely to be effective. Second, because the intended outcome of religious rituals violates normal mechanistic causal expectations, it was predicted that when judging whether a ritual might be effective, people would consider some connection to superhuman agency more important than any other aspect of the ritual, justifying the breach of causal expectations. Third, because the rituals appeal to a superhuman agent to justify their intended consequences, rituals are likely to be represented as social actions. Consequently, when judging whether a ritual is effective, people would regard having an appropriate intentional agent as relatively more important than the particular action, as is the case in social exchanges. The results of the experiments supported all three predictions.

Regarding the first prediction, Protestant Christians unfamiliar with the fictitious rituals converged in their intuitions about which elements of the ritual structure were most important for the rituals' success. Participants could have simply guessed somewhat at random if they possessed no intuitions about the fictitious rituals. Had this been the case the results would have produced mean ratings hovering around the mid-point of the scales. But clearly, participants did have some opinions about the relative importance of different factors. Experiment 2 demonstrated that the convergence of expectations was not an artifact of the items used or exhibition of a cultural bias. Depending on the cover story used, relative judgments changed dramatically.

Bearing on the second prediction, participants seemed to understand that for an action to produce non-natural consequences, superhuman agency must be involved in some way, and this connection with superhuman agents was the best predictor of success. In Experiment 1, participants could have simply rated the rituals that best matched the prototype as most likely to be effective, ignoring the importance of "special"-markers. They did not. Similarly, participants did not simply adopt a strategy of reversing their intuitions about causal events when considering strange, special, or other-worldly actions. When evaluating the relative contributions of different elements for the success of an action, participants demonstrated converging intuitions that varied predictably with context.

Participants rated action forms with "special" agents or "special" instruments (when specialness was defined as having been endowed with unusual properties from the gods) as more likely to result in non-natural actions than ordinary actions. This much is fairly trivial. However, this finding is more meaningful because of the further relative judgment that having "special"-markers was more important than any other component of the action sequence. It could have been, as in many mundane actions, that performing the correct action was what was most important with connection to superhuman agency occupying secondary importance. However, participants answered that whether or not the ritual had a "special"-marker was more important than the particular action, instrument, or agent involved.

Once recognizing the actions as importantly tied to superhuman agency, participants also regarded having an appropriate intentional agent initiate the action as more important to the success of a ritual than the particular action, supporting the third prediction. This judgment is not trivial. A common caricature of rituals is that their actions are highly formulaic and carefully following each step is what leads to success. While the actions of any given ritual are important, participants' judgments align with the suggestion that participants import social-causal intuitions for evaluating religious rituals. As in ordinary social action, having an agent that intends the consequences of the actions is more important than the actions themselves in determining a successful outcome. In the "other-world" condition of Experiment 2, the connection with superhuman agency was removed, rendering the events as instances of odd mechanistic causation. Consequently, participants rated the agent as significantly less important than in the "religious" condition and less important than the particular action.

That judgments pertaining to religious rituals are informed by ordinary cognition regarding social actions should not be confused with the claim that cultural knowledge is irrelevant. Surely explicit tuition regarding the efficacy of rituals plays a central role in ritual practitioners' thought about their rituals. However, the role of ordinary cognition would be expected to exert pressure on religious ritual practices in at least three ways. First, as new rituals are developed, intuitive expectations generated by an ordinary action representation system would guide what become official judgments about the relative importance of the ritual components. Theological and doctrinal positions that are at least somewhat intuitive would be more likely to be suggested and embraced. Further, teachings regarding rituals that resonate with intuitive expectations are more likely to be remembered, resist distortion, and be passed on than concepts with no basis in ordinary representations (Boyer 1994). Likewise, when thinking about rituals in the absence of doctrinal instruction or in situations for which no relevant precedence is salient, ordinary cognition is likely to generate expectations, predictions, and inferences. Suppose a rarely performed ritual fails and there is no orthodox explanation for such a failure. In this case, the search for explanations would begin with ordinary conceptions. Based on the results of the present experiments, "Was the agent who performed the ritual really qualified?" would be asked more frequently than, "Did the person perform the action correctly?" to determine the cause of failure.

In addition to supporting the claim that religious rituals are represented using general conceptual structures for action representation, these studies lend credence to the contention of various scholars of religion that cognitive and psychological factors should occupy more attention in the study of religion and culture (Boyer 1994; McCauley and Lawson 1993; Sperber 1975). Relying only on cultural factors to explain culture is not the only, nor necessarily the best, available option.

Acknowledgment

The authors thank Pascal Boyer for comments and suggestions.

Note

* This article was originally published in *Journal of Cognition and Culture* 1(2) (2001): 183–201.

References

Barrett, J. L. 1999. Theological Correctness: Cognitive Constraints and the Study of Religion. *Method & Theory in the Study of Religion* 11(4): 325–39.

—2000. Exploring the Natural Foundations of Religion. *Trends in Cognitive Sciences* 4: 29–34.

—2001. Do Children Experience God Like Adults? Retracing the Development of God Concepts. In *Religion in Mind: Cognitive Perspectives on Religious Experience*, ed. J. Andresen. Cambridge: Cambridge University Press.

Barrett, J. L., and F. C. Keil. 1996. Conceptualizing a Non-natural Entity: Anthropomorphism in God Concepts. *Cognitive Psychology* 31: 219–47.

Barrett, J. L., R. A. Richert, and A. Driesenga. 2001. God's Beliefs Versus Mother's: The Development of Natural and Non-natural Agent Concepts. *Child Development* 72(1): 50.

Bartlett, F. C. 1932. *Remembering: A Study in Experimental and Social Psychology*. Cambridge: Cambridge University Press.

Boyer, P. 1994. *The Naturalness of Religious Ideas: A Cognitive Theory of Religion*. Berkeley, CA: University of California Press.

—1995. Causal Understandings in Cultural Representations: Cognitive Constraints on Inferences from Cultural Input. In *Causal Cognition: A Multidisciplinary Debate*, ed. D. Sperber, D. Premack, and A. J. Premack. New York: Oxford University Press.

—2000. Evolution of a Modern Mind and the Origins of Culture: Religious Concepts as a Limiting Case. In *Evolution and the Human Mind: Modularity, Language and Meta-Cognition*, ed. P. Carruthers and A. Chamberlain. Cambridge: Cambridge University Press.

Lawson, E. T., and R. N. McCauley. 1990. *Rethinking Religion: Connecting Cognition and Culture*. Cambridge: Cambridge University Press.

McCauley, R. N., and E. T. Lawson. 1993. Connecting the Cognitive and the Cultural: Artificial Minds as Methodological Devices in the Study of the Socio-cultural. In *Minds: Natural and Artificial*, ed. R. Burton, 121–45. Albany: State University of New York Press.

Sperber, D. 1975. *Rethinking Symbolism*. Cambridge: Cambridge University Press.

Ward, T. B. 1995. What's Old about New Ideas? In *The Creative Cognition Approach*, ed. S. M. Smith, T. B. Ward, and R. A. Finke, 157–78. Cambridge, MA: MIT Press.

10

COGNITIVE AND CONTEXTUAL FACTORS IN THE EMERGENCE OF DIVERSE BELIEF SYSTEMS: CREATION VERSUS EVOLUTION[*]

E. Margaret Evans

Abstract

The emergence and distribution of beliefs about the origins of species is investigated in Christian fundamentalist and non-fundamentalist school communities, with participants matched by age, educational level, and locale. Children (n = 185) and mothers (n = 92) were questioned about animate, inanimate, and artifact origins, and children were asked about their interests and natural history knowledge. Preadolescents, like their mothers, embraced the dominant beliefs of their community, creationist or evolutionist; 8- to 10-year-olds were exclusively creationist, regardless of community of origin; 5- to 7-year-olds in fundamentalist schools endorsed creationism, whereas non-fundamentalists endorsed mixed creationist and spontaneous generationist beliefs. Children's natural history knowledge and religious interest predicted their evolutionist and creationist beliefs, respectively, independently of parent beliefs. It is argued that this divergent developmental pattern is optimally explained with a model of constructive interactionism: Children generate intuitive beliefs about origins, both natural and intentional, while communities privilege certain beliefs and inhibit others, thus engendering diverse belief systems.

℘ ☾

The ideological banners raised by supporters at either end of the creationist–evolutionist debate mark extreme positions of one of the most strident of arguments about the nature of science in the 20th century. Scientific creationism has been declared an oxymoron (Numbers 1992), and creationists have been viewed as a group of "ignorant fools" who are "abusing science" (Godfrey 1984). Creationist scientists have been equally caustic, dismissing evolutionary explanations as mere theory (Cavanaugh 1985) and accusing evolution scientists of Satanism: "Satan himself is the originator of the concept of evolution" (Morris 1975, cited in Kehoe 1995). Distortion of an opponent's position is typical of "partisans to ideological disputes" (Keltner and Robinson 1996, 105) but behind the rhetoric lies an interesting question, to be examined in this study: How can both of these incompatible beliefs receive such widespread support? The present paper examines the natural history of these ideas, their emergence and distribution in a population of school-age children.

The dissemination of evolutionist and creationist beliefs in the population at large, it will be argued, is a testament not only to their public availability but also to their cognitive appeal (see Shore 1996; Sperber 1996; Strauss and Quinn 1997). The claim that creationist ideas are intuitively plausible while Darwinian concepts are intuitively opaque (e.g., Dawkins 1987) suggests that cognitive constraints facilitate or limit the adoption of these explanations. On the other hand, it could also be claimed that the spread of such beliefs is simply a function of social forces. By charting the emergence of beliefs about origins in children from families where these beliefs are endorsed to different degrees such as Christian fundamentalist and comparable non-fundamentalist families, these competing claims can be examined in detail. To provide a context for interpreting the empirical findings a brief background to the ideological dispute will first be given. This will then be followed by a summary of some recent theoretical and empirical approaches that provide a rationale for the various measures and analyses employed in the empirical study.

Evolutionists and Creationists

Although evolution science and creation science are both 20th-century products, both have their roots in earlier controversies about the nature of biological kinds (e.g., Evans 2000b; Mayr 1982; Numbers 1992). The cornerstone of modern biological explanation is evolutionary science, which arises from the synthesis of Darwinian theory and Mendelian genetics (Mayr 1997); its central tenet is that all species, including the human, have a common descent extending over millions of years, and that distinct species arise through natural adaptive processes. In the theistic form of evolution science, embraced in some form by most Western religions, evolution is accepted as a valid scientific truth, but the originator of the process is considered to be a Supreme Being. In contrast, creation science, which receives its strongest support from Christian fundamentalism, holds to the biblical dictum that each biological kind or species was created individually by God about 6000 years ago: Biblical literalism (Numbers 1992). A cornerstone of this world view is the immutability of species; new kinds could be created by God but never by natural means (Kehoe 1995). Essentialistic explanations of this type, though, do allow for an inbuilt God-given capacity for limited change within a species, which permits some diversity in intraspecies phenotypes (Morris and Parker 1982).

Modern creation science owes its resurgence to a series of influential books by Christian Fundamentalists John C. Whitcomb and Henry M. Morris, published in the 1960s and 1970s. In these books the Noachim Flood is invoked to explain the fossil record and flood geology to explain the geological column (Kehoe 1995; Numbers 1992). The translation of this creationist literature into many languages fostered the rebirth and subsequent spread of creationist beliefs across the industrialized world (Cavanaugh 1985). Within the United States, creationist and evolutionist beliefs are almost evenly distributed in the population at large, though there are regional variations (Cavanaugh 1985; Miller 1987; Numbers 1992). Although those with a college education are somewhat less likely then those with only a high school education to hold creationist beliefs (Miller 1987), such beliefs are, in general, remarkably resistant to instruction. Thirty-eight percent of undergraduates who had taken relevant courses in anthropology, for example, still held that the Garden of Eden was the origin of human life (Almquist and Cronin 1988). However, students with creationist beliefs are in general no more antiscientific than the rest of the undergraduate population, nor are they any more likely to believe in the paranormal (Harrold, Eve, and Goede 1995; Numbers 1992).

In contrast to creationist ideas, modern evolutionary explanations, in particular Darwinian natural selection, appear to be very difficult to grasp (e.g., Ferrari and Chi 1998; Greene 1990; Samarapungavan and Wiers 1997). Students from a variety of backgrounds, including school-age pupils, undergraduates, and even advanced biology and medical students, often default to a form of "Lamarckian" theorizing to explain adaptive change in species. The crux of the problem seems to be that natural selection requires students to accept strongly counterintuitive notions concerning random change and variation occurring at the level of a population. In spite of focused instruction (e.g., Bishop and Anderson 1990), such students are more likely to believe in the inheritance of acquired characteristics, i.e. that changes in an animal population result from individual adaptations to novel environmental conditions, which are then passed on to offspring. (The giraffe, for example, stretches its neck to reach high vegetation; its offspring inherit this characteristic.)

It took the genius of Lamarck to theorize that such a mechanism could give rise to different species. It is not clear from the research on students' conceptions whether they reason that new kinds arise in this manner, or consider that what emerge are different versions of the same kind. Unlike Darwinian theory such explanations tend to be teleological in nature, in that they invoke adaptation as a solution to the needs and purposes of individual organisms (Evans 2000b; Mayr 1982). In contrast to that of creationist explanation, Lamarck's notion of teleology or purpose is dissociated from that of intention or desire, insofar as he eschewed anything other than material explanations (e.g., fluid dynamics) in his efforts to explain the apparent goal directedness of organisms (Atran 1990; Gould 1999).[1]

Source Analogies for the Origins of Species

When reasoning about an ill-defined or novel problem, such as the origins of species, scientists, theologians, and lay-people alike resort to analogy, which makes the unfamiliar known (Holyoak and Thagard 1995). Analogical reasoning is ubiquitous and appears to underlie many problem-solving capacities including the generation of explanation. A good source analog should match its target (i.e., the novel problem) in terms of feature similarity, structural relations, and purpose, which are hypothesized to act synergistically to constrain its use (Holyoak and Thagard 1995). By the time they are in elementary school, children are competent analogical reasoners, provided the source analog is grounded in familiar domains of knowledge (Gentner and Rattermann 1991; Goswami et al. 1998). Accordingly, elementary school children should be capable of constructing explanations for the origins of living beings without direct adult tutoring, at least to the extent that the source analogs cognitively available to them facilitate such constructions.

From the above description of the ideological dispute, two distinct theories about the origins of species are clearly identifiable in the population at large, namely creation and evolution. However, there is a third version, spontaneous generation, the idea that "living beings could arise from non-living matter" (Roger 1986). Spontaneous generation was a feature of early Greek thought (Mayr 1982), though it reappears in various guises over the centuries. Of the three versions, the creation story is the only one that overtly invokes an intentional and purposeful being; the others are naturalistic and nonintentional.

Many have speculated that the source analogy for creationism is human action (e.g., Guthrie 1993; Holyoak and Thagard 1995; Piaget 1929). There has been little empirical research on the topic but findings to date seem persuasive. For example, while most would claim that God has special powers, on a recall task for stories in which God was depicted as all-powerful and all-knowing many undergraduates defaulted to a view of God as a human with limited capacities (Barrett and Keil 1996). If creationism is rooted in human experience then developmentally one might expect younger children to conflate God and human, with God depicted as an all-powerful parent. On the basis of interviews with children of different ages, Piaget (1929, 356–85) concluded that children are able to distinguish between the powers of God and those of the human only after they understand the limitations of human (parent) capacities, which happens around the early-to-mid elementary school years (see also Evans and Gelman 2001). More recent conceptualizations of children's intuitive beliefs view the latter as naive theories focused on specific ontological domains (e.g., Wellman and Gelman 1997). Numerous studies in this constructivist mode indicate that by the late preschool years children's understanding of their fellow humans, that is, children's naive psychology or theory of mind, is relatively advanced when compared to that of adults (Carey 1985; Wellman and Gelman 1997). Findings such as these indicate a firm basis for a source analogy from which children could construct an understanding of creation, with God as a special kind of human with the power to create living beings the way humans make artifacts. This is a version of the classic argument from design (e.g., Dawkins 1987; Holyoak and Thagard 1995).

In contrast to the difficulties of learning Darwinian concepts, the idea of inheriting acquired features appears to be intuitive, found from the "ancients to the nineteenth century" (Mayr 1982) and even in present-day preschoolers (Springer and Keil 1989). This suggests that children's intuitive ontologies might reference a natural mechanism, the inheritance of acquired features, which, even though incorrect, could be employed to explain the creation of new species. However, there is a crucial corollary: children must also accept the premise that members of a kind can change in a fundamental way. This premise, though, is unlikely to be a part of young children's repertoire of intuitive explanations, as it requires the overturning of their strongly held essentialist beliefs in the immutability of living beings (Gelman, Coley, and Gottfried 1994; Gelman and Hirschfeld 1999; Keil 1989; Mayr 1991). Because of their staunch essentialism, preschool and early-to-mid elementary school children would be unlikely to endorse any kind of natural explanation that involves species transformations. Nevertheless, one may ask whether there are any circumstances under which children might be induced to revise their implicit beliefs in the stability of species.

The intuitive basis for the claim that the inheritance of acquired characteristics could be a mechanism of species creation may arise from two source analogies. The first is the cultural transmission of knowledge. The second is gained from direct exposure to the natural world, and is probably more appropriate as an analogy. Observers of nature are routinely confronted with evidence of change in the characteristics of an animal population over brief periods of time, such as seasonal change (feather color) and meta-morphosis (caterpillar/butterfly). Moreover, fossil knowledge along with examples of adaptation provided the material evidence that convinced scientists of the validity of evolutionary claims (Mayr 1982). This analysis suggests that children's essentialist beliefs might be able to be modified by exposure to the fossil evidence or to evidence that animal populations apparently acquire new adaptive features in response to environmental change (dynamic adaptation: Evans 2000b).

For spontaneous generation, the obvious source analogy could also be derived from direct experience of the natural world. Consider that after a spring thaw or a rainy period new life apparently spontaneously emerges from the earth. Although it preexisted in embryonic forms such as seeds or eggs, this might not be obvious to the casual observer. Unlike Lamarckian evolution or creation, spontaneous generation explanations are nonteleological in that they do not directly invoke purpose or an underlying design (Mayr 1982). Instead, such explanations comprise a variety of proximal causes that describe how an organism, including a new species, becomes perceptible. One of the more complex examples of spontaneous generation reasoning is provided by Anaximander (ca. 610–546 BC), an early Greek philosopher (Mayr 1982, 302):

> The first animals were generated in the moisture, and were enclosed within spiny barks ... men were formed within these [fish-like creatures] and remained within them like embryos until they had reached maturity. Then at last the creatures burst open, and out of them came men and women, who were able to fend for themselves.

Source Analogies: Developmental Evidence

A recent study of the emergence of beliefs about the origins of species in public elementary school children (Evans 2000a) revealed a consistent pattern: The youngest children (5–7 years) endorsed mixed creationist and spontaneous generationist beliefs; children in the middle elementary-school years (8- to 10-year-olds) were exclusively creationist; whereas the oldest children (10.5- to 12-year-olds) were almost exclusively evolutionist with a smaller number being creationist. These children were from a university town in the mid-western United States and although their parents' beliefs were not assessed it would be reasonable to assume that the majority endorsed evolution. A second study (Evans 2000a) was carried out in rural and suburban areas of the Midwest, where, on average, adults had fewer years of education than those in the first study. Results for the two studies were similar, except that of the oldest children and their parents in the second study about half were evolutionist and the other half were creationist; a distribution also found in surveys of the population at large (e.g., Numbers 1992).

In the above studies it was not until early adolescence that children began to articulate evolutionary ideas, albeit of a Lamarckian variety. Moreover, in the second study, the degree to which parents endorsed evolutionary ideas and the degree to which children accepted the evidence for evolution, such as the fossil record, and endorsed beliefs in the inheritance of acquired characteristics (dynamic adaptation), were reliable predictors of the adoption of evolutionist explanations. Children are apparently able to suppress their essentialistic beliefs in the constancy of living kinds when confronted with convincing evidence that animals can change (Evans 2000a). Although there appeared to be a convergence between parents' ideas about the origin of species and those of their preadolescents, parents' beliefs bore little relationship to their younger children's explanations. These findings lead one to ask what system of intuitive beliefs could account for the pattern of responses found among the younger children.

It has already been suggested that children's intuitive ontologies readily provide a source analogy for creationism in the form of a naive psychology. However, even though young children, like creation scientists, appear to adhere to the premise that species are immutable, this does not explain why they shift toward exclusive creationism rather than persisting with naturalistic spontaneous generationist explanations into the middle elementary school years. Essentialism is compatible with either explanation. Two possible reasons have been proposed, one centering on the intuitive appeal of creationist explanations, as just described, and the other on the implausibility of spontaneous generationist explanations for the origins of species (Evans 2000a, b).

In the studies mentioned above, children's spontaneous generationist explanations drew on a variety of natural nontransformational mechanisms to describe how new species originated: "Grew on earth from eggs ...;" "Born in the land and crawled out;" "just appeared" (Evans 2000a). One unusually sophisticated response was similar to that of Anaximander (see above):

> ... they [dinosaurs] looked like small spiky balls that eventually unfolded themselves and grew to enormous size and split themselves into plant and animal eaters—and the ones that just couldn't cope with life and they died out. (G, 10 years old)

Notably, such explanations fail to address the underlying premise of questions about species origins: how and why did "the very first X" get to be there in the first place? One interpretation of the above findings is that young school-age children's naive biology is limited to proximate cause mechanisms, such as growth or birth, that could explain how an organism achieves its mature or perceptible form, but not how it comes into being (Evans 2000a). To appreciate the final cause nature of the origins question, children must first realize that a particular kind was once nonexistent (an idea that might well be incompatible with essentialist notions of the stability of the world)—the existential question. Once this question has been broached, children are likely to wonder what purpose is served by their existence—the design stance (Dennett 1987; Keil 1994; Kelemen 1999a, b). Spontaneous generation fails as a source analogy and as an explanation to the extent that it fails to address these issues. Younger children's adoption of spontaneous generation explanations may indicate that they have difficulty appreciating the nuances of the origins question. Creationist explanations, on the other hand, not only sanction essentialistic beliefs in the stability of species, they address the notion of original design (Evans 2000b), and, as such, provide greater explanatory coherence (Thagard 1989).

Study Rationale: Cognition in Context

These findings, although provocative, were based on children's open-ended responses to questions about the origins of species. They imply that the developmental sequence emerged from interactions between changes in children's knowledge structures and the social and natural contexts in which the children were reared. However, until the study is expanded to include children from homes where creationism is fully sanctioned, as found in Christian fundamentalist communities, only limited conclusions can be drawn. Moreover, although children may not have been able to spontaneously invoke creationist or evolutionist ideas using an open-ended interview technique, they may well have endorsed such explanations had they been presented in a forced-choice or closed-ended format. The latter techniques act, in effect, as scaffolds (Rogoff 1990), reminding children of explanations that are present publicly, which they may not have accessed without such support. Both of these drawbacks are addressed in the current study.

If ideas about the origins of species are in part derived from natural and social source analogs, as described earlier, then the extent to which children are exposed to and value those sources and associated areas of inquiry should be causally linked to children's adoption of these beliefs. To investigate these propositions in more detail, this study included some limited measures of the custom complex, that is the interconnected practices, beliefs, and values in which the child is embedded (Shweder et al. 1997). The adoption of creationist beliefs, for example, should be positively related to the degree to which religious activities and interests are endorsed by the child and family, but not to interest in fossils or to unrelated interests, such as in cars or music. On the other hand, finely tuned interests in the natural world, as evidenced by children's knowledge of fossils and adaptation, and parental encouragement of such interests, should be positively related to the degree to which evolutionary ideas are endorsed.

One unexpected finding of the second of the two earlier studies (Evans 2000a) was that about a third of the older elementary school children and adults endorsed mixed evolutionist and creationist beliefs. Some of the respondents may have embraced theistic evolution, which, as described earlier, is a coherent belief system. It is also possible that some respondents believed that humans and other animals have different origins: creationist for humans and evolutionist for other animals. However, most of these participants appeared to be struggling with what they viewed as incompatible concepts, suggesting that neither provided explanatory coherence (Thagard 1989). Given that a putative source analogy for creationism is artificialism, an indicator of a coherent creationism should be the extent to which these ideas are clearly demarcated: God (but not humans) should be credited with the capacity to create natural kinds (both inanimate, e.g., rocks, and animate, e.g., animals); whereas, humans (but not God) should be credited with the capacity to create artifacts. Measures testing these propositions will also be included.

In sum, the current study draws from matched Christian fundamentalist and non-fundamentalist school communities and includes, in addition to the original open-ended origins questions, closed-ended questions targeting artifacts, inanimate and animate natural kinds, as well as some measures of the custom complex. For the purposes of this study, fundamentalist communities were defined as school communities in which biblical literalism was embraced. Analyses will be of two kinds. First, community and age group comparisons will be made to verify that these two custom complexes vary in ways that are likely to support the differential spread of creationist and evolutionist beliefs. An often unrecognized problem with this approach, however, is that each community is treated as if individual members comprised a single group with a uniform belief system (D'Andrade 1990). As described above, even within the non-fundamentalist populations there are a range of beliefs about origins. Therefore the second set of analyses will focus on the age-related and experiential factors that relate to individual rather than to group belief patterns.

Method

Subjects

Christian fundamentalist children (n = 102: 48 females, 54 males) and their parents were recruited from two private Christian academies (69%) and a

Christian home-schooled group (31%). Their homes were in 26 rural and suburban towns and cities in one Midwestern state. The non-fundamentalist children (n = 83: 45 females, 38 males) and their parents, matched (to the extent possible) by age and locale to the fundamentalist children, were recruited from the same or adjacent towns and cities (18 in all) using a fan-out method: 88% went to public schools, and 12% to parochial schools. Wherever possible, entire families were recruited: in the non-fundamentalist group, 95% of children had a parent who participated (n = 45); in the fundamentalist group, 68% of children had a parent who participated (n = 47). The final set of analyses focused on complete data from family groups, only.

All schools, private and public, participated in state-mandated achievement tests that included a test of scientific knowledge, which differed by grade, and included fossils, dinosaurs, and natural history. Moreover, all the schools tended to use the same science textbooks, even though the actual curriculum varied by school. However, religious studies, including a literal interpretation of the Bible, were a regular part of the curriculum of the Christian fundamentalist schools only.

The children were divided into three age groups following Evans (2000a): (1) Young Group (Grades K–2) with a mean age of 6.8 years and a range of 5.3–7.9 years (non-fundamentalist, n = 25; fundamentalist, n = 38). (2) Middle Group (Grades 3–4) with a mean age of 9.1 years and a range of 8.1–10.2 years (non-fundamentalist, n =29), with a mean age of 9.0 years, and a range of 8.2–10.3 years (fundamentalist, n = 34). (3) Older Group (Grades 5–7) with a mean age of 11.5 years and a range of 10.3–12.9 years (non-fundamentalist, n = 29), and a mean age of 11.9 years and a range of 10.3–13.4 years (fundamentalist, n = 30). There was also an Adult Group comprising 45 non-fundamentalist and 47 fundamentalist parents (one father; the rest, mothers or female guardians).

Demographic Information
The educational level of all adults in the household was supplied by the parent respondent. Using a five-point scale (1, Some High School; 2, High School; 3, Two-Year College; 4, Four-Year College; 5, Some Graduate School), the mean completed educational level of the fundamentalist mothers was 3.4 (SD = .9); the fathers, 3.7 (SD = 1.0); and the predicted completed educational level for the child, according to the parent, 4.2 (SD = .7). Levels for the non-fundamentalist families were comparable: mothers, 3.2 (SD = 1.2); fathers, 3.3 (SD = 1.3); and predicted completed level for the child 4.2 (SD = .8). There were no significant differences in parental educational levels of children from the two school communities. Seventy-two percent of the children from the fundamentalist school communities attended a Christian fundamentalist church (e.g., Church of Christ, Southern Baptist), 11% attended a non-fundamentalist church (e.g.,

Catholic, Jewish, Methodist), and 11% did not attend church regularly. In contrast, of the children attending non-fundamentalist schools, 24% attended a fundamentalist church, 42% a non-fundamentalist church, and 34% did not attend church regularly. Churches, like the schools, were grouped as fundamentalist only if they were judged likely to embrace biblical literalism (for example, not all Southern Baptists are biblical literalists, whereas some conservative Catholics are).

General Procedure

All child interviews were conducted by the investigator and two female research assistants and lasted approximately 30 min. Sixty percent of the interviews were conducted in the child's home, 3% in the town library, and 37% in the child's school during regular school hours. For the in-home interviews, the mother (or guardian) filled in the parent questionnaire either while the child was interviewed in a separate room or after the child interview. Following the school interviews a parent questionnaire was sent home (including a stamped, addressed envelope) with each child. The numbers of adults completing each measure varied as not all parents completed all parts of the questionnaire. The interview was developed in collaboration with members of the Christian fundamentalist communities to ensure that the wording was acceptable. To verify interview reliability and to check the accuracy of the transcripts, all interviews were audiotaped with the permission of the parent and the child. Coding of the open-ended questions was done by coders blind to both the nature of the hypotheses and the group of the subject. The specific tasks and coding criteria for both children and parents will be described in four sections: (1) Open-ended origins task; (2) Closed-ended origins task; (3) Is the human a special case? (4) Natural-history knowledge, interests, and activities.

Task Order

After the child was asked some initial demographic questions, the first task focused on the child's interests. This was followed by the open-ended origins task, the close-ended origins task, and the natural-history questions. For the parents the task order was similar, except that following the demographic questions parents were given a closed-ended task that probed whether their origins explanations differed depending on the target (human versus dinosaur) and the age of the child. In place of the natural-history questions given to the child, parents were asked what activities and interests they encouraged in their children, as the focus of the interviews was on the child's knowledge and interests (not the parent's).

Origins Explanations: Open-Ended

The children's task was introduced with the following statement that was worded to draw their attention to the idea that a species may not have existed in the past (Evans 2000a). "I am going to ask you some questions. There are no right or wrong answers to these questions, just different kinds of ideas. Think about how the very first things got here on earth. A long, long time ago there were no things on earth. Then there were the very first things ever. Now, think about the *Target Item [Target Item description]*. How do you think the very first *Target Item* got here on earth?" (if no answer was elicited, there were two probes). The three target items were the sun bear [a kind of bear from Asia], the tuatara [a kind of lizard from New Zealand], and the human. All items were presented verbally only. The human was always last, with the order of the other two targets alternated between subjects. The tuatara and sun bear were considered to be unfamiliar and unlikely to elicit well-rehearsed knowledge.

The parent questionnaire included the following statement: "Imagine you were teaching a 10- to 12-year old child you know, and he or she had asked you the following questions. Please briefly write down your answers." The questions were "How did the very first *Target Item [Target Item description]* get here on earth?" The target items, which were presented in a fixed order, were tuatara, sun bear, and human. The age of the target child was based on results from earlier studies (Evans 2000a), in which it appeared that by 10–12 years of age children had converged on the beliefs of the adult population.

Coding Criteria

Responses to both the parent and the child origins questions were coded into four explanation patterns (as well as Don't Know and Other), as in Evans (2000a): Spontaneous Generation, responses indicating a natural but non-transformational origin for species (e.g., "grew from the earth," "born in the earth," "appeared"); Creation, responses indicating that God, a human, or another creature, created, planned, or put a species on earth; Evolution, responses indicating the transformation from one distinct animal kind into another (indicated by different species names, e.g., gorilla to a person or fish to a dinosaur); Hybridization, responses indicating that new species arose because of the interbreeding of two different species.

All responses were coded by two people. Inter-rater agreement for the assignment to explanation pattern for the origins questions for the first 100 subjects (approximately half fundamentalist and half non-fundamentalist) was as follows: tuatara origins (86%); sun bear origins (94%); human origins (97%). All disagreements were subsequently resolved by discussion.

Origins Explanation: Closed-Ended

The intent of this task was to investigate children's origins explanations with a forced-choice, recognition technique and to investigate the extent to which subjects' explanations were similar across diverse entities, representing different domains (animate, artifacts, inanimate). For all the explanations, prototypic exemplars were selected from children's open-ended responses given in earlier studies (e.g., Evans 2000a). Owing to the diversity of children's spontaneous generationist explanations, two exemplars were chosen, both of which could be applied to any type of entity (they did not reference a biological process such as growth or birth); the selected evolutionist explanation overtly repudiated the essentialist notion of immutability. To represent the putative source analogy for creationism (God-made), an artificialist (human-made) explanation was also included. Pilot testing indicated that among adults the creationist exemplar was likely to elicit a positive response from biblical literalists but not from theistic evolutionists, who did not find this form of creationism acceptable.

Task

The children viewed seven pictures, randomly selected one at a time from a bag, consisting of three animate entities (sun bear, tuatara, human), two inanimate entities (rock, crystal), and two simple artifacts (toy chair, doll). For each pictured Target Item, children were asked to what extent they agreed or disagreed with five statements (also randomly ordered) about the origins of the entity. Children used an Agree–Disagree card with a four-point scale to indicate how much they agreed with each statement. On the card there were four expressive faces indicating either disagreement (1, a lot; 2, a little) or agreement (3, a little; 4, a lot). Children were first trained to use the card, and no child had problems with its use. If any question elicited a "don't know" response the question was repeated twice; if the child persisted with a "don't know" response, a neutral 2.5 was assigned for that explanation and target (this happened rarely; less than 0.5% of cases). The origins question was always: "How did the very first *Target Item* get here on earth?" The origins explanations consisted of the following: Creationist ("God made it and put it on earth"), Artificialist ("A person made it and put it on earth"), Evolutionist ("It changed from a different kind of animal that used to live on earth"), two spontaneous-generationist explanations ("It just appeared"; "It came out of the ground").

Adults were given the same task in a questionnaire format. For the adults the entities were presented in a fixed order (doll, tuatara, rock, crystal, sun bear, chair, human), and for each entity the origins explanations were in a different fixed order. Adults also used the same four-point, agree–disagree scale to indicate the degree to which they would endorse the explanation.

Both adults and children could (and did) designate intermediate points on the scale and their responses were given proportional values (e.g., 3.5).

Is the Human a Special Case?

This measure was designed to elicit possible changes in the way parents explained their beliefs about human origins versus dinosaur origins to children of different ages. If the source analogy for creationism is a folk psychology, then parents might apply creationist explanations more often to the human than to other animals; moreover, even non-fundamentalist parents might be more likely to explain species origins in creationist terms to younger children.

In the questionnaire parents were told, "what follows are some explanations about origins that adults might give to children of different ages. As they are examples of children's answers (from an earlier study), we would not expect adults to give exactly the same explanations. We want to know if you would give similar explanations to your own children." Parents used a five-point scale anchored at 1, I would *never*—; 3, I *might* give—; and 5, I'm *very likely*— (to) give a similar explanation. Parents rated the likelihood of giving these explanations to children in each of the following age groups: 3–5 years, 6–9 years, 10–12 years (preschool, early–mid elementary, late elementary). Twelve explanations for dinosaur origins were followed by 12 explanations for human origins; they comprised the following groups, with no two explanations from the same group appearing next to each other: (1) Spontaneous generationist—four items (e.g., came alive suddenly; they were just born in a cave; could have just appeared), (2) Creationist—four items (e.g., God made the dinosaurs; God made the humans and put them on earth), (3) Evolutionist—four items (e.g., a long time ago dinosaurs began as sea-animals; humans evolved from other creatures such as the ape).

Natural-History Knowledge, Interests, and Activities

Children (but not parents) were given 12 randomly ordered statements on natural history, which were based on typical misconceptions exhibited by children in earlier studies (Evans 2000a): six were true and six were false. Responses to nine statements on fossils and deep time were grouped into a measure called Fossil Expertise. The three remaining statements probed for children's agreement with the idea that animals acquire new features in response to changed environmental conditions, called Dynamic Adaptation (see Appendix). Children used the previously described Agree–Disagree card (with the same four-point scale) to indicate how much they disagreed or agreed with each statement.

Children also participated in four tasks in which they were shown five randomly ordered pictures of specific interests and activities common to children in this age range. They rank ordered the pictures from those they liked the most (to read about, to collect, to visit, etc.), to those they liked the least; each interest was then assigned a number from 1 (the least) to 5 (the most), for each task (several were filler items). In addition, children used a five-point scale (1, Never; 3, Once or more a year; 5, Once or more a week) to indicate how often they engaged in five different activities. Conceptually related items from these tasks were grouped (3–5 items per group) into four measures of interest (Range, 1–5): (1) Religious (e.g., like to read Bible stories; like to go to church; frequency of church attendance); (2) Fossil (e.g., like to read about fossils and rocks; like to collect fossils and rocks); (3) Dinosaur (e.g., like to collect model dinosaurs; like to go to dinosaur museums); (4) General (e.g., like to read make-believe stories; like to collect stamps; like to go swimming; like to go to the movies).

Parents rated the importance of 25 potential child interests and activities (including three practice items) using a five-point scale anchored at 1, Not at all Important; 3, Important; and 5, Very Important—for their "child to do or to have." The activities were presented in a fixed order (with the constraint that no two activities from the same group appeared successively) and comprised the following groups (5–6 items per group): (1) Musical (e.g., to learn how to sing; to play a musical instrument), (2) Religious (e.g., to learn about Jesus and other religious figures; to go to a church, synagogue, or other place of worship regularly), (3) Fossil and Dinosaur (e.g., to go to rock and fossil museums; to have books on dinosaurs), (4) Nature (e.g., to have their own plants; to go on nature walks).

Results and Discussion

Part One: Community Comparisons

Origins Explanations: Open-ended

The main question addressed in this analysis is whether previous age-related patterns of explanation for the origins of species found in non-fundamentalist school communities (Evans 2000a) are also found in the fundamentalist school community. The findings indicate that creationist responses predominate in each age group in the fundamentalist community, while naturalistic responses (evolution and spontaneous generation) are rarely endorsed. This is unlike the pattern for the non-fundamentalist population where the dominant response depended on the age of the participants.

The basic measure, called frequency of explanation, was computed by recording the number of times participants invoked each of the explanations of interest (evolution, creation, spontaneous generation) across the three animate exemplars (human, sun bear, tuatara); the hybridization explanation was invoked too rarely to be included in the analysis. The possible range of scores for each explanation was 0–3. Mean frequency scores (and standard errors), by age group, in the non-fundamentalist and fundamentalist communities can be seen in Fig. 1. The origins-explanation frequency scores were analyzed in a 2 (Community: Fundamentalist, Non-fundamentalist) × 4 (Age group: Young, Middle, Older, Adult) × 3 (Explanation: Evolution, Creation, Spontaneous Generation) mixed-design analysis of variance (ANOVA),[2] with origins-explanation as the repeated measure. There was a main effect for origins-explanation, $F(2, 510) = 230.8$, $p \leq .0001$, and three significant interactions: origins-explanation × age group, $F(6, 510) = 10.7$, $p \leq .0001$; origins-explanations × community, $F(2, 510) = 50.4$, $p \leq .0001$; and origins-explanations × age group × community, $F(6, 510) = 7.5$, $p \leq .0001$. (A separate repeated measure ANOVA, without the adult group, included gender and found no significant main effects or interactions with gender.) To clarify the nature of the interactions, post hoc Scheffé comparisons were carried out separately within each school-community by age group, and then certain hypothesis-related comparisons were made between communities within each age group to verify the reported pattern. The overall focus was on the pattern of explanation preferences characterizing a particular age group (see Fig. 1).

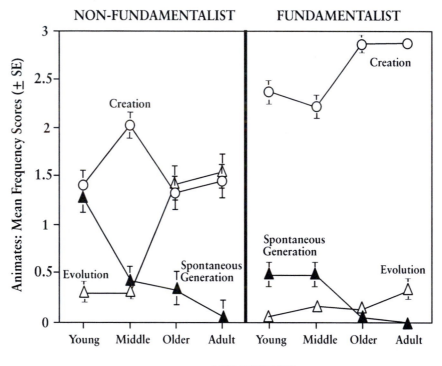

Figure 1. *Mean frequency scores for three explanations for the origins of species in fundamentalist and non-fundamentalist elementary school communities, by age group*

Non-fundamentalist school community. Among the young age group, creation and spontaneous generation were favored over evolution (p's ≤ .007), with no significant difference between creation and spontaneous generation. For the middle age group, in contrast, creation was favored over both evolution and spontaneous generation (p's ≤ .0001), with no significant difference between the latter pair of explanations. In both the older age group and the adults there were no significant differences between creation and evolution and both were favored over spontaneous generation (p's ≤ .02).

Fundamentalist school community. In all age groups, including the adults, creation was favored over both evolution and spontaneous generation (p's ≤ .0001). Of the two least-preferred explanations, the young children tended to invoke spontaneous generation more often than evolution (p ≤ .07), with no significant difference in the middle and older age groups; among the adults, however, evolution was favored over spontaneous generation as a less-preferred explanation (p ≤ .05).

Summary. Comparisons of the results from two school communities (see Fig. 1) suggest that the two natural explanations (evolution and spontaneous generation) were almost completely suppressed in the fundamentalist community relative to the non-fundamentalist community. Thus, creationist explanations predominated in every age group among the fundamentalists, but in the non-fundamentalist school community it was only in the middle age group that creation was the single most favored explanation. Confirming the latter pattern, with the exception of the middle age group, significant differences were found between the two communities in each age group for the frequency of creationist explanation (p's ≤ .0002).

Origins Explanations: Closed-ended
The next set of analyses focused on whether the same patterns of explanation would be found with the use of a forced-choice rather than an open-ended method. In addition, adults and children were asked to what extent they agreed that natural (evolution, spontaneous generation) or intentional (creationist, artificialist) origins explanations could be applied not only to animate natural kinds, but also to artifacts and to inanimate natural kinds. The use of closed-ended or forced-choice questions gave participants the opportunity to explicitly consider all explanations, making it possible for explanations that are not easily invoked in an open-ended recall procedure to be endorsed when using a closed-ended recognition procedure.

As can be seen in Fig. 2, although the same overall pattern is apparent with the use of the forced-choice procedure for the animate entities, there is an increase in creationist responses, especially among younger non-fundamentalist children. Additionally, there is an effect of domain with spontaneous generation favored for inanimate entities and artificialism for artifacts.

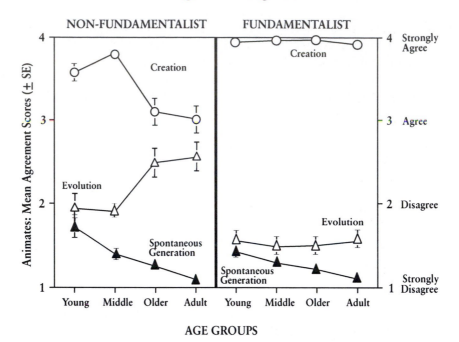

Figure 2. *Animate origins: Mean agreement scores for three explanations, in fundamentalist and non-fundamentalist elementary school communities, by age group*

A measure termed *origins-explanation agreement* was constructed for each origins explanation; this was the mean level of agreement (scale, 1–4) with each origins explanation for each of the three domains: animates, artifacts, and inanimates. In order to limit the number of analyses, only one of the two spontaneous generation exemplars, "It came out of the ground," was used to represent that explanation (the results for both exemplars were similar for the animates). For each domain the origins-agreement scores were analyzed in a 2 (Community: Fundamentalist, Non-fundamentalist) × 4 (Age group: Young, Middle, Older, Adult) × 4 (Explanation: Creation, Evolution, Spontaneous-Generation, Artificialist) mixed-design ANOVA, with explanation as the repeated measure. Where there were significant interactions, post hoc Scheffé comparisons focused on the pattern of explanation preferences characterizing a particular age group; differences between explanations that were rejected by the participant (disagree on the Agree–Disagree scale) will not be reported in any detail, but they do provide evidence that children were evaluating the explanations appropriately. As before, selected further comparisons were made between communities within each age group to verify the reported pattern.

Animate origins. There were significant main effects for community, $F(1, 268) = 4.8$, $p \leq .03$, age group, $F(3, 268) = 10.6$, $p \leq .0001$; and explanation,

F(3, 804) = 765.0, p ≤ .0001; means and standard errors can be seen in Fig. 2 (artificialism was rejected: means ≤ 2). Additionally, there were significant interactions: explanation × age group, F(9, 804) = 8.3, p ≤ .0001; explanation × community, F(3, 804) = 33.93, p ≤ .0002; and explanation × age group × community, F(9, 804) = 3.7, p ≤ .0003. In the young and middle non-fundamentalist age groups, creation was favored over all other explanations (p's ≤ .0001). In the older age group and the adults there was no significant difference between creation and evolution and both were favored over both spontaneous generation and artificialism (p's ≤ .0001). In all age groups in the fundamentalist school community, creation was the most strongly endorsed of all explanations (p's ≤ .0001). Between-community comparisons showed significant differences in each age group for creation (fundamentalists higher, p's ≤ .0003) and evolution (non-fundamentalists higher: young-group, p .05; the other age groups, p's ≤ .009).

Artifact origins. There were significant main effects for community, F(1, 268) = 4.3, p ≤ .04, age group, F(3, 268) = 20.0, p ≤ .0001, and explanation, F(3, 804) = 861.8, p ≤ .0001; means and standard errors can be seen in Fig. 3 (spontaneous generation was rejected: means ≤ 2).

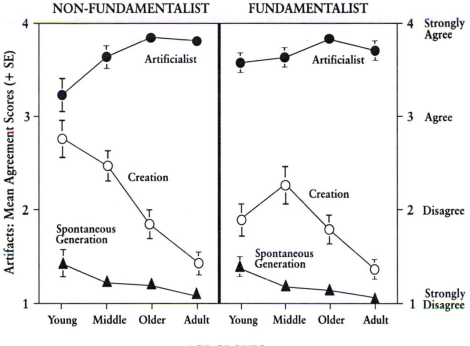

Figure 3. *Artifact origins: Mean agreement scores for three explanations, in fundamentalist and non-fundamentalist elementary school communities, by age group*

Additionally, there were significant interactions: explanation × age group, $F(9, 804) = 13.8$, $p ≤ .0001$; explanation × community, $F(3, 804) = 2.8$, $p ≤ .04$, and explanation × age group × community, $F(9, 804) = 2.5$, $p ≤ .007$. In both communities artificialism was favored over all other explanations ($p's ≤ .0001$), with the exception of the young non-fundamentalist children, for whom creationist and artificialist origins were preferred equally. Between-community comparisons within each age group for artificialism and creation showed differences in the young age group only, with creation more likely to be endorsed in the non-fundamentalist community ($p ≤ .006$). (This interesting result will be investigated in more detail later.)

Inanimate origins. There were significant main effects for age group, $F(3, 268) = 15.9$, $p ≤ .0001$, and explanation, $F(3, 804) = 362.0$, $p ≤ .0001$; means and standard errors can be seen in Fig. 4 (evolution was rejected: means ≤ 2). Additionally, there were significant interactions: explanation × age group, $F(9, 804) = 3.3$, $p ≤ .0007$; explanation × community, $F(3, 804) = 39.0$, $p ≤ .0001$; and explanation × age group × community, $F(9, 804) = 2.3$, $p ≤ .02$. In the fundamentalist community, creation was the explanation of choice for all age groups ($p's ≤ .0001$), though spontaneous

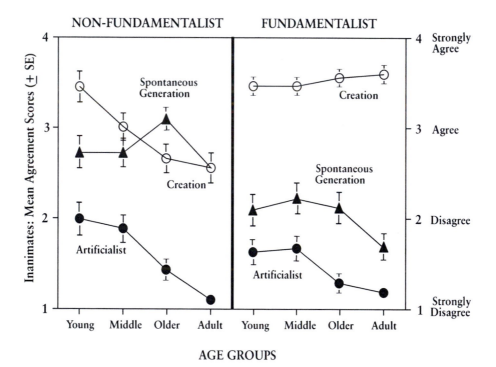

Figure 4. *Inanimate origins: Mean agreement scores for three explanations, in fundamentalist and non-fundamentalist elementary school communities, by age group*

generation was significantly preferred over artificialism and evolution (p's ≤ .02). Among the non-fundamentalists, spontaneous generation and creation were both strongly endorsed by all age groups. For the older age group, spontaneous generation was favored over creation (p ≤ .05), whereas for all the other age groups both explanations were equally endorsed. Between-community comparisons within age groups reveal that with the exception of the young age group, where spontaneous generation and creation were both endorsed equally, creation was more likely to be endorsed in the fundamentalist than in the non-fundamentalist community (p's ≤ .007). On the other hand, with the exception of the middle age group, where they were endorsed equally, spontaneous generation was more likely to be endorsed in the non-fundamentalist community (p's ≤ .04).

Summary. The overall developmental pattern for animate entities with the forced-choice questions was similar to that found with the open-ended questions, with the interesting exception of the younger non-fundamentalist children: they were more likely to endorse creation and less likely to endorse spontaneous generation with the forced-choice paradigm. Notably, however, the younger children still did not endorse evolution. The lack of endorsement for spontaneous generation could result from several factors, which will be discussed in some detail later. One possibility, however, is that the exemplar "came out of the ground" was too specific, although it was a frequent response to the open-ended questions. However, the second spontaneous generation exemplar "it just appeared" potentially had a broader appeal, yet the pattern of responses for the two exemplars was very similar, especially for the animate entities. Of course, it is possible that the spontaneous generationist exemplar (came out of the ground) would have been deemed plausible as an explanation for animate origins by more children if it had been linked to a biological cause (growth, birth), which was done by some children in the open-ended measure.

An interaction between domain and explanation was also found. For artifacts, members of all communities endorsed artificialism, again with the exception of the young non-fundamentalists who appeared to conflate artificialism and creationism. On the other hand, spontaneous generation was more likely to be endorsed for inanimate natural entities than for animates or artifacts, by all age groups in both communities.

Is the Human a Special Case?

Initial analyses focus on whether the overall pattern of explanations endorsed by parents differed depending on the type of exemplar (human or dinosaur) and the type of school community (fundamentalist and non-fundamentalist). It was found that the type of exemplar does have an effect on parental responses especially in the non-fundamentalist community.

Parental endorsement of each explanation (range 1–5: evolution, creation, and spontaneous generation) was analyzed in a 2 (Community: Fundamentalist, Non-fundamentalist) × 2 (Exemplar: Human, Dinosaur) mixed-design ANOVA, with exemplar as the repeated measure. In this analysis no distinction was made between age groups. As expected, non-fundamentalist parents were much more likely to endorse evolution overall, $F(1, 77) = 35.4$, $p \leq .0001$, but parents from both communities were more likely to apply evolution to the dinosaur (means: 1.6 and 2.9) than to the human (means: 1.3 and 2.2), $F(1, 77) = 39.8$, $p \leq .0001$. On the other hand, fundamentalist parents were more likely to endorse creationism overall $F(1, 77) = 15.4$, $p \leq .0003$, but both groups were more likely to apply creation to the human (means: 3.6 and 4.6) than to the dinosaur (means: 2.9 and 3.6), $F(1, 77) = 94.5$, $p \leq .0001$. Although neither community was likely to endorse spontaneous generation explanations (means: 1.1 to 1.4), when they did, they were more likely to apply them to the dinosaur than to the human $F(1, 77) = 19.5$, $p \leq .0001$.

The next analyses are broken down by the targeted age group: preschool, early–mid elementary, late elementary. Members of the fundamentalist community consistently endorsed creationism, and parents, in general, rarely endorsed spontaneous generation; therefore these analyses focused on non-fundamentalist parents and whether they felt they would tailor their creationist or evolutionist explanations to the age of the child. Non-fundamentalist parents were significantly more likely to explain human and dinosaur origins in evolutionary terms to both age groups of elementary school children, than to their preschool children (F's 16.0 to 19.0; p's $\leq .0001$). Moreover, non-fundamentalist parents were more likely to give creationist explanations for dinosaur origins to their preschoolers, than to the two elementary school groups ($F = 3.1$; $p \leq .05$); they did not discriminate between age groups, however, when giving creationist explanations for human origins.

To confirm this indication that the human is treated as a special case, a secondary analysis of answers to the earlier closed-ended origins questions was conducted to see if this result would hold true across explanations that were identical for human and nonhuman targets. For the closed-ended origins questions reported earlier, the human and the two nonhuman species (tuatara, sun bear) were separated into two measures (human versus nonhuman) and compared using one-tailed, paired t-tests. Overall, evolution, $t(275) = 5.2$; $p \leq .0001$, was more likely to be applied to the nonhuman species, and creation to the human, $t(275) = 2.0$; $p \leq .03$. When the results were broken down by community and age group, a clearer picture emerged for creation. The preferential use of creation for the human was evident only in the middle age groups from both communities and in adult members of the non-fundamentalist community (t's 2.2 to 3.5; p's $\leq .02$ to $\leq .0007$). These results provide corroborative evidence for the previous findings.

Summary. A possible cause of the age-related sequence of beliefs exhibited by non-fundamentalist children is that parents change their explanations depending on the age of the child, though it would be difficult to determine the causal direction of the effect. However, given the inconsistency of the pattern, direct parental input seems unlikely to have contributed much to the developmental sequence. Both measures described above indicate that humans are treated as a special case, especially in non-fundamentalist settings, and are more likely than nonhuman species to elicit creationist origins. Moreover, these results demonstrate that parents, particularly non-fundamentalist parents, are likely to manifest mixed beliefs: evolution applied to nonhuman species and creation to the human.

Natural-History Knowledge, Interests, and Activities

The next analyses targeted some limited measures of the custom complex in fundamentalist and non-fundamentalist homes and schools, to evaluate whether they differed in ways consistent with the differences in beliefs between the two communities. As can be seen in Table 1, this effect is apparent in the expected areas of expertise and interest.

Measure (Range)	Non-fundamentalist	Fundamentalist	F value
Child natural-history knowledge			
Fossil expertise (1–4)	2.9 (.4)	2.7 (.4)	12.5***
Dynamic adaption (1–4)	2.0 (.8)	1.7 (.8)	7.4**
Child interests			
Religious (1–5)	2.8 (.9)	3.5 (.9)	23.9***
Fossil (1–5)	2.9 (.9)	2.6 (.9)	4.9*
Dinosaur (1–5)	2.7 (.9)	2.8 (1.0)	0.2
General (1–5)	3.4 (.9)	3.3 (.7)	1.6
Parent encouragement of child interests			
Religious (1–5)	3.5 (1.0)	4.6 (.5)	41.6***
Dinosaurs/fossils (1–5)	3.6 (.8)	3.1 (.8)	8.7**
Nature (1–5)	3.9 (.6)	3.6 (.7)	6.2*
Music (1–5)	3.4 (.8)	3.2 (.8)	2.7

*p < .05.
**p < .01.
***p < .001.

Table 1. *Natural-history knowledge and interests of elementary-school children in fundamentalist and non-fundamentalist school communities: means (standard deviations)*

Mean scores for the measures of children's natural-history knowledge and interests, and parents' encouragement of child interests, by school community, are presented in Table 1. (The higher the score the more expert or interested they were, depending on the measure, and the more likely they were to endorse the belief in the inheritance of acquired features.) One-way

ANOVAs with Community (2) conducted on each of the measures (F values reported in Table 1) showed that members of these two school communities differed on those interests putatively related to their belief systems (religion, fossils), but not on more neutral interests (general interests, music). Interestingly, although non-fundamentalist children were more knowledgeable about fossils, they were more likely than fundamentalist children to accept the false notion that acquired features could be inherited (dynamic adaptation). Children from both communities were interested in dinosaurs, although they differed in their interest in fossils. This finding fits in with other findings (Evans 2000a) that children's ability to sort and describe dinosaurs does not necessarily entail the knowledge that dinosaurs are an important part of the fossil record.

Analyses of the effects for gender on child interests indicate main effects only: In both communities, females preferred religious activities (F = 10.4; p ≤ .002) and general interests (F = 76.3; p ≤ .0001), and males, fossils (F = 16.3; p ≤ .0001) and dinosaurs (F = 57.5; p ≤ .0001). There were no effects for gender, however, on either measure of child natural-history knowledge.

Summary. Overall, children and parents from fundamentalist communities were more likely to endorse religious interests, whereas those from non-fundamentalist communities were more likely to endorse interests in nature and fossils. Interests in music and more general interests in sports, cars, dolls, etc., were endorsed equally by both communities.

Part Two: Individual Differences

Typology of Belief: Implications for Explanatory Coherence

The above results demonstrate that participants often manifested mixed beliefs with evolution applied preferentially to nonhuman species and creation to the human. As group results obscure individual differences it is not clear whether of the adult non-fundamentalists half were evolutionist and half creationist or whether most endorsed mixed creationist and evolutionist beliefs (see Fig. 1). To examine such individual differences in more detail, composite measures of the consistency of beliefs were derived from the origins questions described earlier and used to create a typology of beliefs for each community; the coherence of these explanatory systems was then explored by comparing these typologies.

Beliefs that appear to contradict one another are defined as incoherent (see Thagard 1989); it would follow that they are unlikely to exist as related concepts within a coherent explanatory framework. The belief that God created each living kind as an exclusive and immutable entity and the belief that each living kind evolved, for example, are mutually exclusive. However, as can be seen in Tables 2–5, the beliefs of many of the participants, particularly those in the non-fundamentalist community, appear to be incoherent in that they endorse both creationist and evolutionist explanations.

Typology	Age group			
	Young	Middle	Older	Adult
Non-fundamentalist school community				
(1) Evolution/No Creation	0	3	34	26
(2) Evolution and Creation	22	21	31	33
(3) Creation/No Evolution	56	76	35	36
(4) Neither	22	0	0	5
Fundamentalist school community				
(1) Evolution/No Creation	0	3	3	3
(2) Evolution and Creation	5	15	10	18
(3) Creation/No Evolution	92	82	87	79
(4) Neither	3	0	0	0

Note. This typology was constructed from the open-ended frequency measure for the animates: Creation frequency–Evolution frequency (see Fig. 1)

Table 2. *Animate origins: a typology of the frequency of evolutionist and creationist beliefs among elementary-school children (young, 5–7 years; middle, 8–10 years; older, 11–13 years) and adults from non-fundamentalist and fundamentalist school communities (percentage of group)*

Typology	Age group			
	Young	Middle	Older	Adult
Non-fundamentalist school community				
(1) Evolution/No Creation	0	0	21	27
(2) Evolution and Creation	20	17	28	25
(3) Creation/No Evolution	76	79	48	48
(4) Neither	4	4	3	0
Fundamentalist school community				
(1) Evolution/No Creation	0	0	0	2
(2) Evolution and Creation	8	9	7	8
(3) Creation/No Evolution	92	91	93	90
(4) Neither	0	0	0	0

Note. This typology was constructed from the closed-ended origins agreement measure for the animates: Creation agreement–Evolution agreement (see Fig. 2)

Table 3. *Animate origins: a typology of evolutionist and creationist beliefs (agreement) among elementary-school children (young, 5–7 years; middle, 8–10 years; older, 11–13 years) and adults from non-fundamentalist and fundamentalist school communities (percentage of group)*

Typology	Age group			
	Young	Middle	Older	Adult
Non-fundamentalist school community				
(1) Artificialism/No Creation	20	45	72	89
(2) Artificialism and Creation	56	41	25	7
(3) Creation/No Artificialism	16	14	0	2
(4) Neither	8	0	3	2
Fundamentalist school community				
(1) Artificialism/No Creation	61	47	73	85
(2) Artificialism and Creation	23	44	27	9
(3) Creation/No Artificialism	3	3	0	4
(4) Neither	13	6	0	2

Note. This typology was constructed from the closed-ended origins agreement measure for the artifacts: Creation agreement–Artificialism (human-made) agreement (see Fig. 3)

Table 4. *Artifact origins: a typology of evolutionist and creationist beliefs among elementary-school children (young, 5–7 years; middle, 8–10 years; older, 11–13 years) and adults from non-fundamentalist and fundamentalist school communities (percentage of group)*

Typology	Age group			
	Young	Middle	Older	Adult
Non-fundamentalist school community				
(1) Spontaneous generation/No Creation	8	21	48	30
(2) Spontaneous generation and Creation	52	34	28	27
(3) Creation/No spontaneous generation	28	28	17	23
(4) Neither	12	17	7	20
Fundamentalist school community				
(1) Spontaneous generation/No Creation	5	6	7	4
(2) Spontaneous generation and Creation	29	39	30	21
(3) Creation/No spontaneous generation	53	44	60	66
(4) Neither	13	11	3	9

Note. This typology was constructed from the closed-ended origins agreement measure for the inanimates: Creation agreement–Spontaneous Generation agreement (see Fig. 4).

Table 5. *Inanimate origins: a typology of spontaneous generationist and creationist beliefs among elementary-school children (young, 5–7 years; middle, 8–10 years; older, 11–13 years) and adults from non-fundamentalist and fundamentalist school communities (percentage of group)*

Animates. Two composite measures of belief consistency (evolution-to-creation) were constructed by combining the evolution and creation responses for the animates. The first measure was based on the frequency scale (0–3) from the open-ended questions (see Table 2) and the second measure on the agreement scale (1–4) from the closed-ended questions (see Table 3). In both cases, the evolution responses (Evolution Frequency or Evolution Agreement) were subtracted from the creation responses (Creation Frequency or Creation Agreement). In the resulting composite measures of belief consistency (evolutionist-to-creationist; range, −3 to +3), higher positive scores indicate more consistent creationism, lower negative scores more consistent evolutionism, with intermediate scores indicating some type of mixed beliefs. Based on these consistency measures (and the original data) typologies were then created in which participants were divided into four groups: pure evolution (no creation), mixed evolution and creation, pure creation (no evolution), and neither evolution nor creation. As the agreement scale spanned a range from (1) strongly disagree to (4) strongly agree, the following criteria were used to construct the "agreement" typology: (1) Evolution (> 2.5), No Creation (≤ 2.5); (2) Evolution and Creation (≥ 2.5 for both); (3) Creation (> 2.5), No Evolution (≤ 2.5). If participants did not agree with either explanation (≤ 2.5 for both explanations, where 2.5 = neither agree nor disagree) they were placed in a "neither" category. The percentage of participants falling into each of these groups in the two communities is presented by age group in Table 2, for the frequency measure, and in Table 3, for the agreement measure. As spontaneous generation was rarely endorsed in the closed-ended animate measures it was not included in these analyses (but see Evans 2000a).

In the open-ended frequency measure participants had to construct rather than recognize explanations, which was presumably a more difficult task than the closed-ended agreement measure where "reminders" were given. The typologies presented in Tables 2 and 3 demonstrate that in both school communities more participants exhibited mixed beliefs with the open-ended frequency measure. With the closed-ended agreement measure, pure creationism was endorsed more strongly by all groups of participants. Moreover, young non-fundamentalist children readily endorsed creationist (but not evolutionist) explanations with the agreement measure even though many of them (22%) failed to generate such a response with the open-ended questions. When creationist explanations were suggested, as in the closed-ended agreement measures, it appears that natural explanations, such as spontaneous generation and evolution, were seen as less viable and suppressed, at least with these populations.

Artifacts. A similar measure of belief consistency (artificialist-to-creationist) was constructed for artifact origins from the origins-agreement measure (see Table 4). Unlike the results for the animates and inanimates, the profiles of the three older age groups in both communities were very similar. With the exception of the young non-fundamentalists, a majority of each group endorsed a pure artificialist explanation for artifact origins. Young non-fundamentalist children, though, were more likely than their fundamentalist counterparts to conflate the power of God and that of the human; God, on this analysis, appeared to be treated as just another human.

In general, the percentage of pure artificialist responses increased steadily by age group, but the middle age group from the fundamentalist community provided an interesting exception. In comparison with the other fundamentalist age groups, they were more likely to endorse mixed artificialist/creationist explanations and less likely to endorse pure artificialism. This finding is in line with earlier analyses demonstrating the preferential use of creation for human origins by the middle age group (but not younger children). Together these results suggest that, unlike their younger siblings, children from the middle age groups may be confronting the issue of final cause, which addresses the question of why something might come into existence in the first place. Having recently come to the conclusion that God creates all animates (including the human) and that humans create artifacts, children from the middle age group could be struggling with the question of whether God created artifacts via human agency; therefore, both artificialism and creationism are valid. In effect, the overall pattern of developmental change suggests a U-shaped curve, with older participants and younger fundamentalists both distinguishing between the powers of God and of the human, but for different reasons. Although the younger fundamentalists appear to be precocious in their use of creation and artificialism, their accomplishment is unlikely to reflect a mature understanding of final cause.

Inanimates. For inanimate origins, a typology of belief consistency (spontaneous generation-to-creation) was constructed from the origins-agreement measure and is presented in Table 5. Comparison of the percentage of participants endorsing creationist and natural explanations for inanimate (spontaneous generation; see Table 5) and animate origins (evolution; see Table 3) yields several interesting findings. The spontaneous generation exemplar, "came out of the ground," was more likely to appeal as a pure natural explanation for inanimate origins, than the natural explanation, evolution, did for animate origins, especially for the older non-fundamentalists. Additionally, the percentage of pure creationist explanations is greater for the animate than for the inanimate entities for each age group in both communities.

Summary. These findings raise intriguing issues as to why creation appears to be a more compelling explanation for animate than for inanimate origins. As many have suggested, the very complexity of animates and their teleological entailments might invoke a teleological explanation (e.g., Dawkins 1987). Relatedly, the natural explanation for animate origins, evolution, seems to be particularly unappealing with its counterintuitive emphasis on species change. On the other hand, the natural explanation for inanimate origins, spontaneous generation, appears to have considerable intuitive appeal for many participants.

Regarding the issue of explanatory coherence, these results indicate that coherent belief systems were evidenced to a greater degree in the fundamentalist communities. Mixed beliefs were less prevalent in the fundamentalist than in the non-fundamentalist communities, especially for animate entities. Moreover, a majority of fundamentalists exhibited coherent belief structures with God, alone, being responsible for the origins of both natural kinds, animate and inanimate, and humans, alone, being responsible for the origins of artifacts.

It could be argued, though, that the mixed beliefs of some non-fundamentalists might well reflect coherent belief systems. As described earlier, some participants, in particular non-fundamentalist adults, endorsed evolution for nonhuman species while reserving creation for human origins. However, if a majority of non-fundamentalist adults had proposed such a solution then the score for evolution should be higher than that for creation in most of the mixed belief cases, given that in this study the proportion of nonhuman species exemplars to human exemplars was 2:1. Yet on the agreement measure (see Table 3) only 36% of the mixed belief cases showed this pattern. Further, theistic evolution, which is a coherent framework in which God plays a more distal role as the originator of an evolutionary process, could well have been endorsed by many of the non-fundamentalists. However, although theistic evolutionists might have expressed mixed beliefs in the open-ended (frequency) measure, they would be unlikely to have endorsed the patently biblical literalist "creationist" exemplars in the closed-ended (agreement) measures.

Nonetheless, differences between measures indicate a decrease in mixed beliefs and an increase in pure creationism from the frequency to the agreement measures. This is the opposite of what would have been predicted if coherent theistic evolutionists had made up a significant proportion of the non-fundamentalist population.

Consistency of Parent Belief, Markers of the Custom Complex, and Children's Beliefs

The subsequent analyses focus on individual belief and the relationship between the consistency of parents' beliefs, various markers of the custom complex, and children's beliefs. Given that children in the two school communities differed on their putative beliefs about origins and related issues but not in terms of parental educational level and general interests, they were combined into one pool. The measure of parent belief-consistency is based on the closed-ended animate agreement score, described above. This particular measure is used as an indicator of parent beliefs for two reasons:

more parents completed the closed-ended measure than the open-ended one, and it forced parents to explicitly consider every explanation for animate origins. It is worth noting that results using closed-ended measures were very similar to those based on the open-ended data. Thirty-nine children were excluded from these analyses as they did not have complete parent data. The remaining child sample (n = 147) included 52 from the young age group (23 non-fundamentalist community; 29 fundamentalist), 51 from the middle age group (27 non-fundamentalist community; 24 fundamentalist), and 44 from the older age group (28 non-fundamentalist community; 16 fundamentalist).

To examine the thesis that consistency of parent beliefs influences the kind of environment provided for children, zero-order correlations between parent evolutionist-to-creationist consistency beliefs, children's beliefs, and the various markers of the custom complex described in the last section (see Table 1) were calculated (see Table 6). A measure of church type was also included, since this is a crude marker of the degree to which biblical literalism may have been encountered in a church setting (1, no church; 2, non-fundamentalist church; 3, fundamentalist church); school type was included as a dichotomous variable (1, non-fundamentalist school; 2, fundamentalist school).

Summary. Consistency of parent beliefs was related to most of the other variables in a predictable manner; for all measures the higher a score the more the environment was saturated with creation beliefs, and vice versa for evolution (see Table 6). The consistency of parent evolutionist-to-creationist beliefs correlated positively with both measures of children's creationist beliefs and negatively with both measures of children's evolutionist beliefs. Moreover, parent beliefs correlated positively with children's religious interest and likelihood of attending a fundamentalist school and church, but negatively with children's fossil expertise. Interestingly, parent beliefs were not related to children's fossil interest or dynamic adaptation endorsement. However, children's age correlated positively with children's fossil interest and negatively with dynamic adaptation endorsement. Additionally, dynamic adaptation correlated negatively with both measures of child creationist beliefs and the likelihood of attending a fundamentalist school or church. On the other hand, dynamic adaptation was positively related to both measures of child evolutionist beliefs.

Developmental Change in the Relationship Between Parent Belief, the Custom Complex, and Children's Beliefs

If cognitive and cultural factors play an interactive role in the expression of beliefs about origins then one might predict that these factors have differential impact depending on the targeted age group. As their knowledge structures mature, children's capacity to respond to social and environmental

Measures	(1)	(2)	(3)	(4)	(5)	(6)	(7)	(8)	(9)	(10)	(11)
(1) Consistency of parent beliefs[a] (Evolution-to-Creation)											
(2) Child age (continuous)	-.12	—									
Child origins explinations											
(3) Evolution frequency	-.42***	.34***	—								
(4) Creation frequency	.37***	-.03	-.61***	—							
(5) Evolution agreement	-.46***	.14	.58***	-.56***	—						
(6) Creation agreement	.42***	-.23**	-.57***	.51***	-.58***	—					
Child knowledge and interests											
(7) Fossil expertise	-.33***	.26**	.46***	-.37***	.44***	-.29**	—				
(8) Dynamic adaption	-.07	-.17*	.17*	-.23**	.39***	-.20*	.09	—			
(9) Fossil interest	-.12	.19*	.12	-.09	.05	-.05	.07	.01	—		
(10) Religious interest	.36***	-.18*	-.20*	.19*	-.24**	.33***	-.17*	-.09	-.29***	—	
Child environment											
(11) School Type (NF-to-F)	.54***	-.13	-.32***	.42***	-.41***	-.42***	-.27***	-.24**	-.15	.36***	—
(12) Church type (NF-to-F)	.53***	.06	-.24**	.29***	-.31***	.27***	-.13	-.28***	-.12	.50***	.52***

[a] Consistency of parent beliefs was derived from the closed-ended origins agreement scores for the animates (Creation agreement—Evolution agreement); range −3 to +3: higher scores equal increasingly consistant creationism: lower scores equal increasingly consistant evolutionism.

*p <.05.

**p <.01.

***p <.001

Table 6. *Zero-order correlations between consistency of parent beliefs[a] (Evolution-to-Creation), child age, child origins explanations, child knowledge and interests, and child environment (n = 146)*

information will also change. In the next analyses the developmental patterns underlying the relationships described in the last section are clarified. Replicating and extending earlier work (Evans 2000a), the most striking finding is that parent beliefs do not contribute directly and independently to the expression of child beliefs until children are early adolescents (10–12 years). This result is now found on both the open-ended and the closed-ended measures.

Furthermore, a more detailed exploration of the effects of the culture complex now reveals subtle age-related effects, especially on the closed-ended measures, with parents exercising indirect influence via the environments they select for their younger children.

The above ANOVAs have demonstrated that children in different age groups differentially endorsed the various origins explanations. In the current analyses, a series of simultaneous multiple regressions is carried out to assess whether variables correlated with children's evolution and creation agreement scores (consistency of parent beliefs, fossil expertise, dynamic adaptation, religious interest, and school-type, see Table 6) impacted differentially on each age group. (Church-type was not included as this information was not available for all participants and religious interest and school type picked up most of the associated variance.) The closed-ended agreement measures are the focus of these analyses and they are summarized in Tables 7 and 8; in the following text, however, the open-ended frequency measures will be brought in as reference marks. (To save space, only results for the animates and artifacts will be reported.) Of particular theoretical interest is the independent contribution of each variable (partialing out the effects of the other variables), as indicated by the standardized regression coefficients (b s).

Animates: evolutionary origins. For each age group, consistency of parent beliefs, fossil expertise, dynamic adaptation, religious interest, and school-type were simultaneously regressed on children's evolution agreement scores. Although in each age group a significant portion of the variance was explained by the joint effects of these variables, the profile differed by age group (see Table 7). Notably, only in the oldest age group did parent beliefs contribute independently to the children's evolution agreement scores; in this age group 71% of the variance in children's scores was explained, with children's dynamic adaptation scores ($\beta = 30$) and parent beliefs ($\beta = -.58$) making significant independent contributions. For the two younger age groups, children's fossil expertise (β s = .28–.30) and, in the middle age group, their dynamic adaptation scores ($\beta = .40$) made significant independent contributions to children's evolution agreement scores. The same variables were simultaneously regressed on children's evolution frequency scores separately for each age group. Essentially the same pattern emerged for the old age group: 67% of the variance was explained (p ≤ .0001), with parent beliefs (β = −.40; p ≤ .004), child fossil expertise (β = .24; p ≤ .04), and dynamic adaptation scores (β = .30; p ≤ .005), making significant independent contributions. For the middle age group the overall regression was not significant, but there was a trend for the young age group (R^2 = .19; p ≤.07).

Predictors	Age group (β)		
	Young	Middle	Older
Consistency of parent beliefs	.04	−.16	−.58***
Child's fossil expertise	.30*	.28*	.09
Child's dynamic adaption score	.25	.40**	.30**
Child's religious interests	.08	−.11	−.07
School type (NF to F)	−.25	.04	−.07
R^2	.30**	.36**	.71***

Note. See Table 6.
*p<.05.
**p<.01.
***p<.001.

Table 7. Animates—Evolutionist origins: multiple regressions on child evolution agreement scores for three elementary-school age groups (standardized regression coefficients)

Animates: creationist origins. Next, for each age group, consistency of parent beliefs, fossil expertise, dynamic adaptation, religious interest, and school-type were simultaneously regressed on children's creation agreement scores (see Table 8). For the young age group, school-type (β = .45) made a significant independent contribution to children's creation agreement scores, whereas for the middle age group only the child's religious interest had an independent effect (β = .39). Interestingly, although all the variables jointly accounted for 47% of the variance in the older age group's scores, none made a significant independent contribution. However, school-type appears to have masked the effects of the other variables; when it was removed from the regression, the overall variance explained decreased minimally to 46% but parent beliefs (β = −.31; p ≤ .05), and child religious interest (β = .29; p ≤ .03) now made significant independent contributions.

When the same variables were simultaneously regressed on children's creation frequency scores for each age group, school-type again made a significant independent contribution to the scores of the young age group (R^2 = .34; p ≤ .0002), but the overall regression was not significant for the middle age group. For the older age group, 76% of the overall variance was explained with all variables in place (p ≤ .0001); significant independent contributions were made by school-type (β = 23; p ≤ .04), parent beliefs (β = 45; p ≤ .0003), and child fossil expertise (β = −.27; p ≤.007). Only

263

after removing school-type from the equation did child religious interests (β = 18; p ≤ .05) make a significant independent contribution.

Predictors	Age group (β)		
	Young	Middle	Older
Consistency of parent beliefs	.06	.24	.25
Child's fossil expertise	.15	.10	−.24
Child's dynamic adaption score	−.17	−.02	−.13
Child's religious interests	−.03	.39**	.24
School type (NF to F)	.45**	−.02	.14
R^2	.24*	.27*	.47***

Note. See Table 6.
  *p <.05.
  **p <.01.
  ***p <.001.

Table 8. *Animates—Creationist origins: multiple regressions on child creation agreement scores for three elementary-school age groups (standardized regression coefficients)*

Animates: spontaneous generation origins. Again, for each age group, consistency of parent beliefs, fossil expertise, dynamic adaptation, religious interest, and school-type were simultaneously regressed on children's spontaneous generation agreement scores. There was a significant overall regression coefficient only for the young age group, $R^2 = .49$ (R = .70); $F(5, 51) = 8.8$, p ≤ .0001 (Adjusted $R^2 = .43$), with dynamic adaptation making a significant independent contribution (β = .63, p ≤ .0001). Similar analyses on children's spontaneous generation frequency scores revealed only a trend, and only for the young age group ($R^2 = .20$; p ≤ .07), with school-type making a significant independent contribution (β = −.34, p ≤ .05). Young children who attend fundamentalist schools were less likely to endorse these ideas, whereas children who are attracted to naturalistic explanations (e.g., dynamic adaptation) were more likely to endorse spontaneous generation explanations.

Artifacts: creationist origins. The same regressions were carried out for the creation agreement scores for the artifacts and a significant overall regression was obtained only for the young age group, $R^2 = .28$ (R = .53); $F(5, 51) = 3.5$, p ≤ .009 (Adjusted $R^2 = .20$); significant standardized regression coefficients were obtained for school-type (β = −.39, p = .02) and dynamic adaptation (β = .34, p ≤ .02). Note that school-type contributed negatively to this equation, indicating that children in fundamentalist schools were unlikely to agree that artifacts were made by God. Given that none of the included variables significantly predicted the creation agreement scores of children from the middle age group, these results provide further evidence for the difference between the creationism of the young age groups and that of the middle age groups, as outlined in the above analyses.

If the younger children's partial conflation of artificialism and creationism was any indication that they were not yet attuned to final cause (creationist) arguments, as argued earlier, then it should follow that the higher their creation agreement score for artifacts the more likely they would be to endorse proximate cause arguments for animate origins (spontaneous generation) and the less likely they would be to endorse final cause arguments (creation). Correlations between the creation agreement scores for artifacts (for the young group only) and the relevant variables provide some evidence that this was the case: *Creation agreement* for artifacts and (1) *spontaneous generation agreement* for animates (r = .27; p ≤ .04); (2) *spontaneous generation frequency* for animates (r = .32; p ≤ .02); (3) *creation agreement for animates (ns)*; (4) *creation frequency for animates* (r = −.32; p ≤ .02). In the case of animates, the significant relationship for the creation-frequency measure and not for the creation-agreement measure probably indicates that the former was a more stringent test of children's understanding of creationism than the latter.

Relations between predictors. The preceding analyses give the overall impression that parent beliefs directly impacted child beliefs only in the case of the older elementary school children. However, although the effect was not direct, the environment provided by parents did appear to influence younger children's beliefs as well. Simultaneous regressions for each age group were computed with three environmental measures (school-type, church-type, and the consistency of parent beliefs) and the child knowledge and interest measures (fossil expertise, dynamic adaptation, religious interest), as predictors on each of the latter child knowledge and interest measures.

Dynamic adaptation was significantly predicted in the middle age group only (R^2 = .46; p ≤ .0001), with school-type (β = −.29, p = .04), church-type (β = −.66, p .0001), and fossil expertise (β = .26, p ≤ .03), as significant independent predictors. For fossil expertise, the overall regressions were significant in both the young and the old age groups (R^2s = .29 to .31; p's ≤ .02); in the young age group, school-type (b = −.38, p = .03) was the most significant independent predictor, whereas in the old age group, parent belief-consistency (b = −.42, p = .02) was the only significant independent predictor. For religious interest, at all ages there were significant overall regressions (R^2s = .35 to .38; p's ≤ .002), with school- and/or church-type (β's = −.37 to .58; p's ≤ .02) contributing independently to the overall score of the two younger groups.

Although children who endorsed dynamic adaptation were more likely to be younger and to go to non-fundamentalist schools and churches, the idea of dynamic adaptation was not one that was likely to receive direct community support, unlike fossil expertise and religious interest (note the lack of a correlation between dynamic adaptation and parent beliefs in Table 6). Dynamic adaptation appears to be an idea that was constructed by children in a (non-fundamentalist) environment that facilitated, or at least failed to inhibit, naturalistic explanations involving change. Unbiased observers of the natural world are sure to be beguiled by the abundant evidence of change in nature from metamorphosis to adaptation, and analyses above have indicated that non-fundamentalist parents were more likely than fundamentalist parents to encourage such naturalistic interests (see Table 1).

Summary. The endorsement of evolutionary ideas for animate origins by children in early adolescence was largely a function of their dynamic adaptationist beliefs and fossil expertise, along with the consistency of their parents' beliefs about evolution, which together explained around 70% of the variance in preadolescents' beliefs. For their younger siblings in the early and middle elementary school years, however, parent beliefs exerted no independent effect, and fossil expertise and dynamic adaptationist beliefs made the most significant contribution. It would be a mistake to assume, however, that the latter variables functioned independently of parental beliefs, for children from fundamentalist homes and schools were less likely to be as knowledgeable about fossils or endorse the idea that acquired features could be inherited (dynamic adaptation). What appeared to be happening was that not until early adolescence were children ready to abandon creationist theories of origins and adopt a naturalistic explanation that violated their strongly held beliefs in the immutability of species. Parental beliefs in evolution presumably fostered this shift both directly, by explicitly endorsing evolution and exposing children to the evidence for evolution, such as fossils, as well as indirectly, by promoting naturalistic interests in general.

For creationist beliefs, the overall picture was somewhat similar, though, in this case, attendance at a Christian fundamentalist school now played a critical role. Among the oldest children, depending on the measure, from 47% (agreement) to 67% (frequency) of the variance in the expression of creationist beliefs could be explained. This large difference between measures is another sign that the open-ended frequency measure was a more stringent indicator of a coherent creationism, whereas the closed-ended agreement measure encouraged the ad hoc espousal of creationist beliefs. The consistency of parent beliefs about creation and, depending on the measure, children's religious interest, contributed positively to the expression of creationist beliefs in preadolescents, whereas fossil expertise appeared to exert a negative influence. Among the two younger age groups, interest in religion contributed positively to the scores of the middle age group, whereas attendance at a fundamentalist school contributed positively to the youngest children's creation scores. That there was an effect of children's religious interest over and above that of parent belief system, suggests that, as for evolutionary ideas, child-driven values and interests played a role in the expression and coherence of these belief systems, especially in older children.

For the expression of spontaneous generationist beliefs, not surprisingly, few measures of the custom complex proved to be valid indicators. For both animate and inanimate origins, depending on the age group, fundamentalist schooling apparently inhibited the expression of spontaneous generationist explanations, which were most likely to be endorsed by young children who were already predisposed toward the kind of naturalistic argument found in dynamic adaptation.

Artificialism: A Source Analog for Creationism?
Previously it was proposed that artificialism might be a source analog for creationism. Although these studies did not specifically address this proposal, further analyses of the relationship between these two constructs do provide support: these constructs are significantly correlated even when the effects of other critical variables are partialed out of the equation. At a minimum, if one construct is an analog of the other then the two constructs should be related; if they are not related then they can hardly be analogs. Further, it is argued that initially a source analog and its target are likely to be conflated and that they become gradually disassociated as more components of the source (such as features, structural relations, etc.) are mapped on to the target. Over time the target and source should become increasingly distinct and coherent structures. This hypothesis is addressed in a developmental framework by constructing measures of coherent artificialism and creationism and assessing their relationship, while partialing out the effects of other variables that could account for this relationship.

Composite measures of coherence were constructed for artificialism and creationism by combining responses for the animates, inanimates, and artifacts for each construct in turn, using the agreement measure. Coherence was operationalized as agreement with the following propositions: (1) Artificialism: humans made the very first artifacts; humans did not make the very first animates or inanimates. (2) Creationism: God made the very first animates and inanimates; God did not make the very first artifacts. The higher the score on each construct (possible range, –3 to 3), the more likely the participant was to agree with each proposition.

Data from children (n = 103) in only the two younger age groups (5.3–10.3 years) were combined and used in these analyses because it is in these age groups that a coherent creationism appeared to be emerging. Coherent artificialism, age, school-type, and parent belief-consistency, were simultaneously regressed on children's coherent creationism scores. There was a significant overall regression coefficient, $R^2 = .44$ (R = .66); $F(4, 98) = 19.1$; $p \leq .0001$ (Adjusted $R^2 = .42$), with coherent artificialism ($\beta = .49$, $p \leq .0001$)

and school-type ($\beta = .34$, $p \leq .001$) making significant independent contributions. In the next analysis, coherent creationism, age, school-type, and parent belief-consistency, were simultaneously regressed on children's coherent artificialism scores. Again, there was a significant overall regression coefficient, $R^2 = .35$ ($R = .59$); $F(4, 98) = 13.1$; $p \leq .0001$ (Adjusted $R^2 = .32$), and, in this case, coherent creationism ($\beta = .56$, $p \leq .0001$), age ($\beta = -.19$, $p \leq .03$), and parent belief-consistency ($\beta = -.19$, $p \leq .05$) made significant independent contributions. Notably a child's age only contributed independent variance to the latter equation, indicating that the apparent effect of age (increasingly coherent creationism over time) was explained by the other variables.

Summary. Children who had a coherent understanding of the powers of God were also likely to have a coherent understanding of the limitations of human capabilities; conversely, children who were confused about God's capabilities were also confused about human capabilities. The positive relationship between artificialism and creationism held true even when other related variables such as age and exposure to creationist beliefs, at home or at school, were partialed out of the equation (though these variables did contribute additional variance). Of course the direction of the effect is not clear from these data, but the significant relationship between artificialism and creationism does provide some support for the proposition that one may be an analog of the other.

This analysis further suggests that an analogical mapping between target and source may have bidirectional effects. In the process of differentiating from its source, the target concept may serve to further specify the nature of the source concept. For example, what might begin as a somewhat inchoate limited artificialism, with God as merely another human sharing a human's creative responsibilities, is later differentiated into two daughter concepts, coherent artificialism and coherent creationism. Exposure to creationist beliefs seems to promote this change. Initially, however, the idea that "God-makes-animals" appears to be loosely associated with the artificialist structure, almost as an ad hoc belief. Further studies involving preschoolers and additional related variables are needed to clarify the nature and direction of the effect.

General Discussion

Why does it appear as if "the human brain is specifically designed to misunderstand Darwinism … ?" (Dawkins 1987). On the surface, at least, Darwinian concepts seem simple and easy to grasp; their complexities are revealed only with more detailed scrutiny (Mayr 1991). Dawkins (1995) claims that the reason adults subscribe to creationist explanations is that they have not yet put away "childish things," that, like young children, they are "gullible ... credulous, ... and faith-filled." Dawkins underestimates both children and adults. Children are not sponges effortlessly absorbing all knowledge, for if they did formal education would scarcely be necessary. They are selective constructivists, rapidly assimilating ideas to the extent that they are congruent with existing knowledge structures, and rejecting others that do not fit in (Piaget 1929). Dawkins' polemic ignores the most interesting feature of this debate: Why are creationist ideas so much more attractive than evolutionist ideas, at least in these communities? The answer is not that adults are like children, even though there are obvious continuities. As this study demonstrates, both children and adults are susceptible to creationist explanations, but adult creationism is more likely to be embedded in a complex knowledge structure. Children's earliest creationist explanations may simply reflect a "transfer of expectations" (Boyer and Walker 2000) from an intuitive ontology, a naive theory of mind (see Evans 2000b).

In this study, cognitive and contextual factors appeared to play an interactive role in the dissemination of beliefs about the origins of species, suggesting a "constructive interactionism" (Wozniak and Fischer 1993). Early adolescents (11 to 13 years), like their parents, embraced the dominant beliefs of their community, be they creationist or evolutionist. Their younger siblings, especially those in the middle elementary school years (8 to 10 years), were more apt to be exclusively creationist, whatever their community of origin. Early elementary school children (5 to 7 years) endorsed creationism more strongly if they had been to a fundamentalist school or if they were reminded of creationist explanations, as in the forced-choice measures. Otherwise, they were likely to endorse mixed spontaneous generationist and creationist beliefs (see also Evans 2000a). Interestingly, even when interviewers suggested evolutionary explanations, as in the forced-choice measures, children in the early-to-mid elementary school years still resisted such ideas.

These results indicate that in comparison with the two naturalistic explanations, creationist ideas are, indeed, far more contagious (Sperber 1996), at least in these communities. An environment imbued with creationism, as in Christian fundamentalist school communities, or even in the case of interviewer suggestion, markedly increases the frequency of creationist responses in all age groups on all measures. In effect, such environments serve to suppress or, at least, fail to facilitate, natural explanations, such as spontaneous generation or evolution. Why is the human mind (at least, the Western protestant mind) so susceptible to creationism and so comparatively resistant to naturalistic explanations for the origins of species? A more detailed examination of these data reveals that this susceptibility is a function of several factors, cognitive and contextual; there is no single explanation.

Cognitive Constraints

The primary argument presented here is that the two staples of Western philosophical thinking, essentialism and final-cause or teleological reasoning, emerge from intuitive propensities of the human mind. Moreover, it is suggested that when these basic modes of construal (Keil 1994) are reified in public representations such as in Western religious or philosophical traditions, they then serve to inhibit the expression of natural explanations for the origins of species.

There is increasing evidence to support the idea that the inferential reasoning capacities of the developing mind are constrained by at least three intuitive modes of construal: essentialism, teleology, and intention (see Atran 1990; Carey 1985; Gelman et al. 1994; Keil 1994; Wellman 1990; Wellman and Gelman 1997). As noted in the earlier discussion of Lamarckian ideas, teleology and intentionality are potentially dissociable although they are often conflated in the literature (see also Kelemen 1999a, b). Moreover, elementary school children have been shown to differentially endorse the three modes when explaining the diverse behaviors of a range of biological kinds (Poling and Evans 2002). In the final cause reasoning of the creationist, however, teleology and intention are linked (God's purpose) and used to explain the presence of previously nonexistent entities. Historically, according to Mayr (1982), if it had not been for the paralyzing effect of monotheistic creationism, spontaneous generation might have been the immediate precursor to evolutionary thinking, for, like evolution, it evokes naturalistic and nonteleological reasoning. The evidence presented in this study from both communities suggests that essentialism, in a specific guise, may well be an impediment to the expression of evolutionary ideas; on the other hand, the final-cause reasoning evident in a creationist account of origins might, under some circumstances, act as a catalyst for the ultimate-cause reasoning evident in evolutionary ideas.

Essentialism

The idea that species are inherently immutable was hypothesized to be a crucial factor in the attractiveness of creationist ideas and the resistance to evolutionary ideas for all children in their early-to-mid elementary school years, and for both children and adults from Christian fundamentalist communities. With creationism the essentialistic beliefs of the early elementary school years (see Gelman et al. 1994; Gelman and Hirschfeld 1999) are not only maintained, they are deified, at least in these Christian fundamentalist contexts.

Moreover, Mayr (1982) has proposed that an essentialistic philosophy, with its insistence on the unchanging essence or side of each and every species, was one of the key historical factors preventing the adoption of evolutionary explanations (but see Atran 1990, for an alternative view). Up to Darwin's time, philosophers "considered species as natural kinds," separable by "bridgeless gaps" (Mayr 1991, 41). Although commensurate with the idea that each species was specially created by God, such beliefs were clearly incommensurate with the idea that a species might change through adaptive processes. At a minimum such essentialistic ideas had to be challenged before evolutionary ideas could emerge. For Lamarck, it was the fossil evidence that opened his eyes to the idea that "efforts to satisfy individual needs" might lead to the gradual transformation of one life-form to another (Mayr 1982). Similarly, Darwin's work among the diverse species of the Galapagos Islands fueled his thesis that nature functions as a selection device operating on the variation apparent in any population to produce new species (Mayr 1982).

Nevertheless, some have argued that essentialistic constraints are never overcome; instead, what is granted essential causal power is transformed with the acceptance of evolution (e.g., Evans 2000a; Gould 1992; Kornblith 1993). Such a view is more in keeping with Atran's (1990) contention that historically a strict version of essentialism was rare among naturalists (p. 84). By attempting to identify those DNA sequences that historically define a species even modern geneticists appear to be susceptible to essentialism. However, this apparent paradox could be resolved by distinguishing between explicit philosophical or religious beliefs in the immutable essence of manifest natural kinds (see Hirschfeld 1996), which was overthrown by evolutionary ideas, versus psychological essentialism (Medin and Ortony 1989), an implicit and basic mode of construal that even contemporary biologists appear to endorse. Young children are likely to endorse the latter (Gelman and Hirschfeld 1999).

In the present study, a further piece of evidence for the crucial role of essentialism in the expression of creationist belief is the resistance to ideas about the inheritance of acquired features (dynamic adaptation) among children in fundamentalist communities. Unlike evolutionary explanations, dynamic adaptation merely suggests that the individual animals acquire new features in response to environmental pressures and that these features are then exhibited in their offspring; it does not address species change. Nonetheless, comments by Christian fundamentalist children implied that such statements were regarded with suspicion: "God made it that way, so it can't change," was one 11-year old's rejoinder when asked if an animal could get a long neck from stretching to reach high vegetation (Evans 2000b). This kind of response indicates that in communities where essentialism is deified, a coherent creationist will reject even the hint of a biological change. The non-fundamentalist children, in contrast, were more open to the possibility of dynamic adaptation, even though the inheritance of acquired features is scientifically incorrect.

Not surprisingly, and unlike children's fossil knowledge, children's endorsement of dynamic adaptation was unrelated to the consistency of their parents' beliefs. However, particularly in the older groups, both fossil knowledge and dynamic adaptation, independently of each other and of parent beliefs, positively predicted children's evolutionary beliefs and negatively predicted their creationist beliefs. This particular pattern of results indicates that these two measures, fossil knowledge and dynamic adaptation, tap different knowledge structures, yet each of them contributes to the increased expression of evolutionary explanations. Such results lend credence to the proposal that exposure to evidence that animals can change allows children to suspend their beliefs in the immutability of manifest species and shift toward an evolutionary explanation, as it apparently did for Lamarck and Darwin. However, although such evidence might be necessary, it is hardly sufficient. A key corollary would be that children should not be blinded to this evidence by a custom complex in which essentialism is not only reified but also deified. In environments in which creationist beliefs are underdetermined, children apparently construct their own evolutionary explanations using as analogies sources present in the natural context (Evans 2000a; Hatano and Inagaki 1996; Samarapungavan and Wiers 1997).

Children in the Christian fundamentalist schools had access to the same science textbooks as the public-school children and they were also taught about fossils and natural history but they were neither as interested in nor as knowledgeable about fossils,[3] and they actively resisted any idea that animals could change. One 12-year-old child reported, "Sometimes the [school] books say ... this guy named Derwin or something has a theory, but the teachers say the theories that disagree with the Bible are not true. His theories are about how some animals changed" (Evans 2000b).

Final Cause Reasoning

Earlier it was proposed that the age-related shift to the exclusive creationism of the middle elementary school years (8- to 10-year-olds) came about because children of this age were beginning to contemplate existential themes such as those of existence and final cause. Questions about the origins of "the very first X" would make little sense to younger children who appear to believe in a static and unchanging world in which species always existed. Once children realize that entities were previously nonexistent the issue of original design is raised and the necessity for a final cause or teleological argument (Why are they here? What are they for?) becomes apparent (Dennett 1995; Kelemen 1999a, b). Children's mastery of the final cause argument of a creationist explanation may, in turn, pave the way for their later acceptance of evolution. The evidence to support this proposal in the present study is derived from two sources: the fate of spontaneous generation explanations, and the nature of the creationism of the 8- to 10-year-old non-fundamentalist children, which contrasts with that of the younger and older age groups.

Creationist explanations for animate origins in this study seemed to drive spontaneous generationist arguments underground. Spontaneous generation was much less likely to be endorsed in fundamentalist communities, and when creationism was suggested, as in the closed-ended questions, spontaneous generation was endorsed less frequently in non-fundamentalist communities as well. The reason for the overpowering effect of creationism in this case is unlikely to be the creationist compatibility with essentialism, as spontaneous generation arguments are also compatible with essentialistic beliefs. Spontaneous generationist explanations, it is contended, yield proximate cause arguments only, characterized by the use of immediately prior (spontaneous appearance) or mechanistic causes (e.g., birth, growth) to explain the origins of animate entities. Unlike creationism, such arguments do not address the issue of how a particular living kind comes into being in the first place. In this respect spontaneous generation fails as a final cause explanation[4] for the origins of species. Once children appreciate the existential nuances of the origins question they appear to reject spontaneous generation in favor of a creationist explanation.

Among non-fundamentalists, a consistent creationism was more likely to be found in the middle elementary school years. Moreover, on most measures of creationism, non-fundamentalist 8- to 10-year-olds were indistinguishable from their fundamentalist counterparts. More revealingly, when asked about the origins of artifacts, the younger non-fundamentalists (5–7 years) were the most likely of all participants to endorse creationist explanations. These findings are consistent with Piaget's thesis that when children initially invoke God, they conflate God with human (1929; Evans 2000a). However, children are also capable of distinguishing between the powers of God and humans, in that they know that humans cannot make natural kinds (see also, Gelman and Kremer 1991; Petrovich 1999), yet God can. The differences between the two age groups suggest that the younger children have yet to grasp the special and purposeful nature of God's powers; in fact, their facile espousal of creationist arguments seems merely to represent the initial adoption of an ad hoc belief (Keil 1998). The increased sensitivity to the complex nuances of a creationist argument by the middle non-fundamentalist age group (8- to 10-year-olds) was evident on several measures. These findings indicate that a coherent knowledge structure is emerging in which the existential question is grasped and God and humans have clearly differentiated powers. More recent studies involving preschool and young elementary school children lend further support to this line of reasoning (Evans and Gelman 2001; Evans, Poling, and Mull 2001).

Summary

A crucial feature of the creationist worldview is that of final cause, specifically, God's purpose. In contrast, it has been argued that modern science does not make any claims about final causes as its activities are limited to an investigation of the mechanisms underlying secondary or proximate causes (Root-Bernstein 1984; Shapin 1996). Mayr (1985), however, disagrees, contending that unlike the physical sciences and indeed the rest of biology, evolutionary biology is not concerned with proximate causes. Ultimate causes are to evolutionists what final causes are to creationists: both answer the question of why something came into existence in the first place. Ultimate causes, however, should not evoke the teleological or purposeful overtones of final causes, for they are purposeless teleonomic naturalistic causes (Mayr 1982; 1985).

Based on results from the present studies, the existence of two distinct structures underlying an everyday biological understanding can be hypothesized. The earliest structure is a proximate-cause biology, followed by a later-emerging structure involving an ultimate-cause evolutionary biology. A proximate-cause biology is consistent with an essentialistic belief in a static and unchanging world, whereas an ultimate-cause biology acknowledges the causal role of the environment in adaptive change. The latter is characterized, initially, by the use of nonintentional but teleological explanations (e.g., the inheritance of acquired features—adaptive change) and later by apparently goal-directed (teleonomic) ultimate-cause explanations (Darwinian). Seen in these particular communities is an apparent explanatory void in natural explanations for species origins between proximate-cause spontaneous generation explanations and ultimate-cause evolutionary explanations; a teleointentional creationist explanation seems to fill the gap. The most parsimonious explanation for this void is that in these populations an evolutionary biology gains explanatory power from a creationist explanation. In short, before conceiving of a nonintentional biological purpose for biological origins, i.e. adaptive change, species origins are first conceptualized in terms of the needs and purposes of an intentional being: God.

Contextual Constraints

It is important to note that the members of the two school communities highlighted in this study, Christian fundamentalist and non-fundamentalist, did not differ on a number of dimensions, such as the educational level of the parents and children's and parents' interests in music and sports (for example). The modal response of members of the communities did differ, however, on several benchmark variables: religious interest, fossil expertise, and beliefs in the inheritance of acquired features (dynamic adaptation), which were a sample representing the broader custom complex. Moreover, a measure of the consistency of parent beliefs, evolutionist-to-creationist, appeared to be a valid indicator of the degree to which children's environments were saturated with the core beliefs of the particular community. Nevertheless, it was only for those children in the oldest age group that the consistency of parent beliefs proved to be a direct indicator of children's beliefs. The younger children endorsed creationist (or spontaneous generationist) beliefs regardless of the prevailing belief systems of their communities. Nonetheless, parents did influence the expression of even their younger children's beliefs by restricting the range of environments to which children were exposed.

A core element in a constructive interactionist position is the notion of variability. Although traditional developmental research characterizes children of specific ages as being in one or another stage of development, a focused analysis is likely to reveal that children of the same age are almost never uniform in their responses; often a single child demonstrates variability even when solving the same task twice (Siegler 1996). As is evident in this study, custom complexes, too, vary in the degree to which they value and shape different behaviors and beliefs (e.g., Gardner 1995; Miller 1997, 1999; Shweder et al. 1997). When the emphasis is placed on the average response of a particular age group or cultural group this variability is necessarily downplayed. However, the notion of variability is a key element in explaining cognitive growth or change (Siegler 1994; Thelen and Smith 1994). Certain responses are more likely to be selected as appropriate adaptations to local conditions, thus initiating a change in overall response pattern.

This variation was exploited in this study with a focus on the factors related to the expression of individual belief. Such an approach challenges the idea that custom complexes exhibit uniformity in their belief systems, even when modal responses might differ between complexes (e.g., D'Andrade 1990). As described earlier, elementary school children have at their disposal a variety of modes of construal that constrain their understanding of the natural and intentional worlds. By selecting a particular range of learning opportunities, the custom complex can restrain or expand the expression of these intuitive explanatory modes. The sanctioning of interests in religion or of natural history, for instance, augments these intuitive propensities, which then undergird the emergence of more sophisticated capacities to engage in religious or scientific dialogs concerning the origins of species.

Theoretical Implications: The Natural History of a Belief (and its Explanatory Coherence)

Though they may disagree about the mechanisms, researchers operating at the interface between anthropology and psychology generally agree that knowledge structures emerge from the interaction between social and cognitive factors (e.g., Cole 1996; Miller 1999; Rogoff 1990; Shore 1996; Shweder et al. 1997; Sperber 1996; Strauss and Quinn 1997). Analogical reasoning in a metaphorical guise is embedded in the social context in a variety of narrative forms such as ritual, literature, art, and comedy (Holyoak and Thagard 1995; Shore 1996). This metaphorical mode of communication potentially provides a powerful medium for the transmission of beliefs as it is effective, generative, and indirect (Holyoak and Thagard 1995). In this paper, several analogies were proposed to help explain the source of three different beliefs about the origins of species. The findings indicated that those beliefs were transmitted to the extent that they were interpretable by the receiver, as well as the degree to which they were instantiated and interpreted by the custom complex (Sperber 1996). A feature of this transmission was that the original beliefs became transformed in the process; mental representations of a belief were not isomorphic copies of their public representations (Shore 1996; Sperber 1996; Strauss and Quinn 1997).

In the case of the creation story, its public representation, as portrayed in the book of Genesis, differed quite dramatically from its representation in the minds of individuals. For many of the youngest children, especially those in the non-fundamentalist community, creationism in the form of "God made it" seemed merely to be an ad hoc belief with little explanatory value. At the other extreme, for many in the Christian fundamentalist community, creationism was a coherent belief structure in which animate entities were imbued with a God-given unchanging essence and purpose. Moreover, for the coherent creationist, inanimate entities were also God-created, whereas artifacts were made only by humans.

Holyoak and Thagard (1995) argue that when a source analog is matched to a target a new schema is formed from the mapping between the two relational structures. As described earlier, such a mechanism could explain the emergence of a creationist belief: In its source analogy, a naive intentional psychology, humans are not ordinarily credited with the capacity to create animals, thus a new schema is formed in which a supernatural human, God, takes on that role. This alternative causal structure (Rosengren and Hickling 2000) provides the basis for new inductive inferences. Such conjectures fit into an emerging paradigm on the cognitive basis of religion in which it is argued that everyday cognitive biases not only constrain the expression of religious belief but are central to its pervasiveness (Barrett 1998; Barrett and Keil 1996; Boyer 1993; Lawson and McCauley 1990).

The relationship between the expression of an evolutionary belief and specific kinds of natural history knowledge appears to be fixed, in part, by the explanatory potential (Thagard 1989) as well as the coherence of the associated natural history knowledge structure (see also Linn and Songer 1993). For example, a reasonably rigorous understanding of fossils and of adaptation entails not only the recognition of the pivotal role of environmental variation in biological change, called here dynamic adaptation (Evans 2000b), but also the recognition that species are limited spatiotemporal entities. Such an understanding, it has been argued, is a necessary corollary of an evolutionary belief. In contrast, creationists (and younger elementary school children) are more likely to endorse static adaptation (Evans 2000b), in which biological features are viewed as fixed adaptations to unchanging environments. In both cases biological features are seen as functional, but only for static adaptationists is that function compatible with derived essentialist notions that manifest species are uniquely designed to fit specific environments.

Initially, children from non-fundamentalist communities seemed responsive to dynamic adaptationist ideas, but without linking this mechanism to evolutionary change. However, among the older children both dynamic adaptation and fossil knowledge were positively associated with the expression of evolutionist explanations (and negatively associated with creationism). For some, of course, this pre-Darwinian (perhaps Lamarckian) version of evolutionary origins segues into a Darwinian structure, which requires, at minimum, a shift to population thinking (e.g., Mayr 1984; Thagard 1989). It is quite possible, however, that there is more than one route to an evolutionary explanation (see Evans 2000a). Complex spontaneous generationist explanations, such as those described earlier and those found in research with Dutch schoolchildren (Samarapungavan and Wiers 1997), may, in certain contexts, yield pre-Darwinian evolutionary explanations. Certainly, the spontaneous generationist response of the 10-year-old described in the Introduction, suggests that he was on the verge of some type of evolutionary explanation.

Why is evolutionary change so difficult to contemplate, whereas intuitive notions of breeding are comparatively so easy to grasp? The answer probably lies in the extent to which variation is allowed in a kind. For creationists, limited deviation from an ideal form, revealed, for instance, in the black and white varieties of a particular kind of moth found in industrial England or in developmental change, are thought to be part of God's plan (Morris and Parker 1982). Such deviations are perfectly compatible with essentialistic beliefs in the immutability of kinds, provided they are confined to visible commonsense species: "interbreeding morpho-geographic communities of organisms" (Atran 1990, 259). However, as is true for breeding programs with contemporary species, the boundaries between manifest kinds should not be violated, for they are seen as bridgeless gaps (Mayr 1991, 41). The sterile mule is a warning of what might happen with such attempts. The transformation of one essential kind into another is considered to be unnatural; indeed for creationists (or, for that matter, young children) it can be accomplished only by a magician or artificer, such as Satan (Kehoe 1995).

For an evolutionist, however, the commonsense understanding of species boundaries is abandoned and replaced by a view of species as temporary spatiotemporal constructs, with boundaries that can be transgressed (Atran 1990). The current data attest to the difficulty of these ideas, for such cognitive biases are not easily forsaken.

Between the ad hoc and coherent beliefs about the origins of species, there were a variety of mixed beliefs. Several non-fundamentalists, in particular, dealt with these incommensurable belief systems by assigning evolutionary explanations to nonhuman species only, and retaining creationism for human origins. Even Wallace, the codiscoverer of evolutionary theory, stopped short of applying this theory to human origins (Mayr 1982). Nonetheless, as can be seen from the typology of these belief systems, there must have been other kinds of mixed beliefs, suggesting that in many cases neither belief system was especially coherent. Anecdotally, several parents conveyed their disquiet with the choice: "One way to avoid two completely contradictory theories is not to think about them"; "I don't know what to believe, I just want my kids to go to heaven" (Evans 2000b).

Conclusion

In this account of the epidemiology of beliefs (Sperber 1996) about the origins of species, neither the custom complex nor individual constructivist capacities appeared to be privileged. Sperber's synthesis of anthropological and psychological approaches to the representation of belief provides an apt epidemiological framework for modeling the spread of beliefs in a population (Sperber 1996). In this synthesis, mental representations that result from the interpretation and internalization of public or cultural representations are termed reflective explanations, whereas representations that are largely the product of an inferential reasoning process are termed intuitive. The above analysis of the ideological dispute suggests that for adults, at least, both reflective and intuitive explanations play a role in the stabilization of creationist and evolutionist ideas in the population. What about children? From an epidemiological perspective, children born into a world of preexisting public representations would not be able to avail themselves of such representations unless they already possessed some system of analogous intuitive beliefs (Sperber 1996, 79). As evidence for this position, the studies just reported suggest that the capacity to access the source analogies present in the natural and social environments is constrained by the inductive potential of children's intuitive ontologies.

A unique feature of this study is that factors related to the acquisition of these diverse belief systems were able to be disassociated from other potentially influential aspects of the custom complex. The coherence of parent creationist and evolutionist belief systems was associated with child environments that were relatively more saturated with the customs and values of the respective custom complexes, which then appear to have served to constrain the expression of children's beliefs. At their extreme, though, the coherence of these systems and the inductive inferences they engendered rendered individuals resistant to contradictory evidence (see also Chinn and Brewer 2000; Holyoak and Thagard 1995).

What might happen if children were reared in custom complexes where, in contrast to Western thought, species were seen as seamlessly interconnected, such as Buddhist philosophies? The present findings suggest that younger children exhibit variable naturalistic or intentional modes of construal and the custom complex privileges the construction of the culturally sanctioned mode and inhibits the construction of the less-preferred mode. More complex forms of reasoning emerge as consequence of this interaction: they are neither preprogrammed nor simply derived from the social environment. Although psychological essentialism might be a universal (e.g., Atran 1990; Gelman and Hirschfeld 1999; Medin and Ortony 1989), only in those environments in which essentialism is deified is a coherent creationism likely to be exhibited by children. Moreover, only in contexts in which intuitive essentialistic beliefs in the stability of manifest species are challenged would coherent evolutionary beliefs be evident. The contexts sampled in this study varied in their endorsement of creationism; nevertheless, even children in the less saturated contexts were exposed to creationism to a degree that might not be found in other cultural settings. Absent that particular environment, naturalistic modes of explanation for the origins of species might then predominate. It is the interaction between cognitive and contextual factors that serves to ensure the existence of culturally valued domains of competence in subsequent generations (Gardner 1995).

Appendix:
Measures of Children's Natural History Knowledge

How much do you agree with the following on a scale of 1–4: (1) Strongly Disagree, (2) Disagree, (3) Agree, (4) Strongly Agree.

Fossil Expertise
  Dinosaurs and people used to live on the earth at the same time.
  A Petoskey stone is a coral that turned into rock, a long time ago.
  A geode is a kind of rock with crystals in it.
  The pteranodon was not a real dinosaur, it was a flying lizard.
  If animals or plants gradually turn into stone, they become fossils.
  Petrified wood is wood that has been kept under water for a long time.
  If the earth changes a lot some animals might become extinct.
  All rocks with strange designs on them are fossils.
  A long long time ago, there was no life on earth.

Dynamic Adaptation
  If an animal swims a lot it might get webbed feet; its babies will have webbed feet, too.
  If an animal breaks its leg and it heals with a big lump, its babies will be born with legs with big lumps on them, too.
  If an animal stretches up into the tree to get food it might get a long neck; its babies will have long necks, too.

Notes

* This article was originally published in *Cognitive Psychology* 42(3) (2001): 217–66.
1. Lamarck, however, did credit God with the establishment of eternal living forms. For reasons of space the complexity of Lamarck's position cannot be conveyed here, but see Atran (1990) for a detailed exposition.
2. Further details of results on this measure (frequency of explanation) with the non-fundamentalist group only can be found in Evans (2000a).
3. It should be noted, however, that the measure of fossil knowledge used in this study would be invalid from the standpoint of creationist theory, according to which, for example, dinosaurs and humans lived at the same time. Therefore children exposed to creationist theory would be unlikely to obtain high scores on the measure of fossil knowledge.
4. Interestingly, animate and inanimate entities seem to be treated differently in this study, with creationist arguments more likely to be applied to the former and spontaneous generation to the latter (at least by non-fundamentalists). It has long been suggested that there is something about animate entities, their apparent design, that invites the artifact analogy; if something is designed, there must be a designer (Dawkins 1987).

References

Almquist, A. J., and J. E. Cronin. 1988. Fact, Fancy and Myth on Human Evolution. *Current Anthropology* 29(3): 520–22.

Atran, S. 1990. *Cognitive Foundations of Natural History: Towards an Anthropology of Science*. Cambridge: Cambridge University Press.

Barrett, J. L. 1998. Cognitive Constraints on Hindu Concepts of the Divine. *Journal for the Scientific Study of Religion* 37(4): 608–19.

Barrett, J. L., and F. C. Keil. 1996. Conceptualizing a Non-natural Entity: Anthropomorphism in God Concepts. *Cognitive Psychology* 31: 219–47.

Bishop, B. A., and C. W. Anderson. 1990. Student Conceptions of Natural Selection and its Role in Evolution. *Journal of Research in Science Teaching* 27: 415–28.

Boyer, P. 1993. *The Naturalness of Religious Ideas: Outline of a Cognitive Theory of Religion*. Los Angeles/Berkeley: University of California Press.

Boyer, P., and S. Walker. 2000. Intuitive Ontology and Cultural Input in the Acquisition of Religious Concepts. In *Imagining the Impossible: The Development of Magical, Scientific, and Religious Thinking in Contemporary Society*, ed. K. Rosengren, C. Johnson, and P. Harris. Cambridge: Cambridge University Press.

Carey, S. 1985. *Conceptual Change in Childhood*. Cambridge, MA: MIT Press.

Cavanaugh, M. A. 1985. Scientific Creationism and Rationality. *Nature* 315: 185–89.

Chinn, C. A., and W. F. Brewer. 2000. Knowledge Change in Science, Religion, and Magic. In *Imagining the Impossible: The Development of Magical, Scientific, and Religious Thinking in Contemporary Society*, ed. K. Rosengren, C. Johnson, and P. Harris. Cambridge: Cambridge University Press.

Cole, M. 1996. *Cultural Psychology: A Once and Future Discipline*. Cambridge, MA: Belknap Press.

D'Andrade, R. 1990. Some Propositions about the Relations between Culture and Human Cognition. In *Cultural Psychology: Essays on Comparative Human Development*, ed. J. W. Stigler, R. A. Shewder, and G. Herdt, 48–65. Cambridge: Cambridge University Press.

Dawkins, R. 1987. *The Blind Watchmaker*. New York: Norton.

—1995. Putting Away Childish Things. *Skeptical Inquirer* 19(1): 31–36.

Dennett, D. C. 1987. *The Intentional Stance.* Cambridge, MA: MIT Press.

—1995. *Darwin's Dangerous Idea: Evolution and the Meanings of Life.* New York: Touchstone.

Evans, E. M. 2000a. The Emergence of Beliefs about the Origins of Species in School-age Children. *Merrill-Palmer Quarterly* 46: 19–52.

—2000b. Beyond Scopes: Why Creationism is Here to Stay. In *Imagining the Impossible: The Development of Magical, Scientific, and Religious Thinking in Contemporary Society,* ed. K. Rosengren, C. Johnson, and P. Harris, 305–33. Cambridge: Cambridge University Press.

Evans, E. M., and S. A. Gelman. 2001. *Revisiting the Argument from Design: Final Cause Reasoning in Young Children and Adults.* In preparation.

Evans, E. M., D. Poling, and M. Mull. 2001. *Confronting the Existential Questions: Children's Understanding of Death and Origins.* Paper presented at the Biennial Meeting of the Society for Research in Child Development, Minneapolis, MN.

Ferrari, M., and M. T. H. Chi. 1998. The Nature of Naive Explanations of Natural Selection. *International Journal of Science Education* 20: 1231–56.

Gardner, H. 1995. The Development of Competence in Culturally Defined Domains: A Preliminary Framework. In *The Culture and Psychology Reader,* ed. N. R. Goldberger and J. Veroff, 222–44. New York: New York University Press.

Gelman, S. A., J. D. Coley, and G. M. Gottfried. 1994. Essentialist Beliefs in Children: The Acquisition of Concepts and Theories. In *Mapping the Mind: Domain Specificity in Cognition and Culture,* ed. L. A. Hirschfeld and S. A. Gelman, 341–66. Cambridge: Cambridge University Press.

Gelman, S. A., and L. A. Hirschfeld. 1999. How Biological is Essentialism? In *Folkbiology,* ed. D. L. Medin and S. Atran, 403–47. Cambridge, MA: MIT Press.

Gelman, S. A., and K. E. Kremer. 1991. Understanding Natural Cause: Children's Explanations of how Objects and their Properties Originate. *Child Development* 62: 396–414.

Gentner, D., and M. J. Rattermann. 1991. Language and the Career of Similarity. In *Perspectives on Language and Thought,* ed. S. A. Gelman and J. P. Byrnes, 225–27. Cambridge: Cambridge University Press.

Godfrey, L. R. 1984. Scientific Creationism: The Art of Distortion. In *Science and Creationism,* ed. A. Montague. New York: Oxford University Press.

Goswami, U., H. Leevers, S. Pressley, and S. Wheelwright. 1998. Causal Reasoning about Pairs of Relations and Analogical Reasoning in Young Children. *British Journal of Developmental Psychology* 16: 553–69.

Gould, S. J. 1992. What is a Species? *Discover* 13: 40–44.

—1999. A Division of Worms: The Use and Disuse of Lamarck. *Natural History* 108: 18–22.

Greene, E. D. 1990. The Logic of University Students' Misunderstanding of Natural Selection. *Journal of Research in Science Teaching* 27: 875–85.

Guthrie, S. E. 1993. *Faces in the Clouds: A New Theory of Religion.* New York: Oxford University Press.

Harrold, F. B., R. A. Eve, and G. C. D. Goede. 1995. Cult Archeology and Creationism in the 1990s and Beyond. In *Cult Archeology and Creationism: Understanding Pseudoscientific Beliefs about the Past,* ed. F. B. Harrold and R. A. Evet. Iowa City: University of Iowa.

Hatano, G., and K. Inagaki. 1996. Cognitive and Cultural Factors in the Acquisition of Intuitive Biology. In *Handbook of Psychology in Education: New Models of Learning, Teaching, and Schooling,* ed. D. R. Olson. Cambridge, MA: Blackwell.

Hirschfeld, L. A. 1996. *Race in the Making: Cognition, Culture, and the Child's Construction of Human Kinds.* Cambridge, MA: MIT Press.

Holyoak, K. J., and P. Thagard. 1995. *Mental Leaps: Analogy in Creative Thought*. Cambridge, MA: MIT Press.

Kehoe, A. B. 1995. Scientific Creationism: World View, not Science. In *Cult Archeology and Creationism: Understanding Pseudoscientific Beliefs about the Past*, ed. F. B. Harrold and R. A. Eve, 11–20. Iowa City: University of Iowa Press.

Keil, F. C. 1989. *Concepts, Kinds and Conceptual Development*. Cambridge, MA: MIT Press.

—1994. The Birth and Nurturance of Concepts by Domains: The Origins of Concepts of Living Things. In *Mapping the Mind: Domain Specificity in Cognition and Culture*, ed. L. A. Hirschfeld and S. A. Gelman, 234–54. Cambridge: Cambridge University Press.

—1998. Cognitive Science and the Origins of Thought and Knowledge. In *Theoretical Models of Human Development: Handbook of Child Psychology*, ed. W. Damon and R. M. Lerner. 5th edn. Vol. 1, 341–414. New York: Wiley.

Kelemen, D. 1999a. The Scope of Teleological Thinking in Preschool Children. *Cognition* 70: 241–72.

—1999b. Why are Rocks Pointy? Children's Preference for Teleological Explanations of the Natural World. *Developmental Psychology* 35: 1440–52.

Keltner, D., and R. J. Robinson. 1996. Extremism, Power, and the Imagined Basis of Social Conflict. *Current Directions in Psychological Science* 5: 101–5.

Kornblith, H. 1993. *Inductive Inference and its Natural Ground: An Essay in Naturalistic Epistemology*. Cambridge, MA: MIT Press.

Lawson, E. T., and R. N. McCauley. 1990. *Rethinking Religion: Connecting Cognition and Culture*. Cambridge: Cambridge University Press.

Linn, M. C., and N. B. Songer. 1993. How Do Students Make Sense of Science? *Merrill-Palmer Quarterly* 39: 47–73.

Mayr, E. 1982. *The Growth of Biological Thought: Diversity, Evolution and Inheritance*. Cambridge, MA: Harvard University Press.

—1984. Typological Versus Population Thinking. In *Conceptual Issues in Evolutionary Biology*, ed. E. Sober, 14–17. Cambridge, MA: MIT Press.

—1985. How Biology Differs from the Physical Sciences. In *Evolution at a Crossroads: The New Biology and the New Philosophy of Science*, ed. D. J. Depew and B. H. Weber, 43–63. Cambridge, MA: MIT Press.

—1991. *One Long Argument: Charles Darwin and the Genesis of Modern Evolutionary Thought*. Cambridge, MA: Harvard University Press.

—1997. *This is Biology: The Science of the Living World*. Cambridge, MA: Belknap/ Harvard.

Medin, D., and A. Ortony. 1989. Comments on Part 1: Psychological Essentialism. In *Similarity and Analogical Reasoning*, ed. S. Vosniadou and A. Ortony, 179–93. Cambridge: Cambridge University Press.

Miller, J. D. 1987. The Scientifically Illiterate. *American Demographics* 9(6): 26–31.

Miller, J. G. 1997. Theoretical Issues in Cultural Psychology. In *Handbook of Cross-cultural Psychology*, ed. J. W. Berry, Y. H. Poortinga, and J. Pandey, Vol. 1, 85–128. Boston: Allyn and Bacon.

—1999. Cultural Psychology: Implications for Basic Psychological Theory. *Psychological Science* 10: 85–91.

Morris, H. M., and G. E. Parker. 1982. *What is Creation Science?* El Cajon, CA: Master Books.

Numbers, R. L. 1992. *The Creationists: The Evolution of Scientific Creationism*. New York: Knopf.

Petrovich, O. 1999. Preschool Children's Understanding of the Dichotomy between the Natural and the Artificial. *Psychological Reports* 84: 3–27.

Piaget, J. 1929. *The Child's Conception of the World*. Trans. Joan and Andrew Tomlinson. Totowa, NJ: Rowman and Allanhead.

Poling, D. A., and E. M. Evans. 2002. Why do Birds of a Feather Flock Together? Developmental Change in the Use of Multiple Explanations: Intention, Teleology, Essentialism. *British Journal of Developmental Psychology* 20(1): 89–112.

Roger, J. 1986. The Mechanistic Conception of Life. In *God and Nature: Historical Essays on the Encounter between Christianity and Science*, ed. D. C. Lindberg and R. L. Numbers, 277–95. Berkeley and Los Angeles: University of California Press.

Rogoff, B. 1990. *Apprenticeship in Thinking: Cognitive Development in Social Context*. New York: Oxford University Press.

Root-Bernstein, R. 1984. On Defining a Scientific Theory: Creationism Considered. In *Science and Creationism*, ed. A. Montagu, 64–93. New York: Oxford University Press.

Rosengren, K. S., and A. K. Hickling. 2000. Metamorphosis and Magic: The Development of Children's Thinking About Possible Events and Plausible Mechanisms. In *Imagining the Impossible: The Development of Magical, Scientific, and Religious Thinking in Contemporary Society*, ed. K. Rosengren, C. Johnson, and P. Harris. Cambridge: Cambridge University Press.

Samarapungavan, A., and R. W. Wiers. 1997. Children's Thoughts on the Origin of Species: A Study of Explanatory Coherence. *Cognitive Science* 21: 147–77.

Shapin, S. 1996. *The Scientific Revolution*. Chicago: University of Chicago Press.

Shore, B. 1996. *Culture in Mind: Cognition, Culture, and the Problem of Meaning*. Oxford: Oxford University Press.

Shweder, R. A., J. Goodnow, G. Hatano, R. A. LeVine, H. Markus, and P. Miller. 1997. The Cultural Psychology of Development: One Mind, Many Mentalities. In *Theoretical Models of Human Development: Handbook of Child Psychology*, ed. W. Damon and R. M. Lerner. 5th edn. Vol. 1, 865–937. New York: Wiley.

Siegler, R. S. 1994. Cognitive Variability: A Key to Understanding Cognitive Development. *Current Directions in Psychological Science* 3(1): 1–4.

—1996. *Emerging Minds: The Process of Change in Children's Thinking*. Oxford: Oxford University Press.

Sperber, D. 1996. *Explaining Culture: A Naturalistic Approach*. Oxford: Blackwell.

Springer, K., and F. C. Keil. 1989. On the Development of Biologically Specific Beliefs: The Case of Inheritance. *Child Development* 60: 637–48.

Strauss, C., and N. Quinn. 1997. *A Cognitive Theory of Cultural Meaning*. Cambridge: Cambridge University Press.

Thagard, P. 1989. Explanatory Coherence. *Behavioral and Brain Science* 12: 435–502.

Thelen, E., and L. Smith. 1994. *A Dynamic Systems Approach to the Development of Cognition and Action*. Cambridge: MIT Press.

Wellman, H. M. 1990. *The Child's Theory of Mind*. Cambridge, MA: MIT Press.

Wellman, H. M., and S. A. Gelman. 1997. Knowledge Acquisition in Foundational Domains. In *Handbook of Child Psychology: Cognition, Perception and Language*, ed. D. Kuhn and R. Siegler, 5th ed., vol. 2. New York: Wiley.

Wozniak, R. H., and K. W. Fischer. 1993. Development in Context: An Introduction. In *Development in Context: Acting and Thinking in Specific Environments*, ed. R. H. Wozniak and K. W. Fischer, xi–xvi. Hillsdale, NJ: Laurence Erlbaum Associates.

11

CHILDREN'S ATTRIBUTIONS OF BELIEFS TO HUMANS AND GOD: CROSS-CULTURAL EVIDENCE[*]

Nicola Knight, Paulo Sousa, Justin L. Barrett, and Scott Atran

Abstract

The capacity to attribute beliefs to others in order to understand action is one of the mainstays of human cognition. Yet it is debatable whether children attribute beliefs in the same way to all agents. In this paper, we present the results of a false-belief task concerning humans and God run with a sample of Maya children aged 4–7, and place them in the context of several psychological theories of cognitive development. Children were found to attribute beliefs in different ways to humans and God. The evidence also speaks to the debate concerning the universality and uniformity of the development of folk-psychological reasoning.

৪০ ৫৪

1. Introduction

Humans routinely attribute intentions, beliefs, and desires in order to interpret the behavior of others. Other humans are seen as agents, that is, as entities that pursue goals in accordance with their beliefs and desires. Attributions of agency are so ubiquitous that they are typically taken for granted in everyday life. These attributions are not always correct in identifying the beliefs and desires that underlie a specific action of an agent; yet, if people did not see others as agents, the capacity to understand their behavior would be severely impaired (for example, people would be surprised when others got up and moved).

Abundant research documents children's acquisition of human agent concepts over the first several years of life (Astington, Harris, and Olson 1988; Perner 1991; Wellman 1990), but there is little work available on the development of non-human agent concepts. Yet, people often attribute intentions, beliefs, and desires to animals as well as to ghosts, gods, demons, and monsters. Scholars have long assumed that children first acquire concepts of human agency and then use them as templates to understand all non-human agents. One exception in this regard is found in the work of Barrett and coworkers (Barrett, Richert, and Driesenga 2001; Richert and Barrett, in press; see also Atran 2002, for an evolutionary account of why children cognize non-human agency).

In this article, we offer further support for Barrett's point of view, showing that Yukatek children do not reason in the same way about the agency of humans and God since early on in development. In the first part, we discuss the development of human agent concepts, specifically with regard to the false-belief task. Then, we outline the predictions implied by several theoretical positions concerning the development of children's understanding of humans' and God's beliefs. After that, we present experimental evidence from a Yukatek Maya sample that supports the hypothesis that young children do not reason about God's beliefs in human terms. Finally, we discuss the theoretical positions and their predictions in light of the results and place the evidence in the larger context of theory of mind research.

2. The Development of Human Agent Concepts

The cognitive literature on child development usually distinguishes three phases in the development of understanding of agency (see, for example, Csibra et al. 1999; Gergely et al. 1995; Gopnik and Meltzoff 1997; Wellman 1990). During the first year or so, children are believed to apply a principle of rational action, that is, they begin to appreciate that humans do not merely propel themselves, but do so in purposeful and rational ways. By the second or third year, children incorporate simple mentalistic attributions into this rational principle: the purposeful and rational action is understood to be driven by desires. Finally, during the fourth or fifth year, the principle of rational action is coupled with representational attributions: agents are seen as pursuing goals in accordance to their *beliefs*.

The emergence of this representational stage, which is a necessary condition for the possession of a full-fledged conception of the mind, is the most relevant to the arguments and experimental results presented in this article. Exactly when this transition takes place has been a matter of considerable debate generating an abundance of research (e.g., Astington et al. 1988; Carruthers and Smith 1996; Whiten 1991). Although some evidence has emerged for the presence of representational reasoning in 3-year-olds (Chandler, Fritz, and Hala 1989; Hala, Chandler, and Fritz 1991; Lewis and Osbourne 1990; Siegal and Beattie 1991), the bulk of the data available suggests that this ability is neither stable nor robust until children are 5 or older (Flavell et al. 1990; Perner, Leekam, and Wimmer 1987; Wellman and Bartsch 1988; Wellman and Wooley 1990; Wimmer and Perner 1983).

Since Premack and Woodruff (1978) started experimenting with non-human primates in order to establish the possibility that they had a "theory of mind," different ways of testing for this have been designed and tried out. As Dennett (1978) pointed out, you can credit an entity with a conception of belief only if there is evidence that it is able to understand that others may entertain <u>false</u> beliefs. Therefore, to probe children's representational understanding of agency—whether they have a conception of belief—it is necessary to ascertain that they figure out that people can have false beliefs and that these *beliefs* can motivate behavior.

A variety of false-belief tasks have been developed in the last 20 years to test children's understanding of beliefs. One such experiment is known as the "Sally-Ann" test (Wimmer and Perner 1983). In this test, the child is made to look at a scene in which two dolls are animated by experimenters. The dolls are used to represent human beings—Wellman, Cross, and Watson (2001) have shown in a meta-analysis of false-belief studies that using a doll as a proxy for an actual human being does not affect the outcome of the experiment. The two dolls enter the stage; one of them (Sally) places an object in one of two containers and leaves the room. While Sally is out, the second doll (Ann) moves the object into the second container. Sally re-enters the stage; at that point, children are asked where Sally, who is unaware that the switch took place, will look for the object. Children, therefore, are asked to infer whether Sally will act according to her false belief (that the object is still in the original container) or not.

Another false-belief task, the one used in the experiments that will be presented later, is known as the "surprising contents" task. In it, children are shown a closed container (usually a cracker box with a conspicuous picture of its contents on the outside) and asked what they believe is in it. The experimenter then opens the box to reveal that the crackers have been removed, and that small rocks (or a similarly unexpected item) have been put in their place. After reclosing the box, the experimenter checks that the children are still clear on what the box contains. The experimenter then introduces a doll who has not seen the inside of the box, and asks what the doll would think is in the container. Again, the point of the experiment is to establish whether children are capable of figuring out that other agents may have false beliefs and act accordingly.

3. The Development of God Concepts

By and large the research pertaining to children's understanding of agent concepts deals exclusively with *human* agent concepts: how children's concepts of human agency become increasingly specialized. In false-belief tasks, as well as in most other studies of children's understanding of agency, experimenters have asked children to reason about human actions, beliefs, desires, and emotions. Very little available research addresses the generalizability of children's understanding of agency to non-human agents in general, and to God in particular. However, by looking at the assumptions of several theoretical positions, we can envisage their predictions concerning the understanding of God in comparison to humans in a false-belief task.

In Fig. 1, we offer a tree diagram to show how these positions are related to each other. The graphs outline predictions of false-belief task performance in relation to humans and God. To illustrate the graphs, consider a surprising contents task: suppose children are presented with a closed cracker box, shown that the box contains small rocks, and then asked what a human and God, who did not have a chance to look inside the box, would think is inside.

In all graphs, the top line represents attribution of beliefs to humans, and the bottom line represents attribution of belief to God. On the y-axis, performance is mapped; the higher the line, the more likely it is that a child would attribute false beliefs to the agent in question—to say that a human or God would think that the box contains crackers. The x-axis shows the developmental time frame. As indicated by the dotted lines, the age range of 4–7 is the most relevant to our discussion, since it is then that children, according to the current literature, come to attribute false beliefs to human agents (see discussion in the previous section).

At the highest level of the tree, the opposition is between similarity and non-similarity perspectives with regard to the way beliefs are attributed to God and humans. From a non-similarity perspective, children would start to differentiate humans and God (attributing more false beliefs to humans than to God) from the very beginning of the developmental stage of our concern. From a similarity perspective, children would attribute either true beliefs or false beliefs to both humans and God *in equal measure, initially, and for at least some part* of this developmental time frame.

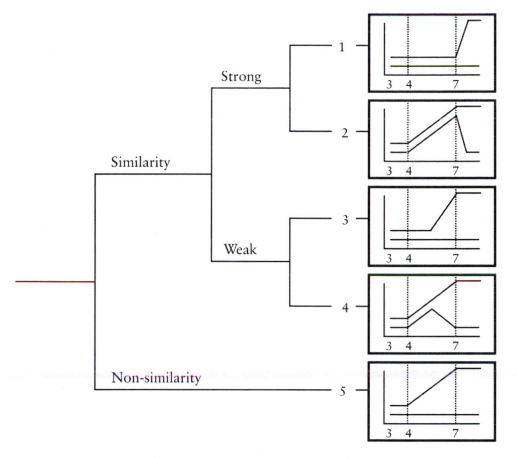

Figure 1. *Predictions of false-belief task performance*

Similarity positions (graphs 1–4) postulate that children initially use humans (or some humans) as an analogical basis to understand God's beliefs. At the very least, we can distinguish two stances: a strong and a weak one. The strong stance is perhaps best represented in Piaget's work (1960). There are two possible interpretations of Piaget's understanding of the development of God concepts. In graph 1, an infallible parent (who is capable of knowing what is inside the box without having to see it) is used as the basis to understand God until quite late in development. At some point, children start to recognize that parents can entertain false beliefs but they do not transfer this characteristic to God, since at this same point they start to learn that God has special qualities such as omniscience. For example, children would initially say that both agents believe that rocks are inside the box, then, only by age 7, they would start to say that humans believe that crackers are inside the box, and God believes that rocks are inside. Conversely, in graph 2, a normal human being is used as the basis to understand God until quite late in development. Then, children start to learn that God possesses certain special characteristics that set God aside from common humans.

The weak stance postulates that children initially use humans as a basis to understand God's beliefs but start to differentiate them earlier in development than Piaget postulated—before reaching the age of 7. In other words, we are envisaging the possibility of Piaget being wrong simply in terms of the onset of the differentiation. In graph 3, an infallible human is used as a basis to understand God. In graph 4, a normal human is instead used as the basis. This explains why both the human and the God line stay flat for some time in the first instance, and climb initially in the second. Although these positions are not well established in the literature, they are possibilities that one should consider when dealing with cross-cultural data. For example, graph 4 can be seen as a plausible representation of people living in a society where the concept of God as omniscient is not very widespread.

Finally, moving on to the last graph in Fig. 1, a non-similarity perspective would predict that children being tested on the false-belief task would start differentiating between humans and God very early in development. This is the position that Justin Barrett and collaborators have been advocating (Barrett et al. 2001; Richert and Barrett, in press; see also Atran 2002). Their main idea is that young children do not need to conceptualize human agency first and then use it as a basis to understand supernatural agency; rather, young children have already the potential to think independently about different types of agents and reason accordingly. In graph 5, the God line remains close to floor level, which signifies that children from an early age attribute mostly true beliefs to God, i.e., that God knows that there are rocks in the box. The human line, on the other hand, starts at the same level as the God line but then by the age of 4 steeply climbs—children increasingly say that humans believe that the box contains crackers, as their capacity to attribute false beliefs improves.

Experimental data from the United States supports the prediction of this non-similarity position (Barrett et al. 2001). In Fig. 2, the results of a surprising contents experiment run with a sample of American children recruited from Reformed and Lutheran Protestant churches are presented. Children in the U.S. sample can be seen to treat humans and God in the same way up to age 4. By age 5, they already sharply differentiate between the two agents. The divergence between God and the mother took place as children started to attribute false beliefs to the latter. A Wilcoxon Signed-Ranks Test for matched pairs comparing "crackers" responses between mother and God at each specific age detected significant differences only for 5- and 6-year-olds ($z = 2.37, p = .018, N = 17$ and $z = 2.93, p = .003, N = 9$, respectively).

However, there is no available cross-cultural evidence that addresses this question. In the next section, we present data on a similar false-belief task run with a sample of Yukatek Maya children, in order to provide a test of these theoretical predictions.

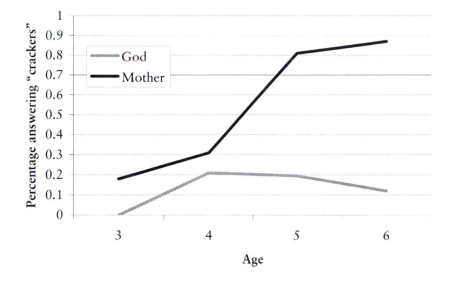

Figure 2. *False-belief task—U.S. children*

4. Methods

The Maya sample consisted of 48 children divided in four age groups: eleven 4-year-olds (4.0–4.11), twelve 5-year-olds (5.0–5.11), twelve 6-year-olds (6.0–6.11), and thirteen 7-year-olds (7.0–7.10). Twenty-six children were male and 22 were female. The experimenter piloted the protocol with some 3-year-olds, but, since most of them seemed to have difficulty in concentrating long enough, they were dropped from the sample. The children resided in four small rural villages in the Quintana Roo state in the Yucatán peninsula (Southeastern Mexico). The overwhelming majority of people living in the rural interior of Quintana Roo are ethnic Maya.

The children generally began attending preschool when they were 4- or 5-years old, and started primary school when they turned six. Both the preschool and the primary school offer bilingual education, in Spanish and Yukatek Mayan. Although many individuals below the age of 50 are reasonably proficient in Spanish, the favored language in the domestic environment is Yukatek. For this reason, most of the children who enter preschool are virtually monolingual in this language. All children were interviewed in Yukatek by a native speaker, who has participated in several other studies in the region and is known to many of the participants' families.

The experiment consisted in a version of the "surprising contents" task. Participants were interviewed either in the hut of the experimenters or in their family's hut. The agents used were a doll named Soledad and the Catholic God (the Maya adopted this religious entity into their pantheon several centuries ago). We decided not to use the mother as stimulus in Yucatán as it proved impossible to interview the children while their mother was away. In this situation, it would not have been feasible to control for the possibility of the child thinking the mother had a chance to see what was inside the container. The researchers used a container made out of a dried squash, known in Yukatek as *ho'ma*, which keeps maize tortillas warm after cooking them. The *ho'ma* has a small opening carved out on top, just large enough to put one's hand through. Every family visited by the experimenters owned at least one and usually several of these containers. Although they may be occasionally used to store other objects, there was high consensus among the participants that the normal, appropriate content was indeed tortillas, as measured by control questions asked at the beginning of the experiment ("What is this container called?"; "What would you usually find in it?").

The *ho'ma*'s opening was closed with a piece of cardboard, so that children could not tell what was inside. One of the experimenters opened the container to reveal a pair of shorts, a most unusual content. The container was closed again and the experimenters then asked the set of questions about the doll and God, in the following form: "What does X think is in the *ho'ma*?" In this experiment, children were not asked questions about other agents' behavior. However, Barrett et al. (2001) obtained very similar results when a sample of U.S. children were asked a question about behavior—"Where would agent X look for object Y?" instead of "Where would agent X think the object is located?"

5. Results

Answers were coded as 1 when children said "tortillas" and 0 when they said "shorts." The percentage of children answering "tortillas" in each age group for the doll and God is shown in Fig. 3.

The answers for the doll showed a statistically significant positive correlation with age [$r(46) = .341$]. Therefore, as age increased, Maya children were more likely to attribute false beliefs to the doll. For example, 33% of the 4-year-olds said that the doll would think tortillas were in the container compared to 77% of 7-year-olds. In contrast, children treated God differently from the doll—as in the U.S., no significant correlation was detected between answers for God and age [$r(46) = .066$]. A Wilcoxon Signed-Ranks Test for matched pairs comparing "tortillas" responses found significant differences between God and the doll for 5-year-olds ($z = -2.000$, $p = .046$, $N = 12$) and 7-year-olds ($z = -2.449$, $p = .014$, $N = 13$), but not for 4- and 6-year-olds.

When looking at the results, some patterns become apparent. The human line follows the same developmental course in both samples, but the Maya children seem to reliably pass the task about a year later than the American children. In the Maya sample, the difference between God and humans is not significant for 6-year-olds, while it is both for 5- and 7-year-olds. Furthermore, Maya children do not seem to reach the near-ceiling levels that are reported for many Euro-American samples of the same age on the "doll" false-belief question: a t-test against chance for 6-year-olds did not reach significance ($t(11) = 0.75$, $p = .082$); even 7-year-olds, while significantly above chance ($t(12) = 0.77$, $p = .047$), are below the performance level of the American sample.

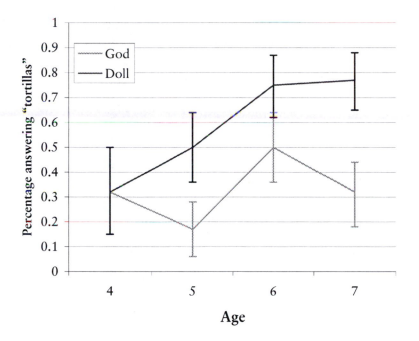

Figure 3. *False-belief task—Maya children. Error bars show ± 1 standard error*

6. Discussion

The vast majority of developmental studies of false-belief understanding in reference to humans focus on samples of Euro-American and East Asian children, often from relatively high socio-economic status (SES) backgrounds (see Wellman et al. 2001). The cross-cultural evidence available from traditional societies so far is incomplete and inconclusive. At any rate, the two available studies of traditional populations (Avis and Harris 1991; Vinden 1996) and the present one seem to show that there is some uniformity in the way false-belief understanding develops, at least where human agency is concerned. However, even a brief inspection of the data presented above reveals that Yukatek children seem to be able to reliably pass a false-belief task only at age 7 (although their performance level is extremely close, though not significantly above chance, a year before); besides, they fail to reach near-ceiling levels at the same age as the children in the American sample. One possible explanation is that children in this community are less familiar than American children with the question/response format that characterizes this experimental task. This suggestion is corroborated by the fact that we were not able to successfully test an adequate number of 3-year-olds due to their shyness, which does not usually pose problems to American experimenters. Another problem, now related to the God results, is the anomalous performance of 6-year-old Maya children. This is less easily explained, but may be due to small sample size. To fully account for the general delay in performance in relation to humans, and the 6-year-olds' performance in relation to God, further studies are needed.

Now, turning to the general discussion of the theoretical positions and their predictions, we can say that, while our results do not address the question of whether children consider the mother as a special kind of agent, they do add to the U.S. findings in speaking against the idea that young children need to use humans as a basis to reason about God, which is the rationale behind all similarity positions. In this sense, the Maya results go in the direction of the non-similarity position, thus providing cross-cultural evidence for the perspective advanced by Barrett and collaborators.

It is important to emphasize that this implies simply that young children do not treat God and humans in the same way in terms of attribution of beliefs. That children truly understand God as a different sort of agent, and not just a human with a few strange properties (e.g., infallible beliefs, ability to make mountains, etc.) is difficult to disambiguate. Also, by no means do the data here support the claim that children's concepts of God are completely independent of their understanding of people in general and their parents in particular. For example, Christian theology teaches about a God who practiced self-anthropomorphization by becoming human in the form of Jesus of Nazareth.

The present results, however, clearly demonstrate that Yukatek young children, as well as American young children, do not treat God as *merely* human. For this reason, this work joins the growing literature that provides evidence against Piaget's notion that young children cannot treat other agents as importantly different from humans. For example, contrary to

Piagetian artificialism (Piaget 1969), Petrovich (1997) found that, although 4-year-olds know that humans make machines and God does not, when asked to account for the origins of natural objects such as large rocks or mountains, they gave God the credit and not people. Similarly, several studies have uncovered evidence that 4-year-old (and, in some cases, older) children believe magicians are a special type of agent able to perform actions that apparently violate natural causation (Chandler and Lalonde 1994; Rosengren and Hickling 1994). Further, recent research suggests that 4- and 5-year-olds appreciate differences in perceptual abilities of different agents across sensory modalities (Richert and Barrett, in press) and appreciate that God is more likely than humans to possess various forms of perceptual knowledge (Barrett et al. 2001).

Note

* This article was originally published in *Cognitive Science* 28 (2004): 117–26.

References

Astington, J. W., P. L. Harris, and D. R. Olson, eds. 1988. *Developing Theories of Mind.* New York: Cambridge University Press.

Atran, S. 2002. *In Gods We Trust: The Evolutionary Landscape of Religion.* Oxford: Oxford University Press.

Avis, J., and P. Harris. 1991. Belief-desire Reasoning among Baka Children: Evidence for a Universal Conception of Mind. *Child Development* 62: 460–67.

Barrett, J. L., R. A. Richert, and A. Driesenga. 2001. God's Beliefs Versus Mother's: The Development of Nonhuman Agent Concepts. *Child Development* 72: 50–65.

Carruthers, P., and P. K. Smith, eds. 1996. *Theories of Theories of Mind.* New York: Cambridge University Press.

Chandler, M., A. S. Fritz, and S. Hala. 1989. Small-scale Deceit: Deception as a Marker of Two-, Three-, and Four-year-olds' Early Theories of Mind. *Child Development* 60: 1263–77.

Chandler, M. J., and C. E. Lalonde. 1994. Surprising, Magical and Miraculous Turns of Events: Children's Reactions to Violations of their Early Theories of Mind and Matter. *British Journal of Developmental Psychology* 12: 83–95.

Csibra, G., G. Gergely, G. Biró, O. Koós, and M. Brockbank. 1999. Goal Attribution Without Agency Cues: The Perception of "Pure Reason" in Infancy. *Cognition* 72(3): 237–67.

Dennett, D. 1978. Beliefs about Beliefs. *Behavioral and Brain Sciences* 1: 568–70.

Flavell, J. H., E. R. Flavell, F. L. Green, and L. J. Moses. 1990. Young Children's Understanding of Fact Belief Versus Value Beliefs. *Child Development* 61: 915–28.

Gergely, G., Z. Nádasdy, G. Csibra, and S. Biró. 1995. Taking the Intentional Stance at 12 Months of Age. *Cognition* 56(2): 165–93.

Gopnik, A., and A. N. Meltzoff. 1997. *Words, Thoughts, and Theories.* Cambridge, MA: MIT Press.

Hala, S., M. Chandler, and A. S. Fritz. 1991. Fledgling Theories of Mind: Deception as a Marker of 3-year-olds' Understanding of False Belief. *Child Development* 62: 83–97.

Lewis, C., and A. Osbourne. 1990. Three-year-olds' Problems with False Belief: Conceptual Deficit or Linguistic Artifact? *Child Development* 61: 1514–19.

Perner, J. 1991. *Understanding the Representational Mind*. Cambridge, MA: MIT Press.

Perner, J., S. R. Leekam, and H. Wimmer. 1987. Three-year-olds' Difficulty with False Belief. *British Journal of Developmental Psychology* 5: 125–37.

Petrovich, O. 1997. Understanding of Non-natural Causality in Children and Adults: A Case Against Artificialism. *Psyche en Geloof* 8: 151–65.

Piaget, J. 1960. *The Child's Conception of the World*. Paterson, NJ: Littlefield, Adams and Co.

—1969. *The Psychology of the Child*. New York: Basic Books.

Premack, D., and G. Woodruff. 1978. Does the Chimpanzee Have a Theory of Mind? *Behavioral and Brain Sciences* 1: 515–26.

Richert, R. A., and J. L. Barrett. in press. Do You See What I See? Children's Predictions of God's Perceptual Abilities. *International Journal for the Psychology of Religion*.

Rosengren, K. S., and A. K. Hickling. 1994. Seeing is Believing: Children's Explanations of Commonplace, Magical, and Extraordinary Transformations. *Child Development* 65: 1605–26.

Siegal, M., and K. Beattie. 1991. Where to Look First for Children's Knowledge of False Beliefs. *Cognition* 38: 1–12.

Vinden, P. G. 1996. Junín Quechua Children's Understanding of Mind. *Child Development* 67: 1707–16.

Wellman, H. M. 1990. *The Child's Theory of Mind*. Cambridge, MA: MIT Press.

Wellman, H. M., and K. Bartsch. 1988. Young Children's Reasoning about Beliefs. *Cognition* 30: 239–77.

Wellman, H. M., C. D. Cross, and J. Watson. 2001. Meta-analysis of Theory-of-mind Development: The Truth about False Belief. *Child Development* 62: 655–84.

Wellman, H. M., and J. D. Wooley. 1990. From Simple Desires to Ordinary Beliefs: The Early Development of Everyday Psychology. *Cognition* 35: 245–75.

Whiten, A., ed. 1991. *Natural Theories of Mind*. New York: Blackwell.

Wimmer, H., and J. Perner. 1983. Beliefs about Beliefs: Representation and Constraining Function on Wrong Beliefs in Young Children's Understanding of Deception. *Cognition* 13: 103–28.

12

THE NATURAL EMERGENCE OF REASONING ABOUT THE AFTERLIFE AS A DEVELOPMENTAL REGULARITY[*]

Jesse Bering and David F. Bjorklund

Abstract

Participants were interviewed about the biological and psychological functioning of a dead agent. In Experiment 1, even 4- to 6-year-olds stated that biological processes ceased at death, although this trend was more apparent among 6- to 8-year-olds. In Experiment 2, 4- to 12-year-olds were asked about psychological functioning. The youngest children were equally likely to state that both cognitive and psychobiological states continued at death, whereas the oldest children were more likely to state that cognitive states continued. In Experiment 3, children and adults were asked about an array of psychological states. With the exception of preschoolers, who did not differentiate most of the psychological states, older children and adults were likely to attribute epistemic, emotional, and desire states to dead agents. These findings suggest that developmental mechanisms underlie intuitive accounts of dead agents' minds.

જ ભ

When one considers the near universality of afterlife beliefs (and of spirituality and religious beliefs in general), it is somewhat surprising that their developmental origins have not received the serious research scrutiny that other culturally recurrent characteristics have. Given their cross-cultural preponderance, afterlife beliefs seem to be excellent candidates for investigation from an evolutionary psychological perspective (e.g., Buss 1995; Cosmides and Tooby 1992), particularly one that emphasizes the role of development in the emergence of evolutionarily significant traits (e.g., Bjorklund and Pellegrini 2002; Geary 1995). One way to explore the natural foundations of belief in life after death is by investigating their emergence in children. Although several researchers (e.g., Barrett 1999; Slaughter, Jaakola, and Carey 1999) have begun investigations on the biological bases of children's understanding of death, the prevalence of afterlife beliefs remains inadequately explained.

Recent empirical attempts to get at children's understanding about life and death are associated with a more general line of investigation meant to determine whether implicit cognitive processes govern individuals' reasoning about the ontological regularities of the natural world. This is especially the case, it seems, among developmentalists interested in determining whether young children possess knowledge—or intuitions—of biological, physical, and social phenomena. Death is a natural phenomenon impinging upon all of these domains. From a fairly early age, children understand that death cannot be avoided, is irreversible, is caused by the breakdown of the body, and leads to complete cessation of function (e.g., Atwood 1984; Barrett 1999; Evans, Poling, and Mull 2001; Lazar and Torney-Purta 1991; Slaughter et al. 1999; Speece and Brent 1984).

Although previous, largely neo-Piagetian, approaches to revealing children's understanding of death have led to scattered findings of coherence of these concepts at about 7 years of age, recent approaches to the problem have found evidence of coherence at earlier ages. Barrett (1999), for example, showed that even preschoolers understand the biology of death when it is placed in the context of predator–prey relationships—such as when a lion attacks and kills a zebra. Four-year-olds reason, for instance, that although the zebra normally grazes in the fields every day, once it is dead it will not be there tomorrow. And, arguing that children's concepts about death are inextricably bound with their understanding of basic life properties (i.e., vitalism), Slaughter and her colleagues (Slaughter et al. 1999; Slaughter and Lyons 2003) showed that the majority of 4- and 5-year-olds who understand the purpose of food, for example, know that dead people do not need to continue eating. Thus, having knowledge of the specific role of certain activities in supporting life seems to provide children with an understanding that such activities will no longer continue after death.

Although it is debatable whether preschoolers' understanding of death, implicit or otherwise, is really equivalent to that of older children, the fact that recent experimental techniques have elicited responses from young children who, not long ago, were thought not to have such concepts, suggests that researchers may have overlooked critical mechanisms involved in children's understanding of death. Might there similarly be "hidden" processes underlying the development of afterlife beliefs, independent of, and possibly collaborative with, sociocultural immersion? The basic attribution of psychological states to deceased agents is a cross-cultural occurrence (Boyer 2001; Hinde 1999). It is perhaps also a defining feature of the human species. No other animal prepares the carcasses of its dead in elaborate rituals that, if nothing else, serve to testify to the species' beliefs in some form of continued existence of the decedent's mind. In both hunter-gatherer and modern societies, fear of ghosts and dead people abounds, rivaling such evolutionarily plausible fears as those of snakes and spiders, and is apparently even more resistant to treatment than fear of strangers (Gullone et al. 2000). Adolescents and adults cram into movie theatres whenever the thematic content of films features ghosts and spirits. And the vast majority of adult Americans believe in some form of life after death (Greeley and Hout 1999).

All of this is puzzling in light of previous findings concerning children's understanding of death. After all, most research has shown that, by age 7, children reportedly have a clear understanding that everything stops functioning at death, something Speece and Brent (1984) have labeled the *non-functionality component* of the mature death concept. Part of the reason that previous work has tended to report that children understand the non-functionality component at around the same age as the other components, such as *finality* and *irreversibility,* may be that such work has tended to concentrate on functions denoting explicit actions (eating, drinking, running) and has often neglected functions denoting either epistemic (knowing, thinking, believing) or psychobiological (thirsty, hungry, sleepy) states, not to mention other psychological state categories (e.g., perceptual, emotional, desire). In the few cases in which psychological state questions were asked in relation to death (e.g., Lazar and Torney-Purta 1991; McIntire, Angle, and Struempler 1972; Slaughter et al. 1999; Smilansky 1987), they were not treated as a distinct category, and so it has been nearly impossible to parcel out the effects of a question such as "Now that X has died, can he still *feel*?" from the effects of a list of primarily action-related nonfunctionality queries (e.g., "... can he still move around?" "... can he still drink water?" "... can he still go to the toilet?"). The actions and thoughts of the dead have been lumped together in a hodgepodge of purported "states" so that it has not yet been possible to understand, really, how children come to view the *minds* of dead organisms.

To our knowledge, Kane (1979) is the only researcher to have systematically distinguished between cognitive and noncognitive functions when asking children about death (labeling the cessation of cognitive and noncognitive functions *insensitivity* and *dysfunctionality*, respectively). Interestingly, she found that children were significantly more likely to attribute to dead organisms continuity of cognitive (e.g., knowing, feeling) states than continuity of noncognitive (e.g., heart beating, breathing) states. Kane explained her findings by suggesting that children have trouble reasoning about more subtle, nonvisible aspects attributable to life. However, Kane did not mention anything about the fact that these more subtle functions are mental states and may therefore be a special case altogether. Because reasoning about invisible causal forces such as beliefs and desires necessitates having a theory of mind, in the context of death reasoning such questions should be especially difficult, because any *theory* of a dead person's mind cannot be adequately validated, or disconfirmed, with behavioral feedback (cf. Gopnik and Wellman 1992). The absence of action does not necessarily imply the absence of intentional states, because one can close one's eyes and lie completely still yet continue to feel and think. Any theory discounting dead agents' capacity to experience these states must therefore arise through means other than those commonly employed in the social domain.

Of course, most children grow up embedded in cultures that support the belief in life after death, making it impossible to separate any purely evolutionarily based mechanisms from purely cultural mechanisms. (In fact, we argue that it is impossible to separate biologic and environmental causation for *any* psychological trait; see Gottlieb 2001.) However, if all that were influencing people's afterlife judgments were mainstream cultural beliefs, with increasing age, children should be more likely to make attributions of psychological continuation following death because of their increasing exposure to cultural norms.

Our first hypothesis was therefore that people's judgments about the continuity of psychological processes following death should actually *decrease* with increasing age, despite the background of cultural influence to the contrary. Because younger children are more likely to have deficient biological knowledge, we predicted that in reasoning about the psychological status of dead agents, they would "default" to the same strategy they use in the social domain—viewing dead agents as still in possession of a mind with all its psychological attributes. As children develop, they tend to acquire explicit biological knowledge, and they likely apply this knowledge when reasoning about the psychological status of dead agents. This should be reflected in an overall age-related decrease in beliefs about the continuity of psychological states in dead agents. What such a decrease would show is that a general belief in the continuity of mental states in dead agents is not something that children *acquire* as a product of their social–religious upbringing but is more likely a natural disposition that interacts with various learning channels.

Our second hypothesis was that these judgments about the continuity of psychological processes following death would also vary as a function of the nature of the mechanisms under question.

For example, ontogenetically, children may begin to reason that dead agents lose the capacity to experience some types of mental states (such as psychobiological and perceptual states) before they reason that dead agents lose the capacity for other types of mental states (such as epistemic, desire, and emotional states). One reason to suspect that such age-related differences in psychological attributions to dead agents may occur is that psychobiological and perceptual states, conceptually at least, appear planted in the physical body. Psychobiological states (e.g., hunger, thirst) are associated with activities that are designed to support life (e.g., finding food, obtaining water). As Slaughter and her colleagues (Slaughter et al. 1999; Slaughter and Lyons 2003) have shown, once children have an understanding of the vitalistic purpose of such activities, they reason that these activities no longer occur at death. To reason that the psychological states accompanying such activities also cease at death would require only one more inferential leap (e.g., "Dead agents do not need to eat. The person is dead. Therefore, the person cannot be hungry."). Similarly, perceptual states (e.g., seeing, hearing) are associated with physical parts of the body (e.g., eyes, ears). If children understand the function of these body parts (e.g., that the eyes are designed to see, the ears are designed to hear, and so on), then reasoning that dead agents lose the capacity for such psychological states should occur when children combine their understanding of the purpose of these body parts, at around 4 years of age (O'Neill and Chong 2001), with their knowledge that the body is rendered nonfunctional at death, at around 6 or 7 years of age (Speece and Brent 1984). Prior to this understanding that the body stops functioning at death, children may find it difficult to understand that the psychological states generated by specific body parts do not occur in dead agents.

Other types of mental states, such as epistemic, desire, and emotional states, are not clearly tied to vitalistic maintenance of the body (as psychobiological states are) or to observable sensory organs (as perceptual states are), and therefore, stating that dead agents have lost the capacity for such states may require more advanced biological reasoning, perhaps knowledge that the brain, which is rendered nonfunctional at death, is responsible for all forms of psychological states (e.g., "The brain is necessary for knowing. The brain stops working at death. Therefore, people who are dead can neither know nor not know."). Such reasoning may be cognitively effortful, as evidenced by recent findings by Bering (2002). Bering found that, when reasoning about the psychological status of a person reportedly just killed in an accident, even adults who characterized themselves as "extinctivists" (individuals who believe that personal consciousness ceases to exist, or becomes extinct, at death; after Thalbourne 1996) were less likely to say that epistemic, emotional, and desire states did not continue after death than they were to say that psychobiological and perceptual states did not continue after death. In fact, 36% of extinctivists' responses to questions dealing with the epistemic status of the dead character (e.g., "Does he *know* that he's dead?") reflected continuity reasoning, whereby they attributed to the dead person the continued capacity to know. In contrast, the same group was at ceiling on discontinuity responses for questions dealing with psychobiological and perceptual states.

The current study is, we believe, the first of its kind to systematically explore the issue of how children represent the minds of dead agents. To obtain a baseline measure of biological knowledge and death, in Experiment 1, we had 4- to 8-year-old children witness a puppet show in which a mouse was killed and subsequently eaten by an alligator. They were then asked a series of questions concerning *biological discontinuity* of function (e.g., "Does the mouse still need to *eat food?*" "Will he *grow up* to be an old mouse?"). The age range selected represents a period that witnesses rapid changes in the core content domain of folk biology such that implicit knowledge about the natural world becomes increasingly explicit (Carey 1991; Carey and Spelke 1994; Keil 1994; Medin and Atran 1999). The types of questions used in Experiment 1 paralleled those used in earlier studies (e.g., Barrett 1999; Mahon, Zagorsky-Goldberg, and Washington 1999; Slaughter and Lyons 2003) and dealt primarily with action-related constructs (e.g., eating food) or purely biological constructs (e.g., growth) that even preschoolers have been shown to understand are clearly interwoven with life (Inagaki 1989; Inagaki and Hatano 1996; Wellman, Hickling, and Schult 1997; see also Medin and Atran 1999).

Experiment 2 was similar to the first experiment with the exception that a new group of children, this time including a third age group of 10- to 12-year-olds, was asked a series of questions concerning *psychological discontinuity* of function involving both cognitive (e.g., "Does the mouse *know* he's not alive?") and psychobiological (e.g., "Is the mouse still *sleepy?*") states. The earliest span of this developmental period—from 4 to 5 years—coincides with the appearance of the ability to represent beliefs and desires, as evidenced by successful performance on traditional false-belief and appearance–reality tasks (for a review, see Flavell 1999). Finally, in Experiment 3, three groups of participants (4- to 5-year-olds, 10- to 12-year-olds, and adults) were confronted with the same basic design but this time were asked whether a wide range of psychological states (i.e., psychobiological, perceptual, emotional, desire, and epistemic) continued after death.

Experiment 1: Discontinuity of Biological Functioning

Method

Participants

Participants were 51 children attending preschool, kindergarten, first grade, and second grade at two university-affiliated schools in a suburban metropolitan area of south Florida. Enrollment at the elementary school (Grades K–8) was based on a community lottery system, and the preschool children were enrolled by their parents. Children came from diverse backgrounds and represented a range of socioeconomic levels. Children were divided into two groups, younger and older. The younger group of children consisted of 26 participants, 12 boys and 14 girls, with an average age of 5 years 6 months (range = 4 years 5 months to 6 years 5 months). There were 25 older children, including 12 boys and 13 girls, with an average age of 7 years 4 months (range = 6 years 6 months to 8 years 9 months).

Materials and Procedure

Children were brought from their classrooms and tested individually in a small, private room in the school library or in a school administrator's private office. All children were asked at the beginning of the experiment whether they would like to watch a puppet show and help the experimenter answer some questions about the puppets. After agreeing to participate, children were instructed to sit in a chair across from the experimenter and on the opposite side of the small puppet theatre display. The puppet theatre display consisted of a green Styrofoam board (75.9 cm × 31.6 cm), wooden fencing around the perimeter of the board, a small plastic tree, artificial grass, two mouse finger puppets (one white and one brown), and an alligator hand puppet. Prior to the puppet show demonstration, participants were introduced to the three puppets (presented separately) and told, "Now we both know that these aren't real mice and this isn't a real alligator, but let's pretend that they're real, ok?" (after Barrett 1999). They were then given the following information about the characters: (a) The alligator's favorite food is mice, and (b) the mice are baby mice. Immediately thereafter, one of the mice was put away (presentation counterbalanced) and the puppet show, involving the remaining mouse and the alligator, was presented to the child.

Enactment of the puppet show involved the following standardized story:

> There's Mr. Alligator hiding behind those bushes. And here comes Brown Mouse [White Mouse]. Brown Mouse doesn't see Mr. Alligator. And Mr. Alligator doesn't see Brown Mouse yet. Brown Mouse is having a very bad day. First of all, he's lost! He has no idea where he is or how to get home. And he's sick! Do you feel good when you're

sick? No! Brown Mouse is very sleepy because he hasn't slept for a very long time. And he's very hungry and thirsty because he hasn't had anything to eat or drink all day. Now do you think Brown Mouse is having a good day? [The experimenter then prompted the participant to repeat Brown Mouse's problems and reiterated them if necessary.] Uh-oh! Mr. Alligator sees Brown Mouse and is coming to get him! [Alligator is shown eating Brown Mouse.] Well, it looks like Brown Mouse got eaten by Mr. Alligator. Brown Mouse is not alive anymore.

Both puppets were then removed from the child's view, and the child was asked whether Brown Mouse was still alive. Only after agreeing that Brown Mouse was not alive did the participant advance to testing. (There were only a few children who answered that the mouse was still alive after watching him get eaten by the alligator, and they were easily persuaded that he was, in fact, dead.) The children were then instructed that they would be asked some questions about Brown Mouse; the experimenter told the children that he or she was only interested in what they thought and that there were no wrong or right answers.

Children were then asked a series of 10 questions pertaining to White/Brown Mouse's biological status (e.g., "Now that Brown Mouse is not alive[1] anymore, do you think that he will ever need to drink water again?"). These questions can be seen in Table 1. Following children's response to each question (usually a "yes" or a "no"), they were asked to provide a justification for their answer (e.g., "Why do you think that?" or "How come?"). Children received the questions in one of four counterbalanced orders. The experimenter's offering of confirmatory but neutral feedback was used to encourage all answers by the children regardless of content, and there were no cases in which the children showed any signs of distress at the questions. The children's answers to the questions were recorded on audiotape for later transcription and were also coded online by the experimenters in the event of audio recorder malfunctioning or inaudible responses.

There were no cases in which it was necessary to use the online data sheets.

Coding
Answers to interview questions were scored according to operational criteria establishing likely *continuity* reasoning (the specific biological imperative was envisioned to function despite the mouse's death) or *discontinuity* reasoning (the specific biological imperative was envisioned to have ceased functioning as a result of the mouse's death). Two percent (1.98%) of the total responses could not be coded because of ambiguity of response or failure of the child to respond. Less than 1% (0.77%) of the data could not be coded because of experimenter error.

"Now that the mouse is no longer alive ..."	Younger	Older
1. Will he ever *be alive* again?"	96	100
2. Will he ever *grow up* to be an old mouse?"	92	96
3. Will he ever need to *go to the bathroom*?"	88	96
4. Do his *ears* still work?"	85	96
5. Will he ever *get sick* again?"	79	91
6. Does his *brain* still work?"	85	81
7. Will he ever need to *drink water* again?"	68	92
8. Do his *eyes* still work?"	68	88
9. Will he ever need to *sleep* again?"	60	84
10. Will he ever need to *eat food* again?"	54	88

Table 1. *Percentages of younger and older children providing discontinuity responses in Experiment 1*

In most cases, initial affirmative answers to the questions were unequivocal evidence of continuity reasoning. For instance, if when asked whether the dead mouse would ever need to drink water again, the child answered "yes" and his or her answer to the follow-up question (e.g., "How come?") matched this affirmative response (e.g., "Because he will"), then a continuity score was coded. Similarly, initial negative answers were usually evidence of discontinuity reasoning. For example, if when asked whether the dead mouse would ever need to go to the bathroom again, the child answered "no" and his or her answer to the follow-up question (e.g., "Why not?") matched this negative response (e.g., "Because when you're dead you don't have to do that"), then a discontinuity score was coded. In those cases in which a child displayed uncertainty by changing his or her response between the target question and the follow-up questions for that item, an unscorable classification was recorded. In those cases in which a child answered "I don't know" to a follow-up question, a discontinuity response was coded if the child responded "no" to the target question, and a continuity response was coded if the child responded "yes" to the target question.

Coding was based on the child's reasoning about specific biological imperatives (e.g., the need to eat food). It was therefore possible for the child to present answers that reflected general afterlife beliefs while maintaining discontinuity reasoning for the item in question (e.g., "Ghosts don't need to eat food"). In other words, individual interview questions were not attempts to discover whether participants believed in life after death; they were attempts to discover whether participants believed in the continuity or discontinuity of each particular biological function after death.

Jesse M. Bering and a second person naive to the purposes of the study served as independent coders for the entire data set. Initial interrater reliability was 95%, and all disagreements were subsequently resolved by reviewing the episodes in question.

Results

Table 1 presents the percentages of scorable discontinuity responses for each of the questions used in Experiment 1, separately for the younger and older children.[2] The analyses of discontinuity responses reported below excluded those responses that could not be coded because of ambiguity or experimenter error (2.75% of all responses). Analysis of the absolute percentages of discontinuity responses, however, produced nearly identical results. In addition, there was no significant difference in the numbers of unscorable responses between the two age groups. Preliminary analyses showed no significant effects of gender, color of the dead mouse (i.e., brown or white), or order of presentation of the questions, and all subsequent analyses were collapsed across these variables.

As can be seen from Table 1, the percentages of discontinuity responses per question ranged from 54% to 96% for the younger children and from 84% to 100% for the older children. A standard t-test produced a significant effect of age, $t(49) = 2.61$, $p <. 05$, with the older children ($M = 91\%$) being significantly more likely to give discontinuity responses than the younger children ($M = 78\%$).

To assess the degree to which children were consistent in their discontinuity reasoning, we classified children as *consistent discontinuity theorists* if they provided discontinuity responses for all questions (excluding those few that could not be scored). Significantly more older children (68%) than younger children (38%) provided discontinuity responses for all of the questions, $X^2(1, N = 51) = 4.53$, $p <.05$, reflecting the fact that the older children were more likely than the younger children to generalize discontinuity reasoning across the biological question set. None of the children in either age group provided continuity responses for all of the questions.

Discussion

As predicted, the older children (6 years 6 months to 8 years 9 months) were significantly more likely than the younger children (4 years 5 months to 6 years 5 months) to state that the biological imperatives no longer applied once the mouse was eaten. This finding was shown both in the overall percentage of questions for which children gave discontinuity responses and in the percentage of children who used discontinuity reasoning for all questions posed (i.e., consistent discontinuity theorists) and is likely the result of a growing biological knowledge base at the start of middle childhood (Keil 1994; Medin and Atran 1999). Importantly, however, even the younger participants demonstrated a relatively firm understanding that normal biological demands associated with living did not apply after death. Half of the total number of questions elicited particularly strong discontinuity responses (i.e.,

> 80%) in the younger group: (a) "Will he ever be alive again?" (b) "Will he grow up to be an old mouse?" (c) "Will he ever need to go to the bathroom?" (d) "Does his brain still work?" and (e) "Do his ears still work?" Only 8% of the younger children, and none of the older children, believed, for instance, that the dead mouse would grow up to be an old mouse. A typical response to this question came from a 6-year-old girl who, after being asked why she answered "no," stated that the mouse would not grow up "because he's already dead."

Other studies have similarly found strong support for preschoolers' understanding of growth and its extension to living organisms (Backscheider, Shatz, and Gelman 1993; Inagaki 1989; Keil 1994). Yet, interestingly, the children's discontinuity reasoning was comparatively meager for the questions related to eating and sleeping—46% of the younger subjects, for example, informed the experimenter that the mouse would continue to need to eat food after its death. This may be at least partially due to the fact that these questions denoted action, whereas most of the other questions (e.g., "Do his ears still work?") had to do with functions. However, at least one of the other questions denoting action rather than function (i.e., "Will he ever need to go to the bathroom?") elicited a high percentage of discontinuity responses (88%) from the younger children. Perhaps, therefore, children's seeming difficulty with reasoning about the cessation of biological functions at death has more to do with the type of actions denoted in the questions than with the simple fact that the actions constitute overt behaviors.

For instance, the data for the "need to sleep" and "need to eat" questions are nearly identical to those obtained by Slaughter et al. (1999), who reported that 44% of their small group of 4- to 5-year-olds believed that people need food when they are dead. The authors interpreted this as evidence that "some young children conceptualize death as living on in altered circumstances, rather than as the cessation of the body machine" (p. 89). With exposure to a vitalistic teaching strategy in which children come to understand that the ultimate function of bodily processes, including nutrient intake and digestion, is to support life, children come to assimilate this knowledge into their maturing concept of death (Slaughter et al. 1999; Slaughter and Lyons 2003). Although this might account for the "need to eat" item in our study as well, it is not as apparent that this argument would apply with equal force to the "need to sleep" item. Perhaps the sleep question is a particularly difficult one for young children to grasp because they equate both death and sleep with physical stillness. Therefore, for preschoolers, stating that the dead mouse will continue to "need to sleep" might be a comment about the perceptually current state of affairs rather than a belief that sleep is required even after death.

We were, however, surprised at the number of children, even among the youngest ones, who correctly reasoned that the mouse's various body parts (e.g., ears, brain, eyes) stopped working after its death. These findings suggest that preschool-age children have some understanding of the nonfunctionality component of the death concept, which previous researchers have reported does not occur until age 6 or 7 (e.g., Speece and Brent 1984). For example, only 15% of the younger children told the experimenter that the mouse's brain continued to work after it had died. This is especially intriguing because other research has shown that even 4-year-olds understand that the brain is for thinking (see Johnson and Wellman 1982). One might therefore reasonably expect children to deny (at the least) higher order cognitive activity to dead agents. In addition, on the basis of these findings, we would expect preschool-age children to apply their knowledge of the nonfunctioning nature of these body parts (i.e., ears, brain, eyes) when reasoning about the capacity for dead agents to experience the types of mental states (i.e., hearing, thinking, seeing) directly associated with those parts. Experiment 2 was designed to test these and related predictions.

Experiment 2: Discontinuity of Psychological Functioning—Cognitive Versus Psychobiological States

Method

Participants

Participants were from the same university-affiliated schools reported in the first experiment and included 82 children ranging in age from 4 years 0 months to 12 years 1 month. Children were divided into three age groups. The youngest group of children, hereafter referred to as "kindergartners," consisted of 29 participants, 19 boys and 10 girls, with an average age of 5 years 3 months (range = 4 years 0 months to 6 years 1 month). There were 33 children from the middle age group, hereafter referred to as the "early elementary" group, including 15 boys and 18 girls, with an average age of 7 years 3 months (range = 6 years 3 months to 8 years 7 months). Finally, the oldest group of children, hereafter referred to as the "late elementary" group, consisted of 20 participants with an average age of 11 years 0 months (range = 10 years 3 months to 12 years 1 month). This group contained 12 boys and 8 girls. None of the children in the present experiment participated in Experiment 1. (See Footnote 2.)

Materials and Procedure

The experiment was conducted identically to the first experiment with two exceptions. First, children in Experiment 2 were asked a series of questions entirely different from those in Experiment 1. Namely, children in the current experiment were asked not about biological functions after death, but rather about psychological functions, including both cognitive (knowing, wanting, seeing, thinking) and psychobiological (hungry, thirsty, sleepy, sick) states (see Table 2). The list of items included a total of nine questions and consisted of five cognitive and four psychobiological questions.[3] Presentation of questions was arranged such that, of four possible order configurations, children never received more than two consecutive questions from the same category. (However, one cognitive question, i.e., "Does he know that he's not alive?," always occurred at the very end of the question set.) Seven of the items were conceptually linked to the list of biological questions from Experiment 1. For instance, the question "Will the mouse get hungry?" from the current experiment was yoked to "Will the mouse ever need to eat food again?" from the first experiment. Second, the children from the two youngest age groups were also presented with a control condition in which a *different* mouse (either white or brown) *escaped* from the alligator and avoided death. This was done in order to assess the likelihood that the children, under conditions in which death did not occur, would easily attribute mental states to a "living" mouse puppet. Because subsequent analyses revealed ceiling performance on this control procedure for the two youngest age groups, it was deemed unnecessary for the oldest children. Presentation of the control condition was counterbalanced so that roughly half of these children witnessed the escape scene before the death scene, and half saw the opposite puppet show order. The control questions were identical to the test questions (minus the experimenter's obligatory preface that the mouse was no longer alive and the question dealing with the mouse's knowledge of its own death).

"Now that the mouse is no longer alive …"	Kindergarten	Early elementary	Late elementary
Psychobiological			
1. Is he still *hungry?*"	39	67	100
2. Is he still *thirsty?*"	33	63	100
3. Is he still *sleepy?*"	39	66	89
4. Does he still *feel sick?*"	21	55	75
Cognitive			
1. Is he *thinking* about the alligator?"	43	73	85
2. Can he *see* this tree?"[a]	50	54	78
3. Does he still *want* to go home?"	28	47	80
4. Does he *know* where he is now?"	36	46	53
5. Does he *know* that he's not alive?"	33	52	35

[a] Refers to the plastic tree placed on the theatre display.

Table 2. *Percentages of children, by age group, providing discontinuity responses in Experiment 2*

As in the first experiment, children were asked to provide a justification for their initial "yes" or "no" response (e.g., "Why do you think that?" or "How come?"), and the experimenter offered confirmatory, neutral feedback regardless of answer content. There were no signs of distress at the questions. The children's answers to the questions were recorded on audiotape for later transcription and were also coded online by the experimenters in the event of audio recorder malfunctioning or inaudible responses. Because of experimenter error in which interview sessions were not recorded, there were two cases in which it was necessary to use the online data sheets.

Coding

As in Experiment 1, answers to interview questions were scored according to operational criteria establishing likely *continuity* reasoning (the specific psychological faculty was envisioned to function despite the mouse's death) or *discontinuity* reasoning (the specific psychological faculty was envisioned to have ceased functioning as a result of the mouse's death). Ten percent (10.2%) of the total responses could not be coded because of ambiguity of response or failure of the child to respond. There were only three cases (out of a total of 733 responses) that could not be coded because of experimenter error.

The criteria used to classify a response as denoting continuity reasoning or discontinuity reasoning are provided in Appendix A along with actual examples of children's responses. As in Experiment 1, initial affirmative ("yes") responses to the test questions were usually considered unequivocal evidence of continuity reasoning. Because of the wording of the questions posed to children in Experiment 2, a "yes" response reflected a belief in the continuity of particular psychological capacities. For instance, if a child responded "yes" to the question "Now that the mouse is no longer alive, is he still hungry?" then the default assumption was that the child was using continuity reasoning. However, in all cases, children were asked follow-up questions after their initial "yes" or "no" response. In the event that a child's answer to a follow-up question did not match his or her initial response, an unscorable classification was recorded for that particular item. If a child answered "yes" to the above question, for example, but for the follow-up question reported "Because when you're dead, you don't get hungry," then the response was considered unscorable. No such cases, however, occurred; children's answers to the follow-up questions categorically matched their initial "yes" or "no" responses along continuity/discontinuity lines. As in Experiment 1, for those cases in which a child answered "I don't know" to a follow-up question, a continuity response was coded if the child stated "yes" to the target question.

Unlike in Experiment 1, negative answers to the initial questions in Experiment 2 required a careful assessment of answers to follow-up questions to determine whether the child was using continuity or discontinuity reasoning. Simply stating "no" in response to the target questions did not offer sufficient evidence of discontinuity reasoning. The participant may have said that the mouse did not know that he was dead but may have based his or her answer on presumed knowledge of the mouse (e.g., "He's confused" or "He thinks he's still alive") rather than on permanent cessation of the dead mouse's capacity to know or not know. To be scored as using discontinuity reasoning, the child was required to respond "no" to the initial target question and then to provide a justification for this response indicating cessation of function for the particular faculty during follow-up questioning. Although individual children's responses were highly variable, Appendix A provides versions of two common answers that would be classified as discontinuity reasoning.

An important caveat with regard to this coding system is that it is not infallible. One of the more frequent discontinuity responses, for instance, was "because he's dead." It is possible to make the case that such a response does not necessarily reflect discontinuity reasoning because it does not carry sufficient linguistic clarity; the child may actually be referring to the temporary suspension or occurrent lack of a particular mental state rather than to the dead agent's incapacity to experience that state (e.g., perhaps the dead mouse was not sleepy not because he lacked the capacity to be sleepy or not sleepy but because he just died and was distracted by goings-on). However, one reason to suspect that this was not the case, and that children who responded in such fashion were indeed relying on discontinuity reasoning, is that when probed for further clarity, children tended to repeat their answer ("because he's dead") rather than to elaborate on the reason they believed the dead mouse was not, at that moment, experiencing the state in question.

Jesse M. Bering and a second person naive to the purposes of the study served as independent coders. Initial interrater reliability (for the death condition only) was 89%, and all disagreements were subsequently resolved by reviewing the episodes in question.[4]

Results

For the control (escape) condition, all children from the kindergarten and early elementary groups provided clear continuity responses, demonstrating that they readily attributed mental states to the "living" mouse puppet. Because both age groups were at ceiling, no analyses were performed on the control trials.

For the test condition, the analyses of discontinuity responses reported here excluded all unscorable responses (10.2% of all responses). However, analysis of the absolute percentages of discontinuity responses produced nearly identical results. In addition, there was no significant difference in the numbers of unscorable responses between the three age groups, nor were unscorable responses more frequent for either question type (i.e., cognitive or psychobiological). Table 2 presents the percentages of scorable discontinuity responses for each question posed to the children in Experiment 2, separately for each age group and question type. Preliminary analyses showed no significant effects of gender, color of the dead mouse (i.e., brown or white), or question order on children's answers, and thus all subsequent analyses were collapsed across these variables. Also, there was no significant effect of order of presentation of the escape and eaten conditions for the two youngest age groups ($p > .05$).

Psychobiological and Cognitive Questions by Age Group
As can be seen from Table 2, the percentages of discontinuity responses per psychological question (collapsing across question type) ranged from 21% to 50% for kindergartners, from 46% to 73% for early elementary children, and from 35% to 100% for late elementary children. A 3 (age group) × 2 (question type: psychobiological vs. cognitive) analysis of variance, with repeated measures on the question-type factor, produced significant main effects of age, $F(2, 79) = 10.51$, $p < .01$ (late elementary [$M = 77\%$] > early elementary [$M = 58\%$] > kindergartners [$M = 32\%$]), and question type, $F(1, 79) = 9.18$, $p < .01$ (psychobiological [$M = 62\%$] > cognitive [$M = 53\%$]), and a significant Age Group × Question Type interaction, $F(2, 79) = 6.88$, $p < .01$. (See Figure 1.) Post hoc analyses of the significant Age Group × Question Type interaction using Bonferroni t-tests revealed that only the 11-year-old group was significantly more likely to use discontinuity reasoning for the psychobiological questions (91%) than for the cognitive questions (66%), $t(19) = 3.38$, $p < .01$. The difference between the psychobiological and cognitive questions was not significant for the early elementary (63% vs. 54%) and kindergarten (33% vs. 38%) groups; in fact, in contrast to the two older groups of children, the kindergartners made slightly more discontinuity responses for the cognitive than for the psychobiological questions. When we looked at changes in the psychobiological and cognitive questions across age groups, Tukey–Kramer tests ($p < .05$) revealed that the percentage of discontinuity responses for the psychobiological questions increased significantly at each age. In contrast, only the comparison between the oldest and youngest children was significant for the cognitive category, with the late elementary group (66%) being more likely than the kindergartners (38%) to give discontinuity responses for these questions.

Consistent Discontinuity Theorizing
To assess the degree to which children were consistent in their discontinuity reasoning overall, and also within question categories (i.e., cognitive and psychobiological), we classified children as consistent discontinuity theorists

if they provided discontinuity responses for all questions (excluding those few that could not be scored). For the analysis of the overall psychological question set, the effect of age group was significant, $X^2(2, N = 82) = 8.83$, $p < .05$. Additional analyses revealed that early elementary children (30%) were significantly more likely than kindergartners (3%) to generalize their discontinuity reasoning across the entire range of psychological questions presented to them, $X^2(1, N = 62) = 8.78$, $p < .01$. The difference between the late elementary (20%) and kindergarten groups approached significance, with the oldest children being somewhat more likely to be classified as consistent discontinuity theorists than the youngest children, $X^2(1, N = 49) = 3.58$, $p = .06$.

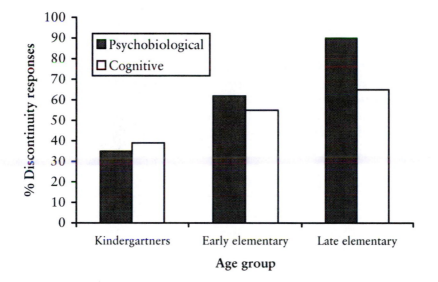

Figure 1. *Percentages of participants providing discontinuity responses for psychobiological and cognitive questions, by age group, in Experiment 2*

Within question-type categories, there were more consistent discontinuity theorists at each age group for the psychobiological questions (43%) than for the cognitive questions (27%). For the psychobiological question set, there was a significant effect of age group, $X^2(2, N = 82) = 20.43$, $p < .01$. Seventy-five percent of late elementary children reasoned that all psychobiological functions ceased at death, whereas only 48% of early elementary children reasoned in this manner, a difference that approached significance, $X^2(1, N = 53) = 3.73$, $p = .05$. The difference between the kindergartners (14%) and both the early elementary and late elementary groups was also significant, $X^2(1, N = 82) = 8.99$, $p < .01$. In contrast to their answers on the psychobiological questions, the late elementary group (30%) was no more likely than the early elementary (33%) and the kindergarten (17%)

groups to be classified as consistent discontinuity theorists for the cognitive question set, $X^2(2, N = 82) = 2.27, p > .05$.

Conceptually Linked Biological and Psychological Factors

To determine the extent to which children answered the yoked questions from the first and second experiments differently, we performed a multivariate analysis of variance (MANOVA) comparing the overall means of these questions from Experiment 1 with those from Experiment 2 for the kindergarten and early elementary age groups. (Recall that a late elementary group was not tested in Experiment 1.) The seven yoked questions included in this analysis are presented in Table 3. Note that for each question pair, for both groups of children, the percentage of discontinuity responses was higher for the biological questions of Experiment 1 than for the corresponding psychological questions of Experiment 2. The MANOVA produced significant effects of age group, $F(1, 6) = 56.82, p < .01$ (early elementary [$M = 75.3\%$] > kindergartners [$M = 54.9\%$]), and question type, $F(1, 6) = 39.76, p < .01$ (biological [$M = 81\%$] > psychological [$M = 49.1\%$]). Although the difference in discontinuity responses between the biological and psychological questions was somewhat greater for kindergartners (72.9% vs. 37.9%) than for the early elementary children (89.1% vs. 61.4%), the Age Group × Question Type interaction was not significant, $F(1, 6) = 1.34, p > .05$.

"Now that the mouse is no longer alive ..."	Kindergarten	Early elementary
1. Will he ever need to *eat food* again?"	54	88
Is he still *hungry?"*	39	67
2. Will he ever need to *drink water* again?"	68	92
Is he still *thirsty?"*	33	63
3. Will he ever need to *sleep* again?"	60	84
Is he still *sleepy?"*	39	66
4. Will he ever *get sick* again?"	79	91
Does he still *feel sick?"*	21	55
5. Does his *brain* still work?"	85	81
Is he still *thinking* about Mr. Alligator?"	43	73
6. Do his *eyes* still work?"	68	88
Can he *see* this tree?"	50	54
7. Will he ever *be alive* again?"	96	100
Does he *know he's not alive?"*	33	52

Table 3. *Means for discontinuity responses for yoked factors in Experiment 1 and Experiment 2*

Discussion

As predicted, children's discontinuity responses for the psychological states increased with age, and this effect was somewhat larger for the psychobiological than for the cognitive questions. (See Figure 1.) Moreover, children in the late elementary age group were significantly more likely to provide discontinuity answers in response to the psychobiological questions than in response to the cognitive questions. Children in the early elementary age group exhibited a similar divergence between the two question-type categories, although the difference did not reach significance. For the kindergartners, the difference between the psychobiological and cognitive question types was negligible and in the opposite direction. This finding was surprising given the high percentage of discontinuity responses on the biological question set among children of comparable ages.

The differences in levels of discontinuity responses between the biological questions of Experiment 1 and the psychological questions (including both psychobiological and cognitive questions) of Experiment 2 were striking. For every biological item that had a corresponding psychological question, kindergartners and early elementary children made more discontinuity responses for the biological item. Although the youngest children from Experiment 1 provided 78% discontinuity responses, in Experiment 2 only 33% of similarly aged children reasoned that psychobiological states ceased functioning at death. The early elementary age group's data show a similar pattern, with 91% of children in Experiment 1 reasoning that biological functions no longer apply at death and only 63% of similarly aged children in Experiment 2 reasoning that psychobiological states cease.

It seems strangely counterintuitive that similarly aged children at these ages stated that dead agents did not need to drink water but answered that it was possible for dead agents to be thirsty. Although younger children may not yet have mastered biological knowledge, even the preschoolers and kindergartners in Experiment 1 gave mostly discontinuity responses, so the comparably young children's performance in Experiment 2 cannot be attributed entirely to impoverishments in the biological domain. Perhaps, ontogenetically, children come to have more control over their biological knowledge when applying it to questions about the mind. Perhaps also the youngest children's high percentage of discontinuity reasoning in the first experiment was due largely to the implicit nature of their biological knowledge—they may not, for instance, have understood why the dead mouse's ears no longer worked aside from the fact that they did not work because the mouse was dead! This interpretation seems to provide support for Atran's (1994) view that preschoolers' folk biology is pretheoretical. It may be that these originally implicit biological concepts become progressively elaborated over time and that only once such knowledge is made explicit can it be applied to questions about the psychological status of dead agents in a fashion reflecting discontinuity reasoning.

Some children from Experiment 2 (particularly among those in the early and late elementary age groups) applied discontinuity reasoning to both psychological state categories. That is, they were consistent discontinuity theorists across the entire field of questions, reasoning not only that psycho-biological experiences cease at death but that all higher order cognitive activities do as well. In effect, these children were classic extinctivists, viewing death as swiftly and sweepingly eliminating the "beingness" of the deceased. One interpretation of these findings is that these children, unlike others, were not attempting to imagine what it feels like to be dead, because in the absence of analogous *conscious* experiences to refer to for help in the matter, such attempts would have failed them and resulted in continuity reasoning, particularly for the cognitive questions (e.g., What does it feel like not to think?). Koocher (1973), for instance, described how a group of children tested on death comprehension reflected upon what it might be like to be dead, "with references to sleeping, feeling 'peaceful,' or simply 'being very dizzy'" (p. 374). Consistent discontinuity theorists may have put such simulations aside and employed their explicit fact-based knowledge in order to make a biologically informed decision concerning the dead agents' current cognitive state, that of nothingness. However, these children were, relatively speaking, few in number, with consistent discontinuity reasoning for the cognitive questions being particularly infrequent. Only 30% of children in the late elementary group consistently reasoned that cognitive states ceased at death, compared with 75% who consistently reasoned that psychobiological states ceased.

Closer inspection of Table 2, however, reveals that the oldest children's pattern of response was driven almost entirely by two questions in particular, and these both dealt with the dead mouse's epistemic access to atypical brands of information (e.g., "Does he *know* where he is now?" "Does he *know* that he's not alive?"). Perhaps, therefore, it is not that the children in the late elementary group had difficulty conceptualizing the dead mouse's lack of ongoing cognitive states, in general, as much as it is that they had difficulty in taking into account the cause of ignorance when death was to blame. To investigate this issue more fully, in Experiment 3 we had both children and adults reason about the functioning of more rigorously categorized psychological states after death, dividing psychological functions into psychobiological, perceptual, emotional, desire, and epistemic states.

Experiment 3: Discontinuity of Variegated Psychological State Categories

Method

Participants
Sixty-six children were recruited from the same university-affiliated schools reported in Experiments 1 and 2. Participants came from ethnically diverse

backgrounds and represented a wide range of socioeconomic levels. None of the children in the current experiment had participated in either of the two previously reported experiments. Children were assigned to one of two groups based on age. The first group (hereafter referred to as "kindergart-ners") consisted of the youngest participants and included 35 preschoolers and kindergartners, 23 boys and 12 girls. The mean age of the children from this group was 5 years 3 months (range = 3 years 2 months to 6 years 10 months). The second group of children (hereafter referred to as "late elementary") consisted of 31 fifth and sixth graders, with a mean age of 11 years 8 months (range = 10 years 6 months to 12 years 10 months). There were 11 boys and 20 girls in this group.

In addition to the children, 20 undergraduate students were also recruited from the psychology subject pool at Florida Atlantic University to serve as participants in the study; these participants were enrolled in a general psy-chology course at the time of testing. The average age of the adult partici-pants in this study was 19 years 1 month (range = 18 years 2 months to 20 years 10 months), and there were 8 men and 12 women. The university is located in a suburban metropolitan area of south Florida, and its student population is highly diverse.

Materials and Procedure

Children were brought from their classrooms or after-school programs and tested individually in a small, private room either inside or neighboring the school library. Adults were tested in a room adjacent to the investigator's laboratory office. As in the foregoing experiments, children were asked at the beginning of their experimental session whether they would like to watch a puppet show and help the experimenter answer some questions about the puppets. Adult participants were told that they would be participating in an experiment designed for children and that the experimenter was interested in determining how adults answered the same types of questions asked of the children.

To minimize experimenter error during enactment of the puppet show and variability in the narration of the scripts, we showed participants in the current experiment a videotaped version of the puppet show. The video showed the same set of materials reported in the Method sections of Experi-ments 1 and 2. The only additions included a blue cardboard cutout that served as the small pond referred to in the puppet-show script and a small gathering of artificial flowers aligned at the perimeter fence in the theatre display, also referred to in the script. Individuals (including the adults) were instructed that although the scene was make-believe, they should pretend that the animals shown in the video were real. All participants observed the same events occurring on-screen, whereby the mouse was eaten and killed by the alligator, but heard one of two script versions (see Appendix B), appropriately matched and counterbalanced across trials, such that each participant heard either Script A or Script B but not both. Different script versions were used in order to determine whether participants were using discontinuity reasoning similarly for specific states (e.g., *taste, see*) within the same state category (e.g., *perceptual*), or if they treated such within-category states differently. We believed that including all states in a single script might exceed the attentional and memory abilities of the youngest children; we thus used two scripts in order to include a broader selection of psychological states. Script versions were randomly assigned to participants.

Following presentation of the video, individuals were asked a series of questions related to the continuity or discontinuity of psychological states or biological imperatives addressed in the script presented to them (see Appendix B). For example, in Script B, the mouse protagonist, prior to being eaten by the alligator, was said to "love how the flowers smell." Participants who heard this version of the story were then asked in the interview whether the dead mouse could "still smell the flowers" after it had died. Each script contained information dealing with five psychological state categories: (a) psychobiological, (b) perceptual, (c) emotional, (d) desire, and (e) epistemic. In addition, each script contained two questions dealing with biological imperatives from Experiment 1 in order to obtain a baseline, within-subject measure of death-related knowledge independent of reasoning about psychological states. Each interview in Experiment 3 therefore contained a total of 12 questions.

The two scripts differed with respect to the particular functions composing each category, such that, for instance, whereas Script A included information dealing with the perceptual states *hear* and *taste*, Script B substituted the perceptual states *smell* and *see*. Both scripts, therefore, contained information dealing with perceptual states. There were two questions for each psychological state category,[5] such that participants were asked a series of 10 questions dealing with the continuity or discontinuity of the psychological functioning of the dead agent. The questions used in this experiment are shown in Table 4. The order of presentation was varied so that questions dealing with the same psychological state categories were never asked consecutively.

As in the previous experiments, participants were asked follow-up questions after providing an initial "yes" or "no" response so that the experimenter could determine whether they were using continuity or discontinuity reasoning. In all cases, experimenters provided neutral, confirmatory feedback to encourage the participants' responses regardless of content and instructed them beforehand that there were no wrong or right answers to the questions.

"Now that the mouse is no longer alive ..."	Kindergarten	Late elementary	Adults
Biological			
1. Will he ever need to *eat food* again?"	76	100	100
2. Does his *brain* still work?"	88	81	82
3. Will he ever *grow up* to be an old mouse?"	59	100	100
4. Will he ever need to *drink water* again?"	63	93	100
Psychobiological			
1. Is he still *thirsty?*"	44	94	100
2. Is he still *hungry?*"	47	100	100
3. Is he still *sleepy?*"	44	86	93
4. Does he still feel *sick?*"	29	87	100
Perceptual			
1. Can he still *hear* the birds sing?"	67	81	82
2. Can he still *taste* the yucky grass he ate?"	83	87	100
3. Can he still *smell* the flowers?"	47	62	89
4. Can he *see* where he is?"	53	77	87
Desire			
1. Does he still *wish* he didn't have a brother?"	60	60	50
2. Does he still *want* to go home?"	24	46	74
3. Does he still *hope* to get better at math?"	23	45	88
Emotional			
1. Is he still *sad* because he can't find his way home?"	38	69	60
2. Is he still *angry* at his brother?"	60	81	70
3. Does he still *love* his mom?"	6	20	36
4. Is he still *scared* of the alligator?"	27	62	100
Epistemic			
1. Is still *thinking* about his brother?"	64	69	64
2. Does he still *believe* he's smarter than his brother?"	53	77	40
3. Does he *know* that he's not alive?"	21	23	60
4. Does he still *believe* his mom is the nicest grownup?"	11	33	56

Note: The first two questions for each question category reported above were from Script A. The remaining questions for each category were from Script B. The exception to this was the Desire question category, in which the question "Does he still *want* to go home?" was included in both scripts.

Table 4. *Percentages of children, by age group, providing discontinuity responses in Experiment 3*

Coding

The coding procedure was identical to the one used in Experiment 2. Jesse M. Bering and a second person naive to the purposes of the study served as independent coders. Initial interrater reliability on a random sample of 20% of the database was 90%, and all disagreements were subsequently resolved by reviewing the episodes in question.

Results

The analyses of discontinuity responses reported here excluded all unscorable responses (8% of all responses). However, a 3 (age group) × 6 (question type) analysis of variance including percentage of unscorable responses as the dependent variable and question type as the repeated measure showed significant effects of age group, $F(2, 83) = 5.44$, $p < .01$ (kindergartners > late elementary children > adults), and question type, $F(5, 408) = 3.90$, $p < .01$ (desire > perceptual > emotional = epistemic > biological > psychobiological), but the interaction was not significant. Further analyses of the main effects using Tukey–Kramer post hoc tests ($p < .05$) revealed that questions dealing with desire states (13%) produced significantly more unscorable responses than those dealing with both biological (3%) and psychobiological (2%) states. All other comparisons between question types produced nonsignificant differences. For the main effect of age group, the youngest children (12%) made significantly more unscorable responses than the adults (3%) but not significantly more than the older children (6%). The older children and adults produced equivalent percentages of unscorable responses.

Preliminary Analyses

Preliminary analyses using the percentage of scorable discontinuity responses as the dependent variable found no significant effects involving gender, so all subsequent analyses were performed collapsed across this factor. Participants received one of two scripts in this experiment, and each script posed questions about the continuity or discontinuity following death of two different processes for each question type (e.g., two questions about emotions, two question about desires). The different questions posed in the two scripts produced different overall levels of discontinuity responses, $F(1, 80) = 4.14$, $p < .01$ (Script A > Script B). The Age Group × Script interaction, $F(2, 80) = 17.34$, $p < .05$, and the Question Type × Script interaction, $F(5, 393) = 2.28$, $p < .05$, were also significant. An examination of performance between the two scripts revealed higher overall discontinuity responses on Script A than on Script B but a similar pattern of discontinuity responses for the various question types in the two scripts (Script A: biological = 89%, psychobiological = 77%, perceptual = 79%, emotional = 61%, desire = 51%, epistemic = 63%; Script B: biological = 83%, psychobiological = 67%, perceptual = 65%, emotional = 33%, desire = 35%, epistemic = 29%). (Percentages of discontinuity responses for individual questions for each age group can be found in Table 4.) Because the patterns of responses among the various question-type categories were similar for the two scripts, all subsequent analyses were collapsed across scripts.

Question Type by Age Group

Figure 2 presents the percentages of scorable discontinuity responses in Experiment 3, separately for each age group and question type. As can be seen in Figure 2, there was a general increase in discontinuity responses with age, and for each age group, discontinuity responses were made more frequently for the biological, psychobiological, and perceptual states than they were for the emotional, desire, and epistemic states. A 3 (age group: kindergartners vs. late elementary children vs. adults) × 6 (question type: biological vs. psychobiological vs. perceptual vs. emotional vs. desire vs. epistemic) analysis of variance with repeated measures on the question-type factor produced significant main effects of age group, $F(2, 83) = 9.40$, $p < .01$ (adults [$M = 78\%$] > late elementary children [$M = 70\%$] > kindergarten children [$M = 43\%$]), and question type, $F(5, 408) = 33.73$, $p < .01$ (biological [$M = 86\%$] = psychobiological [$M = 72\%$] = perceptual [$M = 72\%$] = emotional [$M = 48\%$] = epistemic [$M = 46\%$] = desire [$M = 43\%$]), and a significant Age Group × Question Type interaction, $F(10, 408) = 2.62$, $p < .01$.

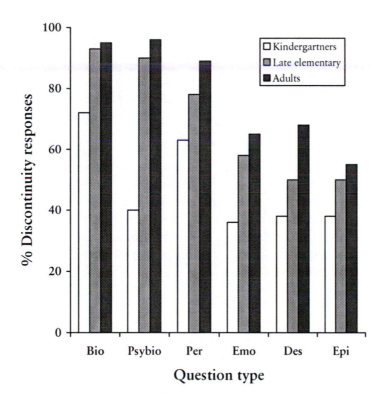

Figure 2. *Percentages of participants providing discontinuity responses, by age group and question type, in Experiment 3. Bio = biological; Psybio = psychobiological; Per = perceptual; Emo = emotional; Des = desire; Epi = epistemic*

Post hoc analyses of the significant Age Group × Question Type interaction using Tukey–Kramer post hoc tests ($p < .05$) revealed significant differences between question types in the predicted direction. For the kindergartners, biological questions elicited the highest levels of discontinuity responses, significantly greater than of the levels for all other questions. Discontinuity responses were statistically equivalent for the psychobiological, emotional, desire, and epistemic questions. The only other significant difference was between the perceptual questions and the emotional and desire questions (i.e., perceptual > emotional = desire). Patterns of performance were similar between the late elementary children and the adults. Both showed high and equivalent levels of discontinuity responses for the biological, psychobiological, and perceptual questions and lower and equivalent levels of performance for the emotional, desire, and epistemic questions. For the late elementary children, both the biological and psychobiological questions elicited significantly greater percentages of discontinuity responses than did the emotional, desire, and epistemic states. For the adults, the psychobiological questions produced significantly higher levels of discontinuity responses than did the emotional, desire, and epistemic questions; the biological questions produced higher levels of discontinuity responses than did the emotional and epistemic questions, with this difference approaching significance for the desire questions.

When contrasting the means for discontinuity responses between the age groups for each question type, we found no significant differences between the adults and the late elementary children for any question type. The biological and psychobiological questions elicited significantly more discontinuity responses among both the late elementary children and the adults than among the kindergartners (i.e., adults = late elementary children > kindergartners). Adults made significantly more discontinuity responses than did kindergartners for the perceptual, emotional, and desire states but not for the epistemic states. None of the differences between the late elementary children and the kindergartners were significant for these latter four categories (i.e., late elementary children = kindergartners, for perceptual, emotional, desire, and epistemic).

Consistent Discontinuity Theorizing
To assess the degree to which children and adults were consistent in their discontinuity reasoning over all questions, and also within each psychological state category (e.g., psychobiological, epistemic), we classified participants as consistent discontinuity theorists if they provided discontinuity responses for all questions, excluding those few that could not be scored within a specified category (see Table 5). As can be seen from Table 5, differences in the percentages of participants classified as consistent discontinuity theorists were small and nonsignificant between the adults and the late elementary children

for each contrast. In all cases, these two groups of older participants were more apt to be classified as consistent discontinuity theorists than were the kindergartners. These latter differences were significant (i.e., both adults and late elementary children > kindergartners via chi-square tests, $p < .05$) for the biological, psychobiological, and desire questions and overall but not for the perceptual ($p = .06$), emotional ($p = .09$), or epistemic ($p = .12$) questions.

Question type	Kindergarten	Late elementary	Adults
All questions	14	35	40
Biological	65	87	90
Psychobiological	34	90	95
Perceptual	55	71	85
Emotional	24	45	50
Desire	21	47	60
Epistemic	26	48	50

Note. Consistent discontinuity theorists were those providing 100% scorable discontinuity responses within a question type.

Table 5. *Percentages of consistent discontinuity theorists by age for all questions and separately for each question type in Experiment 3*

Discussion

The findings show that older children and adults were, overall, more likely to state that both biological imperatives and psychological states ceased at death and were more likely to report that *particular* categories of psychological states (i.e., psychobiological and perceptual states) ended at death than that others did (i.e., emotional, desire, and epistemic states). In contrast, the youngest children in the sample, although acknowledging that biological imperatives no longer applied to the dead agent, failed to distinguish between the different categories of psychological states and were just as likely to report that one type of state (e.g., psychobiological) continued after death as that another one did (e.g., epistemic). This finding may be explained by the implicit nature of the youngest children's knowledge about the biology of death; only after this knowledge has become conceptually enriched and made explicit can it be applied when reasoning about the psychological status of dead agents. However, even when explicit knowledge is in place, reasoning that certain types of psychological states (i.e., emotional, desire, and epistemic states) become extinguished at death appears difficult. Discontinuity reasoning for these types of mental states encounters resistance. The present studies do not address the question of where, precisely, this resistance comes from, but it seems likely that it is the product of both the ephemeral nature of these states (i.e., they are neither clearly tied to vitalistic demands nor directly associated with sensory organs) and an underlying sociocultural endorsement of folk dualism, phenomena that are probably causally linked among themselves.

As the findings strongly suggest, this pattern of response (among the children especially) is sensitive to independent factors such as the specific psychological states (as opposed to the general state category) used in the interview tasks. This is especially apparent for the emotional and epistemic categories. For the emotional questions, for instance, participants more readily attributed positive emotional states (e.g., love) than negative ones (e.g., anger) to the dead mouse. Eighty percent of the older children in Experiment 3 reasoned that the dead mouse had the capacity to love, whereas only 20% of children from the same age group reasoned that it maintained the capacity to experience anger. Similarly, for the question "Now that the mouse is not alive anymore, does he still believe his mom is the nicest grownup?" only 33% of the older children applied discontinuity reasoning, whereas another question dealing with the capacity for belief, "Does he still believe he's smarter than his brother?" evoked 77% discontinuity responses. Together, these data suggest that the emotional valence included in such questions may play an important role in children's answers, with participants being more likely to attribute the capacity to experience positive feelings than negative feelings to dead agents. However, although inherent differences between specific psychological states within the same state category (e.g., the perceptual states of *taste* vs. *see*) could either exacerbate or attenuate the general pattern of discontinuity responses seen here, the overall pattern between state categories remained consistent among older children and adults.

When compared with the findings from the previous two experiments, the findings from Experiment 3 closely approximate the earlier results. For example, the younger children from Experiment 1 produced, on average, 78% discontinuity responses, whereas a sample from that same biological question set in Experiment 3 elicited 74% discontinuity responses from similarly aged children. Likewise, the performance of children in Experiment 2 for the psychobiological questions was very similar to that observed for the kindergartners and late elementary children in Experiment 3 for a sample from the same question set. (Indeed, for the oldest children it was nearly identical.)

In addition, contrary to the findings from Experiment 2 in which the pattern of responses for questions dealing with epistemic access to atypical information (e.g., "Does he know that he's not alive?") was seemingly disparate from the pattern for the rest of the "cognitive" questions, the findings from Experiment 3 indicate that older children and adults' discrimination between psychological state types is driven by factors other than problems in representing the knowledge of dead agents. That is, it is not only the case that children and adults are challenged by reasoning about what a dead agent does or does not know, but they face real challenges when thinking about dead agents' capacity for emotional, epistemic, and desire states more generally. Finally, the pattern of adult discontinuity reasoning for the different question types was similar to that reported in a study by Bering (2002) in which adults were tested on a modified design with a human protagonist as the dead story character, which adds support for the general testing paradigm.

General Discussion

The results from this series of experiments lend support to the initial hypotheses that belief in the continuity of psychological states in dead agents generally decreases over time and that these default "afterlife" beliefs are pruned in a systematic fashion during development so that, in older children and adults, discontinuity reasoning is more likely to be applied to some mental state categories (i.e., perceptual and psychobiological) than others (i.e., epistemic, emotional, and desire). Although even preschool-age children seemed to possess knowledge that parts of the body (e.g., ears, eyes) no longer work after death, and many understood that biological imperatives (e.g., the need to eat, the need to drink) no longer applied after death, they tended to reason that the psychological states associated with these body parts (e.g., hearing, seeing) and these biological activities (e.g., hunger, thirst) continued after death. This finding may suggest that young children's biological knowledge about death is implicit in this regard and that only when such knowledge becomes explicit and declarative can it be logically applied to reasoning about the psychological status of dead agents. Nevertheless, by preschool, most children appear fully appreciative of the fact that, once death is certain, those activities and physical processes essential to the physical maintenance of all organisms cease. Seventy-eight percent of all responses made by the 4- to 6-year-olds in Experiment 1 were classified as reflecting discontinuity reasoning, and a nearly identical percentage (74%) of such responses was found for the youngest children in the final experiment (even though this sample included several 3-year-olds).

Surprisingly little has been reported in the literature specifically addressing children's understanding of biological imperatives and death, but our findings largely support those of Barrett (1999; Barrett and Behne 2001), who found that even 3-year-olds possessed accurate death-related knowledge when the study design was sensitive enough to extract implicit knowledge. Jointly, these findings of such early understanding of death contradict findings from previous work that used Piagetian-type methodologies and suggested that preschoolers are bound to view death as a form of deep sleep or a literal physical absence from the scene of the living (e.g., Koocher 1973;

Nagy 1948). Children understand that, unlike sleep, biological processes no longer apply at death.

Deep sleep is, of course, closely related to a monistic view of death, and in terms of children's attributions of the psychological processes accompanying sleep and death, there may indeed be a common inductive mechanism at work. For example, Flavell, Green, and Flavell (1995; see also Flavell and O'Donnell 1999) found that 5-year-olds were more likely than 8-year-olds to attribute decision-making abilities and self-awareness to a person sound asleep and not dreaming. Flavell et al. (1995) interpreted their findings as evidence of young children's tendency to wrongly attribute mental states when explaining the absence of behavior during unconscious periods and to older children's better understanding of unconsciousness. Because Flavell et al.'s study dealt only with children's reasoning about higher order cognitive activity during sleep, however, it is currently unknown whether children of different ages are more likely to attribute certain types of psychological states (e.g., thinking, knowing) than other states (e.g., being thirsty, hearing) to sleeping agents.

It is also worth noting that both Barrett's (1999) work and the current study placed the death scenario in the context of a predator–prey relationship, something that Barrett proposed is critical to experimentally getting at discontinuity death reasoning at such early ages. Whether this evolutionarily based explanation continues to hold up remains to be seen; nevertheless, it is apparent from the results reported for Experiment 1 that, at least when it comes to strictly biological matters, preschoolers confronted with concrete, visually salient death events apprehend the subject far more clearly than most professionals have been willing to give children their age credit for. And by age 7, nearly all children view death as a collapsing of the biological system and all associated vitalistic demands in individual organisms.

Interestingly, however, only slight deviations from the original biological questions resulted in drastic changes in children's reasoning. Comparisons between the strictly biological questions in Experiment 1 (e.g., "Will he ever need to drink water again?") and the psychological questions from Experiment 2 conceptually linked to them (e.g., "Is he still thirsty?") showed that both the youngest children ($M = 5$ years) and those in the middle age group ($M = 7$ years) produced far fewer discontinuity responses for the psychological questions. Similarly, in Experiment 3, which included questions about the continuity of both biological imperatives and psychobiological states in the same design, the youngest children clearly distinguished between these two categories, readily reporting that biological imperatives ceased at death while psychobiological states still occurred. Clearly, the youngest children had some biological knowledge about death but ran into trouble when applying this biological knowledge to related psychological matters.

Perhaps only after biological knowledge has become elaborated and made increasingly declarative can children apply this knowledge of the nonfunctionality of body parts and the role of vitalistic activities to related psychological states, as evidenced by the performance of the oldest children in Experiments 2 and 3 and the adults in Experiment 3. However, participants in these age groups were more likely to report that psychobiological and perceptual states ceased at death than that emotional, desire, and epistemic states ceased at death, thus showing an underlying cognitive bias that predisposes individuals to entertain the idea of the continuity of certain phenomenological characteristics of dead agents over others.

The current study was not an attempt to explain why individuals believe in life after death per se but rather was an attempt to explain why, when they do harbor such beliefs about the afterlife, these beliefs are characterized by a highly typical complexion: that of a knowing, believing, *mindful* spirit that has shed its biology proper. We do not wish to pit cognitive biases for afterlife beliefs against culture in attempting to explain this nearly universal phenomenon. Narrow scientific philosophizing of this sort rarely proves to be anything but futile (Cosmides and Tooby 1992). As is the case with any complex psychological trait found across cultures, genders, religions, and a host of other dispositional variables, the tendency for people to believe in the continued existence of specific psychological states after death while discounting others cannot be reduced to some instinctive mechanism in isolation from experiential input. Neither, as these data show, can afterlife beliefs be effectively reduced to a product of sheer learning, independent of the organized structure that receives information regarding such beliefs (Bering 2002). If afterlife beliefs were solely a function of social learning, then we should be compelled to ask why early elementary children would provide, in general, more *discontinuity* responses than, say, kindergartners? Likewise, the late elementary children in the current study provided more epistemic discontinuity responses than did the early elementary children (Experiment 2). The vast majority of adults believe in some form of personal consciousness after death, and one would suppose, after all, that the more time children spend in a given socioreligious milieu, the more they should show signs of indoctrination (see also Brent et al. 1996). From a strictly cultural perspective, there is simply no a priori reason to assume that preschoolers, no matter what religious instruction they have thus far received, would be more likely to reason that a dead agent will no longer need to eat food than that a dead agent cannot be hungry.

It is also interesting to note that only a very small percentage of children used any eschatological terms (e.g., *heaven, God, spirit,* and so on) during the course of the study. If children's answers were guided in any significant fashion by what they had learned from religious pedagogy, then one might expect such material to have been more salient in the children's responses.

In contrast, it was conspicuously lacking. This is not compelling evidence of the unimportance of indoctrination in its own right but is only suggestive when viewed in light of the patterns of divergence between children's responses to the various questions posed to them.

Rather, it seems more likely that popular and ecumenical accounts of the afterlife contribute throughout development to the general pattern of reasoning about dead agents' minds, with cultural immersion and religious indoctrination effectively exploiting innate cognitive biases. It may be a simple matter of fact that spirits and ghosts are typified by the possession of certain psychological states, but it is precisely because the disposition of these beliefs about dead agents are so uniform that developmental psychologists must attempt to explain them. Future research should examine the exact role of sociocultural influences on children's intuitive reasoning about the psychological status of dead agents.

Appendix A:
Coding Guidelines for Interview Sessions in Experiment 2

Continuity

The child responds "yes" to the initial, target question and does not contradict this answer in his or her response to the follow-up question(s) (see Example 1a). If the child does not provide an answer at follow-up questioning for the initial "yes" response (shrugs shoulders, states "I don't know," etc.), then a continuity score is recorded (see Example 1b). Also, a continuity score is recorded when the child responds "no" to the initial, target question but his or her answer to subsequent follow-up questioning indicates continuity reasoning (see Example 1c).

Example 1a

Experimenter: "Now that the mouse is not alive anymore, is he thinking about the alligator?"
Child: "Yes."
Experimenter: "Why?"
Child: "Because he scared him."

Example 1b

Experimenter: "Now that the mouse is not alive anymore, does he know where he is now?"
Child: "Yes."
Experimenter: "How come?"
Child: "I don't know."

Example 1c

Experimenter: "Now that the mouse is not alive anymore, can he see this tree?"
Child: "No."
Experimenter: "Why not?"
Child: "He's inside of an alligator's body and can't see anything but his mouth."

Discontinuity

The child responds "no" to the initial, target question and provides a justification for this response indicating cessation of function for the particular faculty during follow-up questioning (see Examples 2a and 2b).

Example 2a

Experimenter: "Now that the mouse is not alive anymore, is he thinking about the alligator?"
Child: "No."
Experimenter: "How come?"
Child: "Because he doesn't have a brain that's attached and working."

Example 2b

Experimenter: "Now that the mouse is not alive anymore, is he still sleepy?"
Child: "No."
Experimenter: "And why not?"
Child: "Because he's dead."

Appendix B:
Afterlife Vignettes and Interview Questions for Experiment 3

Script A

"Hi, I'm going to do a puppet show for you today, and the first thing I'm going to do is introduce you to the two characters. Do you know what kind of animal this is? That's right! It's a mouse. And this mouse is a baby mouse. One day he's going to grow up to become an old mouse. Do you know what kind of animal this is? Right again! It's an alligator. And this alligator's favorite food is baby mice. Now, we both know that these animals aren't real, they're just puppets, but for today let's just pretend that they are real.

"One day, Baby Mouse decides to go for a walk in the woods. While he's walking he's thinking about a lot of things. He's thinking about how angry he is with his brother, because his brother is always fighting with him. Sometimes Baby Mouse wishes he was an only child and didn't have a brother to worry about. Baby Mouse's mom always tells Baby Mouse how smart he is, so Baby Mouse thinks he is smarter than his brother. He's also wondering what his brother is doing right now and what he's thinking.

"Baby Mouse is also thinking about food. He hasn't had anything to eat all day and he's getting very hungry. He decides to eat some grass. But he takes one bite and spits it out because it tastes very gross. Yuck! He's also very thirsty, but he doesn't want to drink out of the pond because the water is dirty. The birds are singing very loud, and Baby Mouse is listening to their songs. Baby Mouse really wants to go home now because he's lost. This makes him very sad. He doesn't know where he is. Just then, he notices something strange. The bushes are moving! An alligator jumps out of the bushes and gobbles him all up. Baby Mouse is not alive anymore."

Script A Interview Questions

Each of the following questions was prefaced with the conditional "Now that Baby Mouse is not alive anymore ..."

Biological
Do you think that Baby Mouse will ever need to *eat* food again?
Do you think that Baby Mouse's *brain* still works?

Psychobiological
Do you think that Baby Mouse is still *thirsty*?

Do you think that Baby Mouse is still *hungry*?

Perceptual
Do you think that Baby Mouse can still *hear* the birds singing?
Do you think that Baby Mouse can still *taste* the yucky grass he ate?

Emotional
Do you think that Baby Mouse is still *sad* that he can't find his way home?
Do you think that Baby Mouse is still *angry* at his brother?

Desire
Do you think that Baby Mouse still *wishes* he had no brother?
Do you think that Baby Mouse still *wants* to go home?

Epistemic
Do you think that Baby Mouse is still *thinking* about his brother?
Do you think that Baby Mouse still *believes* he's smarter than his brother?

Script B

"Hi, I'm going to do a puppet show for you today, and the first thing I'm going to do is introduce you to the two characters. Do you know what kind of animal this is? That's right! It's a mouse. And this mouse is a baby mouse. One day he's going to grow up to become an old mouse. Do you know what kind of animal this is? Right again! It's an alligator. And this alligator's favorite food is baby mice. Now, we both know that these animals aren't real, they're just puppets, but for today let's just pretend that they are real.

"One day, Baby Mouse decides to take a walk in the woods. There are flowers, and Baby Mouse loves how the flowers smell. The flowers smell very nice. While he's walking, he's thinking about a lot of things. He's thinking about his mom, and how much he loves her. He believes his mom is the nicest grownup mouse in the whole world. Baby Mouse wonders where his mom is right now. Baby Mouse is also thinking about numbers. He likes numbers, but he's not very good at using them. He doesn't even understand how to add numbers together. He hopes that one day he'll be better at using numbers. Baby Mouse's feet are very tired, and he wants to go home now. But he realizes that he's lost and he doesn't know how to get back to his house. He's very sleepy and really wants to go to bed.

"Baby Mouse has a sore throat and he feels sick. Maybe if he drinks some water he'll feel better. He goes to drink some water from the pond but before he gets there he notices something funny. The bushes are moving!

An alligator jumps out of the bushes and gobbles him all up. Baby Mouse is not alive anymore."

Script B Interview Questions

Each of the following questions was prefaced with the conditional "Now that Baby Mouse is not alive anymore . . ."

Biological
Do you think that Baby Mouse will *grow* up to be a grownup mouse?
Do you think that Baby Mouse will ever need to *drink* water again?

Psychobiological
Do you think that Baby Mouse still feels *sleepy*?
Do you think that Baby Mouse still feels *sick*?

Perceptual
Do you think that Baby Mouse can still *smell* the flowers?
Do you think that Baby Mouse can *see* where he is now?

Emotional
Do you think that Baby Mouse still *loves* his mom?
Do you think that Baby Mouse is still *scared* of the alligator?

Desire
Do you think that Baby Mouse still *hopes* he gets better at math?
Do you think that Baby Mouse still *wants* to go home?

Epistemic
Do you think that Baby Mouse *knows* he's not alive?
Do you think that Baby Mouse still *believes* his mom is the nicest grownup?

Notes

* This article was originally published in *Developmental Psychology* 40(2) (2004): 217–33.

1. Because of the timing of the research and worldly events, we used the term *not alive* whenever possible rather than *dead*. Parents and teachers expressed greater satisfaction with this terminology, and it likely contributed to the level of parental compliance. It is important to take this into account, however, in interpreting the present findings. It may be that use of more straightforward terms such as *dead, death,* and *kill* would have influenced children's responses.

2. For Experiments 1 and 2, age group classifications were based on the relative age distribution of the sample, such that there was approximately a 2-year age range within each age category. For both experiments, preliminary analyses revealed no significant differences between the youngest half and the oldest half of the children within each age group, indicating that, for the questions posed here, children in each age group were relatively homogeneous in their reasoning.

3. Initial testing included a sixth cognitive question (i.e., "Now that the mouse is not alive anymore, does he like Mr. Alligator?"). However, this question was dropped early during the course of the study because responses from the two youngest groups of children were highly ambiguous, suggesting that the children did not understand the nature of the question (e.g., that it referenced the mouse's state *after* being eaten rather than before or during being eaten). The decision to drop this question was also motivated by comments from several of the older children in which they asked whether the experimenter was referring to the mouse's feelings toward the alligator before or after it had been killed.

4. This reliability does not include responses from the control condition.

5. This was true for all categories except questions dealing with desire states. Both scripts included the question "Does he still want to go home?" because other potential desire state terms (such as *desire, long for,* etc.) were judged to be too sophisticated for the youngest children.

References

Atran, S. 1994. Core Domains Versus Scientific Theories: Evidence from Systematics and Itzaj-Maya Folk Biology. In *Domain Specificity in Cognition and Culture*, ed. L. A. Hirschfeld and S. A. Gelman, 316–40. New York: Cambridge University Press.

Atwood, V. A. 1984. Children's Concepts of Death: A Descriptive Study. *Child Study Journal* 1: 11–29.

Backscheider, A., M. Shatz, and S. Gelman. 1993. Preschoolers' Ability to Distinguish Living Kinds as a Function of Regrowth. *Child Development* 64: 1242–57.

Barrett, C. 1999. *Human Cognitive Adaptations to Predators and Prey*. Unpublished doctoral dissertation, University of California, Santa Barbara.

Barrett, H. C., and T. Behne. August 2001. *Understanding Death as the Cessation of Intentional Action: A Cross-Cultural Developmental Study*. Poster presented at the meeting of the Cognitive Science Society, Edinburgh, Scotland.

Bering, J. M. 2002. Intuitive Conceptions of Dead Agents' Minds: The Natural Foundations of Afterlife Beliefs as Phenomenological Boundary. *Journal of Cognition and Culture* 2: 263–308.

Bjorklund, D. F., and Pellegrini., A. D. 2002. *The Origins of Human Nature: Evolutionary Developmental Psychology.* Washington, DC: American Psychological Association.

Boyer, P. 2001. *Religion Explained: The Evolutionary Origins of Religious Thought.* New York: Basic Books.

Brent, M. W., S. B. Speece, C. Lin, and Q. Dong. 1996. The Development of the Concept of Death among Chinese and U. S. Children 3–17 Years of Age: From Binary to "Fuzzy" Concepts? *Omega: Journal of Death and Dying* 33: 67–83.

Buss, D. M. 1995. The Future of Evolutionary Psychology. *Psychological Inquiry* 6: 81–87.

Carey, S. 1991. Knowledge Acquisition: Enrichment or Conceptual Change? In *The Epigenesis of the Mind: Essays on Biology and Cognition*, ed. S. Carey and R. Gelman, 257–91. Hillsdale, NJ: Erlbaum.

Carey, S., and E. Spelke. 1994. Domain-specific Knowledge and Conceptual Change. In *Mapping the Mind: Domain Specificity in Cognition and Culture*, ed. L. Hirschfeld and S. Gelman, 169–200. New York: Cambridge University Press.

Cosmides, L., and J. Tooby. 1992. The Psychological Foundations of Culture. In *The Adapted Mind*, ed. J. Barker, L. Cosmides, and J. Tooby, 19–136. New York: Oxford University Press.

Evans, M., D. A. Poling, and M. S. Mull. April 2001. *Confronting the Existential Questions: Children's Understanding of Origins and Death.* Paper presented at the biennial meeting of the Society for Research in Child Development, Minneapolis.

Flavell, J. H. 1999. Cognitive Development: Children's Knowledge about the Mind. *Annual Review of Psychology* 50: 21–45.

Flavell, J. H., F. L. Green, and E. R. Flavell. 1995. Young Children's Knowledge about Thinking. *Monographs of the Society for Research in Child Development* 60(1, Serial No. 243): v–96.

Flavell, J. H., and A. K. O'Donnell. 1999. Development of Intuitions about Mental Experiences. *Enfance* 3: 267–76.

Geary, D. C. 1995. Reflections of Evolution and Culture in Children's Cognition: Implications for Mathematical Development and Instruction. *American Psychologist* 50: 24–37.

Gopnik, A., and H. M. Wellman. 1992. Why the Child's Theory of Mind Really is a Theory. *Mind and Language* 7: 145–71.

Gottlieb, G. 2001. A Developmental Psychobiological Systems View: Early Formulation and Current Status. In *Cycles of Contingency: Developmental Systems and Evolution*, ed. S. Oyama and P. E. Griffiths, 41–54. Cambridge, MA: MIT Press.

Greeley, A. M., and M. Hout. 1999. Americans' Increasing Belief in Life after Death: Religious Competition and Acculturation. *American Sociological Review* 64: 813–35.

Gullone, E., N. J. King, B. Tonge, D. Heyne, and T. H. Ollendick. 2000. The Fear Survey Schedule in Children—II (FSSC–II): Validity Data as a Treatment Outcome Measure. *Australian Psychologist* 35: 238–43.

Hinde, R. A. 1999. *Why Gods Persist: A Scientific Approach to Religion.* London: Routledge.

Inagaki, K. 1989. Developmental Shift in Biological Inference Processes: From Similarity-based to Category-based Attribution. *Human Development* 32: 79–87.

Inagaki, K., and G. Hatano. 1996. Young Children's Recognition of Commonalities between Animals and Plants. *Child Development* 67: 2823–40.

Johnson, C. N., and H. M. Wellman. 1982. Children's Developing Conceptions of the Mind and Brain. *Child Development* 53: 222–34.

Kane, B. 1979. Children's Concepts of Death. *Journal of Genetic Psychology* 134: 141–53.

Keil, F. 1994. The Birth and Nurturance of Concepts by Domains: The Origins of Concepts of Living Things. In *Mapping the Mind: Domain Specificity in Cognition and Culture*, ed. L. Hirschfeld and S. Gelman, 234–54. New York: Cambridge University Press.

Koocher, G. 1973. Childhood, Death, and Cognitive Development. *Developmental Psychology* 9: 369–75.

Lazar, A., and J. Torney-Purta. 1991. The Development of the Subconcepts of Death in Young Children: A Short-term Longitudinal Study. *Child Development* 62: 1321–33.

Mahon, M. M., E. Zagorsky-Goldberg, and S. K. Washington. 1999. Concept of Death in a Sample of Israeli Kibbutz Children. *Death Studies* 23: 43–59.

McIntire, M. S., C. R. Angle, and L. J. Struempler. 1972. The Concept of Death in Midwestern Children and Youth. *American Journal of Diseases in Children* 123: 527–32.

Medin, D., and S. Atran. 1999. *Folkbiology*. Cambridge, MA: MIT Press.

Nagy, M. 1948. The Child's Theories Concerning Death. *Journal of Genetic Psychology* 83: 199–216.

O'Neill, D. K., and S. C. F. Chong. 2001. Preschool Children's Difficulty Understanding the Types of Information Obtained through the Five Senses. *Child Development* 72: 803–15.

Slaughter, V., K. Jaakola, and S. Carey. 1999. Constructing a Coherent Theory: Children's Biological Understanding of Life and Death. In *Children's Understanding of Biology, Health, and Ethics*, ed. M. Siegal and C. Peterson, 71–96. Cambridge: Cambridge University Press.

Slaughter, V., and M. Lyons. 2003. Learning about Life and Death in Early Childhood. *Cognitive Psychology* 46: 1–30.

Smilansky, S. N. 1987. *On Death: Helping Children Understand and Cope*. New York: Peter Lang.

Speece, M. W., and S. B. Brent. 1984. Children's Understanding of Death: A Review of Three Components of a Death Concept. *Child Development* 55: 1671–86.

Thalbourne, M. A. 1996. Belief in Life after Death: Psychological Origins and Influences. *Personality and Individual Differences* 21: 1043–45.

Wellman, H. M., A. K. Hickling, and C. A. Schult. 1997. Young Children's Psychological, Physical, and Biological Explanations. In *The Emergence of Core Domains: Children's Reasoning about Physical, Psychological, and Biological Phenomena*, ed. H. M. Wellman and K. Inagaki. New Directions for Child Development, 75. San Francisco: Jossey-Bass.

13

MODES OF RESEARCH: COMBINING COGNITIVE PSYCHOLOGY AND ANTHROPOLOGY THROUGH WHITEHOUSE'S MODES OF RELIGIOSITY

Rebekah A. Richert

Abstract

For the past decade, Whitehouse (e.g., 1995, 2000, 2004) has advanced a cognitive theory of religion, which he has termed *modes of religiosity*. The *modes of religiosity* theory is an account of ritual transmission. This account not only describes the existence of two distinct types of ritual traditions (as has been noted historically throughout literature in anthropology and religious studies), but also goes a step deeper by attempting to explain this dichotomy, and its related social morphologies, in terms of cognitive science. Whitehouse has argued that participation in ritual, and the resulting activation of specific cognitive processes, is instrumental in defining both individual religious experience as well as the distinct forms of religious communities that accompany different ritual traditions. Surrounding the advancement of this theory have been numerous conferences funded by the British Academy, edited volumes (Whitehouse and Laidlaw 2004; Whitehouse and Martin 2004; Whitehouse and McCauley 2005), and journal special issues (Martin and Whitehouse 2004; Martin and Whitehouse 2005; Whitehouse and McCauley 2004) evaluating the validity of the *modes of religiosity* theory from the perspectives of a variety of fields, including anthropology, history of religion, psychology, and cognitive science.

ဆ ಔ

As Barrett (2005) has suggested, the breadth and depth of the *modes of religiosity* theory requires that evidence either in support of or contradicting the hypotheses will emerge from numerous disciplines and in the guise of a variety of empirical methods. This chapter will focus on evidence and experiments in the field of cognitive psychology that address the *modes of religiosity* theory. First, I will provide a brief outline of the key points of the *modes of religiosity* theory. Second, I will explore possible methods for testing some predictions of the theory in the arena of cognitive psychology, as well as some of the difficulties with combining the two disciplines. Third, I will review several experiments that have used methods from cognitive psychology to test predictions from the *modes of religiosity* theory.

Whitehouse's Modes of Religiosity

In his theory, Whitehouse (2004) distinguishes between two *modes of religiosity*: doctrinal and imagistic. Table 1 outlines some of the key differences relevant to cognitive science between Whitehouse's two modes.

	Doctrinal Mode	*Imagistic Mode*
Repetition	Highly repetitive	Very infrequent
Arousal level	Low	High
Memory systems	Semantic schemas and implicit scripts	Episodic/flashbulb memories
Ritual meaning	Learned/acquired	Internally generated
Techniques of revelation	Rhetoric, logical integration, narrative	Iconicity, multivocality, and multivalence

Table 1. *The two modes of religiosity* (from Whitehouse 2004)

The doctrinal mode is characterized by rituals that are repeated frequently, low in emotional arousal, and usually accompanied by verbally transmitted exegesis. For example, the Catholic practice of Holy Communion, given its frequent (weekly) repetition, comparatively low levels of emotional arousal, and accompanying doctrine, forms part of a doctrinal mode of religiosity. According to Whitehouse, by frequently repeating rituals, the ritual procedures are encoded into implicit memory in the form of behavioral scripts and are generally performed without explicit attention to how or why. In addition, the frequent repetition of doctrinal rituals provides the opportunity for the activation of semantic memory systems, making possible the transmission of explicit and complicated doctrinal teachings. In this case, religious leaders have multiple opportunities for transmitting doctrine to ritual participants. Whitehouse argues that the activation of these two types of memory systems ensures the survival of doctrinal rituals; they are performed often, but without internally motivated reflection, and thus provide a prime cognitive environment for learning the doctrine taught by religious authorities.

Whitehouse further explores the consequences of activating these memory systems by suggesting that the presence of religious teachings requires the presence of religious leaders, which in turn requires orthodoxy checks and religious centralization. Adherence to the religious teachings also results in a large, anonymous religious community. The product of these processes is something like the Roman Catholic Church, with the Vatican (religious centralization and orthodoxy checks), bishops and priests (religious leaders), catechism (religious doctrine), weekly rituals and approximately 1 billion members (as reported by the 2005 Pontifical Yearbook). Even though the *modes of religiosity* theory attempts to account for this broad range of social tendencies, at the crux of all these outcomes are basic human cognitive processing tendencies: frequent repetition leads to implicit memory for ritual actions and long-term semantic memory for religious doctrine (Whitehouse 2004).

The imagistic mode, by contrast, is characterized by rituals that are low in frequency, high in emotional arousal, and often involve terrifying ordeals. For example, the initiation rituals of boys in Papua New Guinea are characterized by highly traumatizing experiences of "kidnapping" and torture. Whitehouse argues that verbally transmitted exegesis cannot stabilize in conditions of low-frequency transmission. These ritual experiences are encoded in episodic memory, and participants spontaneously reflect on the meaning of the ritual through a process of analogical reasoning that continues to unfold over the course of a participant's lifetime. Since this process of reflection is internally motivated and unique to each ritual participant, imagistic rituals are accompanied by a diversity of religious representations. The lack of consistent doctrine associated with these kinds of rituals inhibits the presence of dynamic leadership and centralization. However, Whitehouse suggests that the high level of arousal accompanying imagistic rituals fosters a sense of cohesion among cohorts of ritual participants. This combination of factors results in small, localized religious communities, rather than the large, anonymous communities accompanying doctrinal rituals. While the lack of dynamic leadership and authoritative doctrine inhibit the spread of ritual tradition, the high levels of arousal provide a motivating force for the transmission of the ritual within the community itself. Again, the foundation of these outcomes are basic human cognitive processing tendencies: high arousal leads to episodic memory for ritual actions and long-term rumination on ritual meanings (Whitehouse 2004).

In evaluating ways to test predictions from the *modes of religiosity* theory, a key caveat to consider is that Whitehouse allows for the possibility that both of his modes, and their accompanying dynamics, can be present within a single religious community. Members of a religious community easily identified as a doctrinal community (e.g., Turkish Islam) may also participate in rituals considered imagistic (e.g., Muslim circumcision). Given the potential for overlap, a benefit of research in the field of cognitive science is that it explores the effect of ritual participation at the individual level, rather than at the community level. This brings us to a series of general points that are important to keep in mind before embarking on an exploration of how to test predictions of the *modes of religiosity* theory.

Combining Research in Cognitive Psychology and Anthropology

There are a number of challenges to conducting interdisciplinary research that attempt to combine the goals of cognitive psychology and anthropology. However, even though these challenges exist in the underlying assumptions that members of each discipline tend to work from, they are not insurmountable. Dedicated researchers in each field can certainly collaborate to design research programs that are both experimentally informative and meaningful. The majority of challenges to conducting research combining both cognitive psychological and anthropological perspectives arises from the fact that researchers in each field differ in whether they seek to explain uniqueness or universals. The anthropological community tends to conduct research programs intended to describe the uniqueness that occurs within and between various human groups and cultures. Principles of research within the field reflect this priority. Anthropologists are well trained to write thorough, insightful, and creative ethnographies that describe what makes a particular culture or group unique. In contrast, cognitive psychologists tend to operate from the assumption that there are universals in the way that human minds work to process information. Principles of research within the field of cognitive psychology are intended to filter out contextual variation and to isolate basic-level processing universals. Researchers attempting to design studies that overlap between these two disciplines will become all too aware of the tension between these two, potentially polarizing, research goals. The benefit of cross-disciplinary collaboration is that it can keep the research of the cognitive psychologist from seeming irrelevant and ungeneralizable to naturally occurring situations, as well as keep the research of the anthropologist from being too context-specific and ungeneralizable outside of the culture being studied.

With these issues in mind, Barrett (2005) has conducted a thorough analysis of the empirical evidence necessary to support or disprove elements of the *modes of religiosity* theory. Given that the theory sets out predictions for a vast array of factors (e.g., memory processes, emotional arousal, social arrangements, transmission), no single empirical method could address all the hypotheses. In his analysis, Barrett has emphasized that evidence pertaining to Whitehouse's theory should come from studies drawing upon a variety of classes of empirical methods, which Barrett identifies as ethnographic, naturalistic, and experimental. A summary of Barrett's definitions of these methods is included in Table 2.

Method	Definition
Ethnographic	Studies that involve the observation and measurement of naturally occurring human behavior.
Naturalistic	Studies that explore differences between naturally occurring groups within the same population.
Experimental	Studies that are designed with artificially produced materials and measures.

Table 2. *Barrett's (2005) distinctions between various empirical methods*

Traditionally, research on religious rituals has employed either ethnographic or naturalistic methods. Reliance on these methods reflects the demand for ecological validity—that findings in experimental studies should be generalizable to naturally occurring conditions. Achieving ecological validity is a key challenge to conducting experiments on hypotheses generated in a field like the cognitive science of religion. One of the key constraints to bear in mind when designing experiments in the cognitive science of religion is whether the findings from a particular experiment will only reveal how participants respond in a very structured experimental setting, or whether the findings will address broader questions outside the experimental setting and in the "real world." As we move down Table 2 from ethnographic research to experimental research, experimental control and the ability to draw causal conclusions increases, but at the cost of a potential decrease in generalizability. While this is a perfectly valid criticism of experimental research, it is not insurmountable. In his chapter, Barrett (2005) identifies a number of questions generated by the *modes of religiosity* theory that can be answered using experimental research. These are outlined in Table 3.

Prediction (and mode)	Method
Frequent repetition of doctrinal information is required to develop explicit memory for religious teachings (doctrinal).	Explore precisely how much repetition is necessary to remember and transmit the complex ideas in doctrinal systems.
The presence of orthodoxy checks in a religious community encourages centralization of power structures (doctrinal).	Explore whether groups who are strictly instructed to precisely remember and transmit material are more likely to develop some sort of hierarchy for ensuring accuracy than groups who are given less strict requirements on accuracy.
Implicit memory for the procedures of ceremonies reduces individual reflection and innovation regarding theological justifications for the ceremonies, thereby increasing acceptance of orthodox interpretations (doctrinal).	Explore the relationship between procedure learning and reflection by having participants perform a mock ritual multiple times and journal their reflections on the ritual; then test whether the amount of reflection decreases with performance frequency.
Episodic memory for religious events (arising from emotionally arousing religious experiences) promotes spontaneous exegetical reflection (SER) (imagistic).	If one could overcome the obstacles presented by an inherent lack of personal meaning in experimentally derived rituals, one could compare participants' reflections on two different versions of a ritual: one that is highly emotionally arousing and one that is not.
SER spawns a diversity of understandings of the same religious event (imagistic).	The exploration of this question could be included in the same experiment as the test for whether episodic memory for religious events promotes SER.
Participants in a high-arousal religious ceremony tend to enjoy relatively intense social cohesion after the fact (imagistic).	Explore the role that various psychological mechanisms play in creating group cohesion to isolate both whether and how highly emotionally arousing experiences create intense social cohesion.

Table 3. *Summary of the areas in which the* modes of religiosity *predictions can be experimentally tested* (Barrett 2005)

Thus, despite the fact that there are challenges to combining the research goals of cognitive psychologists and anthropologists, there is also the potential for rich collaboration between the two disciplines. Following is a review of four experiments that demonstrate potential for this kind of collaboration by testing predictions of the *modes of religiosity* theory.

Testing Modes of Religiosity Predictions

Included in this section of the chapter are four experiments, two of which are considered pilot research, that have used methods in the field of cognitive psychology to test specific predictions stemming from Whitehouse's (2004) *modes of religiosity* theory.

Pilot Research

Whitehouse (2004) reports on two pilot studies he has conducted that address predictions of his *modes of religiosity* theory. The first pilot study was intended to test the prediction that memory for ritual procedures will vary based on self-ratings of emotion. It also addressed the prediction that "frequent repetition is required to develop explicit memory for religious teachings" (Barrett 2005). In this study, conducted with Barrett (Whitehouse 2004, 84), 150 university students participated in an artificial ritual in which they were instructed to perform a series of unusual actions. The students were told that the purpose of performing the ritual was to learn about the stress ethnographic field researchers are likely to experience when performing strange activities. They were also given a "theological" interpretation of the ritual and a short questionnaire in which they indicated their emotional reaction while performing the ritual. After seven weeks, the participants were asked to complete a second questionnaire in which they reported on the sequence of actions in the ritual, the purpose of the experiment, and the theological interpretation of the ritual. The students almost perfectly remembered the ritual itself, but almost none of the students correctly remembered the purpose of the experiment or the theological interpretation of the ritual. While the initial attempt to explore the relationship between emotional arousal and memory for ritual actions was unsuccessful (given an essentially ceiling effect in students' memories of the ritual procedures), Whitehouse suggests that the results may indicate that reproducing ritual actions does not require a high degree of frequency, but that memory for exegetical concepts likely requires repetition and rehearsal.

The second pilot study Whitehouse (2004, 98) reviews also explored the relationship between repetition and memory for religious doctrine. In the study, an instructor recited the four noble truths of Buddhism two times a week for four weeks to a class of undergraduate university students. They were asked to recall the truths at three intervals: after the second repetition, after the eighth repetition, and after six weeks during which the students did not hear the noble truths reviewed at all. The findings revealed that participants' recall was best after eight repetitions (40%), and was quite poor after only two repetitions and again after the six weeks of not hearing the noble truths. Whitehouse suggests these results reveal that a rather large amount of repetition is necessary to encode doctrinal material into memory, and that once exposure to doctrinal teaching has ceased, there will be a rapid decay in memory for the doctrine.

Even though they offer suggestive conclusions, these pilot studies reveal some of the weaknesses of drawing anthropological conclusions from research in the field of cognitive psychology. Whitehouse (2004) himself acknowledges that members of a religious community have a certain level of personal motivation for learning doctrine and remembering rituals that is not inherent in the participants of these studies. In addition, the time scale of the studies, where participants were questioned after only a few months, is far shorter than the actual experience of people learning religious doctrine or participating in religious rituals. The purpose of mentioning these criticisms is not to imply that the studies are not useful or informative, but to point out some of the necessary considerations and inherent difficulties that are present when designing this kind of experimental research. With these issues in mind, the following is a review of how one particular aspect of cognitive psychology, that of analogical reasoning, has been employed to test one of the predictions of the *modes of religiosity* theory.

Analogical Reasoning and Spontaneous Exegetical Reflection

Richert, Whitehouse, and Stewart (2005) have recently conducted two experiments to directly test one of the *modes of religiosity* predictions. They explored whether arousal level at the time of ritual participation influences the volume and depth of reflection that ritual participants have on their ritual experiences. To test this question, they focused on one of the cognitive processes key to Whitehouse's theory, that of the human tendency toward analogical reasoning. In particular, analogical reasoning comes into play in the *modes of religiosity* theory in the hypothesized Spontaneous Exegetical Reflection, or SER (Richert et al. 2005; Whitehouse 2004). SER is Whitehouse's term to describe participants' attempts to make sense of highly arousing ritual experiences. Traditionally, analogical reasoning is understood to be the process of understanding one situation in terms of another (e.g., Gentner and Markman 1997; Holyoak and Thagard 1997). Analogies can involve the application of a solution, principle, or general relational structure from a past experience to a present experience. Analogical reasoning is used to solve problems, build arguments, and most importantly for this paper, in the construction of explanations (Gentner and Markman 1997). In terms of Whitehouse's SER, a ritual participant will engage analogical reasoning to explain novel ritual elements based on their relation to other, more familiar experiences.

Richert et al. (2005) framed their study in terms of Holyoak and Thagard's (1997) *multiconstraint theory* of analogical reasoning. According to the *multiconstraint theory*, there are three general constraints that guide the selection of analogical comparisons: similarity, structure, and purpose. The constraint of *similarity* focuses on the fact that analogies are often guided by the direct similarities between two analogs. For example, a spider web and a fishing net are similar in appearance in that both are comprised of interconnected strands of thin material. The *structural* constraint acknowledges that an analogy is not limited to superficial similarity, but capitalizes on parallels in the relational structure of the elements in the two analog domains (Holyoak and Thagard 1997). This constraint indicates that despite the infinite number of superficial or surface similarities between two analogs, the most meaningful and informative analogies are those in which the analogs share connected systems of relations, resulting in deeper parallels (Gentner and Markman 1997). For example, a spider web and a fishing net are both structurally similar in that they are both smaller than the Taj Mahal, but a more useful and informative structural similarity is that they are both used to trap food.

The third constraint mentioned by Holyoak and Thagard (1997) is *purpose*. Holyoak and Thagard (1997) assert that the purpose behind creating an analogy will influence the types of analogies that people make. This constraint is particularly relevant to the Richert et al. (2005) experiments. Recall the two *modes of religiosity* that Whitehouse distinguishes: doctrinal and imagistic. Rituals in the doctrinal mode (high frequency, low arousal rituals) are usually accompanied by verbally transmitted explanations. According to Whitehouse, the routinization of these rituals activates implicit procedural memory for ritual actions, suppressing the rate and volume of spontaneous reflection on the ritual meaning and increasing each participant's susceptibility to verbally transmitted, authoritative exegesis. Thus, in terms of analogical reasoning in the doctrinal mode, routinized rituals may not be expected to spur analogical reasoning because they are missing the element of purpose. According to Whitehouse, the doctrinal ritual experience does not spur analogical reasoning either because the explanation is provided in authoritative exegesis or the ritual practice has become such a habitual part of life that it does not strike one as an experience that needs an explanation.

In contrast, the combination of factors constituting the imagistic mode results in the element of purpose for analogical reasoning, that of explaining a particularly bizarre ritual experience. In the case of imagistic mode rituals (low frequency, high arousal), Whitehouse has suggested that a ritual event which encompasses the combination of high emotional arousal and little doctrinal exegesis produces a prime cognitive environment for creating explanations and meaning, spurring the natural cognitive tendency toward analogical reasoning, or comparisons with other events or environments that may help to explain the ritual.

As Barrett (2005) points out, one of the key predictions of the modes of religiosity theory is that "episodic memory for religious events promotes spontaneous exegetical reflection (SER)." SER plays a crucial role in the imagistic mode, as it is in place to account for both encoding into semantic memory and attributions of meaning and purpose to imagistic rituals. The claim is that through this process ritual participants develop diverse and elaborate exegetical interpretations of ritual activities, resulting in a lack of dynamic leadership, which in turn has its own consequences in the shaping of a religious community. These SER outcomes are in contrast to the type of reflection afforded doctrinal rituals, which converge on the exegesis provided by religious authority. Thus, it is of considerable importance to establish whether imagistic ritual practices do indeed spur the level of SER that Whitehouse predicts.

Two Experiments Testing the Role of Analogical Reasoning in the Modes of Religiosity

The purpose of the following two experiments was to define and measure participants' Spontaneous Exegetical Reflection (SER) for high and low arousal rituals (Richert et al. 2005). In the first experiment, referred to as the Propagation Ritual experiment, participants were placed in one of two groups to enact a ritual: a high arousal form of the ritual or a blander version of the same ritual (Richert et al. 2005). In order to ensure a level of ecological validity, the ritual was conducted outdoors in a large field surrounded by trees. To control for type of exegesis, both groups were provided the same, minimal, amount of information about the ritual, namely that the experimenters were interested in testing the efficacy of certain ritual procedures, and that this particular ritual was derived from propagation rituals in Amazonia, often conducted to increase hunting success. Participants were told that they would be directed through some simple ritual actions and then asked to fill out some questionnaires. Following this introduction, participants were led through the ritual itself. There were two key differences between the high and low arousal groups. First, participants in the *low arousal* condition performed the ritual in the afternoon, and participants in the *high arousal* condition performed the ritual at dusk. Second, at a particular point in the ritual, participants in the *high arousal* group were given blindfolds to wear, but participants in the *low arousal* group did not wear blindfolds.

Immediately after the ritual, all participants were given an emotional rating form. Additionally, two and a half months after the ritual performance, participants returned for a follow-up interview. In this final interview, participants were asked to recall freely the events of the evening or afternoon that they participated in the ritual. They were also asked to indicate what thoughts crossed their mind while performing the ritual and if anything struck them as being particularly important to the ritual. If participants did not expand on a ritual action, the interviewer questioned them directly on whether that action seemed important and for what reason.

Richert et al. (2005) coded these interview responses for volume of reflection (the number of actions to which participants attributed meaning) and use of analogies. The specific analogs were given a score of 2 each, and all other meanings were given a score of 1. These scores were then totaled for a cumulative SER score for the final interview. Based on arousal groups created *post-hoc* from participants' ratings of fright intensity, the cumulative SER scores were compared for participants deemed to have had low and high arousal reactions to ritual participation. Results revealed that participants who had a strong emotional reaction to the ritual attributed meanings to a greater number of ritual elements than participants who had a minimal emotional reaction to the ritual participation when interviewed two and a half months after their initial ritual participation. In addition, participants who had a strong emotional reaction demonstrated higher cumulative SER scores. This experiment offers tentative support for Whitehouse's hypothesis. However, Richert et al. (2005) note that a key limitation to generalizing from this study was that the measure of participants' emotional reaction to the ritual depended on participants' self-report, which may have been an unreliable measure.

To correct for this limitation, and to attempt to replicate the findings from the Propagation Ritual experiment, Richert et al. (2005) conducted a second experiment. In the second experiment, which they label the Altar Ritual, the experimenters recruited over twice as many participants, used extreme sound and lighting differences to vary arousal level, and assessed participants' actual emotional arousal levels while performing the ritual through a galvanic skin response (GSR) measure. GSR is a measure of skin conductivity. It is obtained by sending a small electric pulse between two fingers and measuring the skin's resistance to the pulse. Higher GSR levels indicate that the skin is conducting greater levels of electricity, which constitutes a well-established indication of emotional arousal. In contrast to the Propagation Ritual, participants performed the ritual alone, rather than in groups. Furthermore, the ritual was performed indoors in a university-owned sonic arts research facility. While the experimenters admit that this location was not ideal for ecological validity, it was chosen because of the extensive capabilities for manipulating sound and lighting, which were utilized in manipulating participants' arousal levels.

Also in contrast to the Propagation Ritual, participants in the Altar Ritual were not asked to accept that the ritual may have some sort of real-world effect. Instead, they were told that, following the ritual, the experimenters wanted to obtain their feedback about what purpose they thought this ritual may have served in its original cultural setting. Participants were told that, while the experimenters knew the actions of the ritual, they were uncertain about their meanings or the purpose of the ritual as a whole. Participants performed the ritual in front of an "altar" draped in Hessian fabric that had been placed in the center of a large room at the sonic arts research facility. Participants were directed through the ritual itself by reading directions as they were flashed onto a screen. For an accurate measure of participants' galvanic skin response, their index and middle fingers on their left hands were connected to two sensors. The experimenters collected three measures of GSR: a baseline measure, collected while participants were standing still for three minutes before the ritual began, and two arousal measures, coordinated with the playing of music and drums at two points in the course of the ritual, as described below. These two points were chosen because they were parts of the ritual that were expected to produce strong emotional reactions in the high arousal ritual condition.

There were four key differences between the high arousal and low arousal versions of the ritual. First, at the start of the ritual for the high arousal group, the house lights were turned off and the room became red. In contrast, for the low arousal group, the house lights remained on and red lights were turned on at a very low setting. Second, at two points in the ritual, either music or drums were played. At both times for the low arousal group, the music and drums were played softly through one small speaker in front of the participants. For the high arousal group, the music and drums were played very loudly and in surround sound. In addition, for the high arousal condition, the drumming steadily increased in intensity and pace; however, in the low arousal condition, the drumming maintained an even tempo. A third key difference between the two groups occurred when the music was playing for the first time. In both cases, a man entered the room carrying a box. In the high arousal condition, he walked slowly, stood at the table until the music had ended, and then proceeded to walk behind the participant and shake a rattle. In the low arousal condition, he walked more quickly and shook the rattle while standing in front of participants. The fourth difference between the conditions involved the box brought in by the man. After the drumming stopped, participants were instructed to place their hand inside the box. In the case of high arousal ritual, the lid of the box could not be removed and participants had to place their hand through a hole in the side of the box without being able to see what was inside. In the case of the low arousal ritual, the lid was removed from the top of the box, and participants could simply reach inside.

Different from the Propagation Ritual, where participants simply filled out a survey rating their emotional reaction to the ritual, immediately following their performance of the ritual, participants in the Altar Ritual were directly interviewed by an interviewer. As in the Propagation Ritual experiment, participants were asked to rate the intensity of several emotions. Richert et al. (2005) focus their report on participants' ratings of fright and surprise. Following the reports of their emotional reaction, participants were asked to recall freely the procedures of the ritual and to offer some suggestions as to what they thought the purpose of the ritual may have been and what the various steps of the ritual may have meant. Participants then returned one month later for a follow-up interview. They were asked the same questions as in the first interview as well as whether they had any significant moments of insight about the ritual, and to reflect on the process by which they came to decide on particular ritual meanings.

Both the initial interview and the one-month follow-up interview were coded for volume of reflection and use of analogies in the same way as the interviews from the Propagation Ritual. All general meanings were given a score of 1 each, and specific analogs were given a score of 2 each. These scores were then totaled for a cumulative SER score for each of the interviews. In addition, since both interviews were the same, a difference score was computed for the volume of reflection and use of analogies to explore whether there were different degrees of change over time for the participants experiencing high and low arousal reactions to the ritual experience.

As with the Propagation Ritual, Richert et al. (2005) explored differences based on participants' actual emotional reaction to the ritual experience instead of the arousal version of the ritual that they performed. To create the *high arousal* and *low arousal* groups, the experimenters compared three measures of emotional arousal for consistency: self-report ratings of fright intensity and the changes in GSR during the music and drum sequences. A participant was placed in the low arousal group if at least two of the three measures indicated an emotional reaction below average in intensity, and a participant was placed in the high arousal group if at least two of the three measures indicated an above average emotional reaction. Results revealed that participants who had a stronger emotional reaction to the ritual also demonstrated a greater increase in both their volume and depth of reflection on the ritual between their initial interview and the follow-up interview.

In summary, these two experiments offer tentative support for one of Whitehouse's *modes of religiosity* predictions, namely that emotionally arousing religious experiences promote spontaneous exegetical reflection (Barrett 2005). Results from the Propagation Ritual Experiment revealed that participants with stronger emotional reactions to the ritual demonstrated greater volume and depth of reflection on the meaning of the ritual. Furthermore, in the Altar Ritual Experiment, participants with stronger emotional reactions to the ritual demonstrated a greater *increase* in volume and depth of reflection on the ritual. These findings suggest that both volume and depth of reflection on rituals vary with the level of emotional arousal (Richert et al. 2005).

Richert et al. (2005) acknowledge some limitations to the generalizibility of their findings. One of the key limitations is that, because the rituals were fabricated for the purpose of the experiment, they lacked the element of personal consequentiality for the participants. The experimenters suggest that this limitation only muted their findings, however, and that personal consequentiality would actually increase the volume and depth of reflection, making the differences in arousal groups more profound. A second limitation to this research, not mentioned by Richert et al. (in press), is that it does not address the impact of the ritual actions directly, but rather participants' reactions to the ritual actions. More specifically, some participants performing high arousal versions of the ritual had a very minor emotional reaction to the experience. Thus, the results generalize to naturally occurring imagistic rituals only if one accepts the assumption that a strong majority of the participants in imagistic rituals have a strong emotional reaction to the ritual performance.

Given the ethical constraints of designing experiences intended to evoke strong negative reactions, further research into the effect of personal consequentiality and highly arousing ritual experiences will likely need to be conducted using what Barrett (2005) identifies as naturalistic and ethnographic methods. For example, whether personal consequentiality would indeed increase the volume and depth of SER could be explored by comparing reflections on a ritual experience from ritual participants who are members of the ritual community to ritual participants who are not members of the community but who perform the ritual actions. Furthermore, one could recruit participants in naturally occurring imagistic rituals and track their reflections on the experience (although this approach presents its own difficulties given the secret nature of many rituals, as well as taboos on talking about rituals that are commonly in place).

Despite these limitations, the four experiments described above are examples of research programs attempting to cross the disciplinary boundaries. In the long term, methods from these experiments can be adapted to analyze ethnographic interviews for naturally occurring rituals. This research could also be expanded to consider other variables that are important to the *modes of religiosity* theory. For example, the last two studies reviewed considered only the arousal level of ritual participants; however, frequency of participation is also a key factor in the predicted outcomes of Whitehouse's theory. Thus, these studies represent a starting point, not an end point, in research on this topic. In addition, they point to the possibility for successful cross-disciplinary research, even beyond that which could be accomplished by continued collaboration between cognitive psychologists and anthropologists.

Acknowledgments

The funding to write this chapter was provided by a National Science Foundation International Post-doctoral Research Fellowship (INT-0301330) to the author. The author would also like to thank Justin Barrett, Suzanne Duke, and Elizabeth Pasquini for their comments on various drafts.

References

Barrett, J. 2005. In the Empirical Mode: Evidence Needed for the Modes of Religiosity Theory. In *Mind and Religion: Psychological and Cognitive Foundations of Religiosity*, ed. H. Whitehouse and R. N. McCauley. Walnut Creek, CA: AltaMira Press.

Gentner, D. 1983. Structure-mapping: A Theoretical Framework for Analogy. *Cognitive Science* 7: 155–70.

Gentner, D., and A. B. Markman. 1997. Structure Mapping in Analogy and Similarity. *American Psychologist* 52: 45–56.

Holyoak, K. J., and P. Thagard. 1997. The Analogical Mind. *American Psychologist* 52: 35–44.

Martin, L. H., and H. Whitehouse. 2004. *Implications of Cognitive Science for the Study of Religion*. Special Issue of *Method and Theory in the Study of Religion* 16(3).

—2005. *History, Memory, and Cognition*. Special issue of *Historical Reflections/Réflexions Historiques* 31(2).

Richert, R. A., H. Whitehouse, and E. Stewart. 2005. Memory and Analogical Thinking in High-arousal Rituals. In *Mind and Religion: Psychological and Cognitive Foundations of Religiosity*, ed. H. Whitehouse and R. N. McCauley. Walnut Creek, CA: AltaMira Press.

Spellman, B. A, and K. J. Holyoak. 1996. Pragmatics in analogical mapping. *Cognitive Psychology* 31: 307–46.

Whitehouse, H. 1995. *Inside the Cult: Religious Innovation and Transmission in Papua New Guinea*. Oxford: Oxford University Press.

—2000. *Arguments and Icons: Divergent Modes of Religiosity*. Oxford: Oxford University Press.

—2004. *Modes of Religiosity: A Cognitive Theory of Religious Transmission*. Walnut Creek, CA: AltaMira Press.

Whitehouse, H., and J. Laidlaw. 2004. *Ritual and Memory: Towards a Comparative Anthropology of Religion*. Walnut Creek, CA: AltaMira Press.

Whitehouse, H., and L. H. Martin. 2004. *Theorizing Religions Past: Archeology, History, and Religion*. Walnut Creek, CA: AltaMira Press.

Whitehouse, H., and R. N. McCauley. 2004. *The Cognitive Foundations of Religiosity*. Special Issue of *Journal of Cognition and Culture* 4(3).

—2005. *Mind and Religion: Psychological and Cognitive Foundations of Religiosity*. Walnut Creek, CA: AltaMira Press.

Index of Authors

Abelson, R. 150
Ackerman, B. P. 183
Almquist, A. J. 233
Anderson, K. 64
Angle, C. R. 299
Anderson, C.W. 233
Argyle, M. 118
Armstrong, S. L. 61
Astington, J. 286, 287, 295
Atran, S. 48, 49, 63, 71, 74, 76, 78, 100, 104, 234, 270, 271, 277–79, 286, 290, 295, 302
Atwood, V. A. 298

Backscheider, A. 307
Baillargeon, R. 100
Ball, S. 118
Barrett, H. C. 298, 302, 325, 326
Barrett, J. L. 3–7, 86, 88–90, 94, 103–105, 109, 116, 138, 149, 151, 169, 179–84, 200, 203, 204, 215, 216, 235, 276, 285, 286, 290, 294, 295, 338, 341–43, 345, 349, 350
Bartlett, F. C. 150, 152–56, 182
Bartsch, K. 287
Bassett, R. L. 142
Beattie, K. 108, 287
Behne, T. 325
Behrend, D. A. 62
Bellugi, U. 58
Benson, P. L. 118
Bergman, E.T. 182
Bering, J. 8, 109, 301, 305, 311, 319, 325, 327
Berlin, B. 49, 50, 70, 71, 75
Biederman, I. 77
Biró, G. 295
Bjorklund, D. 8, 297, 298
Bloch, M. 179, 206

Bloom, P. 73, 106, 195
Boland, J. E. 205
Boster, J. 76
Boyer, P. 6, 8, 72, 89–91, 104, 105, 119, 120, 140, 141, 150–53, 158, 169, 179–83, 187–89, 195, 196, 216, 229
Brandon, S. G. F. 139
Bransford, J. D. 120, 151
Breedlove, D. 70
Brent, S. B. 298, 299, 301, 308, 327
Brewer, W. F. 150, 182, 183, 279
Briky, I. T. 118
Brockbank, M. 295
Bromberger, S. 27, 28, 34
Bulmer, R. 71
Buss, D. M. 298

Caporael, L. A. 139
Carey, S. 49, 50, 64, 77, 106, 107, 110, 140, 180, 235, 270, 298, 302
Carnap, R. 26, 34
Carruthers, P. 91, 287, 295
Casler, K. 106, 110
Cavanaugh, M. A. 232, 233
Chandler, M. 108, 287, 295
Chi, M. T. H. 66, 73, 76, 79, 117, 233
Chinn, C. A. 279
Chomsky, N. 56–59, 67, 76
Chong, S. C. F. 301
Churchland, P. M. 23, 26
Churchland, P. S. 23
Cole, M. 276
Coley, J. D. 235
Colker, L. 152
Cosmides, L. 69, 298, 327
Crick, F. 31
Cromer, R. F. 58
Cronin, J. E. 233

Index of Subjects

Index of Subjects

Breinigsville, PA USA
11 January 2010
230569BV00002B/3/A